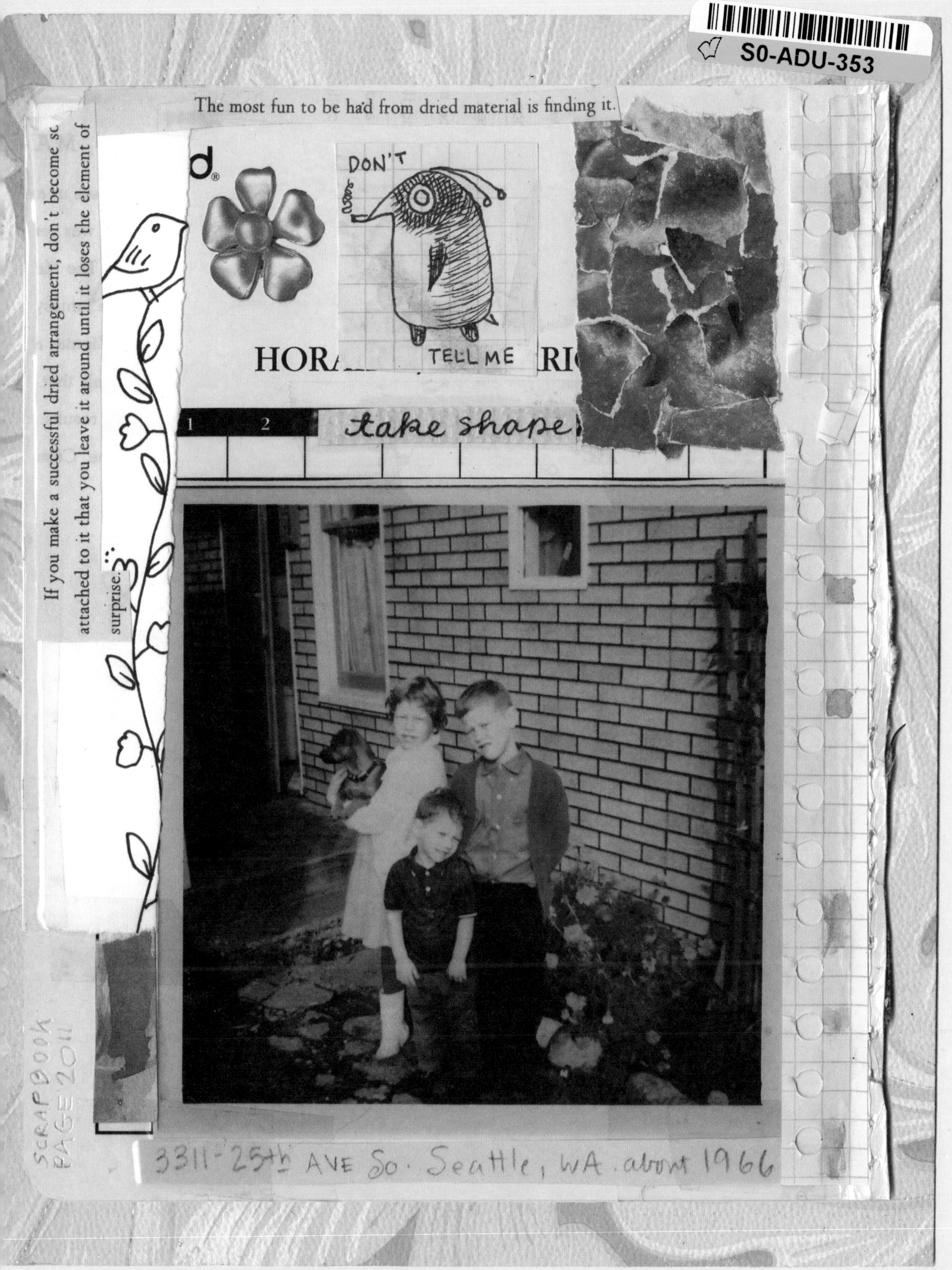

The most fun to be had from dried material is finding it.
If you make a successful dried arrangement, don't become sc
attached to it that you leave it around until it loses the element of
surprise.
d®
DON'T
TELL ME
HORA
RI
1
2
take shape
SCRAPBOOK PAGE 2011
3311-25th AVE So. Seattle, WA. about 1966

The JOURNAL Staff

BOBO

Here we are, the Fall Quarter Cooper Point Journal staff. Clockwise from left to
News Editor Steve Kruse, Feature Editor Matt Groening, Editor Jill Stewart, Adver
Mgr. Brock Sutherland, Ad Salesman Leo Rogers, Business Mgr. David Judd, Sec
Jeanne Hansen, and Production Mgr. Curtis Milton.
  The Journal will be published each Thursday until Christmas vacati~

MATT AT
THE EVERGREEN
STATE COLLEGE
ABOUT 1976

ABCDEFGHIJKLMNOPQRSTUVWXYZ123456789

this book is FOR MATT GROENING FUNK LORD OF USA

who is ~~NORWEGIAN~~ ~~BAD AND BLOWING~~

A GOOD FRIEND AND A ~~GOOD~~ INFLUENCE

~~REALLY BAD~~
~~FANTASTIC~~
~~GOOD~~ ~~FOXY~~
~~Horrible~~ LOVING
~~Important~~
religious
~~OK~~ BAD and GOOD
AQUARIUS
GOOD

ABCDEFG
HIJKLM
NOPQR
STUV
WXYZ

I WOULD ALSO LIKE TO THANK
JOHN KEISTER and THE TEACHERS at SEATTLE'S
KIMBALL ELEMENTARY, ASA MERCER JR. HIGH,
FRANKLIN HIGH AND ROOSEVELT HIGH - AND
ALL OTHER PUBLIC SCHOOL TEACHERS AND ALL
LIBRARIANS and LIZ DARHANSOFF and
SUSAN GRODE and MARILYN FRASCA AND
everyone at DRAWN + QUARTERLY and
MOST OF ALL Thank You TO MY DEAR
HUSBAND, KEVIN KAWULA

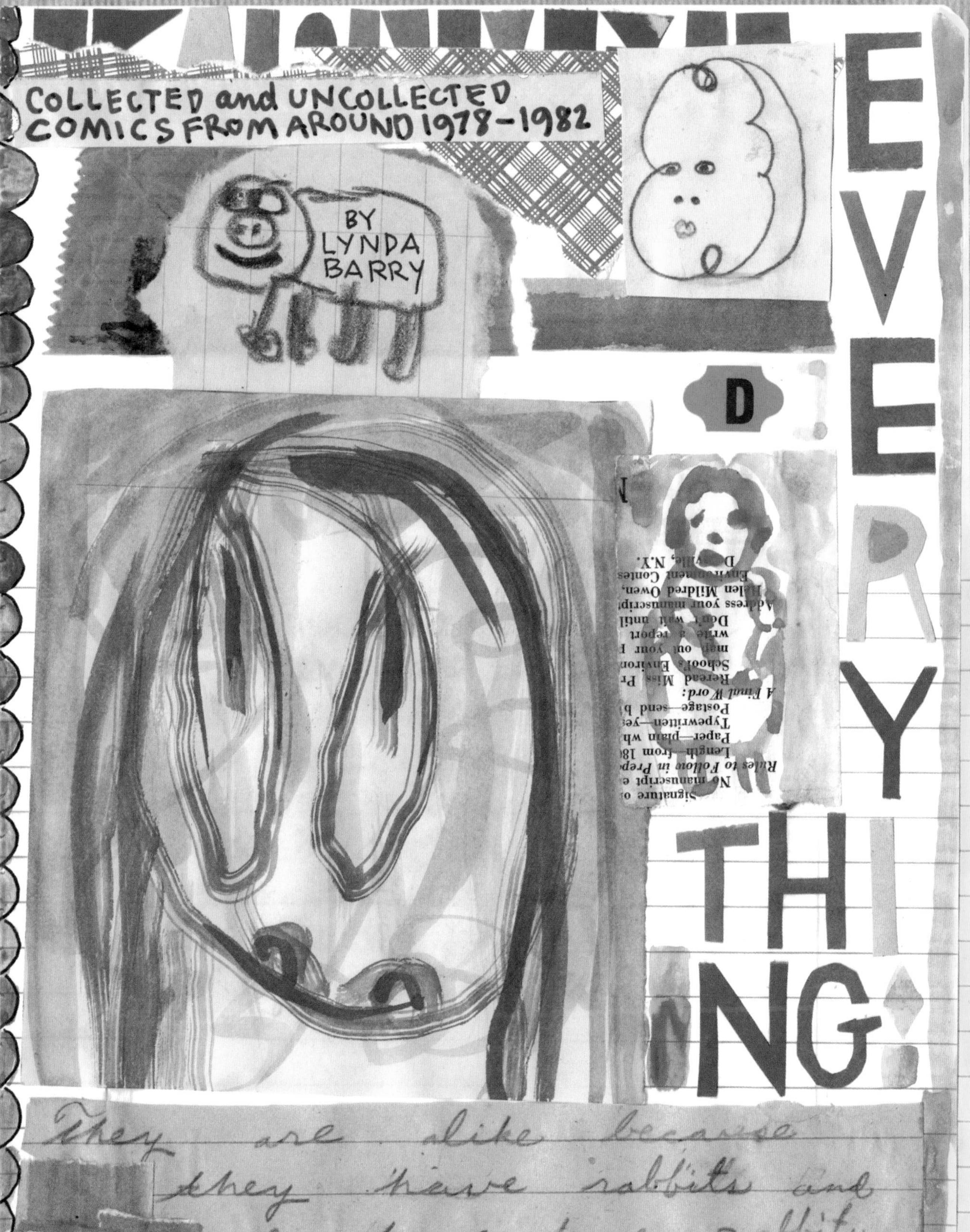
COLLECTED and UNCOLLECTED
COMICS FROM AROUND 1978-1982
BY LYNDA BARRY
EVERYTHING
D
They are alike because they have rabbits and we have have rabbits.
DRAWN + QUARTERLY • montreal
2011

FROM MY DRAWING BOOK FROM 1972

PLEASE NOTE THIS VOLUME OF 'EVERYTHING' isn't FOR EVERYBODY. There is BAD DRAWING and mature CONTENT!

THIS BOOK IS NOT FOR KIDS UNLESS THEY HAVE FOUND IT AND ARE sneak-reading it BECAUSE YOU DIDN'T HIDE IT WELL ENOUGH FROM KIDS

Campbell's condensed TOMATO MONSTER SOUP

net wt 10¾ oz

©1972 Heath-ie

I DREW THIS IN THE 9TH GRADE AND FELT INCREDIBLE AFTERWARD.

1972

Drawn & Quarterly. Post Office Box 48056 Montreal, Quebec Canada H2V 4S8 www.drawnandquarterly.com

First edition: October 2011 Printed in China 10 9 8 7 6 5 4 3 2 1 Library and Archives Canada Cataloguing in Publication Barry, Lynda, 1956– Blabber Blabber Blabber / Lynda Barry. ISBN 978-1-77046-052-2 (v. 1) I. Title. PN6727.B36E94 2011 741.5'973 C2011-901766-0 Distributed in the USA by: Farrar, Straus and Giroux 18 West 18th Street New York, NY 10011 Orders: 888.330.8477 Distributed in Canada by: Raincoast Books 2440 Viking Way Richmond, BC Orders: 800.663.5714 V6V 1N2

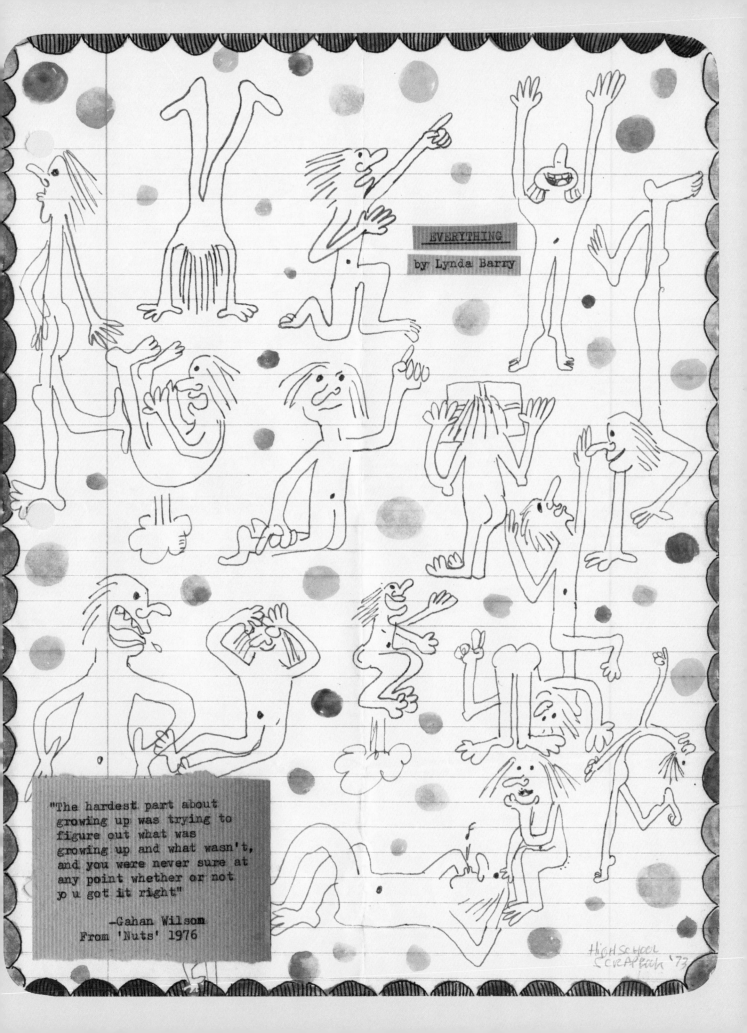

EVERYTHING

by Lynda Barry

"The hardest part about
growing up was trying to
figure out what was
growing up and what wasn't,
and you were never sure at
any point whether or not
you got it right"

—Gahan Wilson
From 'Nuts' 1976

HIGH SCHOOL
SCRAPBOOK '73

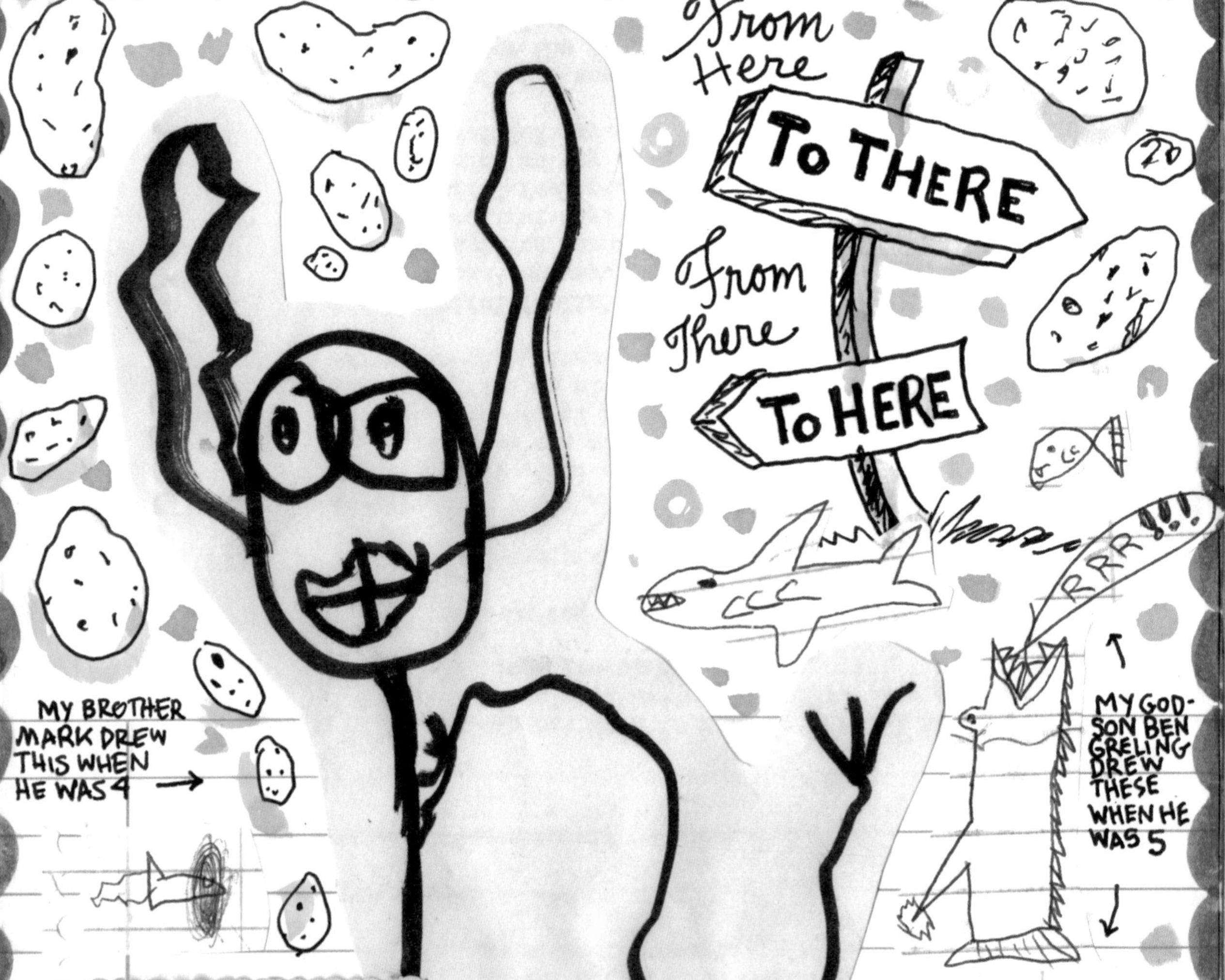
From Here
To THERE
From There
To HERE
RRR!!!
MY BROTHER MARK DREW THIS WHEN HE WAS 4
MY GOD-SON BEN GRELING DREW THESE WHEN HE WAS 5

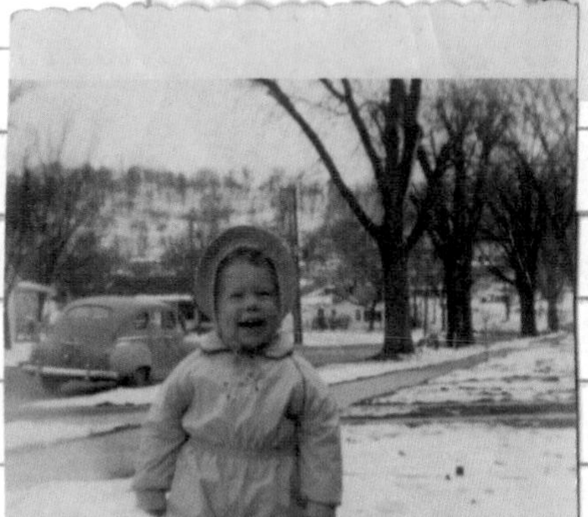

RICHLAND CENTER, WI 1958

I don't have any drawings from when I was a kid but I remember scribbling, the feeling of it being so alive and unpredictable and also surprising. I'm told I really liked drawing potatoes.

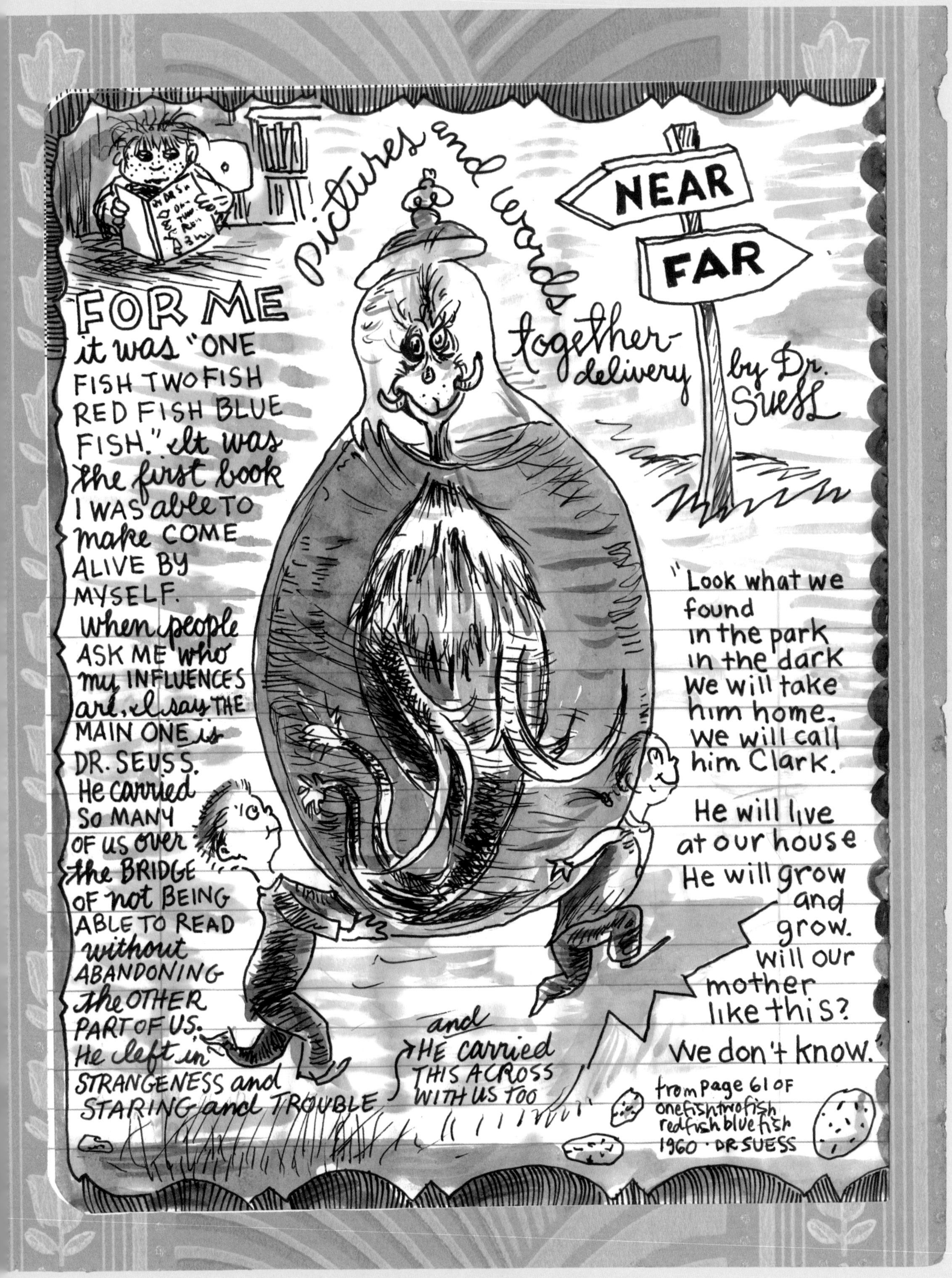
pictures and words together- delivery by Dr. Suess
NEAR
FAR
FOR ME
it was "ONE FISH TWO FISH RED FISH BLUE FISH." It was the first book I WAS able TO make COME ALIVE BY MYSELF.
When people ASK ME who my INFLUENCES are, I say THE MAIN ONE is DR. SEUSS.
He carried SO MANY OF US over the BRIDGE of not BEING ABLE TO READ without ABANDONING the OTHER PART OF US.
He left in STRANGENESS and STARING and TROUBLE
and HE carried THIS ACROSS WITH US TOO
"Look what we found in the park in the dark We will take him home. We will call him Clark.
He will live at our house He will grow and grow. Will our mother like this?
We don't know."
from page 61 of onefishtwofish redfish bluefish 1960 · DR SUESS

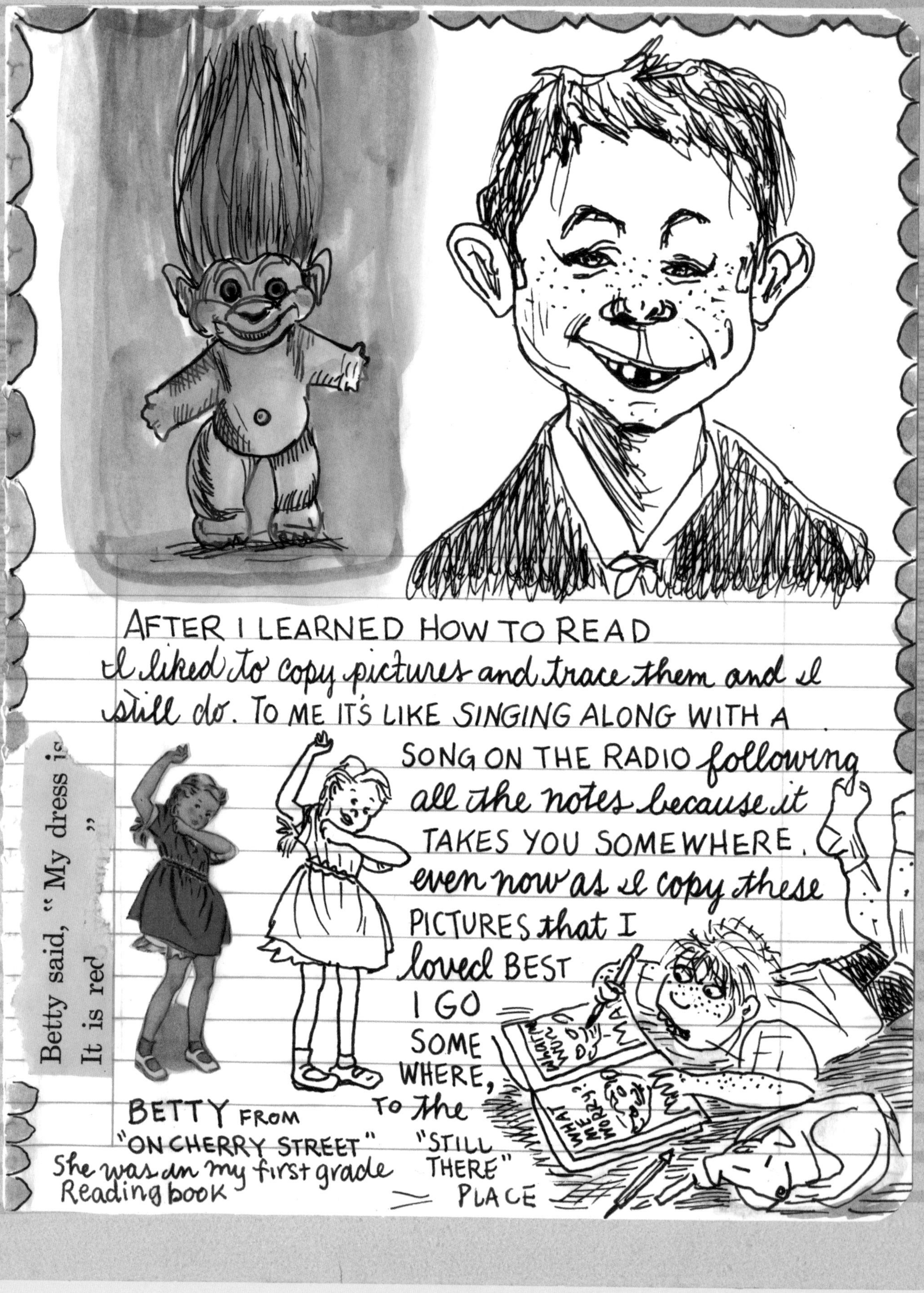
AFTER I LEARNED HOW TO READ
I liked to copy pictures and trace them and I still do. TO ME IT'S LIKE SINGING ALONG WITH A SONG ON THE RADIO following all the notes because it TAKES YOU SOMEWHERE. even now as I copy these PICTURES that I loved BEST I GO SOME WHERE, to the "STILL THERE" PLACE
Betty said, "My dress is
It is red"
BETTY FROM "ON CHERRY STREET"
She was in my first grade Reading book
WHAT ME WORRY?

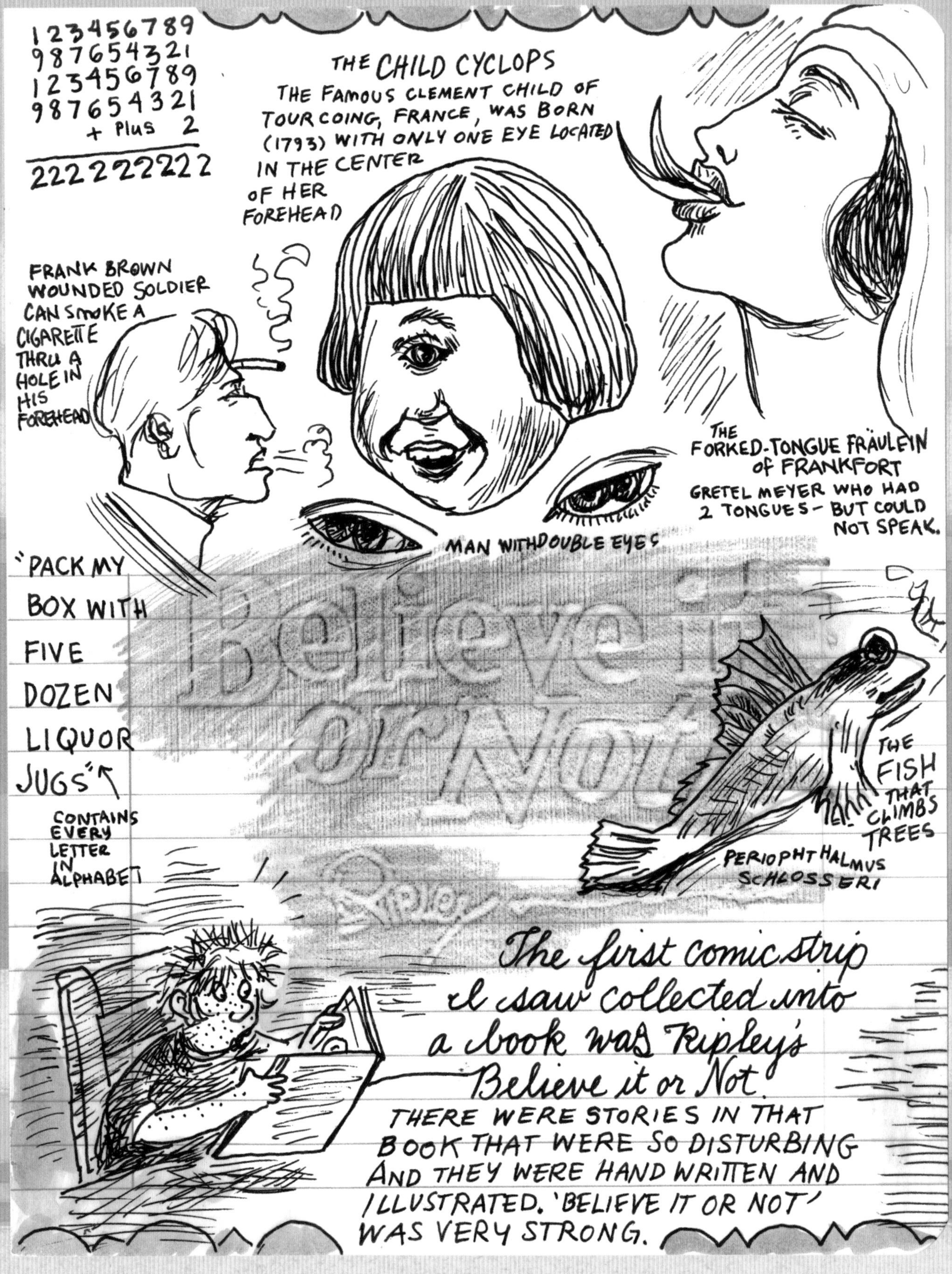
123456789
987654321
123456789
987654321
+ Plus 2
2222222222
THE CHILD CYCLOPS
THE FAMOUS CLEMENT CHILD OF TOURCOING, FRANCE, WAS BORN (1793) WITH ONLY ONE EYE LOCATED IN THE CENTER OF HER FOREHEAD
FRANK BROWN WOUNDED SOLDIER CAN SMOKE A CIGARETTE THRU A HOLE IN HIS FOREHEAD
THE FORKED-TONGUE FRÄULEIN OF FRANKFORT
GRETEL MEYER WHO HAD 2 TONGUES - BUT COULD NOT SPEAK.
MAN WITH DOUBLE EYES
"PACK MY BOX WITH FIVE DOZEN LIQUOR JUGS"
CONTAINS EVERY LETTER IN ALPHABET
Believe it or Not
Ripley
THE FISH THAT CLIMBS TREES
PERIOPHTHALMUS SCHLOSSERI
The first comic strip I saw collected into a book was Ripley's Believe it or Not.
THERE WERE STORIES IN THAT BOOK THAT WERE SO DISTURBING AND THEY WERE HAND WRITTEN AND ILLUSTRATED. 'BELIEVE IT OR NOT' WAS VERY STRONG.

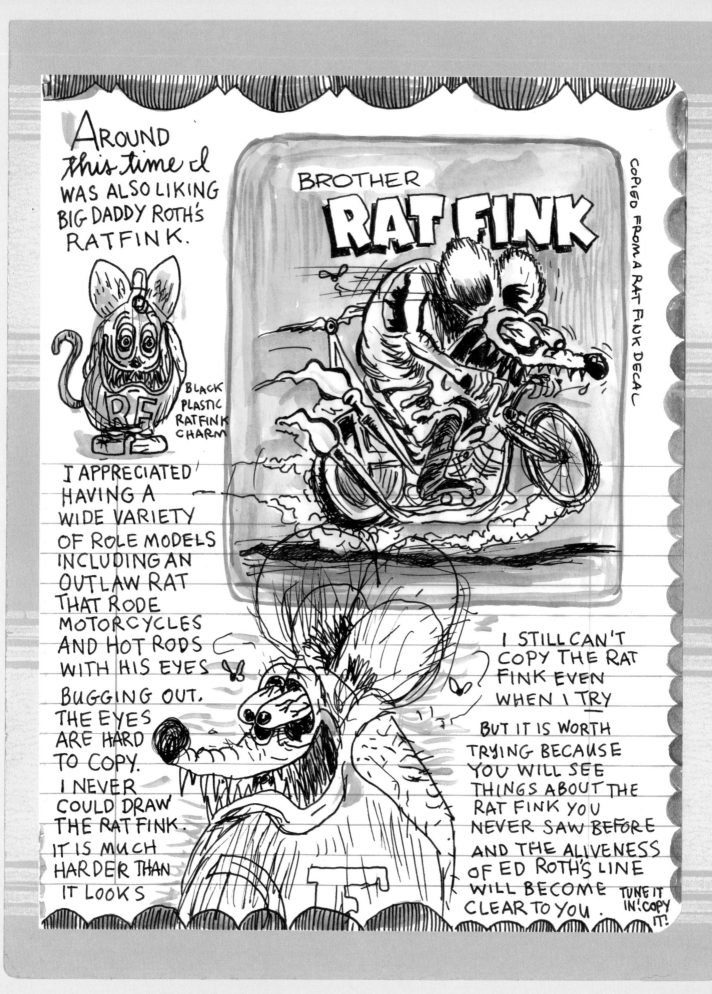

Around this time I was also liking Big Daddy Roth's Ratfink.

BLACK PLASTIC RATFINK CHARM

I APPRECIATED HAVING A WIDE VARIETY OF ROLE MODELS INCLUDING AN OUTLAW RAT THAT RODE MOTORCYCLES AND HOT RODS WITH HIS EYES BUGGING OUT. THE EYES ARE HARD TO COPY. I NEVER COULD DRAW THE RAT FINK. IT IS MUCH HARDER THAN IT LOOKS

BROTHER RAT FINK

COPIED FROM A RAT FINK DECAL

I STILL CAN'T COPY THE RAT FINK EVEN WHEN I TRY

BUT IT IS WORTH TRYING BECAUSE YOU WILL SEE THINGS ABOUT THE RAT FINK YOU NEVER SAW BEFORE AND THE ALIVENESS OF ED ROTH'S LINE WILL BECOME CLEAR TO YOU.

TUNE IT IN! COPY IT!

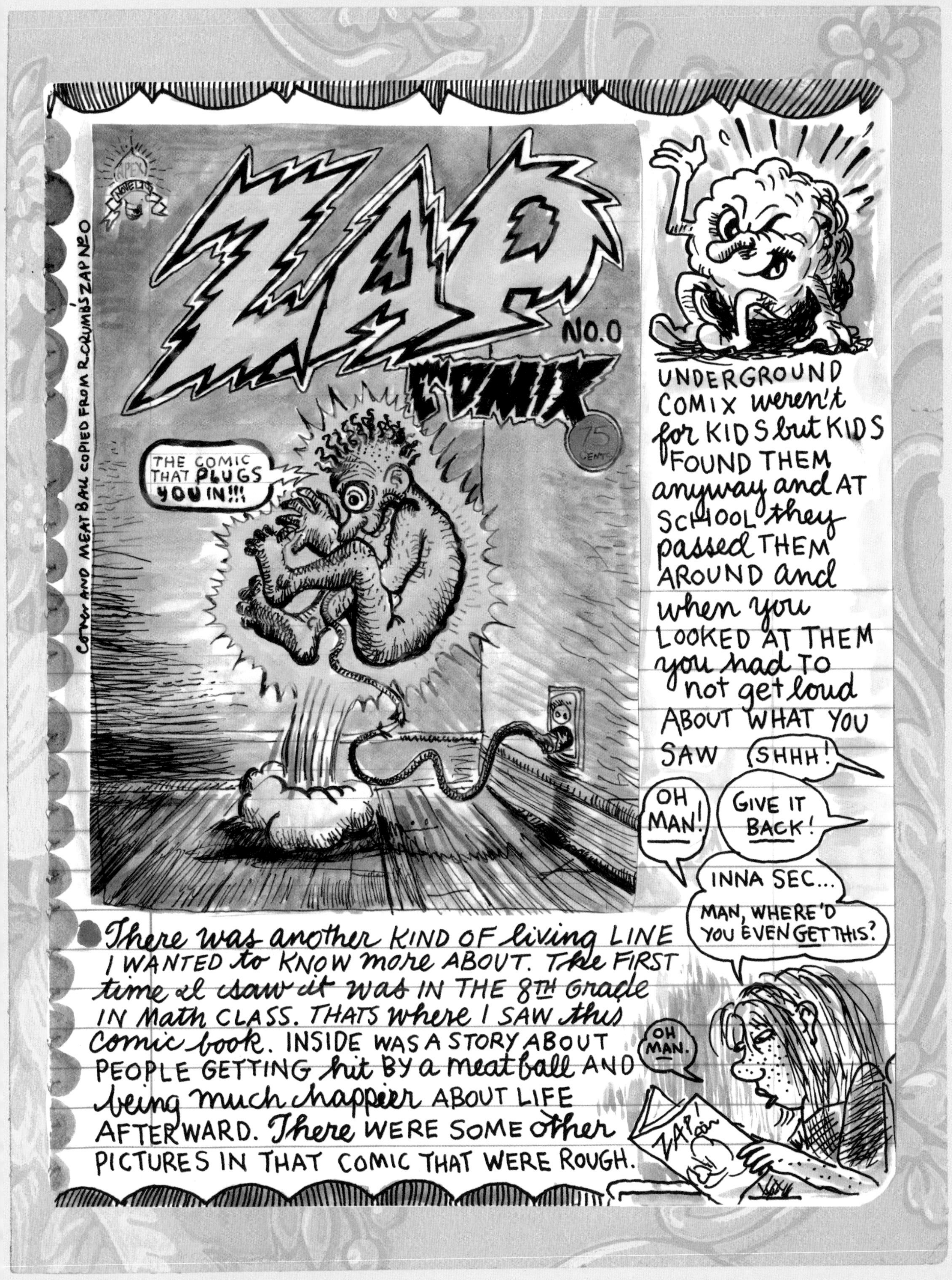
COVER AND MEAT BALL COPIED FROM R. CRUMB'S ZAP NO 0
APEX NOVELTIES
ZAP
NO. 0
COMIX
75 CENTS
THE COMIC THAT PLUGS YOU IN!!!
UNDERGROUND COMIX weren't for KIDS but KIDS FOUND THEM anyway and AT SCHOOL they passed THEM AROUND and when you LOOKED AT THEM you had to not get loud ABOUT WHAT YOU SAW
SHHH!
OH MAN!
GIVE IT BACK!
INNA SEC...
MAN, WHERE'D YOU EVEN GET THIS?
There was another KIND OF living LINE I WANTED to KNOW more ABOUT. The FIRST time I saw it was IN THE 8TH Grade IN Math CLASS. THATS where I SAW this comic book. INSIDE WAS A STORY ABOUT PEOPLE GETTING hit BY a meatball AND being much happier ABOUT LIFE AFTERWARD. There WERE SOME other PICTURES IN THAT COMIC THAT WERE ROUGH.
OH MAN.
ZAP!

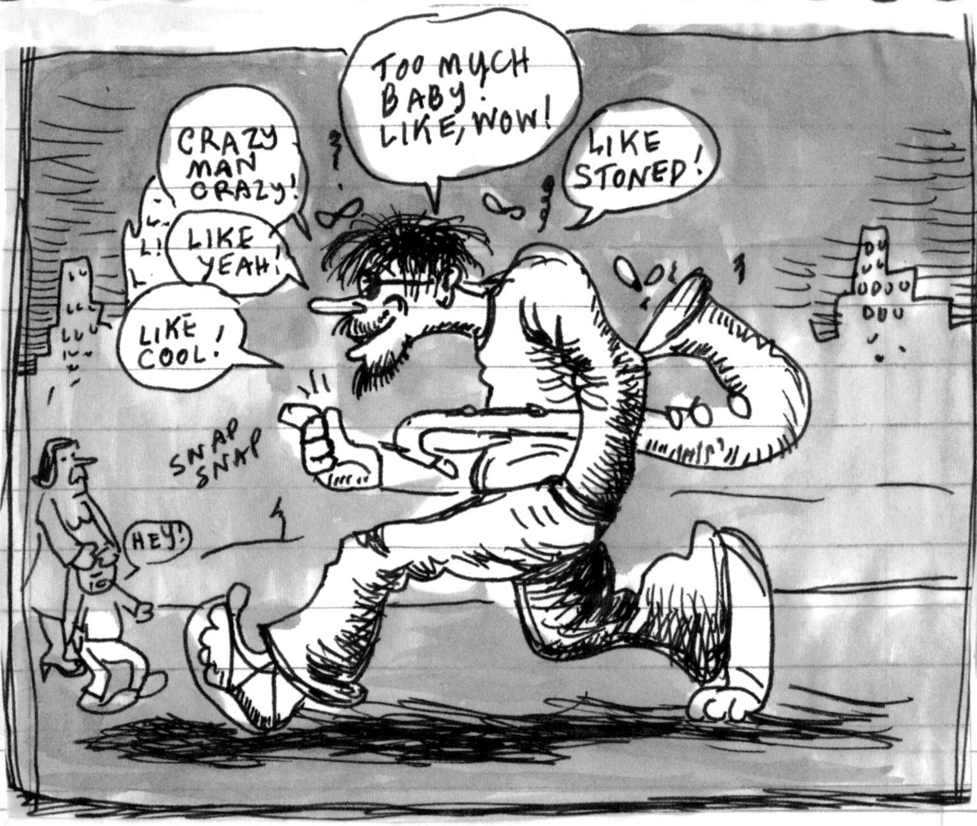
CRAZY MAN CRAZY!
TOO MUCH BABY LIKE, WOW!
LIKE STONED!
LIKE YEAH!
LIKE COOL!
SNAP SNAP
HEY!

COPIED FROM "MEATBALL" ZAP#0 ROBERT CRUMB

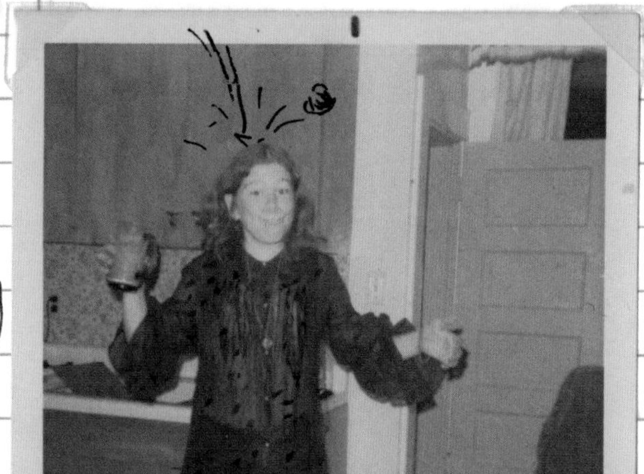

I WAS too YOUNG to GO WHERE underground comix took ME BUT EVERYTHING that WAS going ON AROUND ME seemed TO be IN that Comic. IT both SCARED ME and MADE ME brave. IT made me REALIZE you COULD DRAW anything IN a COMICSTRIP. Even VERY MESSED UP things FOUND IN THE PARK in the DARK A COMPLETELY NEW set of things I'D NEVER dealt WITH BEFORE.

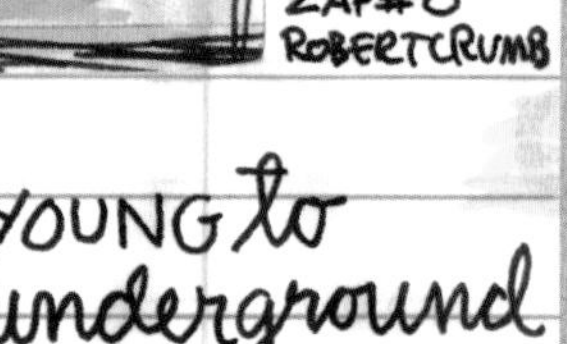

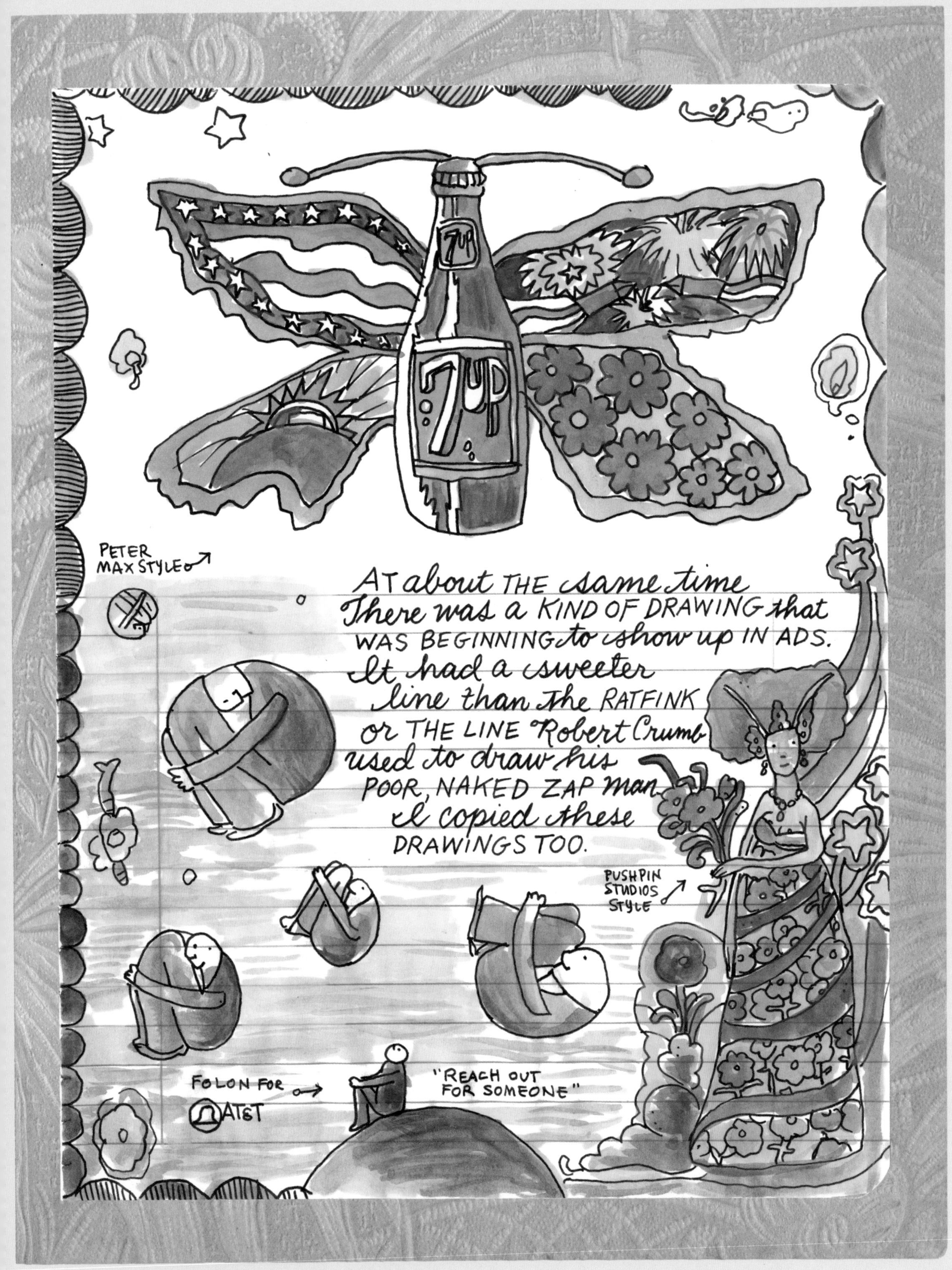
7UP
7UP
PETER MAX STYLE
AT about THE same time There was a KIND OF DRAWING that WAS BEGINNING to show up IN ADS. It had a sweeter line than the RATFINK or THE LINE Robert Crumb used to draw his POOR, NAKED ZAP man. I copied these DRAWINGS TOO.
PUSHPIN STUDIOS STYLE
FOLON FOR AT&T
"REACH OUT FOR SOMEONE"

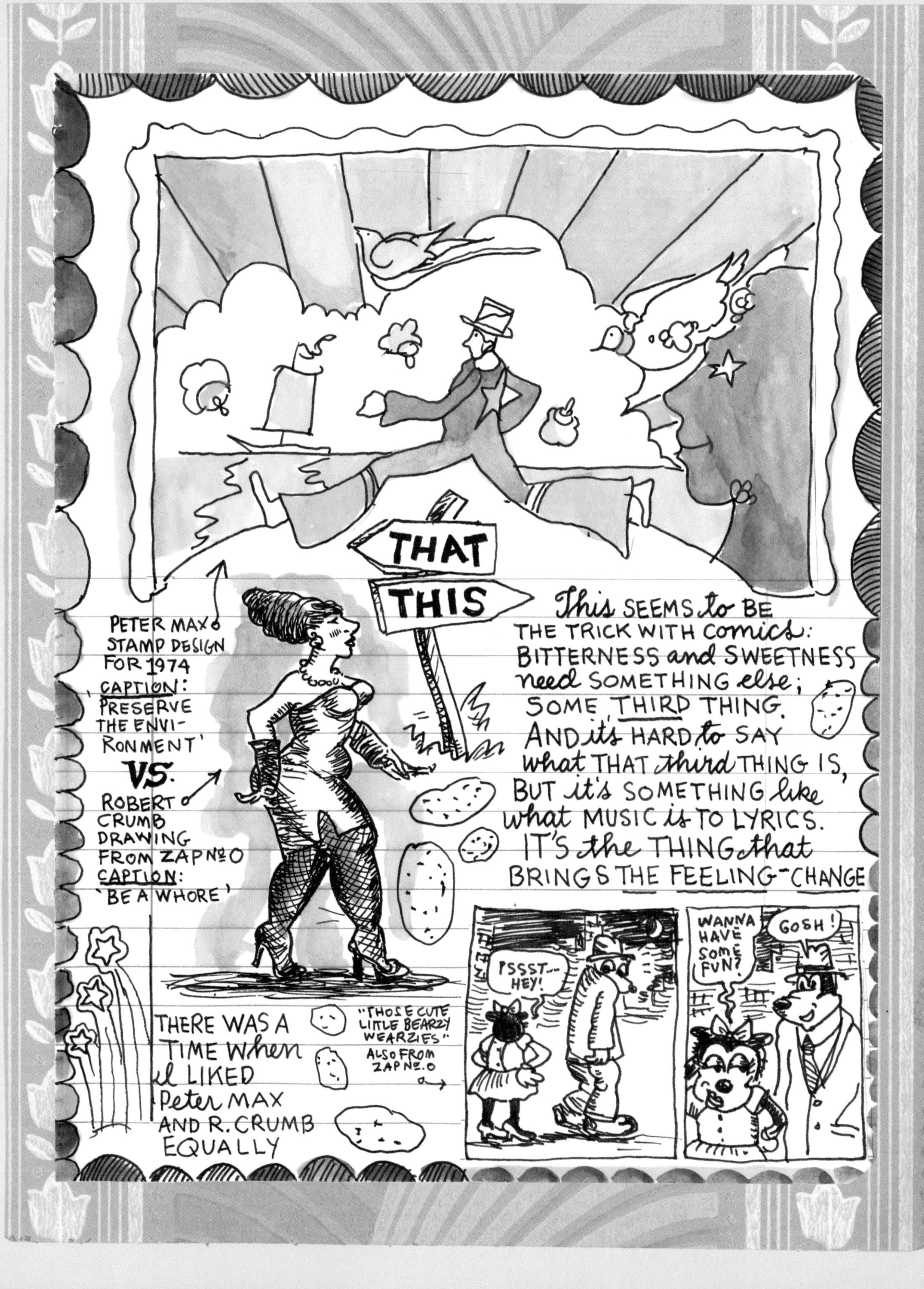
THAT
THIS
PETER MAX STAMP DESIGN FOR 1974
CAPTION: 'PRESERVE THE ENVIRONMENT'
VS.
ROBERT CRUMB DRAWING FROM ZAP No. 0
CAPTION: 'BE A WHORE'
This SEEMS to BE THE TRICK WITH comics: BITTERNESS and SWEETNESS need SOMETHING else; SOME THIRD THING. And it's HARD to SAY what THAT third THING IS, BUT it's SOMETHING like what MUSIC is TO LYRICS. IT'S the THING that BRINGS THE FEELING-CHANGE
THERE WAS A TIME When I LIKED Peter MAX AND R. CRUMB EQUALLY
"THOSE CUTE LITTLE BEARZY WEARZIES" ALSO FROM ZAP No. 0
PSSST... HEY!
WANNA HAVE SOME FUN?
GOSH!

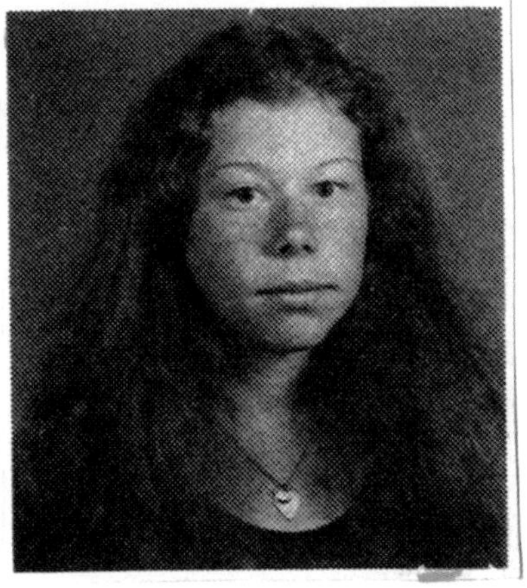

CLASS OF 1974

BY THE TIME I GRADUATED FROM *highschool* I KNEW *about* BITTER *and* SWEET. BUT THANKS TO *cartoonists* LIKE M.K. BROWN, GAHAN *Wilson*, *and* ED SUBITZKY *I also knew about* WEIRD *and* RARE *and* HILARIOUS WAYS OF CHANGING *one* INTO *the* OTHER. *These three cartoonists taught me to* WATCH *the* PEOPLE AROUND *me* AND *Listen* TO *how* THEY *talk* AND *to write down* WHAT THEY SAY!

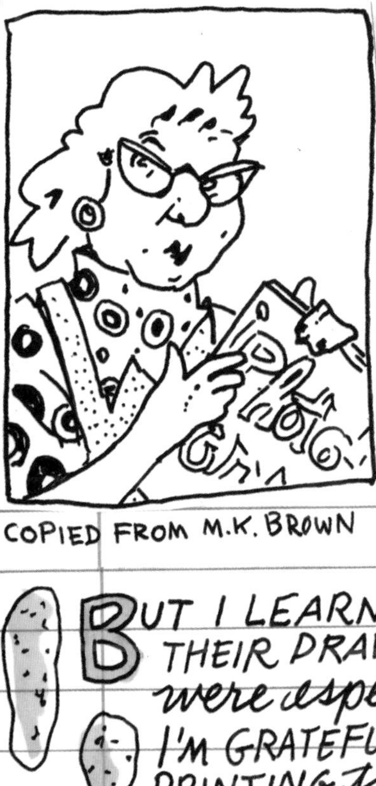

COPIED FROM M.K. BROWN

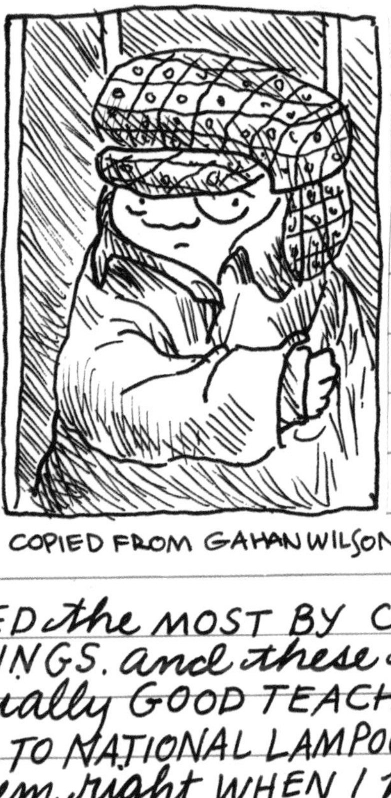

COPIED FROM GAHAN WILSON

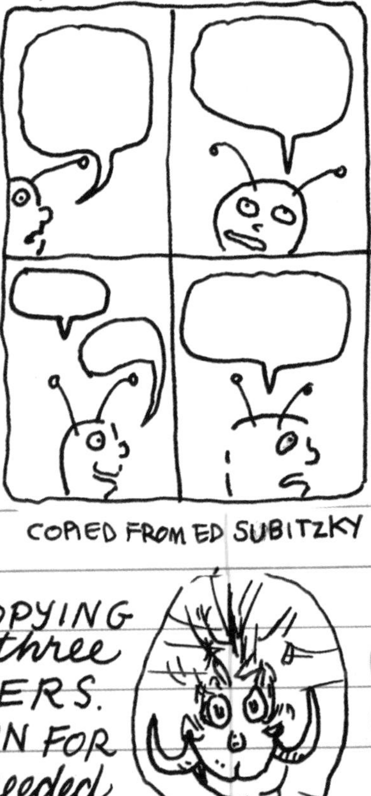

COPIED FROM ED SUBITZKY

BUT I LEARNED *the* MOST BY COPYING THEIR DRAWINGS. *and these three were especially* GOOD TEACHERS. I'M GRATEFUL TO NATIONAL LAMPOON FOR PRINTING *them right* WHEN I *needed them*: ALL OF THE ARTISTS WHOSE WORK I'VE RECOPIED *here made* ME WANT TO KEEP DRAWING *and* WRITING. AND DRAWING AND WRITING SAVED MY LIFE.

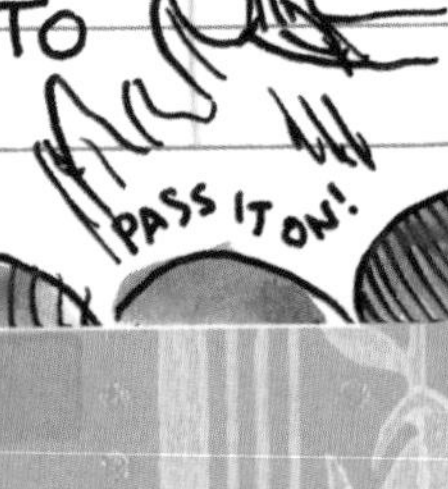
PASS IT ON!

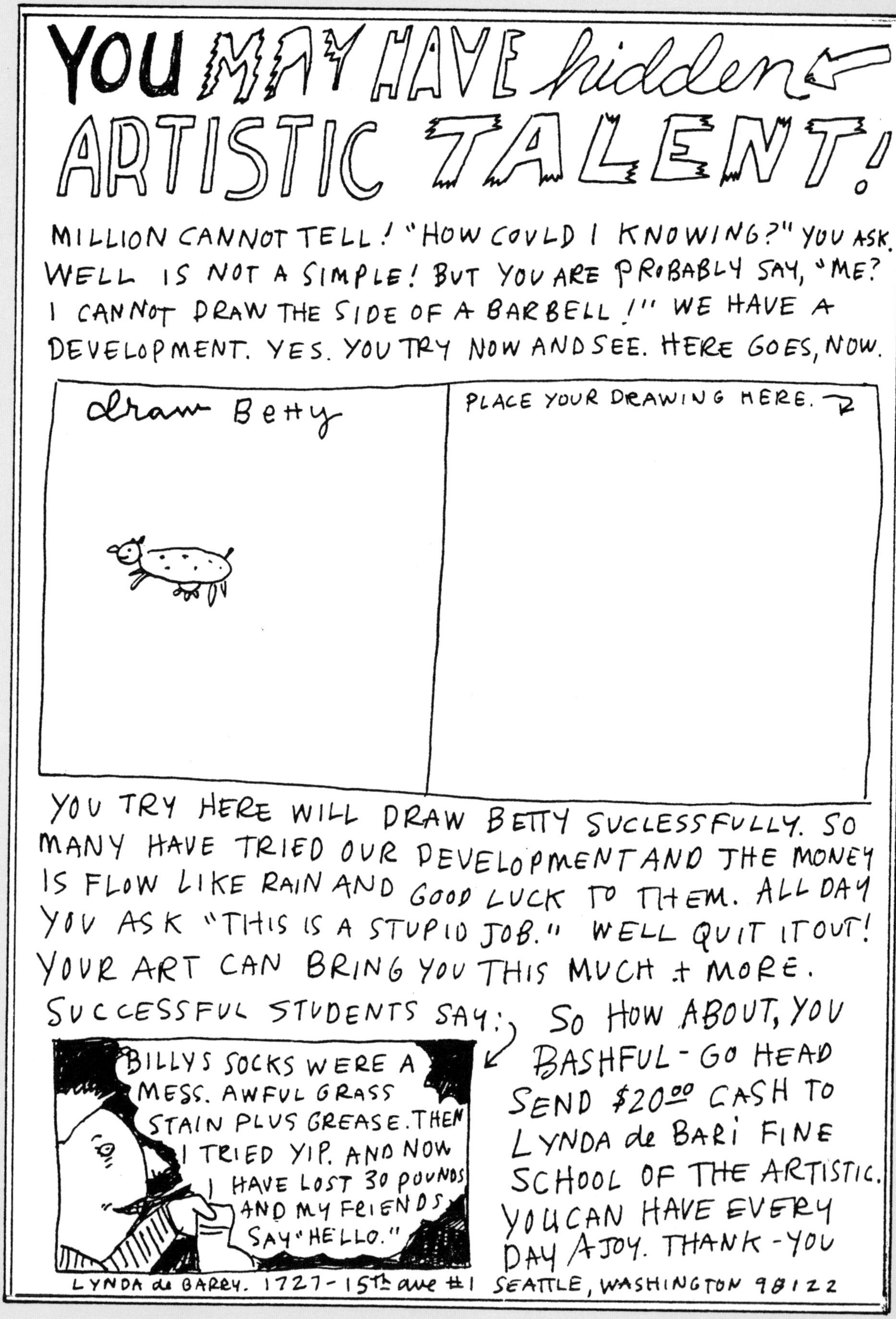
YOU MAY HAVE hidden ARTISTIC TALENT!
MILLION CANNOT TELL! "HOW COULD I KNOWING?" YOU ASK. WELL IS NOT A SIMPLE! BUT YOU ARE PROBABLY SAY, "ME? I CANNOT DRAW THE SIDE OF A BARBELL!" WE HAVE A DEVELOPMENT. YES. YOU TRY NOW AND SEE. HERE GOES, NOW.
draw Betty
PLACE YOUR DRAWING HERE.
YOU TRY HERE WILL DRAW BETTY SUCLESSFULLY. SO MANY HAVE TRIED OUR DEVELOPMENT AND THE MONEY IS FLOW LIKE RAIN AND GOOD LUCK TO THEM. ALL DAY YOU ASK "THIS IS A STUPID JOB." WELL QUIT IT OUT! YOUR ART CAN BRING YOU THIS MUCH + MORE.
SUCCESSFUL STUDENTS SAY:
BILLYS SOCKS WERE A MESS. AWFUL GRASS STAIN PLUS GREASE. THEN I TRIED YIP. AND NOW I HAVE LOST 30 POUNDS AND MY FRIENDS SAY "HELLO."
SO HOW ABOUT, YOU BASHFUL - GO HEAD SEND $20.00 CASH TO LYNDA de BARI FINE SCHOOL OF THE ARTISTIC. YOU CAN HAVE EVERY DAY A JOY. THANK-YOU
LYNDA de BARRY. 1727-15th ave #1 SEATTLE, WASHINGTON 98122

Test Your Sense of Humor!
ERNIE POOKS COMICS by LYNDA-JEAN BARRY
1.
2.
WHICH ONE IS FUNNY?
☐ 1. HULA CHICKEN
☐ 2. A GLASS of MILK

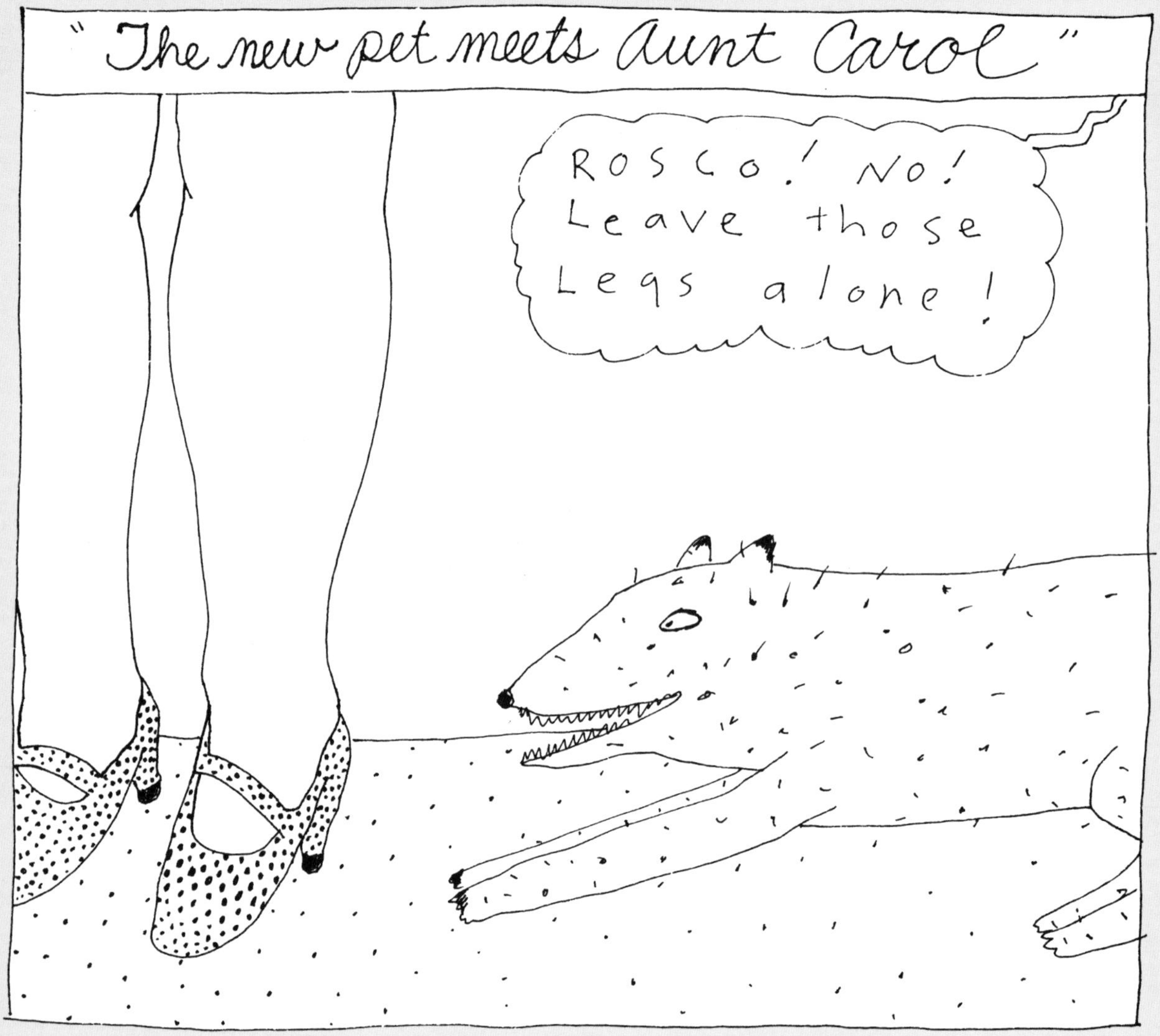
"The new pet meets Aunt Carol"
ROSCO! NO! Leave those Legs alone!

ERNIE POOK'S COMICS
WATCHING OUT NOW YOU ARE THAT THESE NOT JUST BANANA WHISTLE DIXIE IN MY HANDS HERE THIS MINUTE NOW FELLOW. SO THEN I ASKING WHERE IS GIRL?
DON'T SHOOTING ME NOW! I WILL TELLING YOU THIS MINUTE NOW!
L. BARRY/78

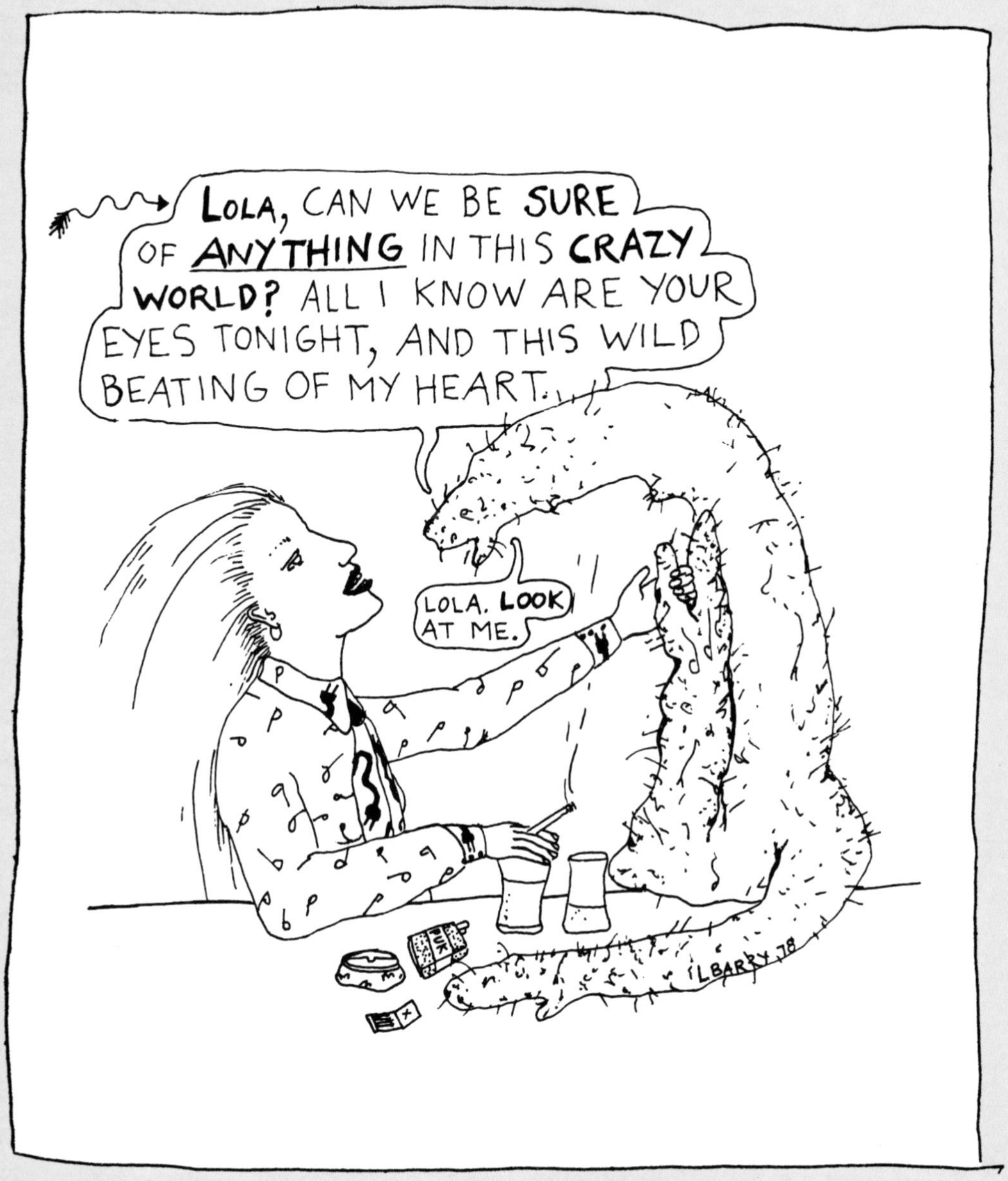

LOLA, CAN WE BE SURE OF ANYTHING IN THIS CRAZY WORLD? ALL I KNOW ARE YOUR EYES TONIGHT, AND THIS WILD BEATING OF MY HEART.
LOLA. LOOK AT ME.
LBARRY 78

EMERGENCY WARD FOR ERNIE POOK
AN ALMOST TRUE COMIC BY Lynda Barry '80 (a girl)
GOOD ONE ERNIE. I JUST SCREWED UP MY FOOT. I SHOULD GO TO THE HOSPITAL
PART 1
MR. POOK?
YES?
THIS GENTLEMAN WAS JUST STABBED IN THE NECK. DO YOU MIND IF HE GOES A HEAD OF YOU?
FISK
NO GOOFING OFF IN THE WHEELCH
NO.
BOY I WONDER WHAT THEY'RE GONNA DO TO ME.
WELL AT LEAST I WASN'T STABBED IN THE NECK. BOY.
UT NO JOKING A
NO SCREAMING
MR. POOK IN ORDER TO TREAT YOU IM AFRAID WE WILL BE FORCED TO STAB YOUR NECK
OH GOD
WE'RE SORRY
NO JOKING AROUND
NO SC
HA HA HA

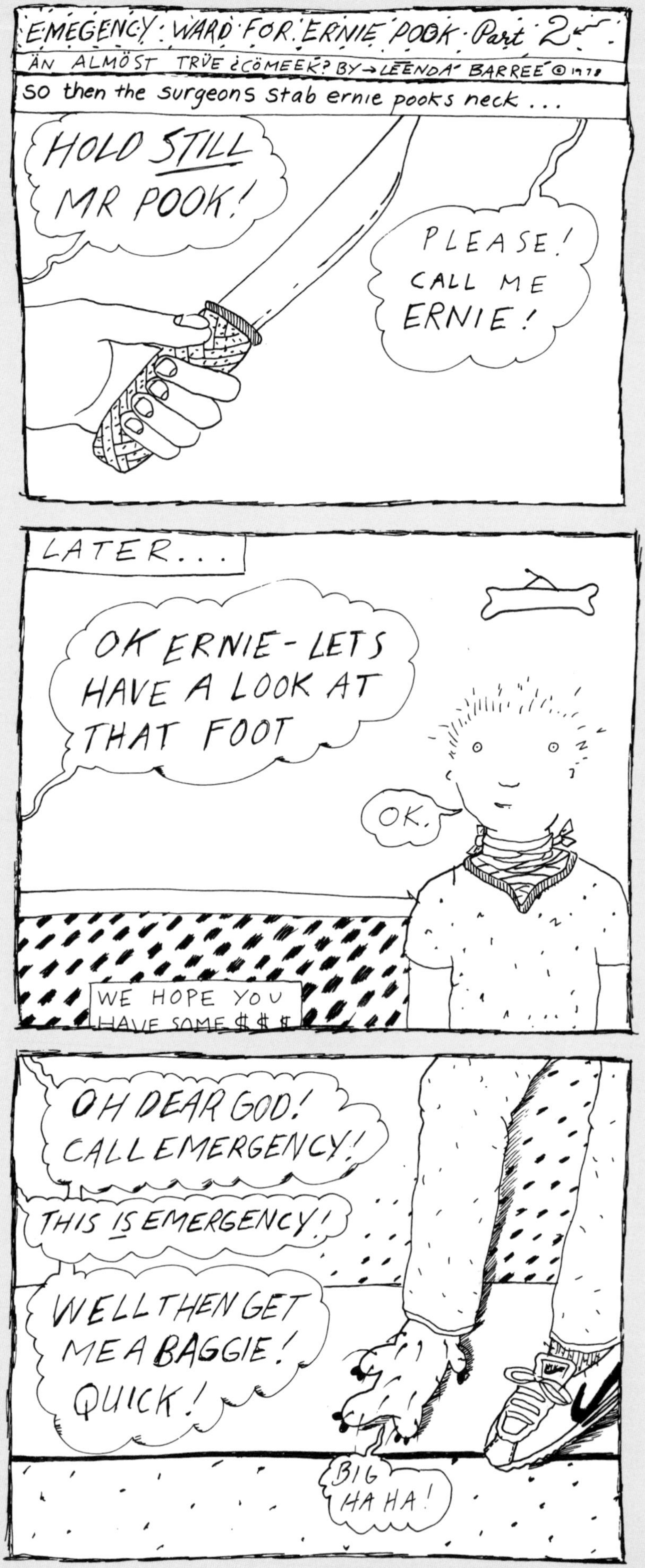
EMEGENCY WARD FOR ERNIE POOK Part 2
ÄN ALMÖST TRÜE ¿CÖMEEK? BY → LEENDA BARREE © 1978
so then the surgeons stab ernie pooks neck . . .
HOLD STILL MR POOK!
PLEASE! CALL ME ERNIE!
LATER . . .
OK ERNIE - LETS HAVE A LOOK AT THAT FOOT
OK.
WE HOPE YOU HAVE SOME $ $ $
OH DEAR GOD! CALL EMERGENCY!
THIS IS EMERGENCY!
WELL THEN GET ME A BAGGIE! QUICK!
BIG HA HA!

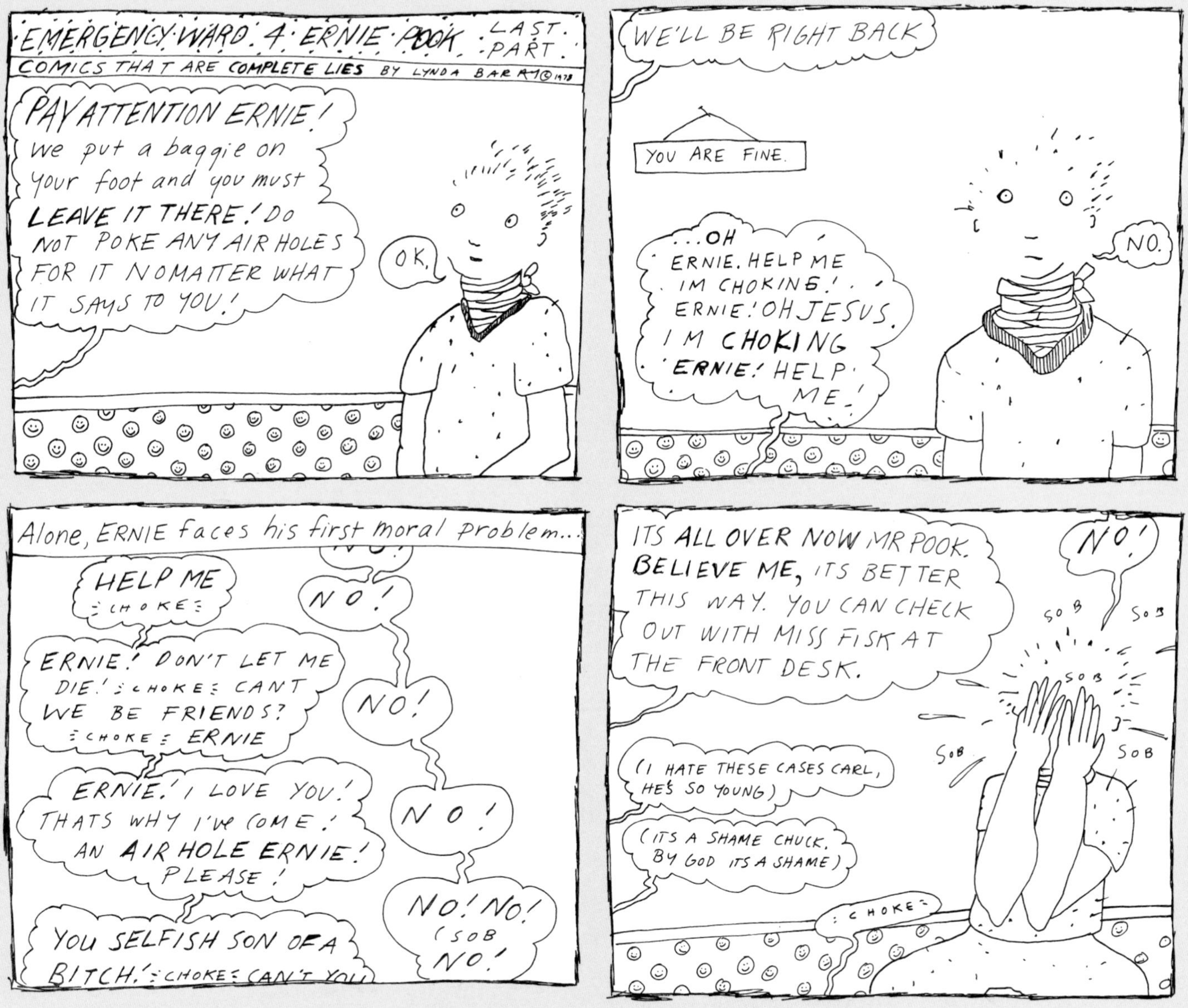
EMERGENCY WARD 4 ERNIE POOK LAST PART
COMICS THAT ARE COMPLETE LIES BY LYNDA BARRY ©1978
PAY ATTENTION ERNIE! We put a baggie on your foot and you must LEAVE IT THERE! DO NOT POKE ANY AIR HOLES FOR IT NOMATTER WHAT IT SAYS TO YOU!
OK.
WE'LL BE RIGHT BACK
YOU ARE FINE.
...OH ERNIE. HELP ME IM CHOKING! ERNIE! OH JESUS. I M CHOKING ERNIE! HELP ME!
NO.
Alone, ERNIE faces his first moral problem...
HELP ME :CHOKE:
NO!
ERNIE! DON'T LET ME DIE! :CHOKE: CANT WE BE FRIENDS? :CHOKE: ERNIE
NO!
ERNIE! I LOVE YOU! THATS WHY I'VE COME! AN AIR HOLE ERNIE! PLEASE!
NO!
You SELFISH SON OF A BITCH! :CHOKE: CAN'T YOU
NO! NO! (SOB NO!
ITS ALL OVER NOW MR POOK. BELIEVE ME, ITS BETTER THIS WAY. YOU CAN CHECK OUT WITH MISS FISK AT THE FRONT DESK.
NO!
SOB SOB SOB SOB SOB
(I HATE THESE CASES CARL, HE'S SO YOUNG)
(ITS A SHAME CHUCK. BY GOD ITS A SHAME)
:CHOKE:

ERNIE POOK'S VAGUE CHILDHOOD MEMORIES
My yellow pillow
(© 1978 LYNDA BARRY)
My Uncle Jerry's Nose
The scariest thing in the world.
Ivan Burke
(My brother Mike's scariest thing in the world)

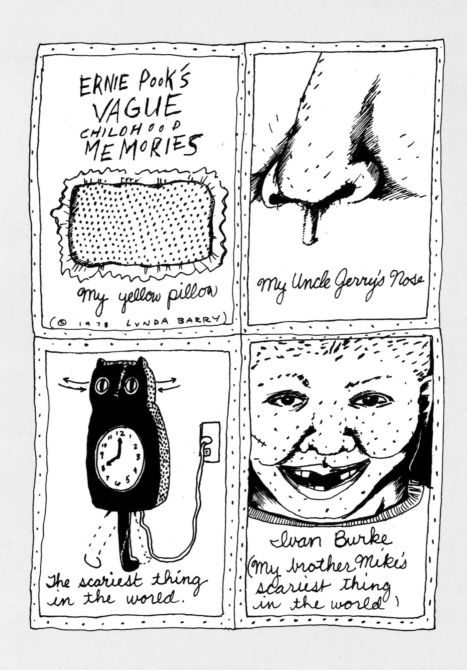

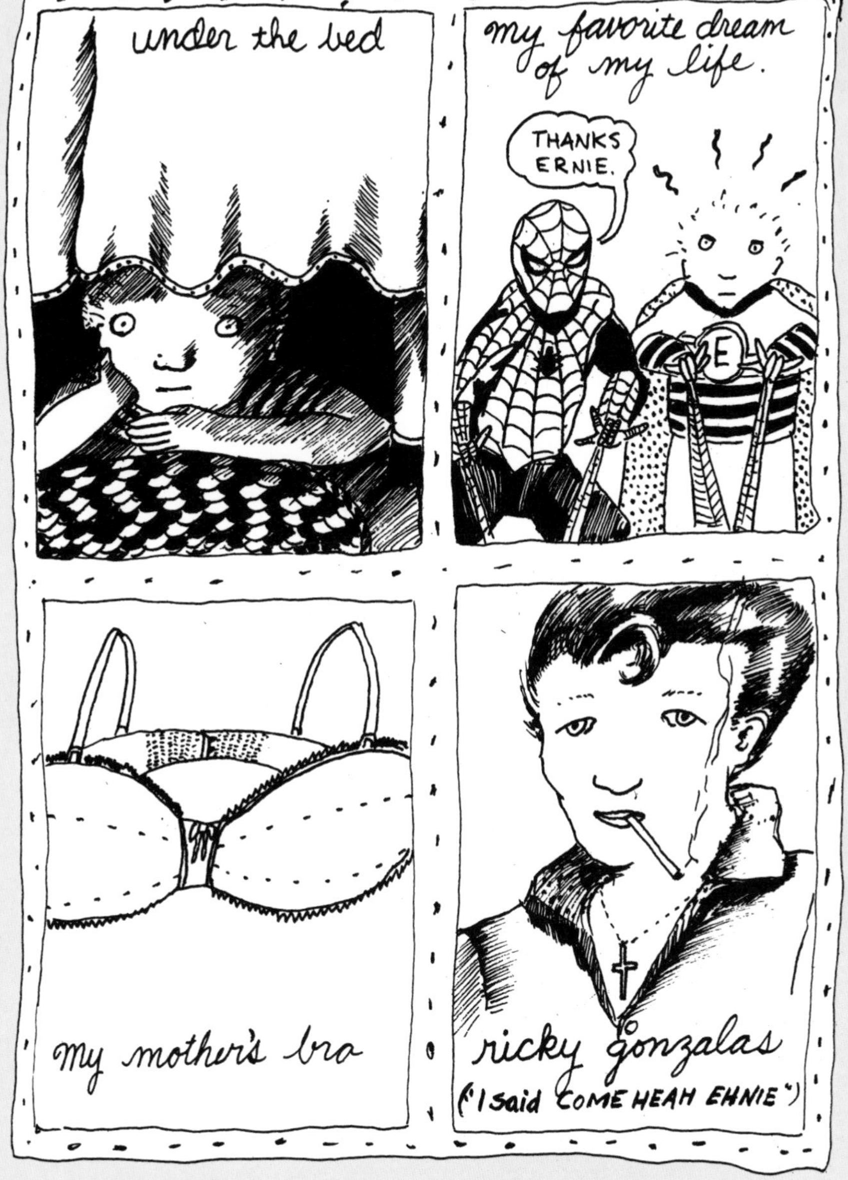
under the bed
my favorite dream of my life.
THANKS ERNIE.
E
my mother's bra
ricky gonzalas
("I said COME HEAH EHNIE")

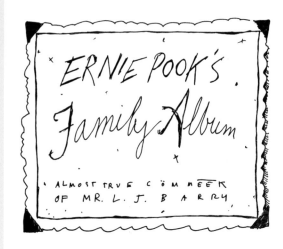

ERNIE POOK'S
Family Album

ALMOST TRUE CÖMÑEEK
OF MR. L. J. BARRY

ROBERT W. POOK "NATURE BOY" 1959

My father was a kind man who loved to shoot pool, play the horses, get drunk and tell jokes.

My mother was an accordian owned by Anita Getz. We tried several times to buy her but Anita wouldn't sell.

"in the back yard" Roy - 1976

My 12 year old brother Roy is the youngest drag queen in Seattle and just loves Pioneer Square and the new Annie Hall look.

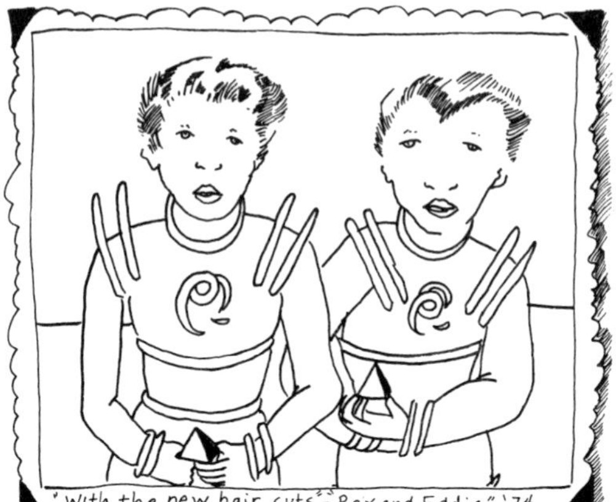

"With the new hair cuts"-Rex and Eddie" '74

My brothers Rex and Eddie are convinced they are from another planet. Dad said something about clones and "goofing off in the basement" but he won't tell us how he did it. Rex and Eddie are very excited about the King Tut exhibit.

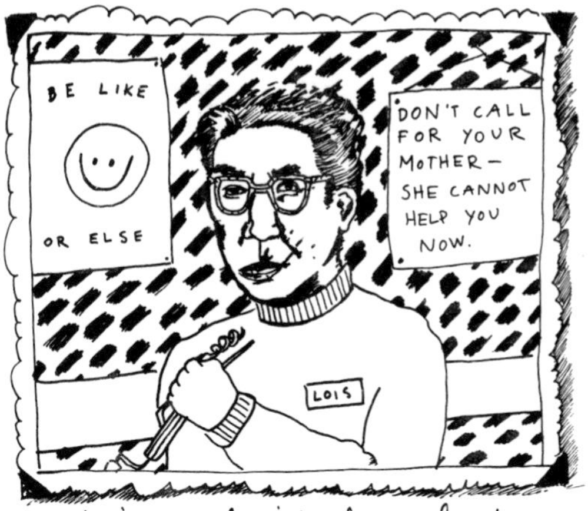
BE LIKE
OR ELSE
DON'T CALL FOR YOUR MOTHER— SHE CANNOT HELP YOU NOW.
LOIS

This is my dentist who made us call him lois when mama couldn't come. He was a psychopath and is in jail now. I was kinda scared of him. He called novocaine the love pinch.

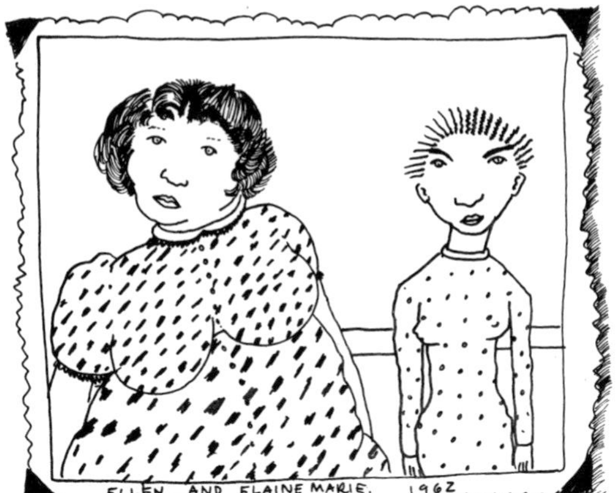

ELLEN AND ELAINE MARIE. 1962

Auntie ellen and auntie elaine marie live together. They have a condominium in West Seattle and go to Honolulu every year. They dont look so happy here but it is because my uncle george who is taking the picture is calling them names.

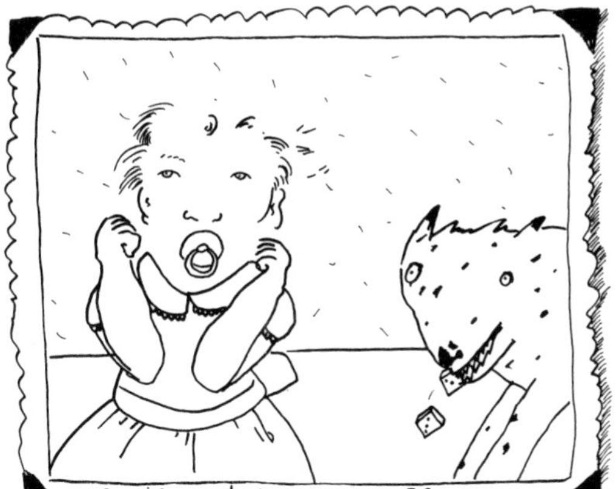

ernie and Joe — 1959

This is me and my dog Joe Paluka. My father taught me how to box and all the words to Jailhouse Rock. He taught Joe Paluka to throw dice with his mouth, but he never made any money off of him.

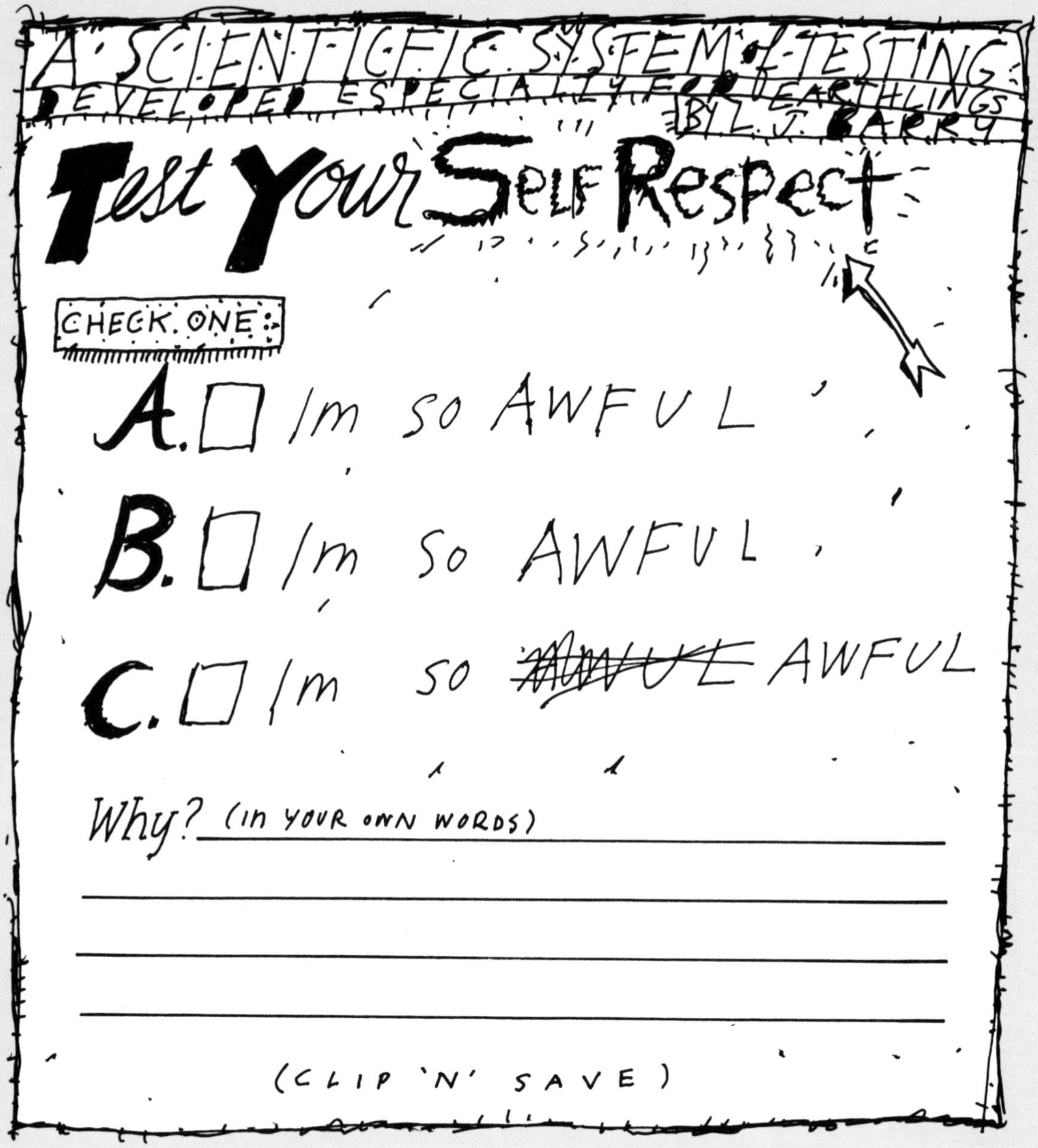

A SCIENTICFIC SYSTEM of TESTING
DEVELOPED ESPECIALLY FOR EARTHLINGS
BY L. J. BARRY
Test Your Self Respect
CHECK ONE:
A. ☐ Im so AWFUL
B. ☐ Im so AWFUL
C. ☐ Im so ~~AWFUL~~ AWFUL
Why? (in your own words)
(CLIP 'N' SAVE)

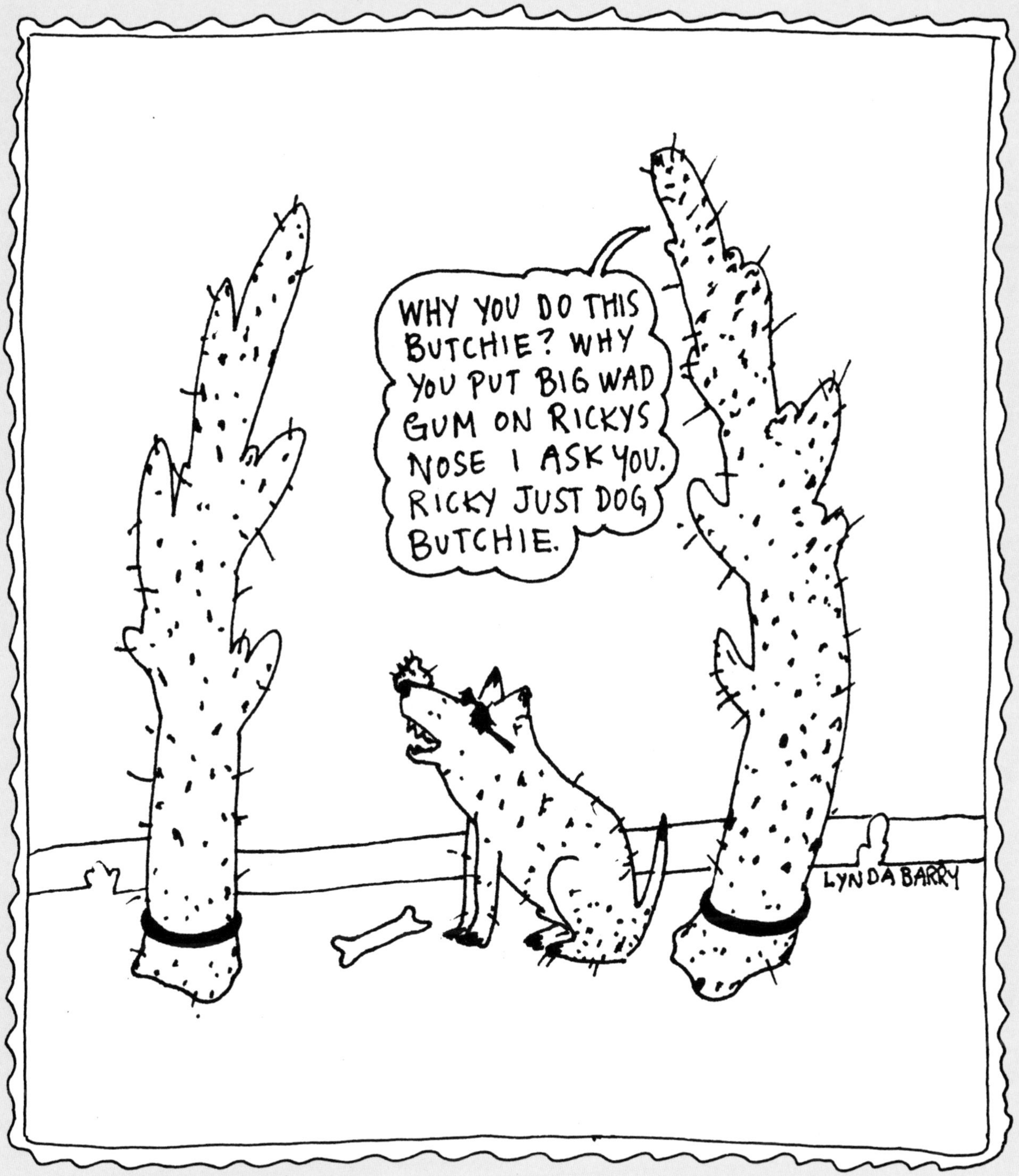
WHY YOU DO THIS BUTCHIE? WHY YOU PUT BIG WAD GUM ON RICKYS NOSE I ASK YOU. RICKY JUST DOG BUTCHIE.
LYNDA BARRY

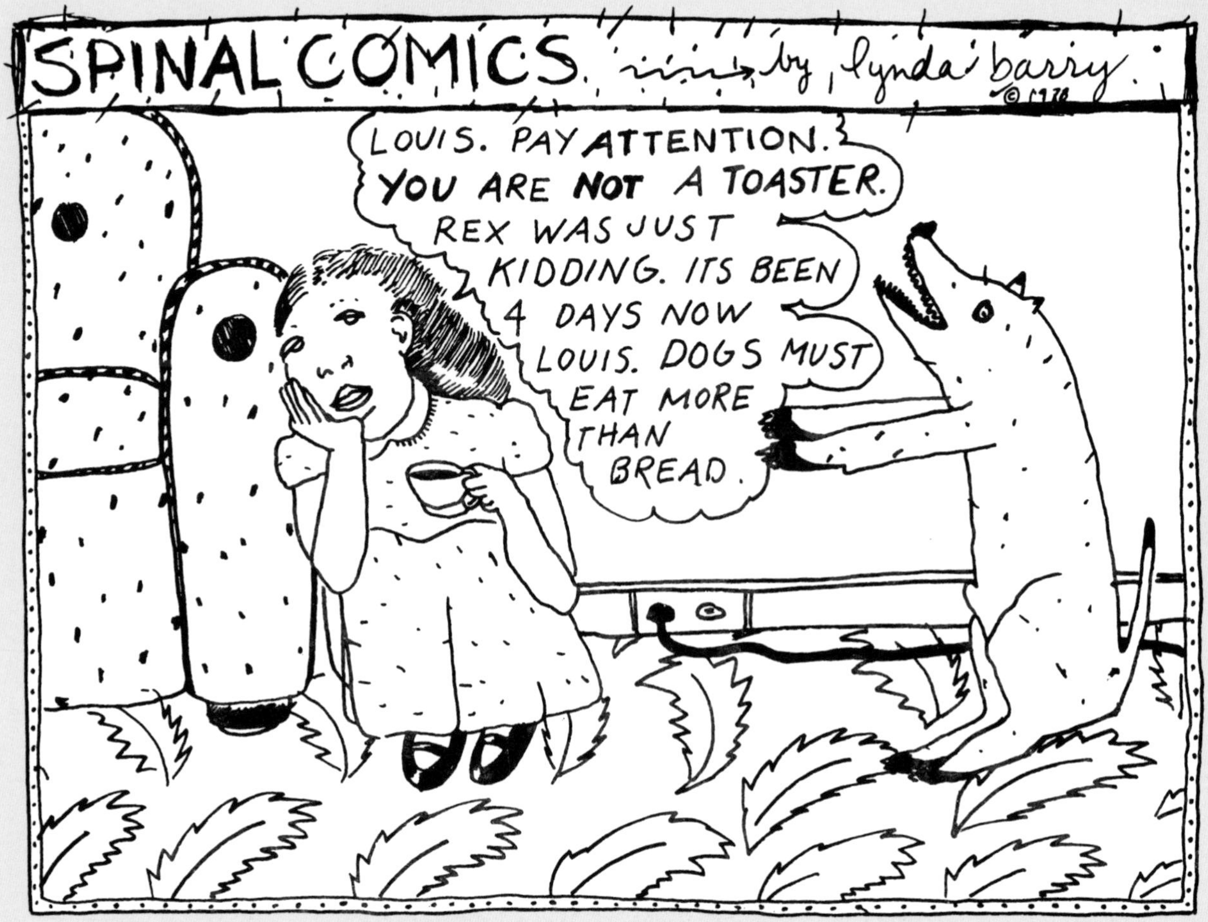
SPINAL COMICS by lynda barry © 1978
LOUIS. PAY ATTENTION. YOU ARE NOT A TOASTER. REX WAS JUST KIDDING. ITS BEEN 4 DAYS NOW LOUIS. DOGS MUST EAT MORE THAN BREAD.

ERNIE POOK REMEMBERS
FAT LEO
LATER
TOO LATE
LYNDA BARRY

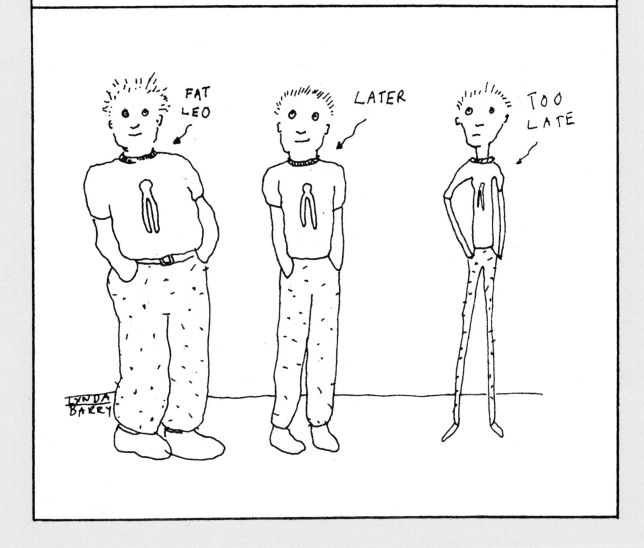

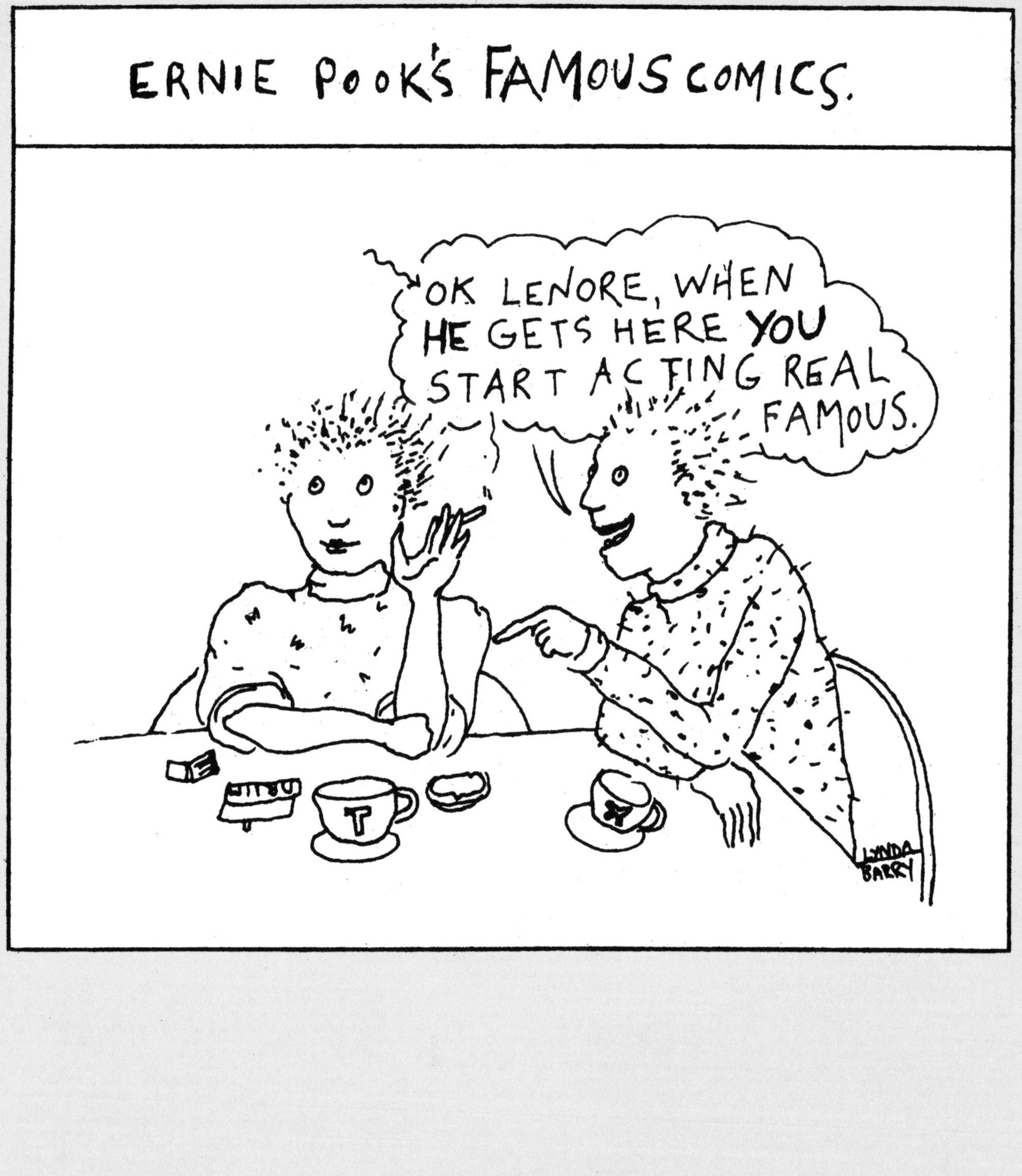
ERNIE POOK'S FAMOUS COMICS.
OK LENORE, WHEN HE GETS HERE YOU START ACTING REAL FAMOUS.
LYNDA BARRY

rita and Evette's
FUN QUIZ!
©1978
FOR MARK BARRY
HOUSEHOLD COMEEKS by LYNDA BARRY
the D ENTURES
LITTLE DICKY
A CANADIAN JUMBO
SISTER DIANA
A 10 PIN
10
Match the objects.
draw lines between ones that go together.

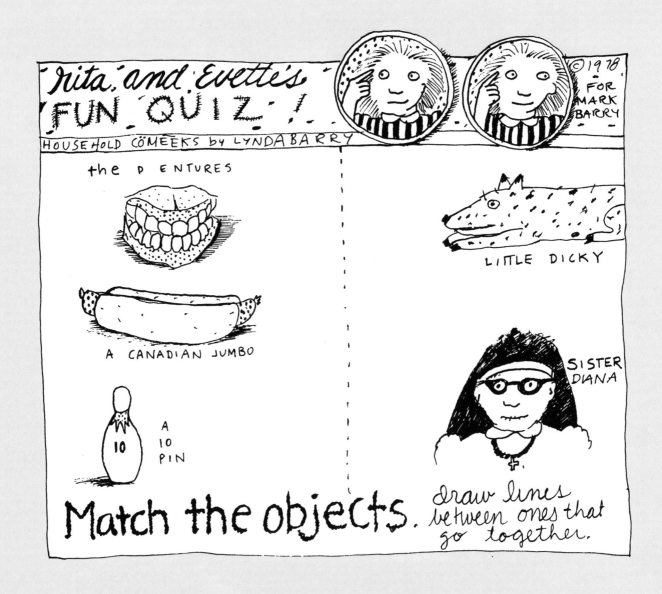

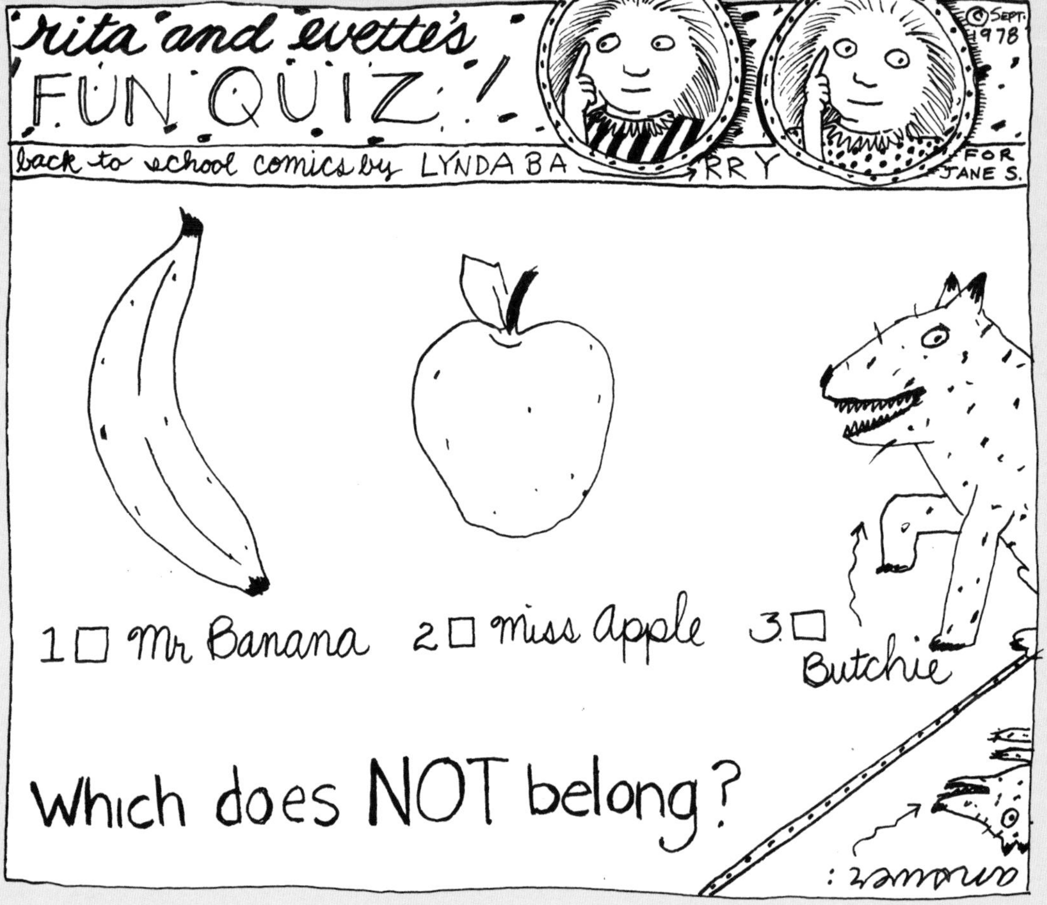
rita and evette's
FUN QUIZ!
© SEPT. 1978
back to school comics by LYNDA BARRY
FOR JANE S.
1 ☐ Mr Banana
2 ☐ miss Apple
3. ☐ Butchie
Which does NOT belong?
answer:

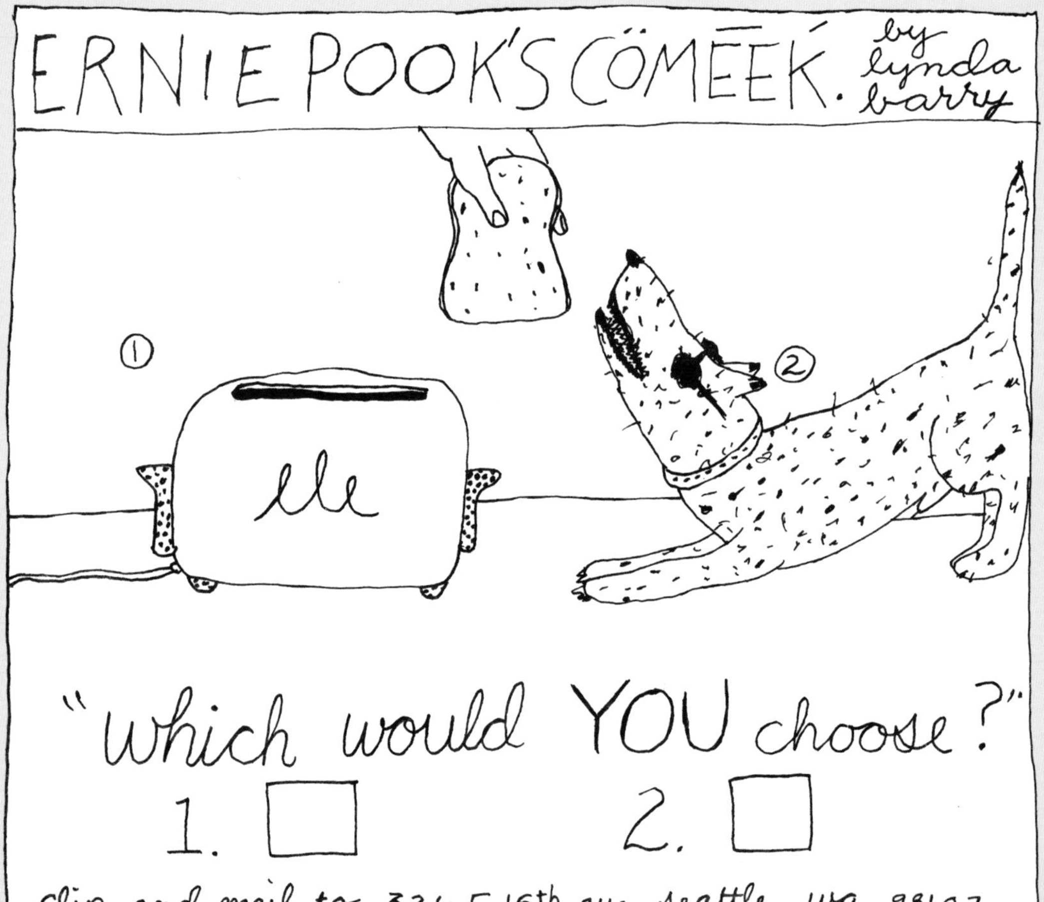
ERNIE POOK'S COMEEK.
by lynda barry
①
②
"Which would YOU choose?"
1. ☐
2. ☐
clip and mail to 326 E 15th ave seattle, wa 98102

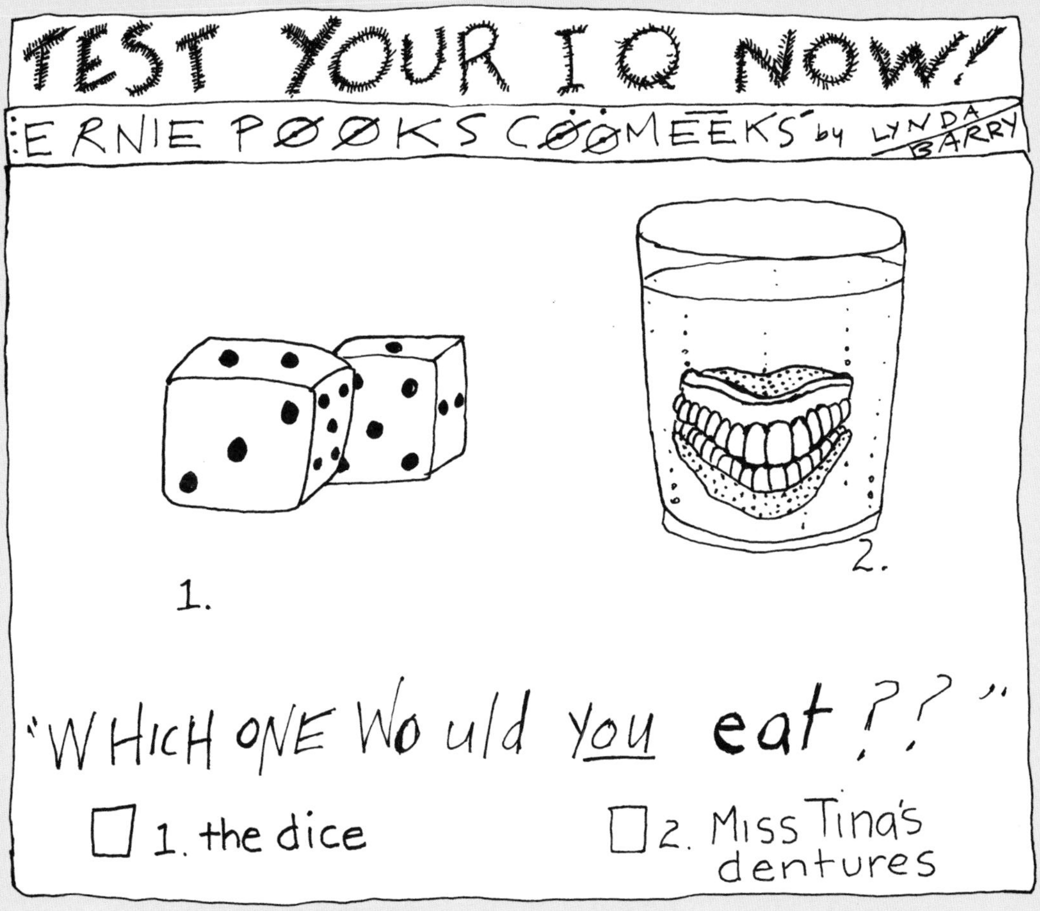
TEST YOUR I Q NOW!
ERNIE PØØKS CØØMEEKS by LYNDA BARRY
1.
2.
"WHICH ONE Would YOU eat??"
1. the dice
2. Miss Tina's dentures

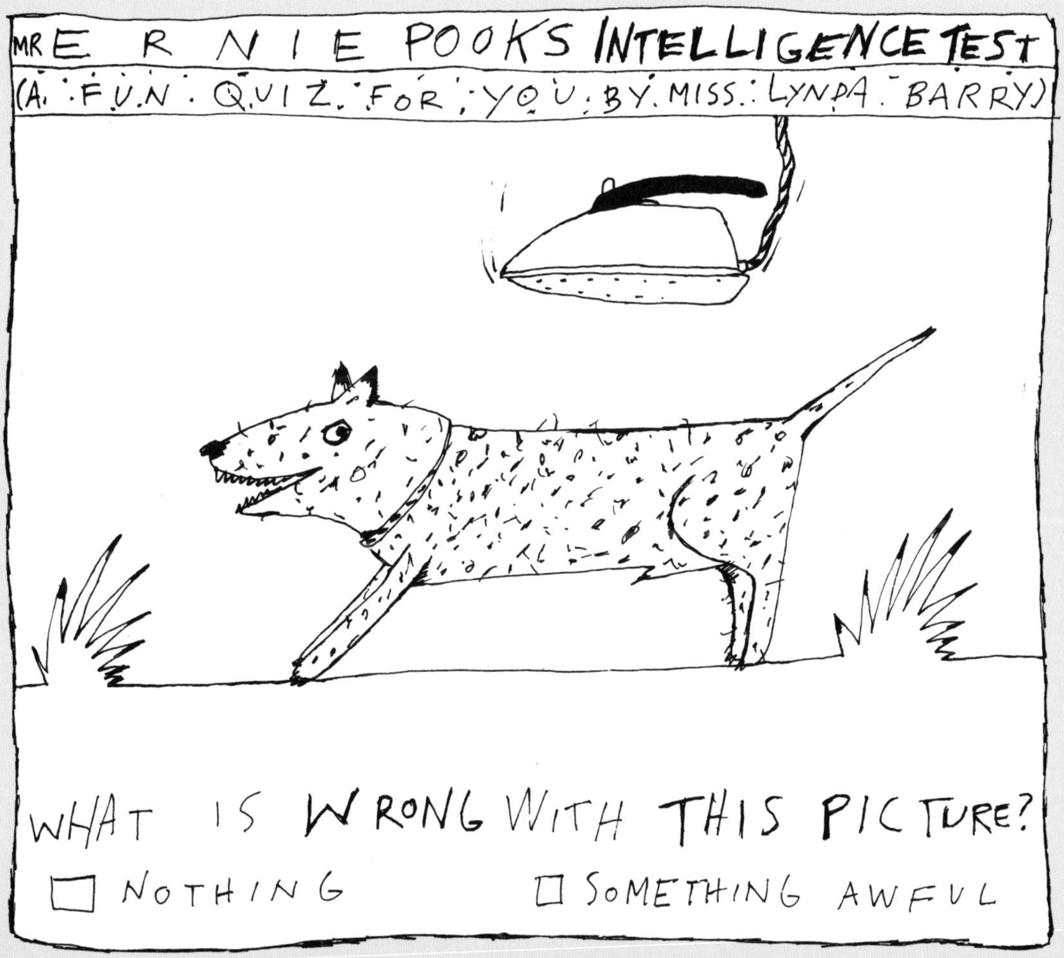
MR ERNIE POOKS INTELLIGENCE TEST
(A FUN QUIZ FOR YOU BY MISS LYNDA BARRY)
WHAT IS WRONG WITH THIS PICTURE?
NOTHING
SOMETHING AWFUL

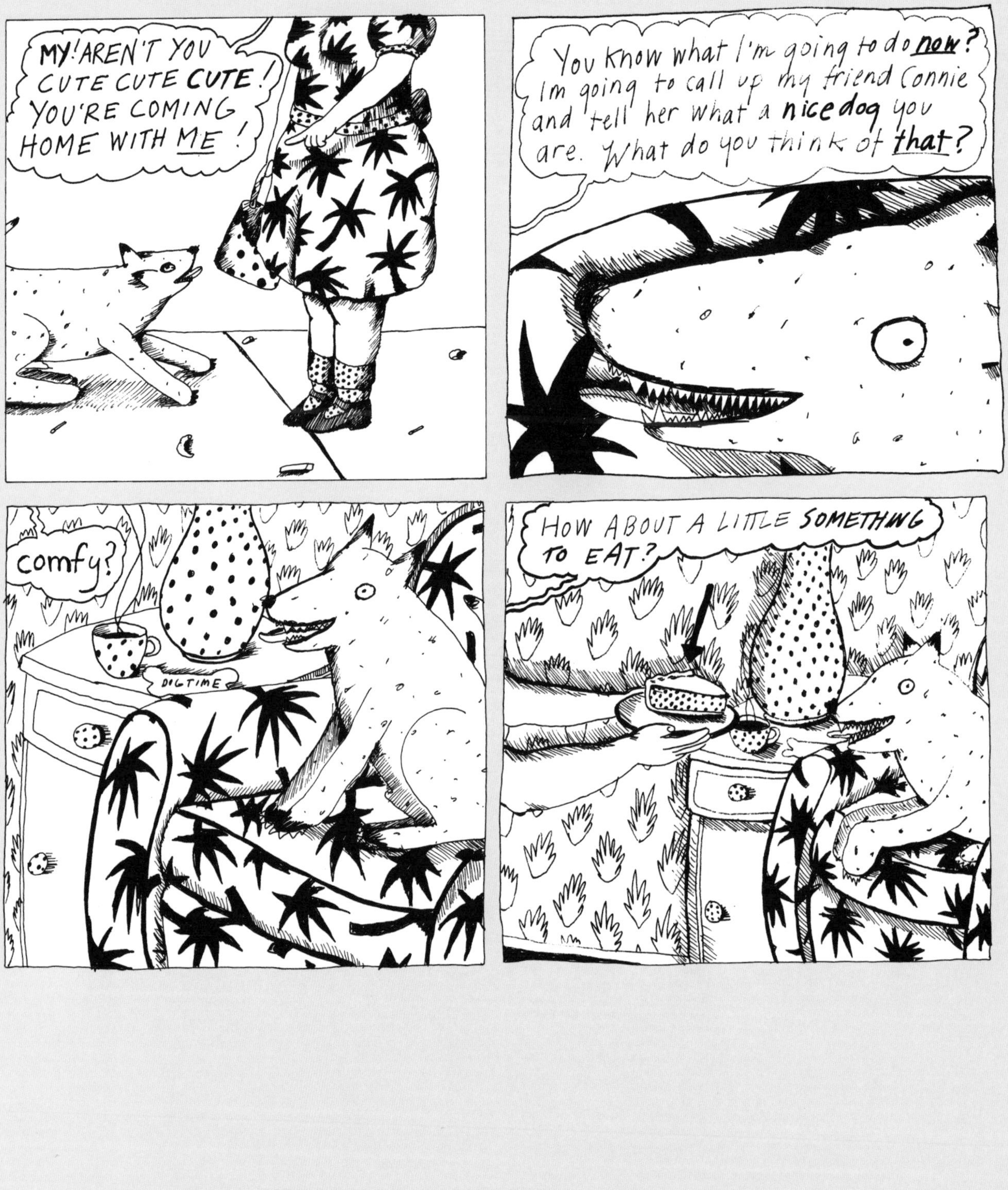
MY! AREN'T YOU CUTE CUTE CUTE! YOU'RE COMING HOME WITH ME!
You know what I'm going to do now? I'm going to call up my friend Connie and tell her what a nice dog you are. What do you think of that?
comfy?
DOGTIME
HOW ABOUT A LITTLE SOMETHING TO EAT?

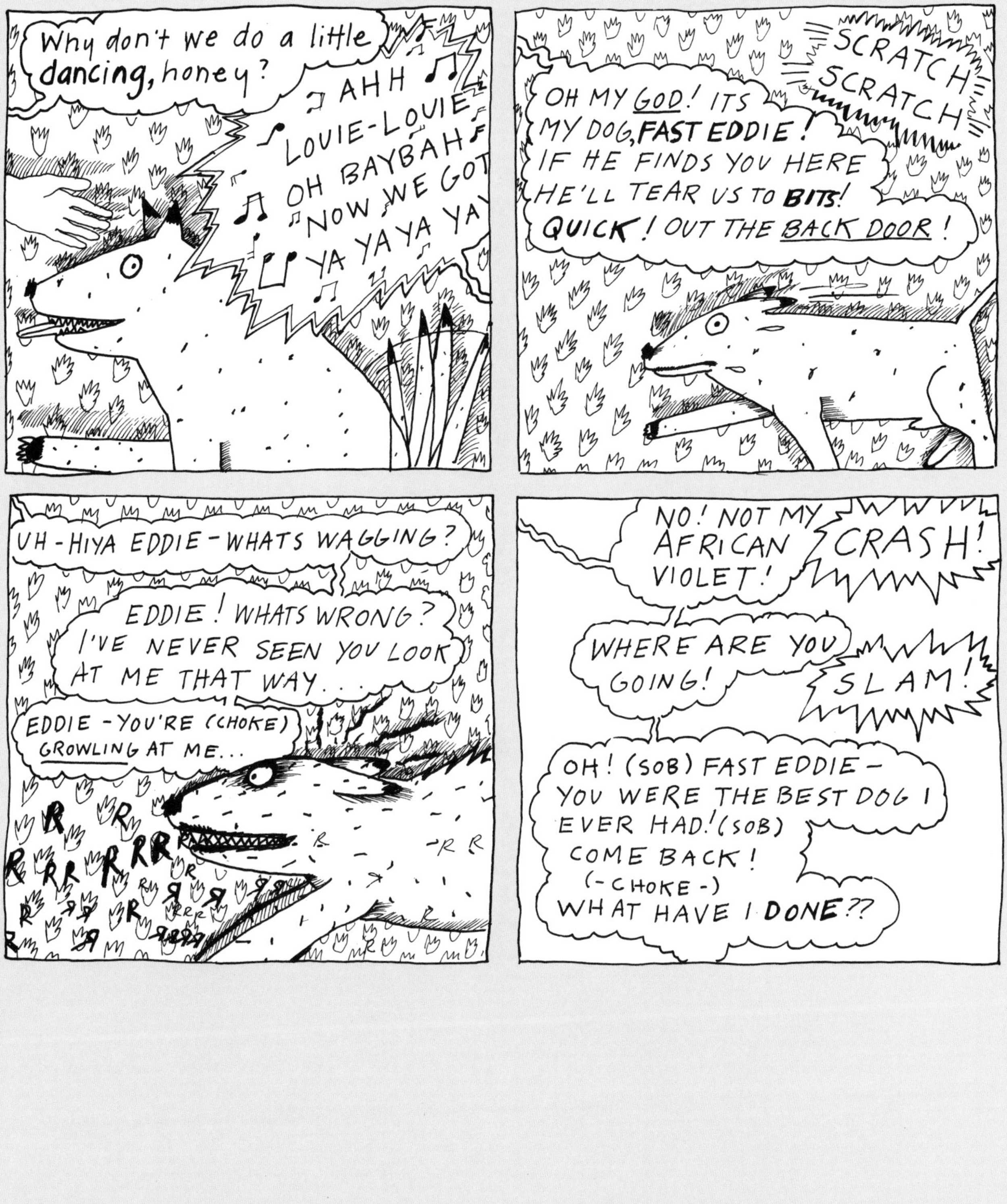
Why don't we do a little dancing, honey?
AHH LOUIE-LOUIE OH BAYBAH NOW WE GOT YA YA YA YA
SCRATCH SCRATCH
OH MY GOD! ITS MY DOG, FAST EDDIE! IF HE FINDS YOU HERE HE'LL TEAR US TO BITS! QUICK! OUT THE BACK DOOR!
UH-HIYA EDDIE - WHATS WAGGING?
EDDIE! WHATS WRONG? I'VE NEVER SEEN YOU LOOK AT ME THAT WAY...
EDDIE - YOU'RE (CHOKE) GROWLING AT ME...
RRRRRR
NO! NOT MY AFRICAN VIOLET!
CRASH!
WHERE ARE YOU GOING!
SLAM!
OH! (SOB) FAST EDDIE - YOU WERE THE BEST DOG I EVER HAD! (SOB) COME BACK! (-CHOKE-) WHAT HAVE I DONE??

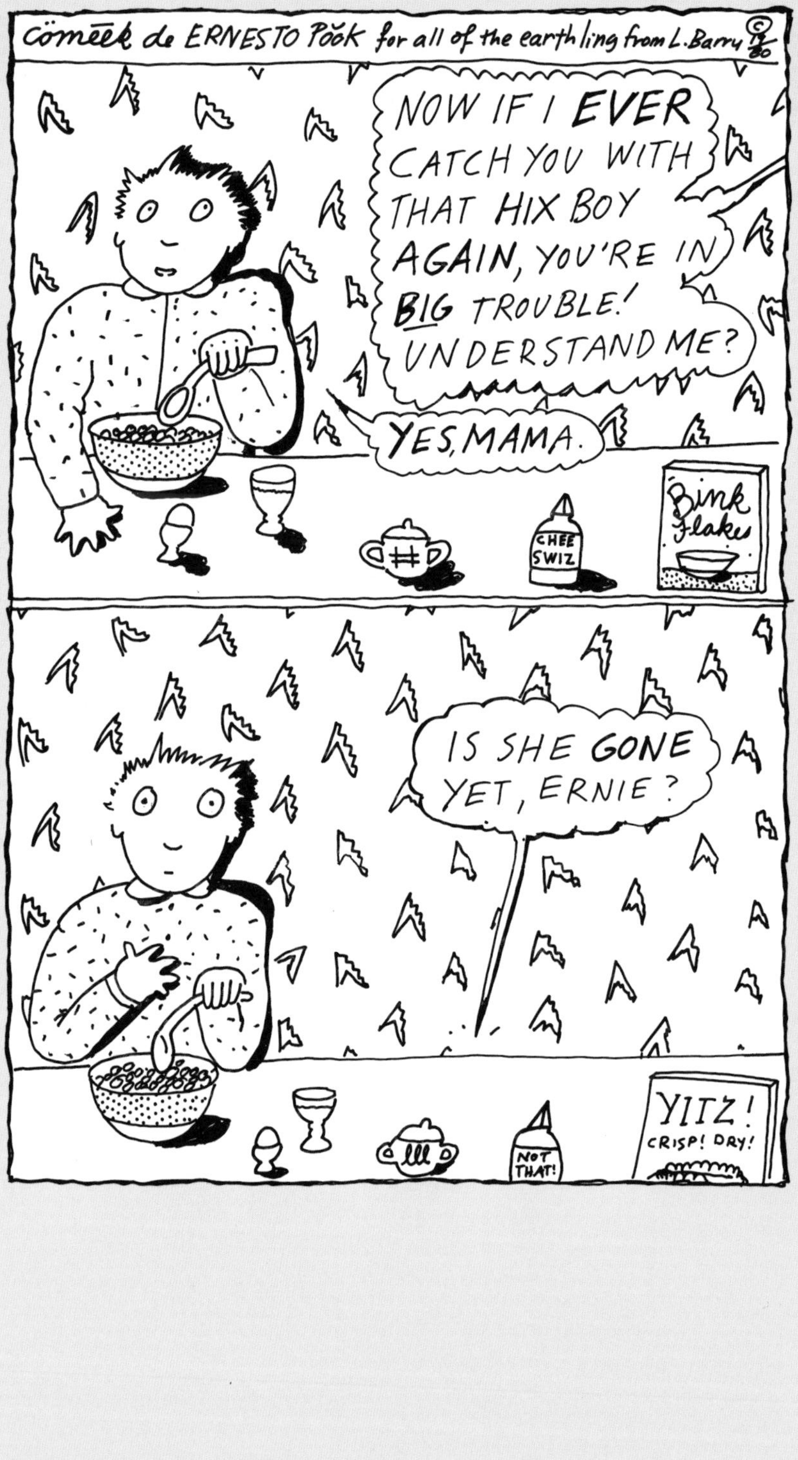
Cömēēk de ERNESTO Pŏŏk for all of the earthling from L. Barry © 80
NOW IF I EVER CATCH YOU WITH THAT HIX BOY AGAIN, YOU'RE IN BIG TROUBLE! UNDERSTAND ME?
YES, MAMA.
CHEE SWIZ
Bink Flakes
IS SHE GONE YET, ERNIE?
NOT THAT!
YITZ! CRISP! DRY!

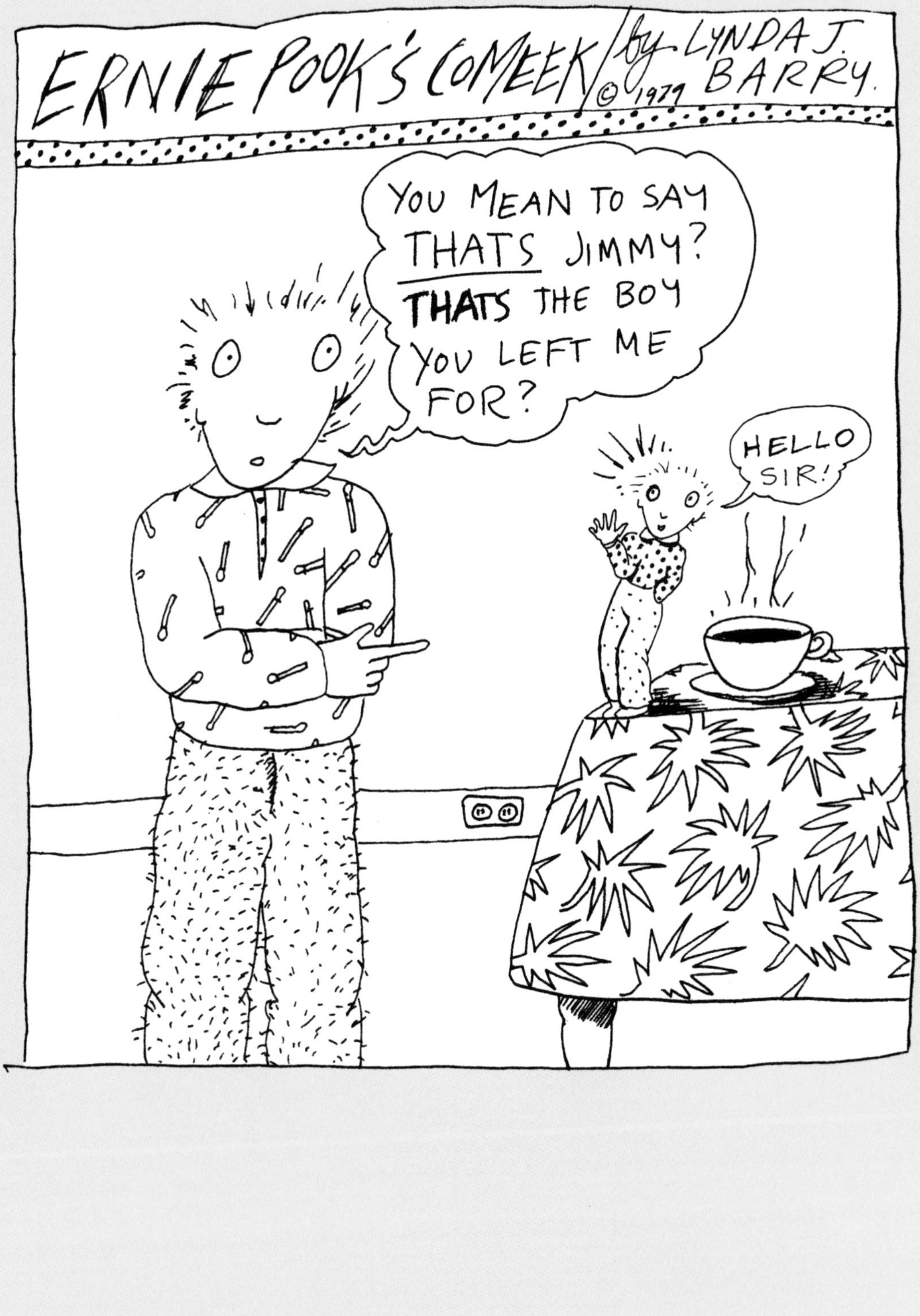
ERNIE POOK'S COMEEK
by LYNDA J. BARRY. © 1979
YOU MEAN TO SAY THATS JIMMY? THATS THE BOY YOU LEFT ME FOR?
HELLO SIR!

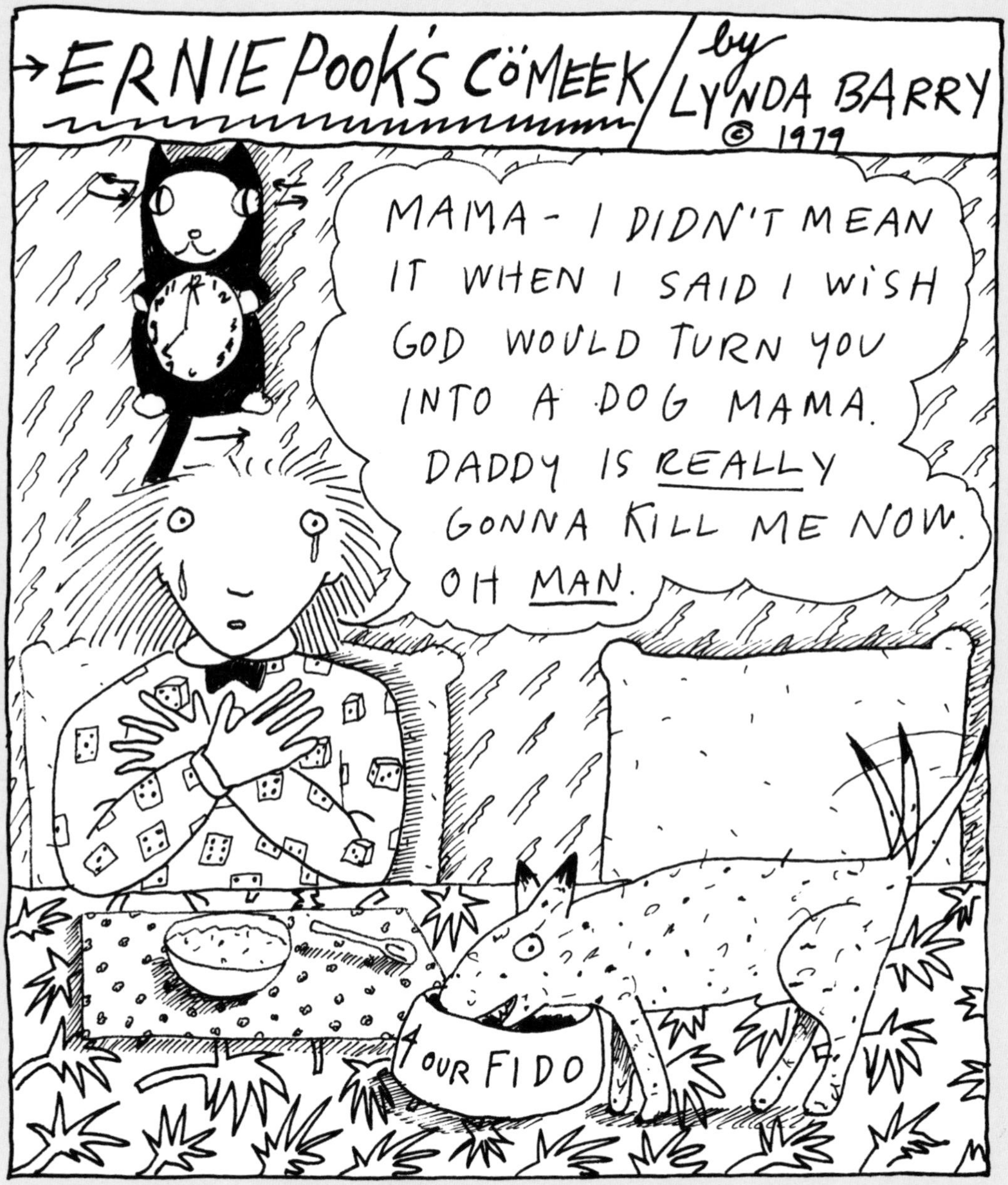
ERNIE POOK'S CÖMEEK
by LYNDA BARRY © 1979
MAMA - I DIDN'T MEAN IT WHEN I SAID I WISH GOD WOULD TURN YOU INTO A DOG MAMA. DADDY IS REALLY GONNA KILL ME NOW. OH MAN.
4 OUR FIDO

ernie pook's fun times
©1979
COMEK 4 PEOPLE OF EARTH / DR. BARRY
HEY- WHY DON'T YOU LIKE LOBOTOMIZE YOUR DOG, PAL
I'LL LOBOTOMIZE YOUR FACE MAN- GET YOUR DOG AWAY FROM MY DOG'S ASS MAN
SNIFF. UH UH UH UH
SNIFF
THAT GUY WAS A REAL DICK, WASN'T HE STINKY? THERE-THERE
whine
IT WAS A BAD MOVE THOUGH SNIFFING THAT STRANGE DOGS ASS. I LIKE YOU STINKY - But you got NO SENSITIVITY.
UH/UH

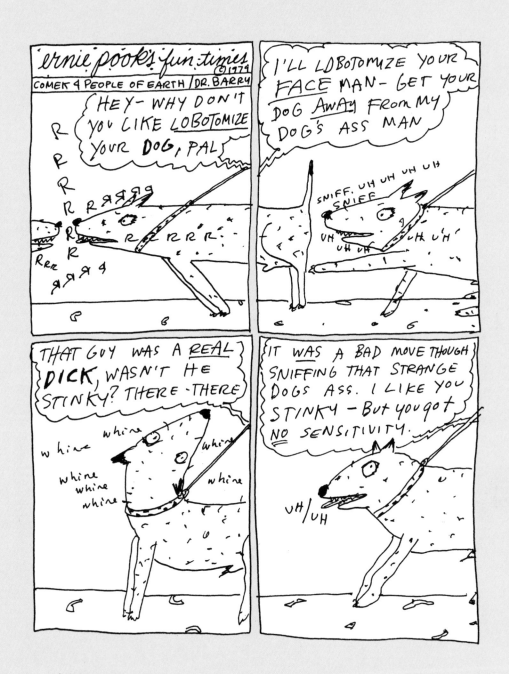

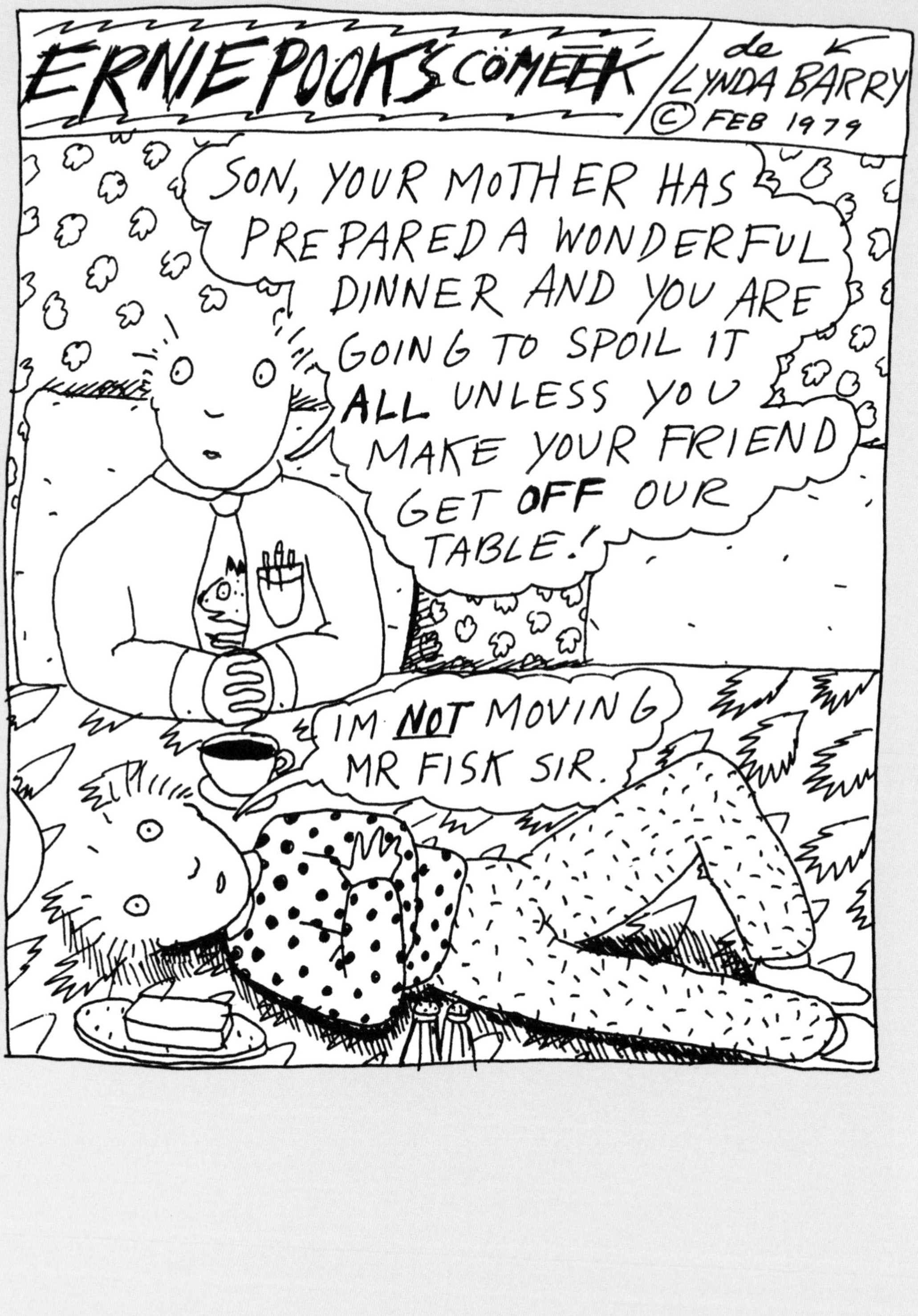
ERNIE POOK'S CÖMEEK
de LYNDA BARRY © FEB 1979
SON, YOUR MOTHER HAS PREPARED A WONDERFUL DINNER AND YOU ARE GOING TO SPOIL IT ALL UNLESS YOU MAKE YOUR FRIEND GET OFF OUR TABLE!
IM NOT MOVING MR FISK SIR.

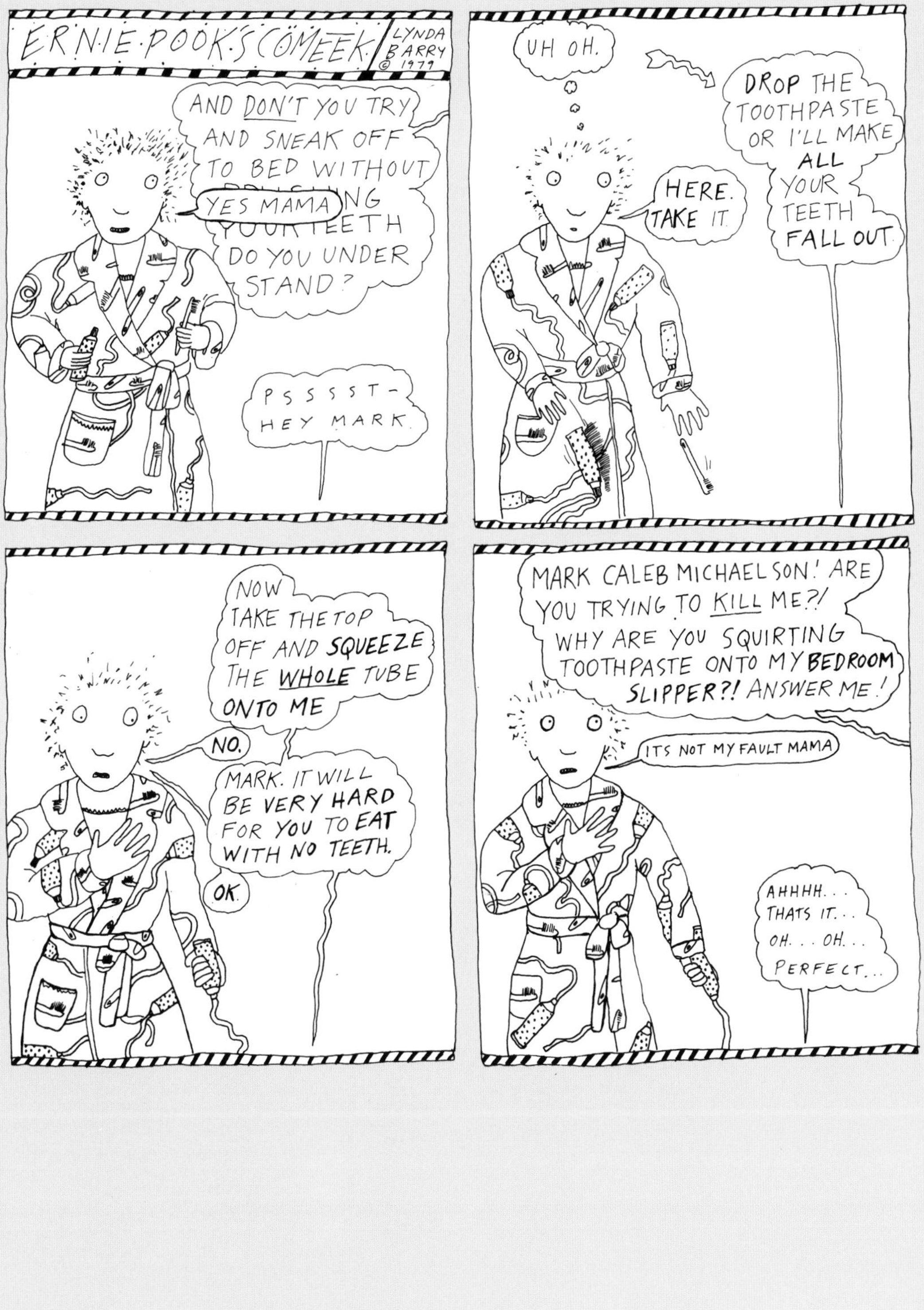
ERNIE·POOK'S·COMEEK
LYNDA BARRY © 1979
AND DON'T YOU TRY AND SNEAK OFF TO BED WITHOUT BRUSHING YOUR TEETH DO YOU UNDERSTAND?
YES MAMA
PSSSST- HEY MARK.
UH OH.
DROP THE TOOTHPASTE OR I'LL MAKE ALL YOUR TEETH FALL OUT.
HERE. TAKE IT.
NOW TAKE THE TOP OFF AND SQUEEZE THE WHOLE TUBE ONTO ME
NO.
MARK. IT WILL BE VERY HARD FOR YOU TO EAT WITH NO TEETH.
OK.
MARK CALEB MICHAELSON! ARE YOU TRYING TO KILL ME?! WHY ARE YOU SQUIRTING TOOTHPASTE ONTO MY BEDROOM SLIPPER?! ANSWER ME!
ITS NOT MY FAULT MAMA
AHHHH... THATS IT... OH... OH... PERFECT...

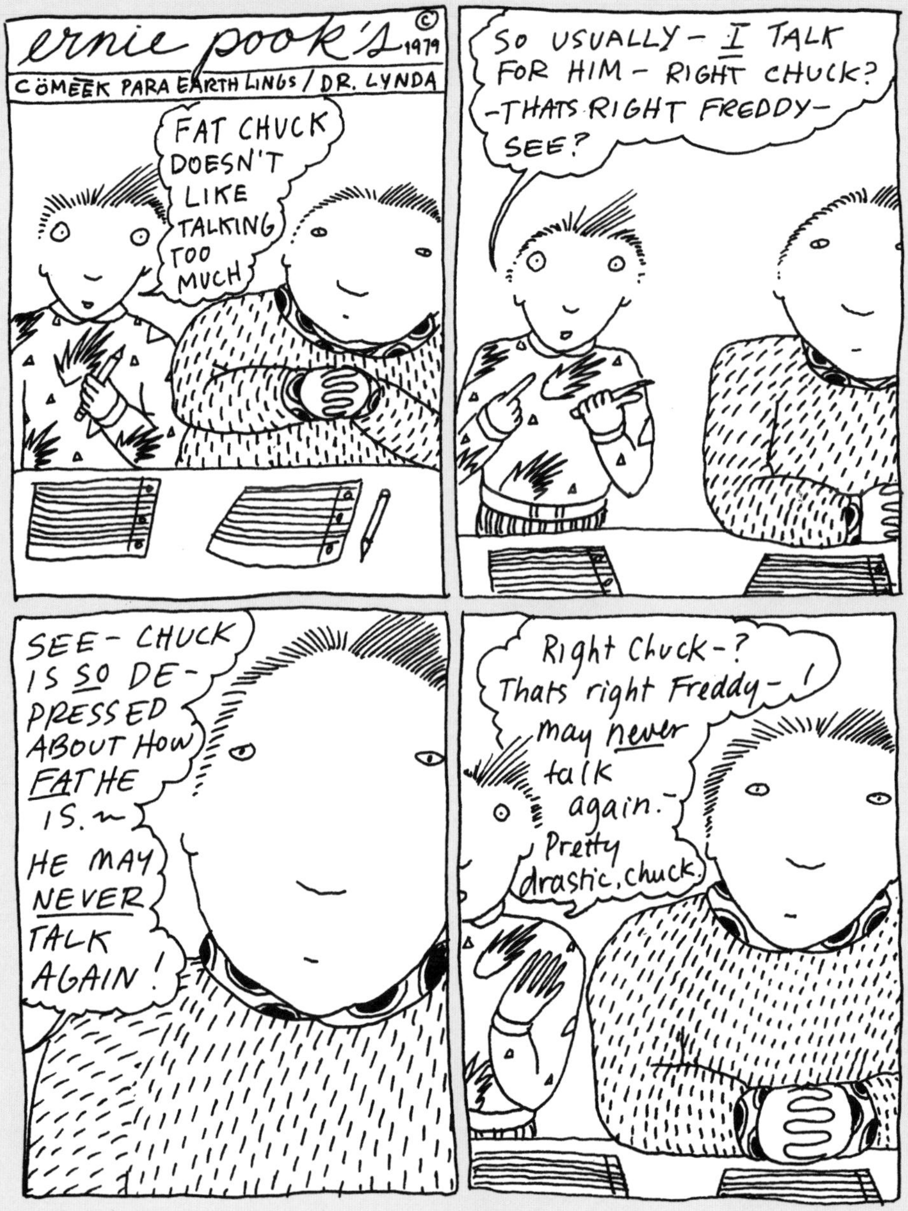
ernie pook's © 1979
CÖMEEK PARA EARTH LINGS / DR. LYNDA
FAT CHUCK DOESN'T LIKE TALKING TOO MUCH
SO USUALLY - I TALK FOR HIM - RIGHT CHUCK? -THATS RIGHT FREDDY- SEE?
SEE - CHUCK IS SO DE-PRESSED ABOUT HOW FAT HE IS. ~ HE MAY NEVER TALK AGAIN!
Right Chuck-? Thats right Freddy-I may never talk again.- Pretty drastic, chuck.

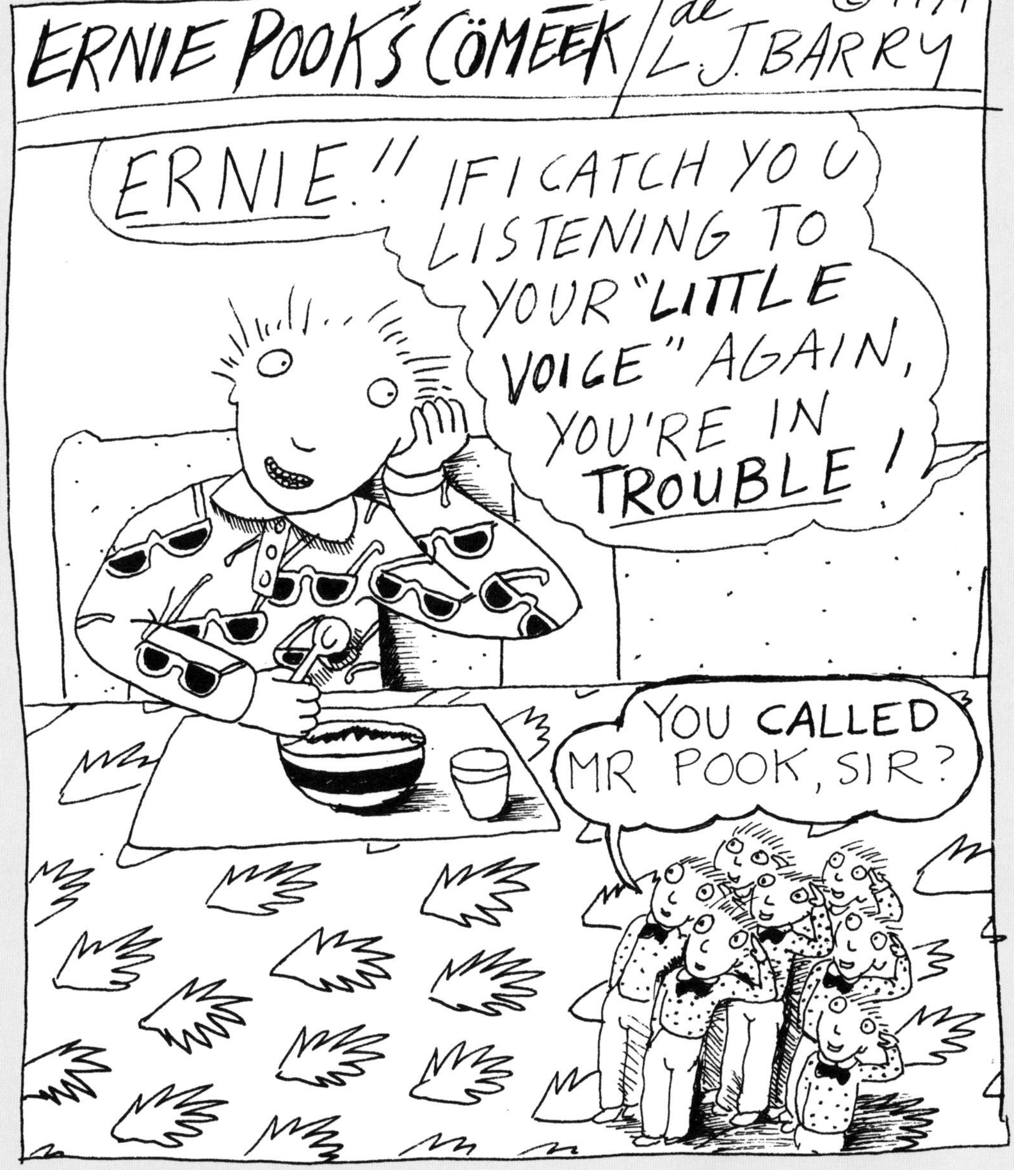
ERNIE POOK'S CÖMEEK
de L.J. BARRY
© 1979
ERNIE!! IF I CATCH YOU LISTENING TO YOUR "LITTLE VOICE" AGAIN, YOU'RE IN TROUBLE!
YOU CALLED MR POOK, SIR?

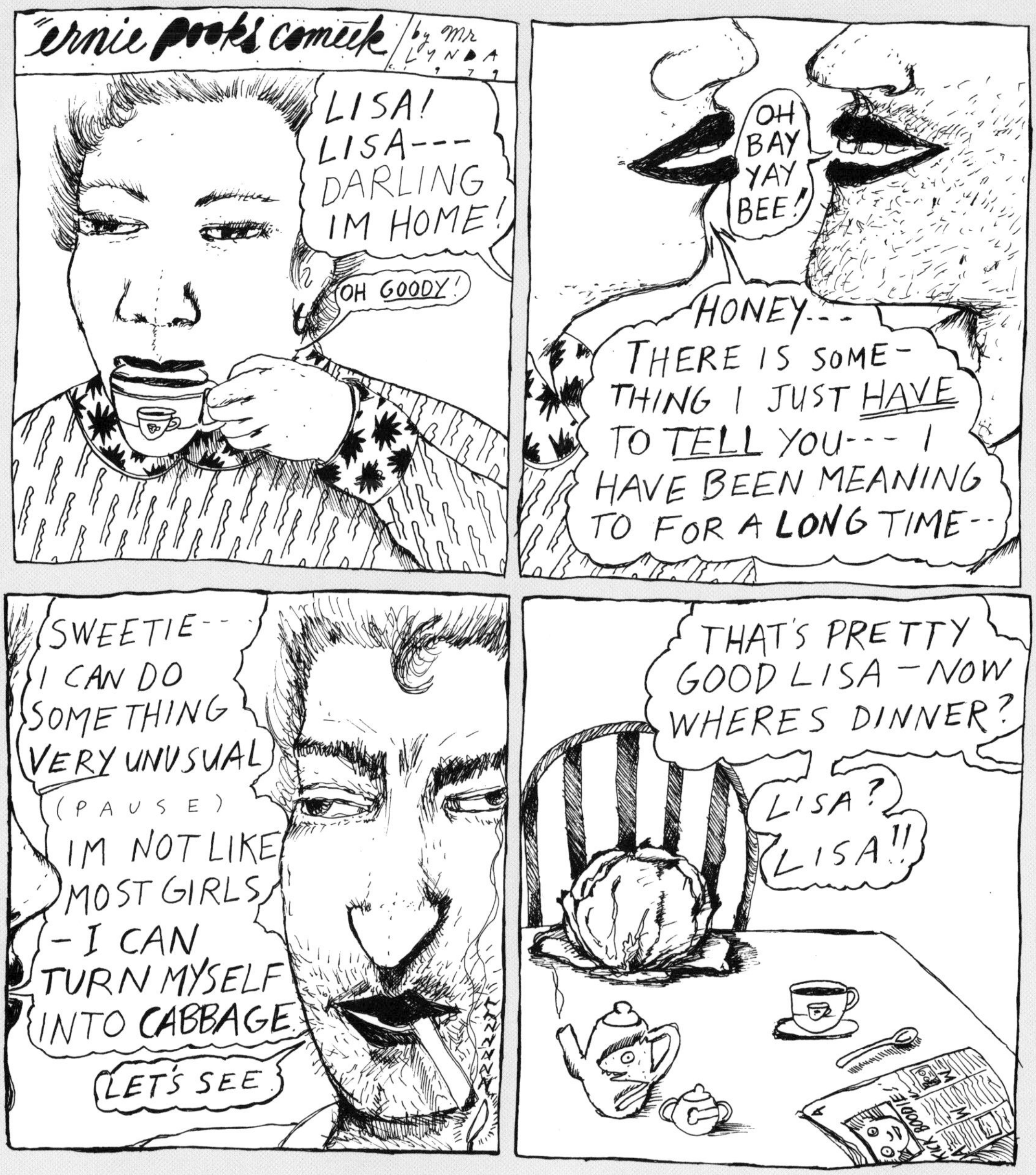
"ernie pooks comeek
by Mr LYNDA c. 1979
LISA! LISA--- DARLING IM HOME!
OH GOODY!
OH BAY YAY BEE!
HONEY--- THERE IS SOMETHING I JUST HAVE TO TELL YOU--- I HAVE BEEN MEANING TO FOR A LONG TIME--
SWEETIE-- I CAN DO SOMETHING VERY UNUSUAL
(PAUSE)
IM NOT LIKE MOST GIRLS -I CAN TURN MYSELF INTO CABBAGE
LET'S SEE
THAT'S PRETTY GOOD LISA - NOW WHERES DINNER?
LISA? LISA!!

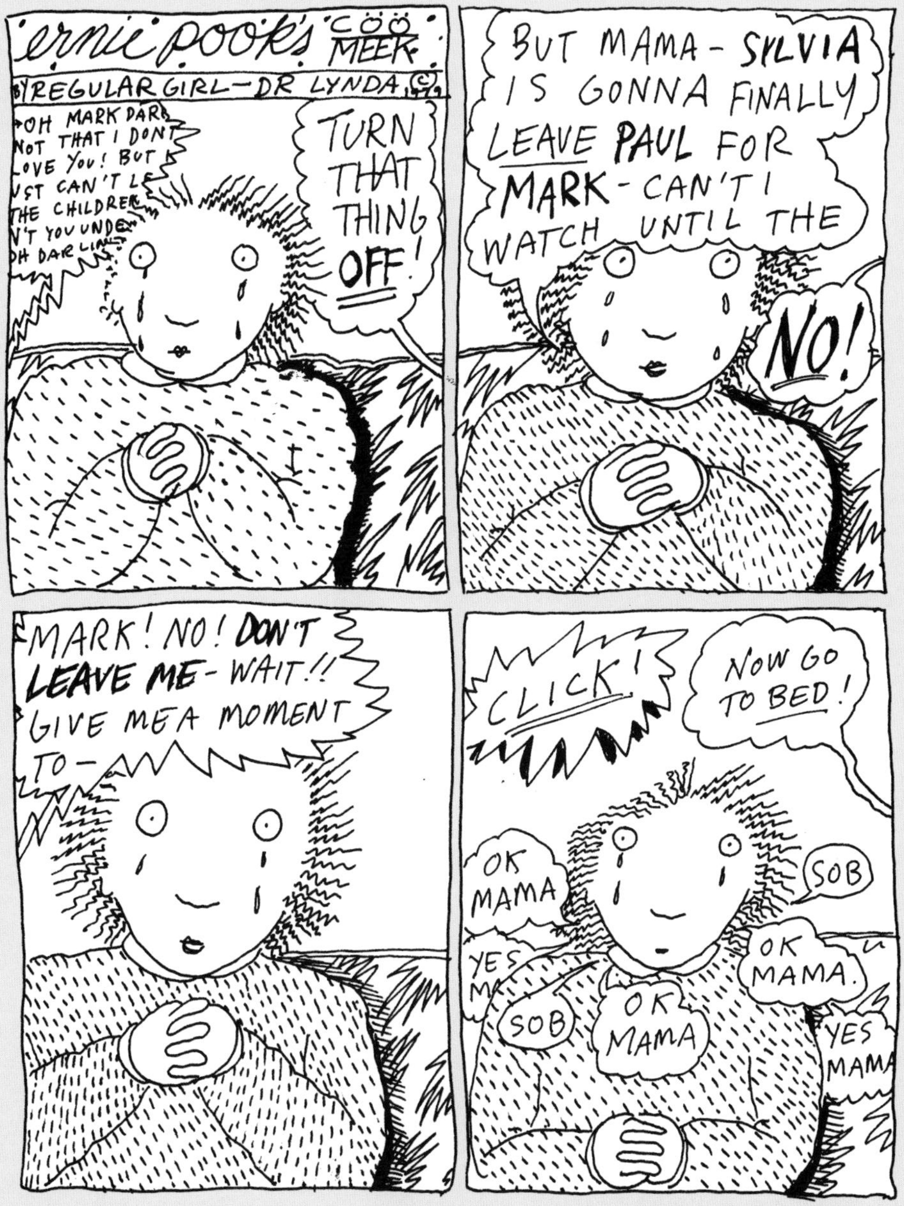
ernie pook's CÖÖ MEEK
BY REGULAR GIRL—DR LYNDA ©
OH MARK DAR
NOT THAT I DONT
LOVE YOU! BUT
UST CAN'T L
THE CHILDREN
N'T YOU UNDE
OH DARLIN
TURN THAT THING OFF!
BUT MAMA-SYLVIA IS GONNA FINALLY LEAVE PAUL FOR MARK-CAN'T I WATCH UNTIL THE
NO!
MARK! NO! DON'T LEAVE ME-WAIT!! GIVE ME A MOMENT TO-
CLICK!
NOW GO TO BED!
OK MAMA
SOB
YES
SOB
OK MAMA
OK MAMA.
YES MAMA

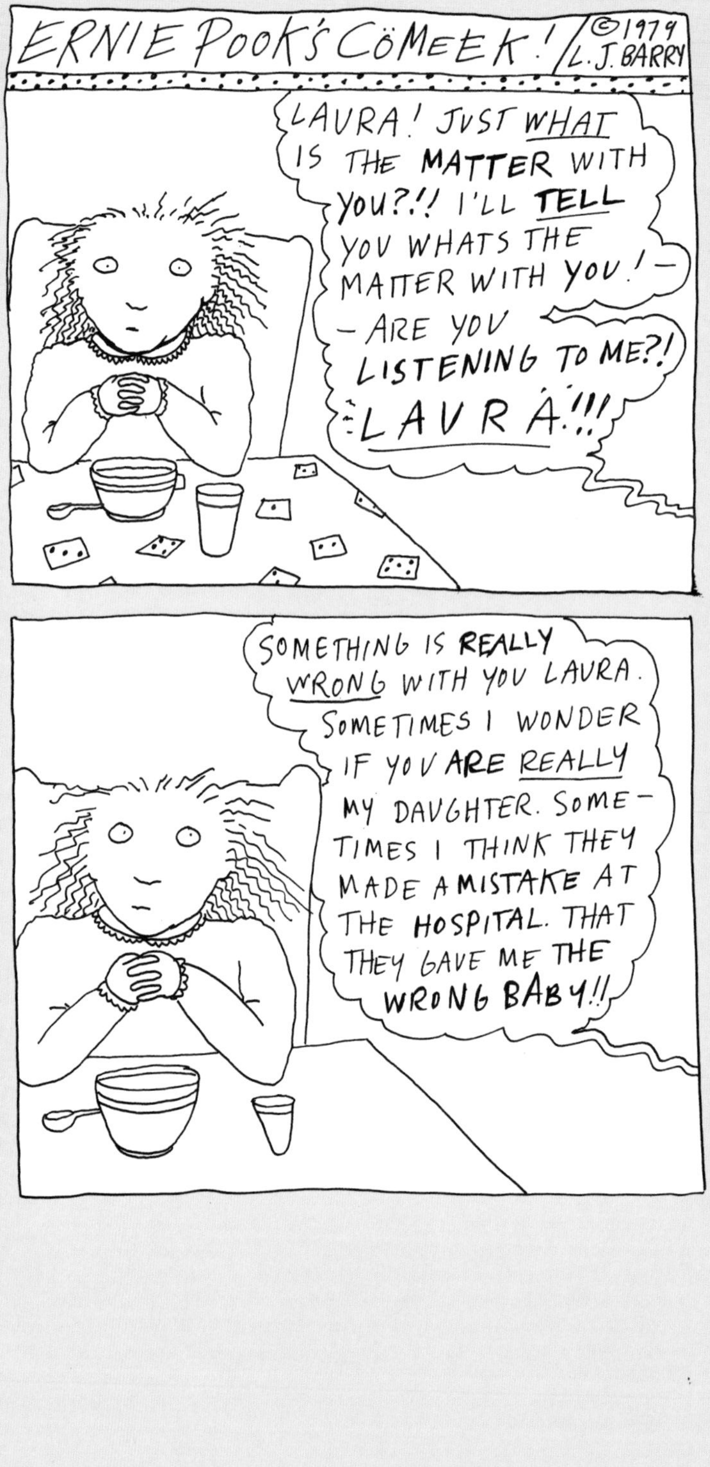
ERNIE POOK'S CÖMEEK!
©1979 L.J. BARRY
LAURA! JUST WHAT IS THE MATTER WITH YOU?!! I'LL TELL YOU WHATS THE MATTER WITH YOU!— —ARE YOU LISTENING TO ME?! LAURA!!!
SOMETHING IS REALLY WRONG WITH YOU LAURA. SOMETIMES I WONDER IF YOU ARE REALLY MY DAUGHTER. SOMETIMES I THINK THEY MADE A MISTAKE AT THE HOSPITAL. THAT THEY GAVE ME THE WRONG BABY!!

ERNIE POOK'S CÖMEEK / LYNDA J. BARRY © 1979
THIS IS WHAT I WILL LOOK LIKE IN MY COFFIN
RING!! RING!!
IF I HAVE TO SIT IN MATH ANOTHER DAY AND SEE RANDY HOLDING HANDS WITH SUSAN KOPINSKI I'LL, I'LL
IMPOSSIBLE MATH. DON'T EVEN TRY THIS BOOK.
ITS SUSAN KOPINSKI HONEY- SHE WANTS TO KNOW IF YOU WANT A RIDE TO SCHOOL—
SHE WOULD
NO MAMA - TELL HER I ALREADY HAVE A RIDE
BUT YOU DON'T
BUT TELL HER I DO
YOU TELL HER YOURSELF - IM NOT GOING TO LIE FOR YOU!!
SHE HUNG UP! SUSAN KOPINSKI HUNG UP ON ME!!
SHE PROBABLY HEARD YOU! IT SERVES YOU RIGHT FOR LIEING!
ALL I SAID WAS HELLO AND THEN SHE HUNG UP.
Now isn't Susan Kopinski that nice slender attractive blonde girl Randy has been seeing lately? - Why wouldn't you want to ride to school with her?
BECAUSE IM A LUNATIC MAMA - I WOULDN'T WANT TO PUT TEETH-MARKS IN HER UPHOLSTERY.
HEATH 4 U
Nothing will ever be the same again. you should quit now

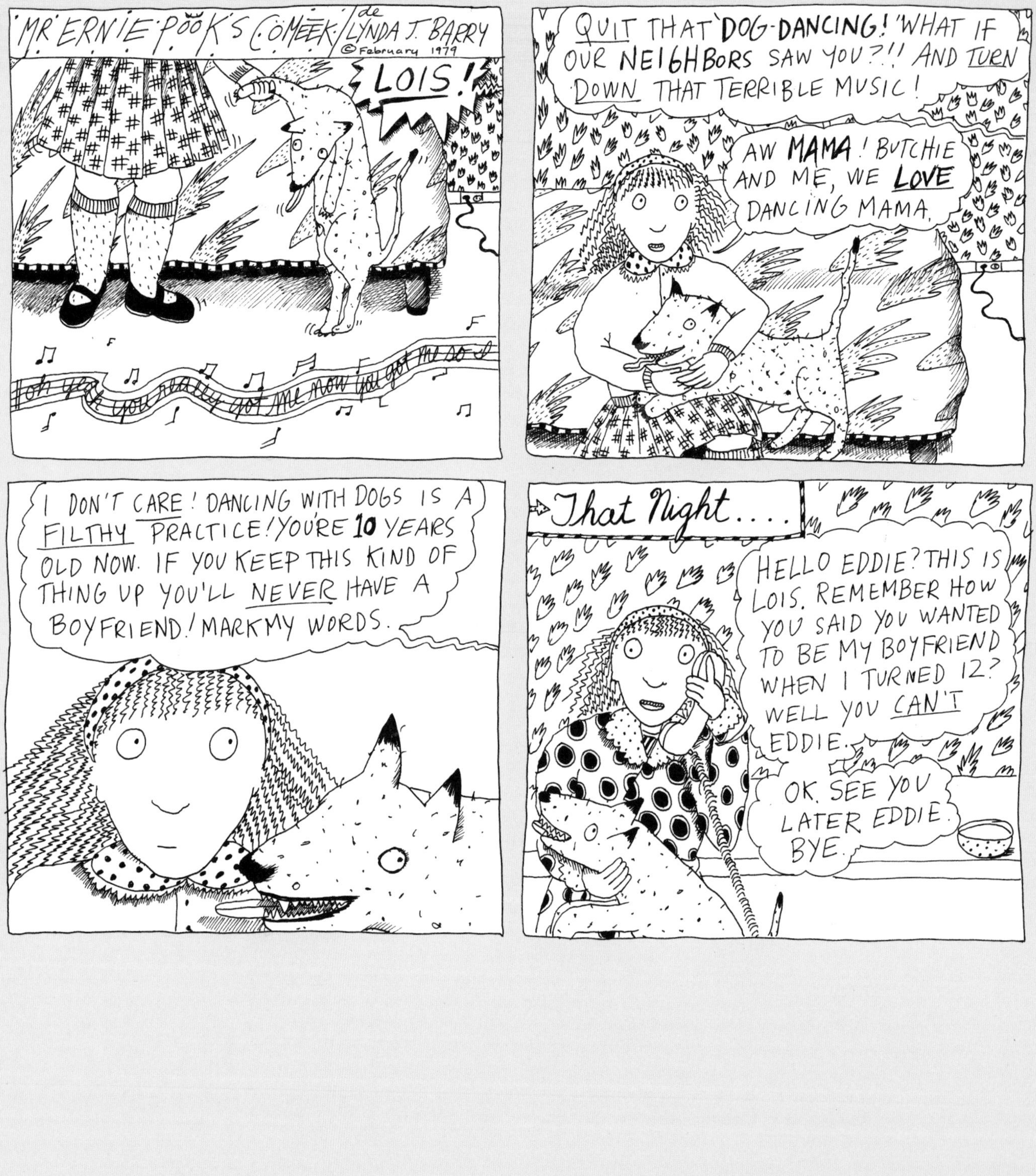
MR ERNIE POOK'S COMEEK
de LYNDA J. BARRY
© February 1979
LOIS!
oh yeah you really got me now you got me so
QUIT THAT DOG-DANCING! WHAT IF OUR NEIGHBORS SAW YOU?!! AND TURN DOWN THAT TERRIBLE MUSIC!
AW MAMA! BUTCHIE AND ME, WE LOVE DANCING MAMA.
I DON'T CARE! DANCING WITH DOGS IS A FILTHY PRACTICE! YOU'RE 10 YEARS OLD NOW. IF YOU KEEP THIS KIND OF THING UP YOU'LL NEVER HAVE A BOYFRIEND! MARK MY WORDS.
That Night....
HELLO EDDIE? THIS IS LOIS. REMEMBER HOW YOU SAID YOU WANTED TO BE MY BOYFRIEND WHEN I TURNED 12? WELL YOU CAN'T EDDIE.
OK. SEE YOU LATER EDDIE. BYE.

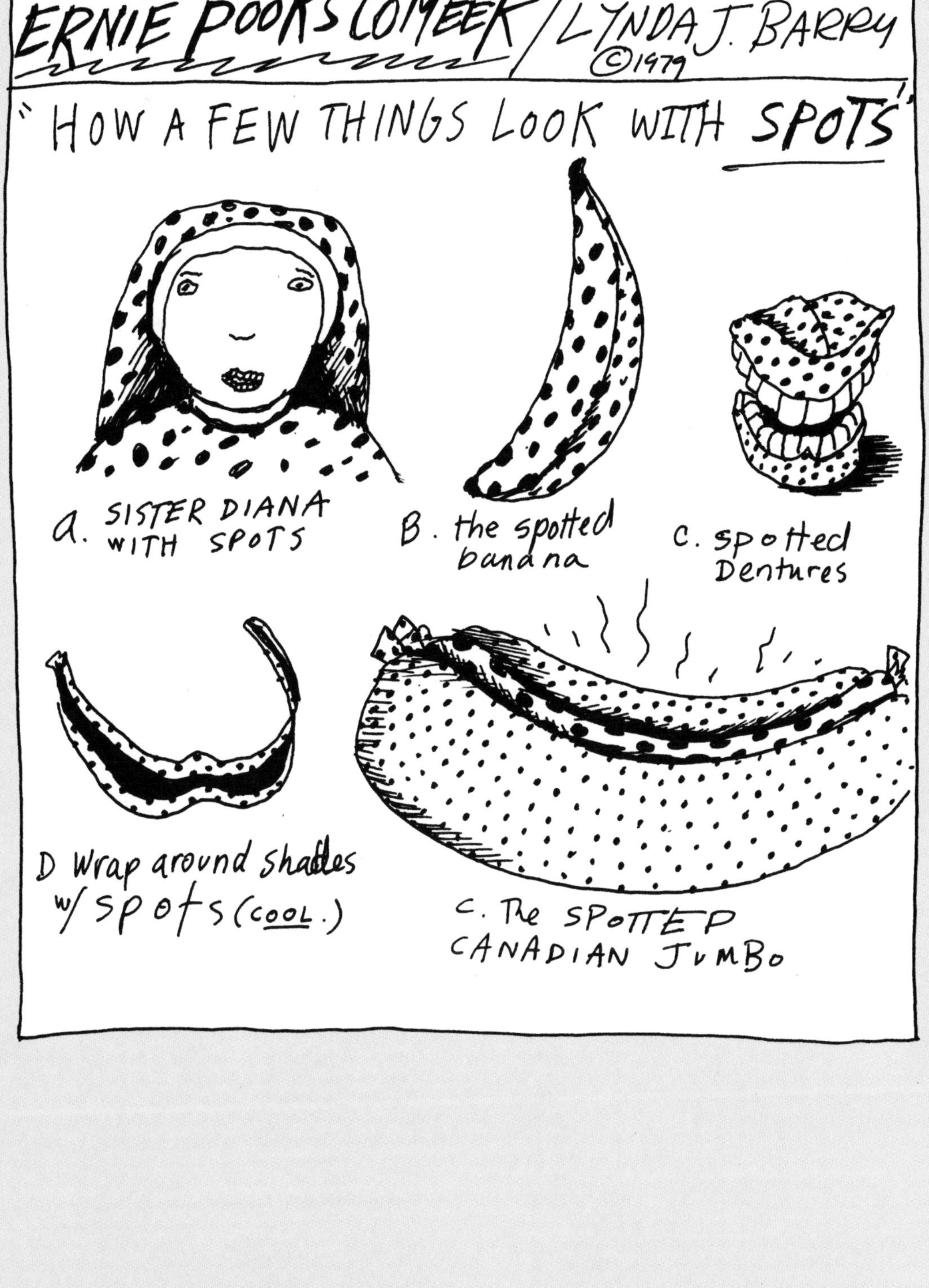

ERNIE POOKS COMEEK
LYNDA J. BARRY ©1979
"HOW A FEW THINGS LOOK WITH SPOTS"
a. SISTER DIANA WITH SPOTS
B. the spotted banana
c. spotted Dentures
D Wrap around shades w/ spots (COOL.)
c. The SPOTTED CANADIAN JUMBO

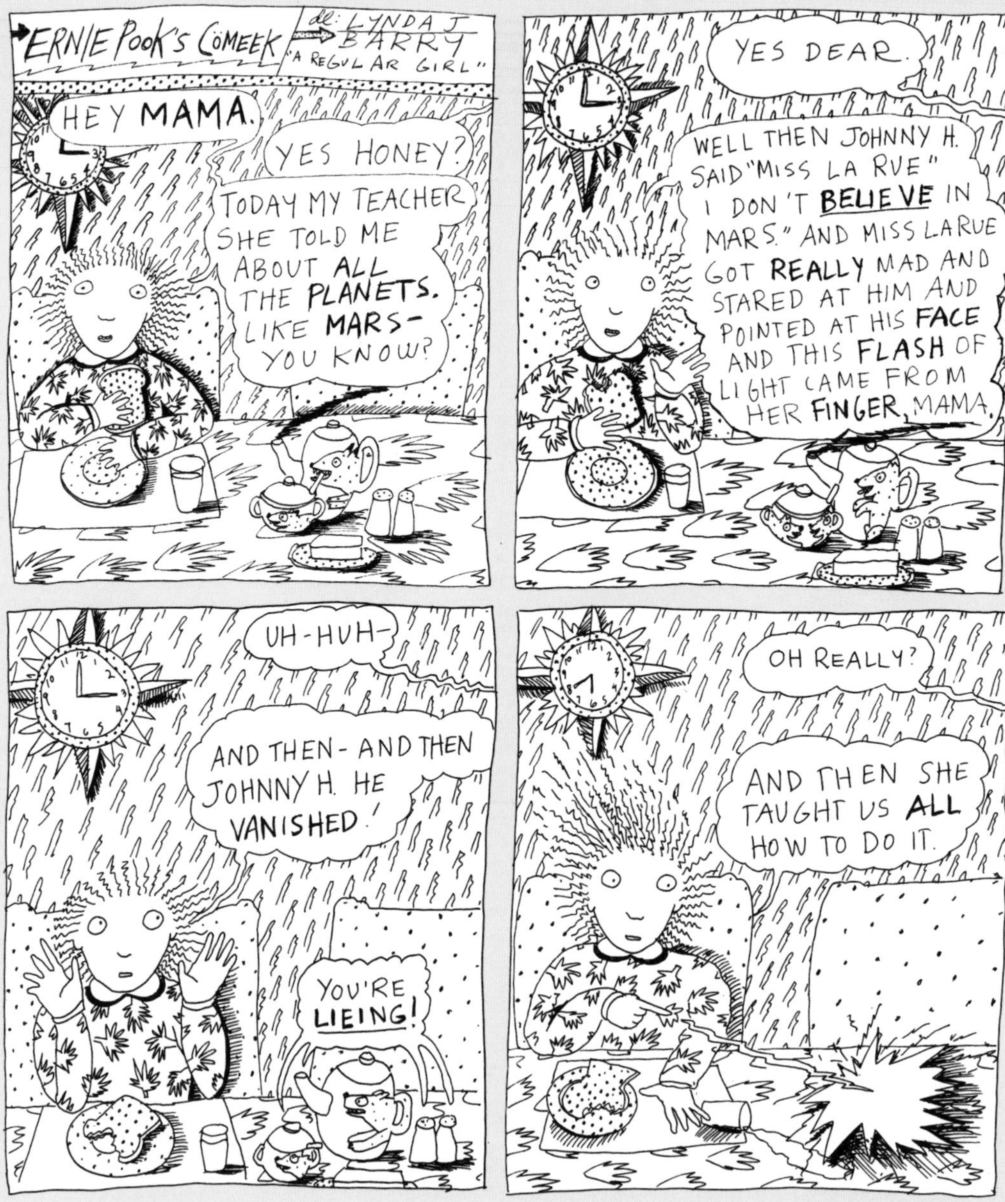
ERNIE POOK'S CÖMEEK
dr: LYNDA J BARRY
"A REGULAR GIRL"
HEY MAMA.
YES HONEY?
TODAY MY TEACHER SHE TOLD ME ABOUT ALL THE PLANETS. LIKE MARS- YOU KNOW?
YES DEAR.
WELL THEN JOHNNY H. SAID "MISS LA RUE" I DON'T BELIEVE IN MARS." AND MISS LARUE GOT REALLY MAD AND STARED AT HIM AND POINTED AT HIS FACE AND THIS FLASH OF LIGHT CAME FROM HER FINGER, MAMA.
UH-HUH-
AND THEN- AND THEN JOHNNY H. HE VANISHED!
YOU'RE LIEING!
OH REALLY?
AND THEN SHE TAUGHT US ALL HOW TO DO IT.

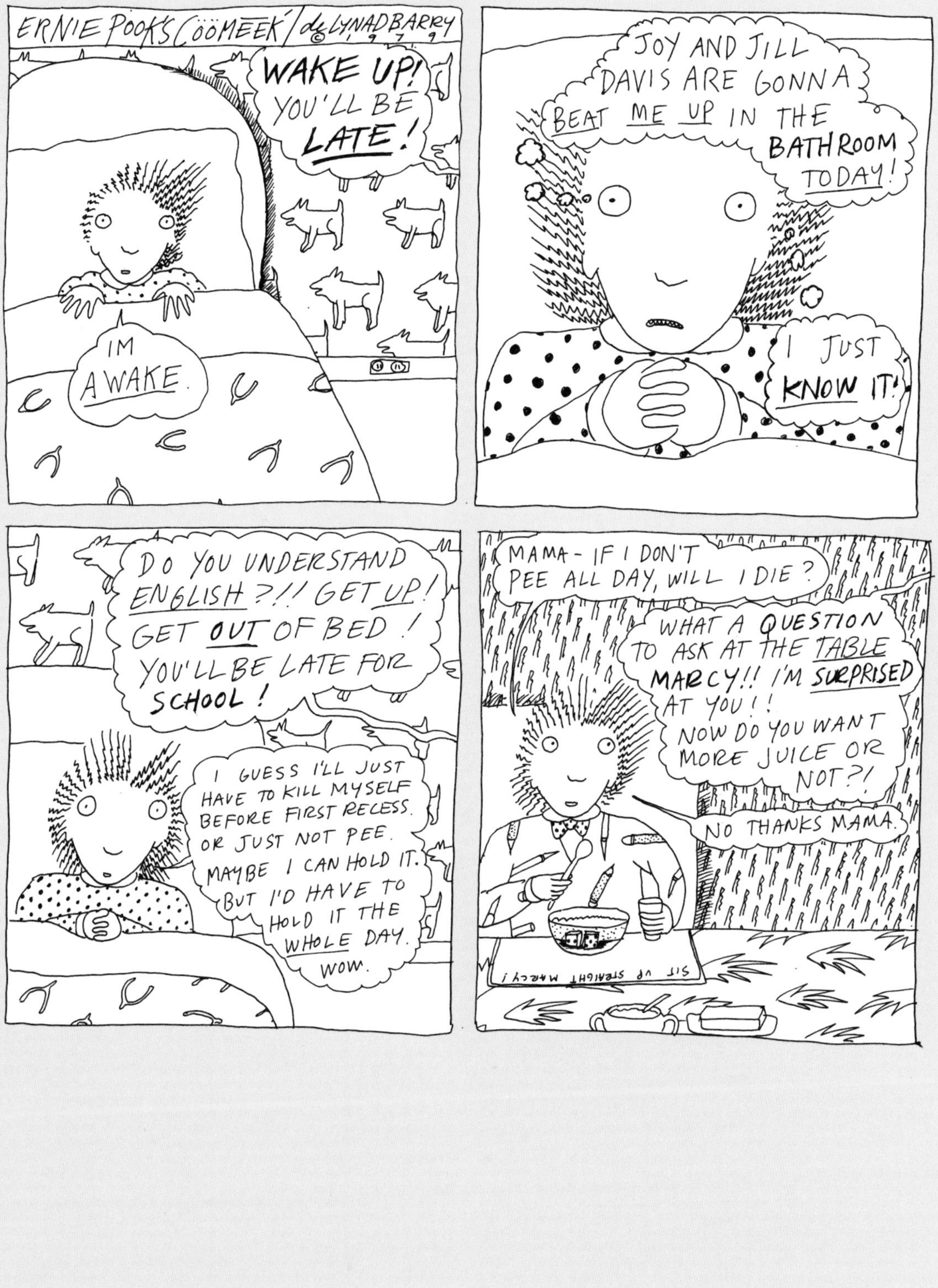
ERNIE POOK'S CÖÖMEEK
© LYNDA BARRY 1979
WAKE UP! YOU'LL BE LATE!
IM AWAKE.
JOY AND JILL DAVIS ARE GONNA BEAT ME UP IN THE BATHROOM TODAY!
I JUST KNOW IT!
DO YOU UNDERSTAND ENGLISH?!! GET UP! GET OUT OF BED! YOU'LL BE LATE FOR SCHOOL!
I GUESS I'LL JUST HAVE TO KILL MYSELF BEFORE FIRST RECESS. OR JUST NOT PEE. MAYBE I CAN HOLD IT. BUT I'D HAVE TO HOLD IT THE WHOLE DAY. WOW.
MAMA - IF I DON'T PEE ALL DAY, WILL I DIE?
WHAT A QUESTION TO ASK AT THE TABLE MARCY!! I'M SURPRISED AT YOU!! NOW DO YOU WANT MORE JUICE OR NOT?!
NO THANKS MAMA.
SIT UP STRAIGHT MARCY!

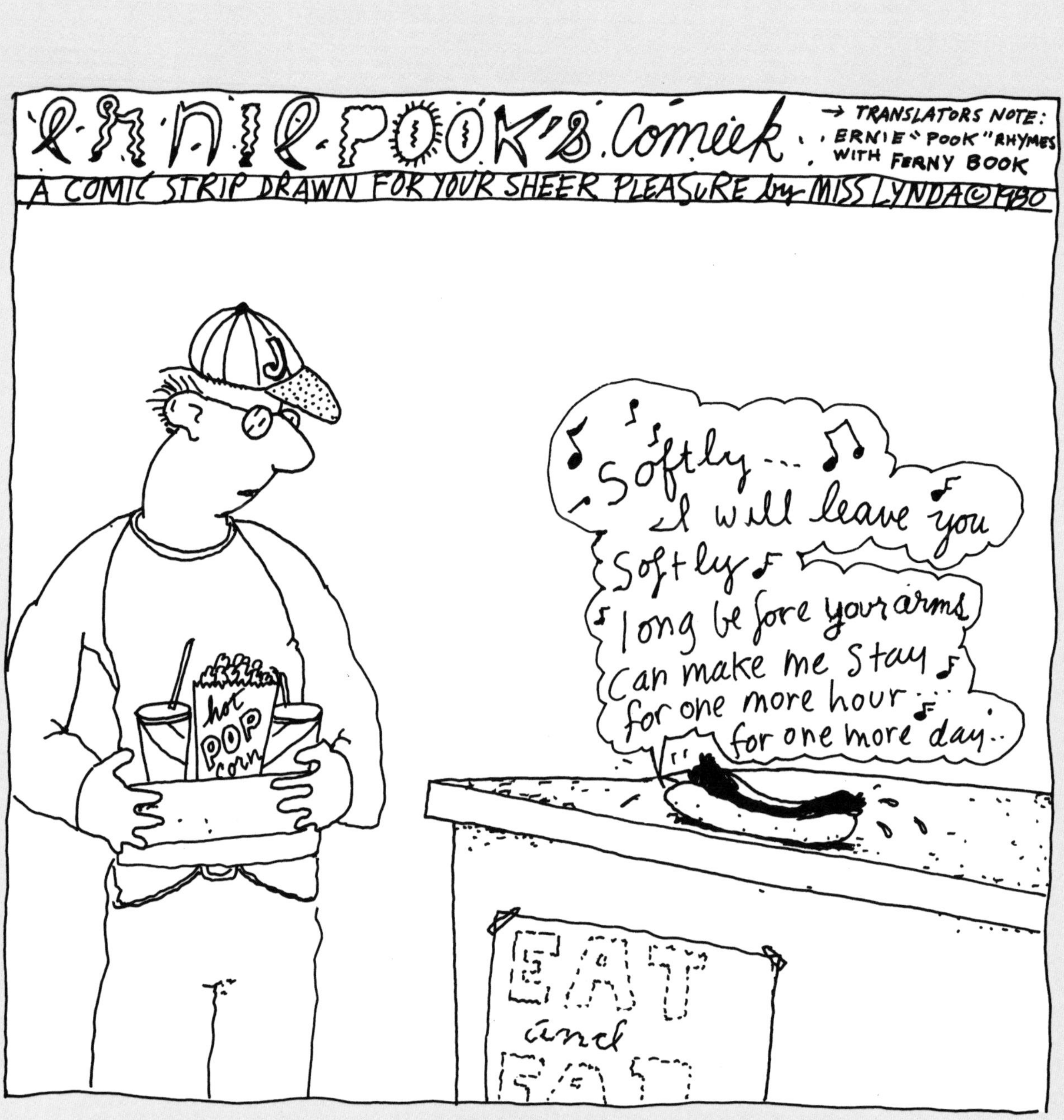
ERNIE POOK'S COMEEK
→ TRANSLATORS NOTE: ERNIE "POOK" RHYMES WITH FERNY BOOK
A COMIC STRIP DRAWN FOR YOUR SHEER PLEASURE by MISS LYNDA © 1980
J
Softly... I will leave you softly long before your arms can make me stay for one more hour for one more day...
hot POP corn
EAT and EAT

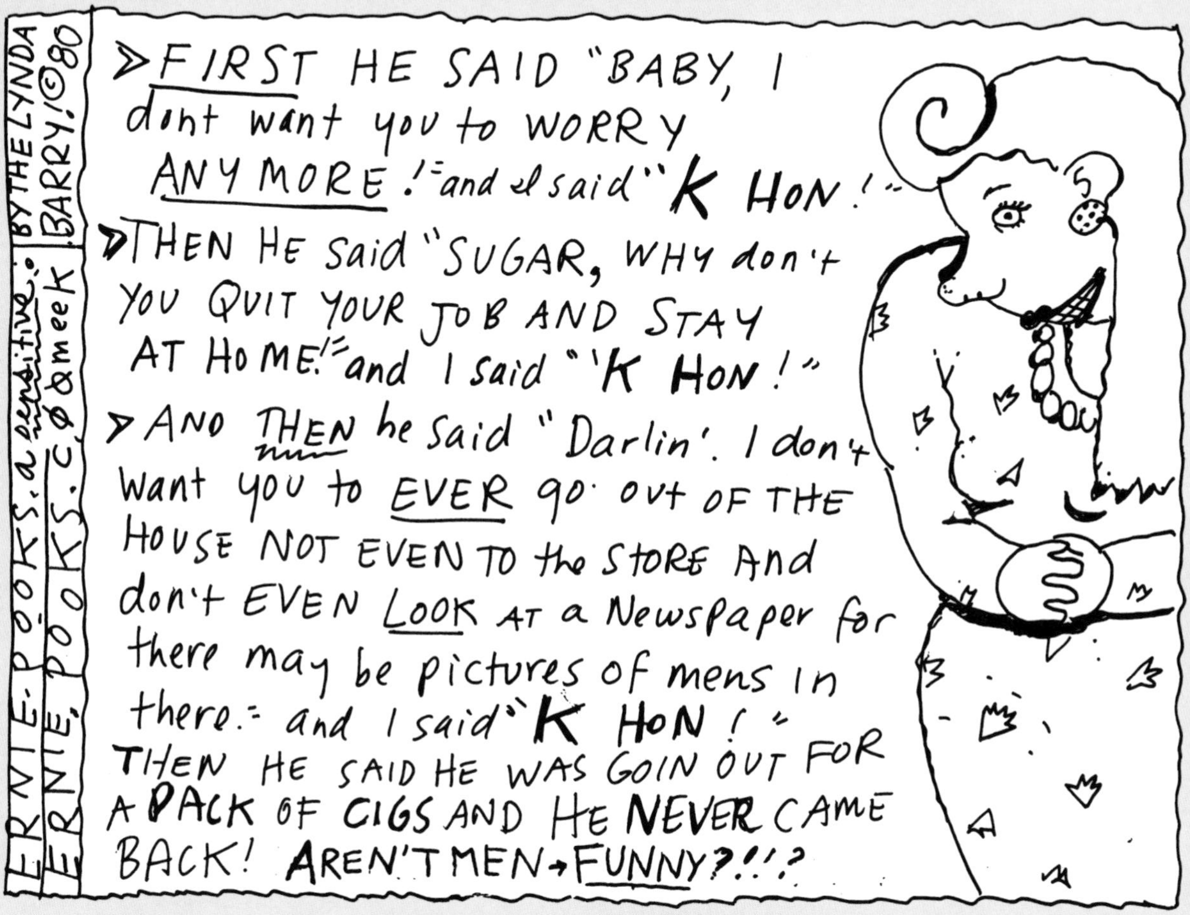
ERNIE POOK'S, a sensitive ERNIE POOK'S COMEEK BY THE LYNDA BARRY! ©80
FIRST HE SAID "BABY, I dont want you to WORRY ANYMORE!" and I said "K HON!"
THEN HE said "SUGAR, WHY don't YOU QUIT YOUR JOB AND STAY AT HOME!" and I said "'K HON!"
AND THEN he said "Darlin'. I don't want you to EVER go out OF THE HOUSE NOT EVEN TO the STORE And don't EVEN LOOK AT a Newspaper for there may be pictures of mens in there." and I said "K HON!"
THEN HE SAID HE WAS GOIN OUT FOR A PACK OF CIGS AND HE NEVER CAME BACK! AREN'T MEN FUNNY?!!?

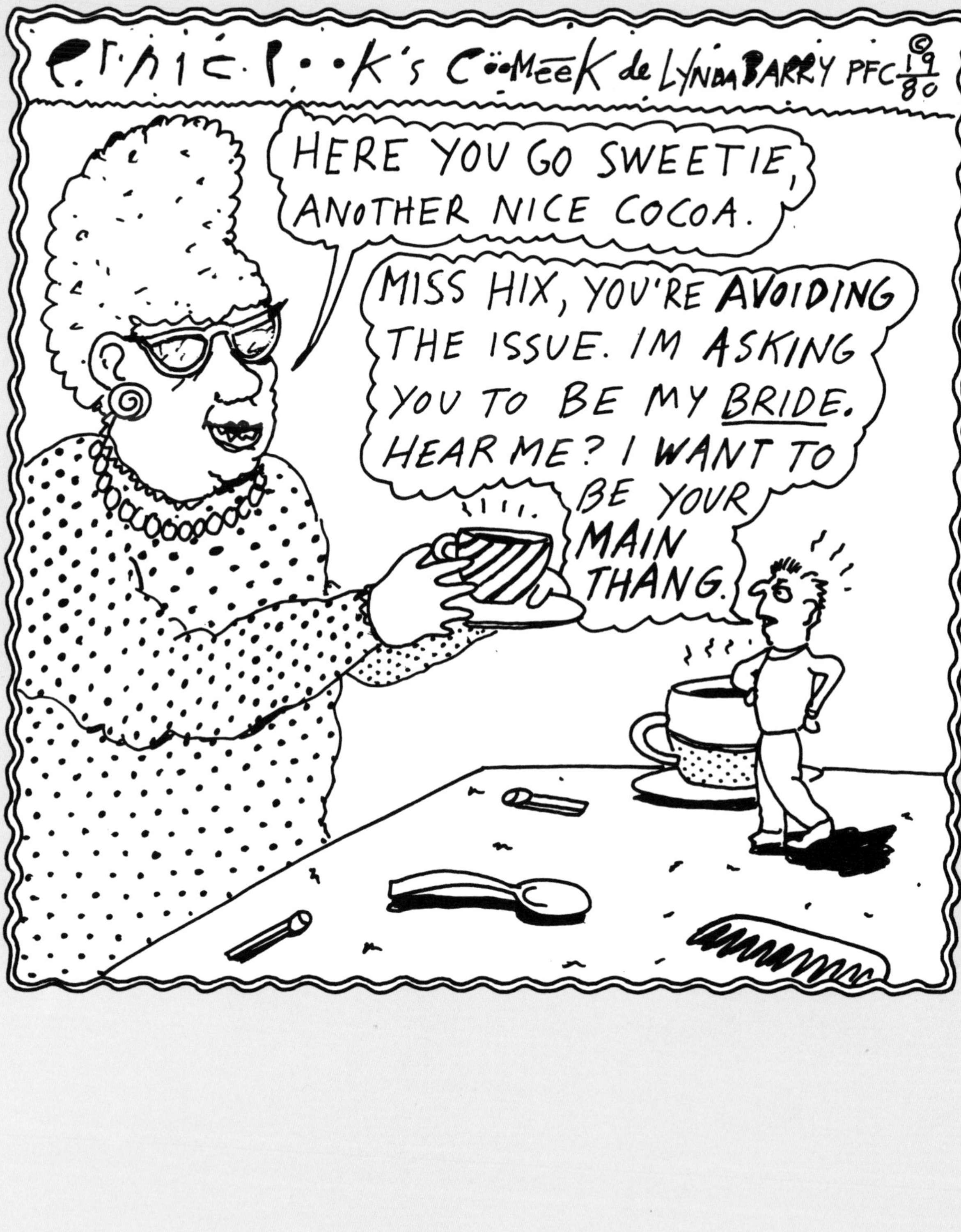
ERNIE POOK'S COMEEK de LYNDA BARRY PFC © 1980
HERE YOU GO SWEETIE, ANOTHER NICE COCOA.
MISS HIX, YOU'RE AVOIDING THE ISSUE. IM ASKING YOU TO BE MY BRIDE. HEAR ME? I WANT TO BE YOUR MAIN THANG.

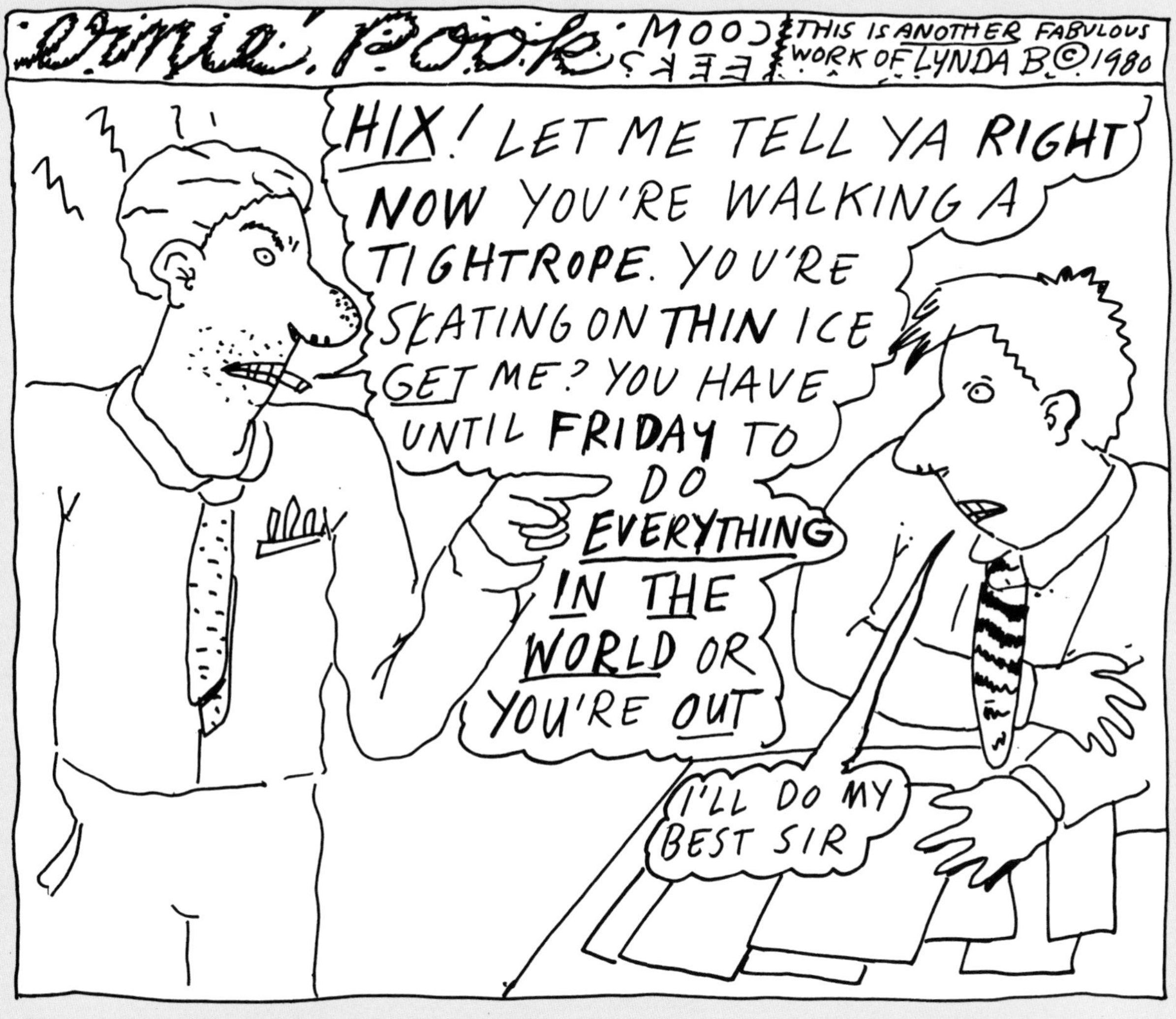
THIS IS ANOTHER FABULOUS WORK OF LYNDA B. ©1980
HIX! LET ME TELL YA RIGHT NOW YOU'RE WALKING A TIGHTROPE. YOU'RE SKATING ON THIN ICE GET ME? YOU HAVE UNTIL FRIDAY TO DO EVERYTHING IN THE WORLD OR YOU'RE OUT
I'LL DO MY BEST SIR

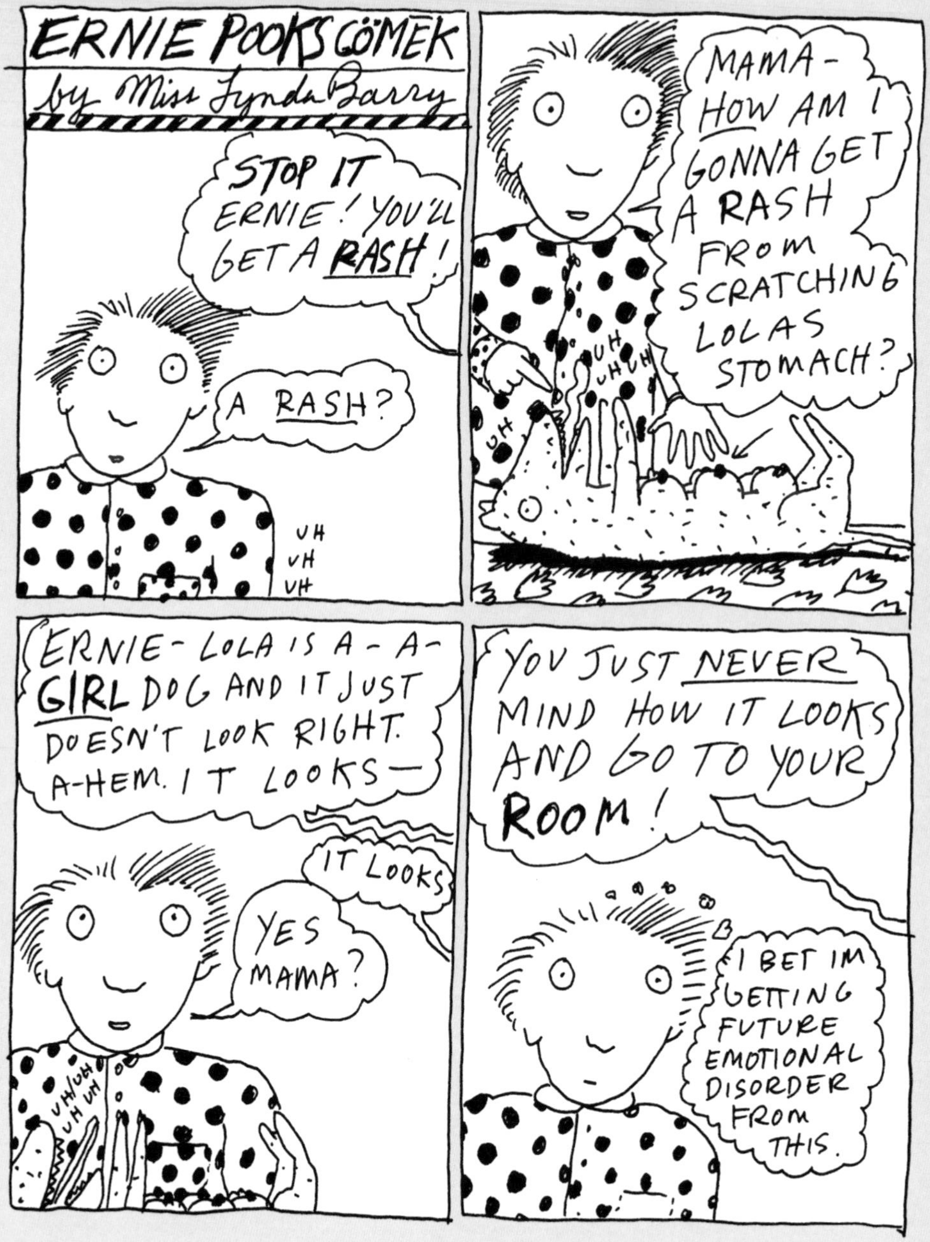
ERNIE POOKS CÖMEK
by Miss Lynda Barry
STOP IT ERNIE! YOU'LL GET A RASH!
A RASH?
UH UH UH
MAMA- HOW AM I GONNA GET A RASH FROM SCRATCHING LOLAS STOMACH?
UH UH UH
UH
ERNIE- LOLA IS A - A- GIRL DOG AND IT JUST DOESN'T LOOK RIGHT. A-HEM. IT LOOKS—
IT LOOKS
YES MAMA?
UH UH UH UH
YOU JUST NEVER MIND HOW IT LOOKS AND GO TO YOUR ROOM!
I BET IM GETTING FUTURE EMOTIONAL DISORDER FROM THIS.

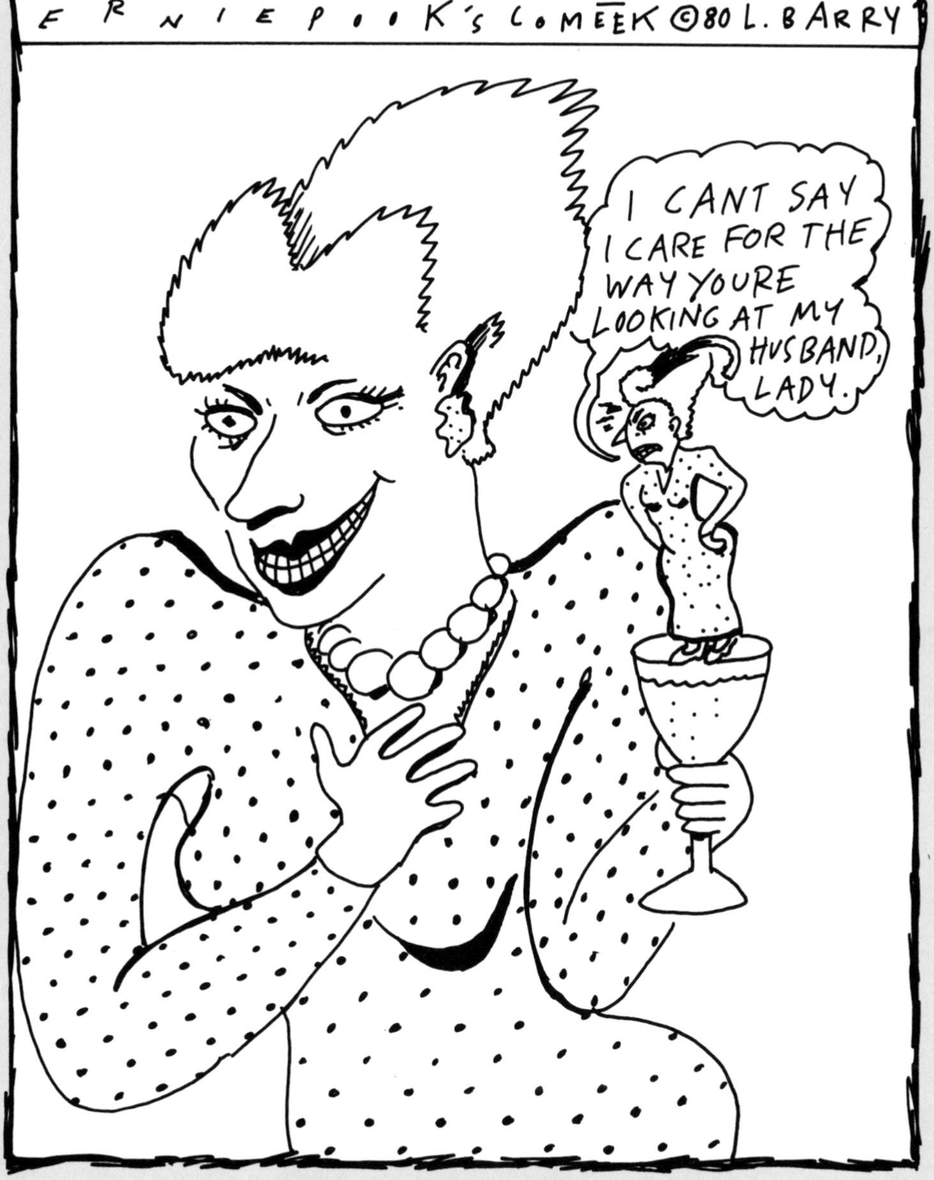
ERNIE POOK'S COMEEK ©80 L. BARRY
I CANT SAY I CARE FOR THE WAY YOURE LOOKING AT MY HUSBAND, LADY.

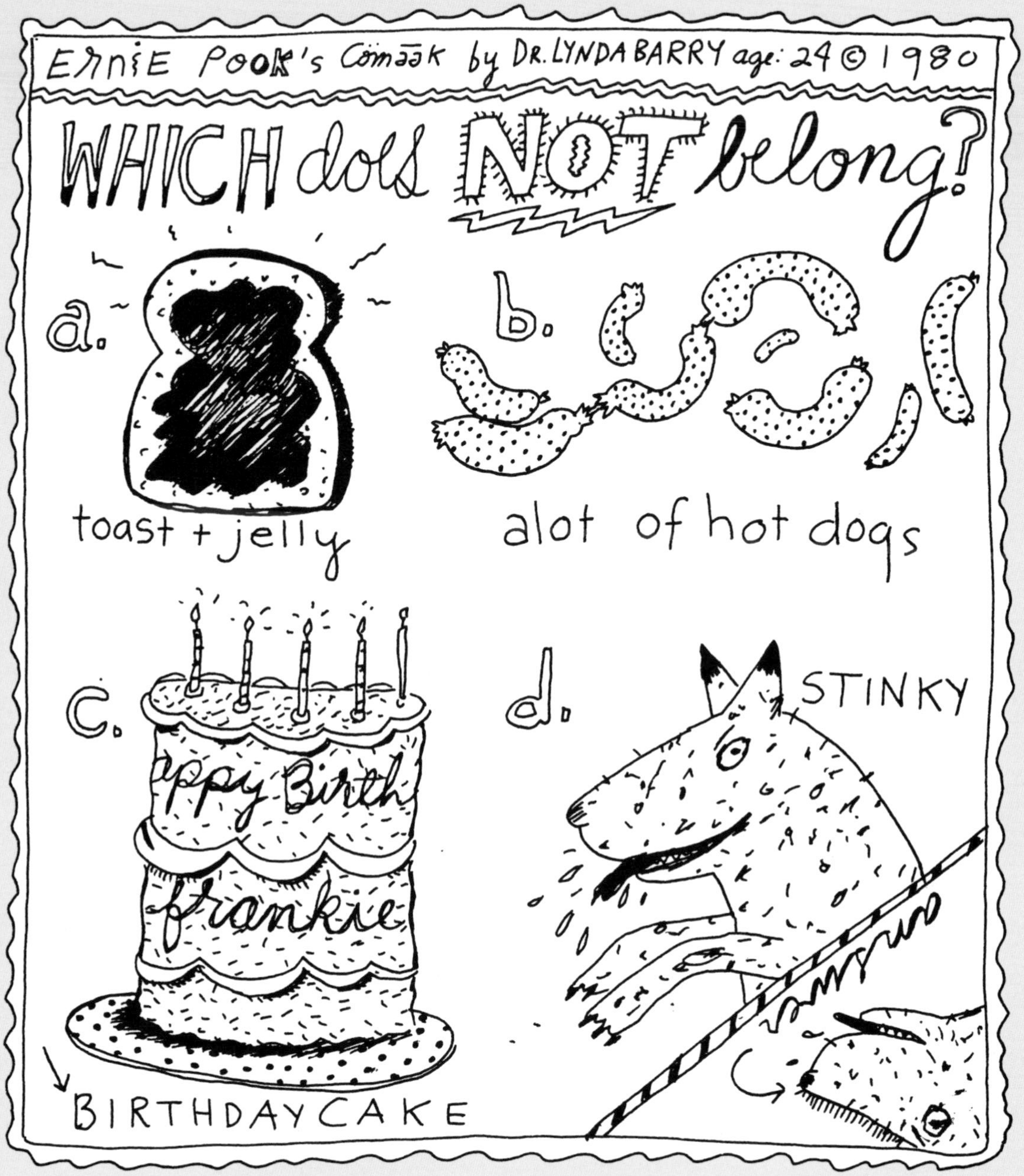
ErNiE POOK's Cömääk by DR. LYNDA BARRY age: 24 © 1980
WHICH does NOT belong?
a.
toast + jelly
b.
alot of hot dogs
c.
appy Birth
frankie
BIRTHDAYCAKE
d.
STINKY

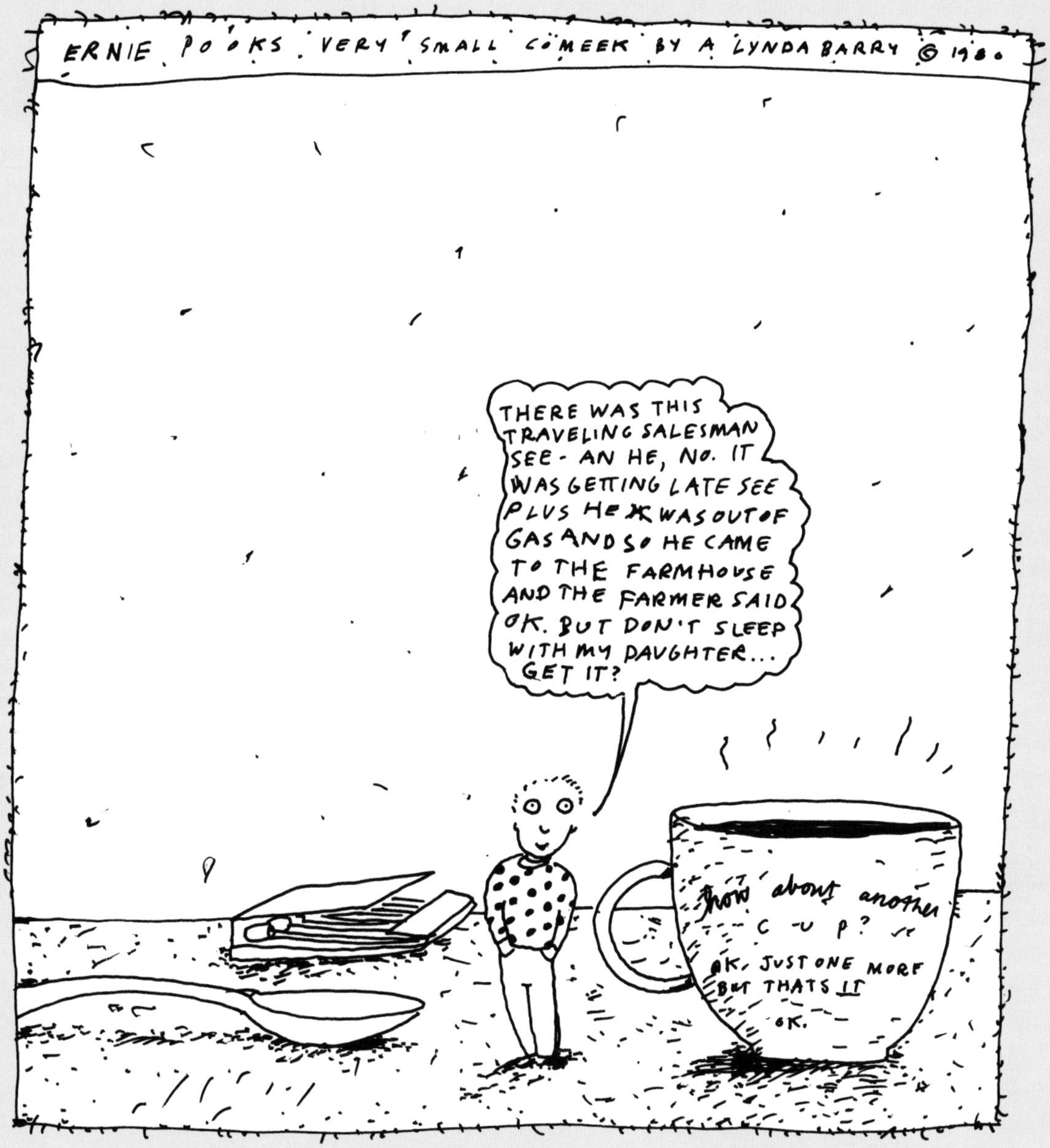
ERNIE POOKS VERY SMALL COMEEK BY A LYNDA BARRY © 1980
THERE WAS THIS TRAVELING SALESMAN SEE - AN HE, NO. IT WAS GETTING LATE SEE PLUS HE WAS OUT OF GAS AND SO HE CAME TO THE FARMHOUSE AND THE FARMER SAID OK. BUT DON'T SLEEP WITH MY DAUGHTER... GET IT?
How about another C U P?
OK, JUST ONE MORE BUT THATS IT
OK.

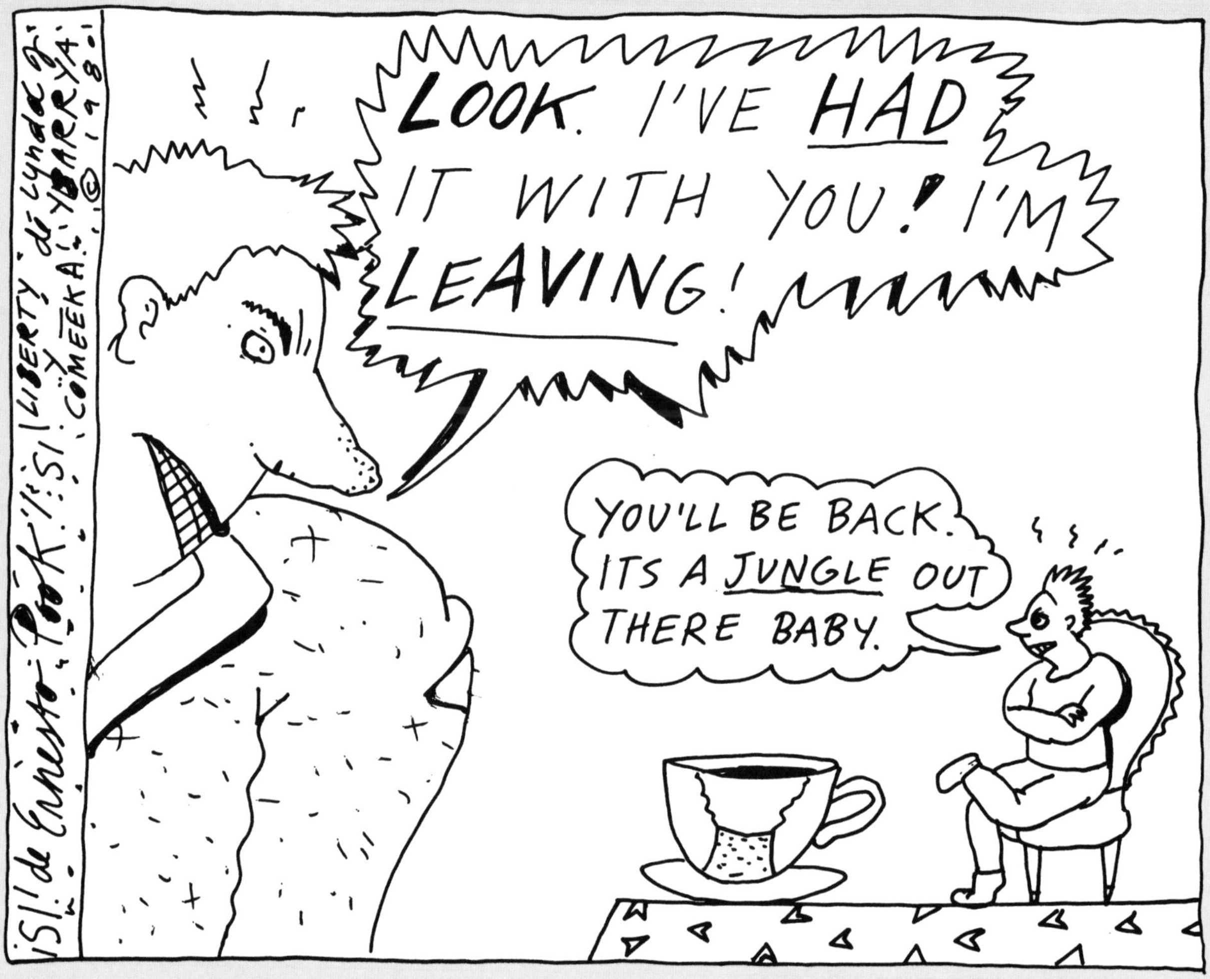
¡SI! ¡de Ernesto Pook! ¡SI! ¡LIBERTY di Lynda J. YBARRYA!
¡COMEEKA! © 198
LOOK. I'VE HAD IT WITH YOU! I'M LEAVING!
YOU'LL BE BACK. ITS A JUNGLE OUT THERE BABY.

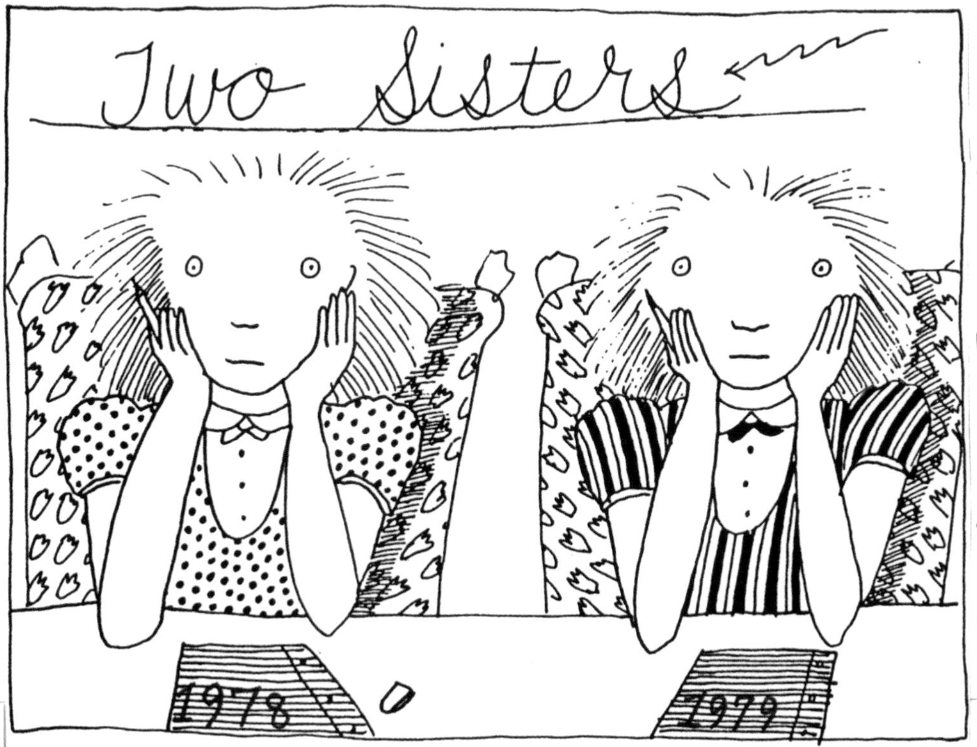
Two Sisters
1978
1979

IN 1978, AFTER I'D BEEN DOING A *weekly* COMIC STRIP FOR *a* FEW *months*, I BEGAN *writing* MORE *about* TWO PARTICULAR CHARACTERS *who had* SHOWN UP *in* MY STRIPS NOW *and* THEN: TWO SISTERS.

They WERE TWINS *named* RITA *and* EVETTE FISK.

The STRIP *Ran* FOR *about* A YEAR *in* A LONG-GONE SEATTLE WEEKLY CALLED "THE SEATTLE SUN."

PHOTOCOPY SHOPS *were* OPENING AROUND *then* *and* FOR THE FIRST *time*, *anyone* COULD EASILY MAKE THEIR *own* COMIC BOOKS.

MY FIRST BOOK *was made this way*. COPYSHOP, COPIES OF THE TWO SISTERS STRIPS *with* A HAND-COLORED *and* HAND DECORATED 'COVER' *which* WAS A MANILA ENVELOPE WITH A DRAWING TAPED ON IT. IT INCLUDED *an* 'AUTHOR PORTRAIT' DRAWN BY MY LITTLE BROTHER:

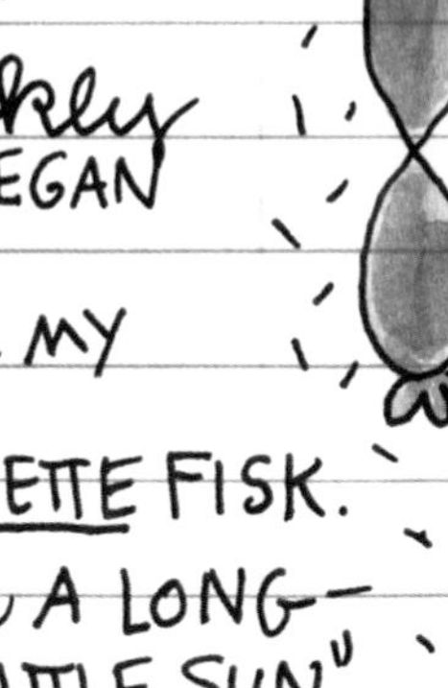

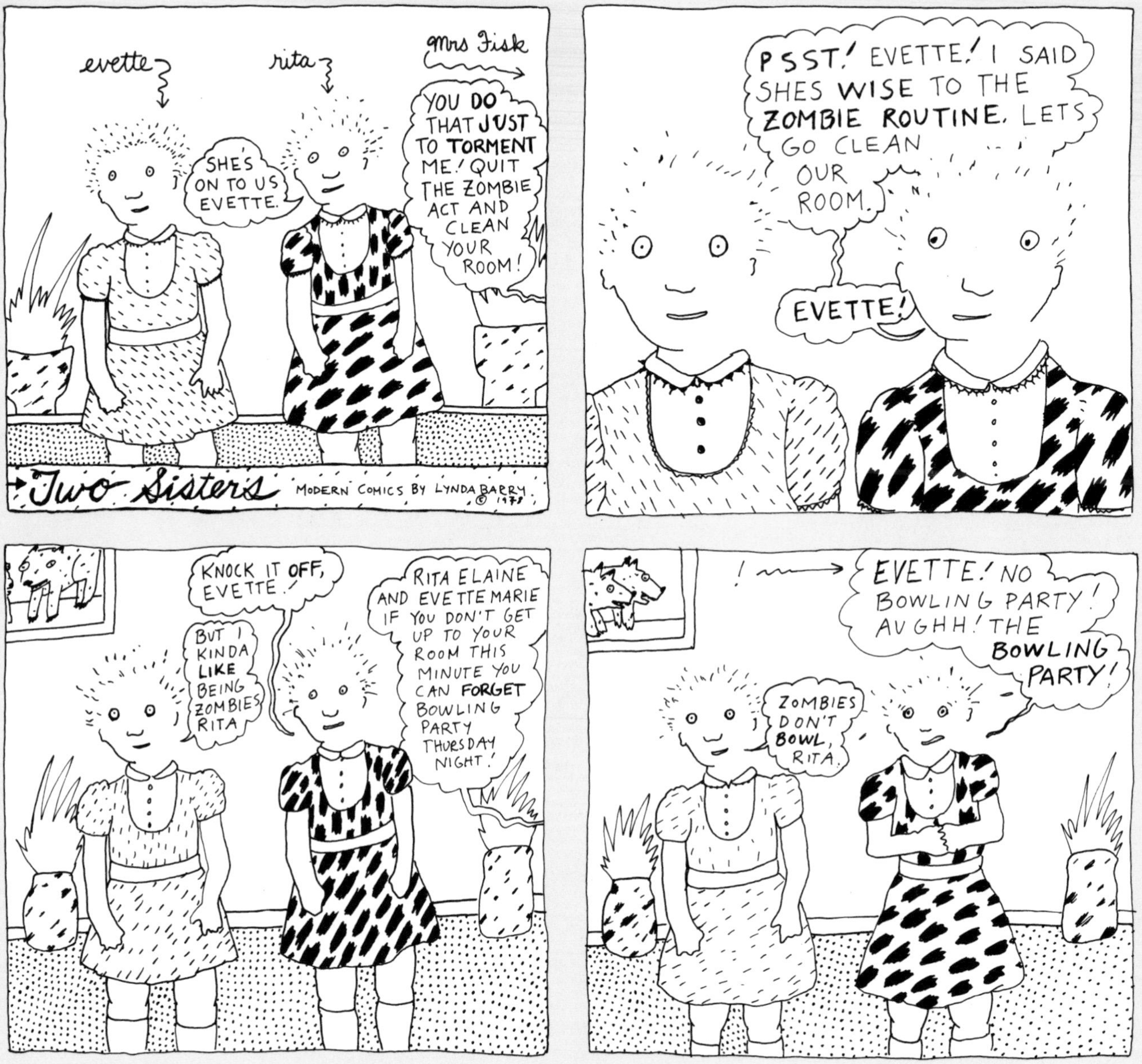
evette
rita
Mrs Fisk
SHE'S ON TO US EVETTE.
YOU DO THAT JUST TO TORMENT ME! QUIT THE ZOMBIE ACT AND CLEAN YOUR ROOM!
Two Sisters
MODERN COMICS BY LYNDA BARRY ©
PSST! EVETTE! I SAID SHES WISE TO THE ZOMBIE ROUTINE. LETS GO CLEAN OUR ROOM.
EVETTE!
KNOCK IT OFF, EVETTE!
BUT I KINDA LIKE BEING ZOMBIES RITA
RITA ELAINE AND EVETTE MARIE IF YOU DON'T GET UP TO YOUR ROOM THIS MINUTE YOU CAN FORGET BOWLING PARTY THURSDAY NIGHT!
EVETTE! NO BOWLING PARTY! AUGHH! THE BOWLING PARTY!
ZOMBIES DON'T BOWL, RITA.

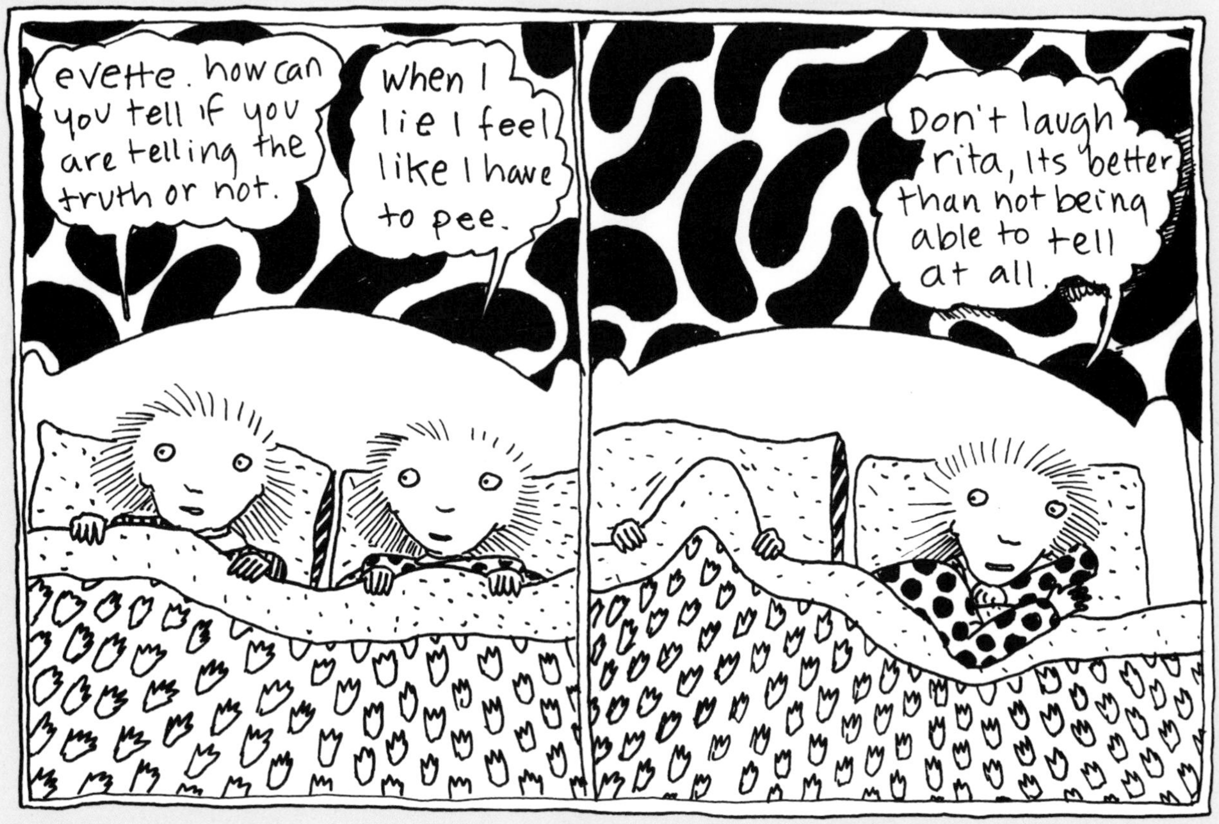
evette. how can you tell if you are telling the truth or not.
When I lie I feel like I have to pee.
Don't laugh rita, Its better than not being able to tell at all.

Two Sisters
MODERN COMICS BY LYNDABARRY
© 1978
rita
and
evette
oh evette! You look beautiful!
MY GOD EVETTE! YOU LOOK LIKE A TWO PENNY TART! WASH YOUR FACE AND GO TO YOUR ROOM.

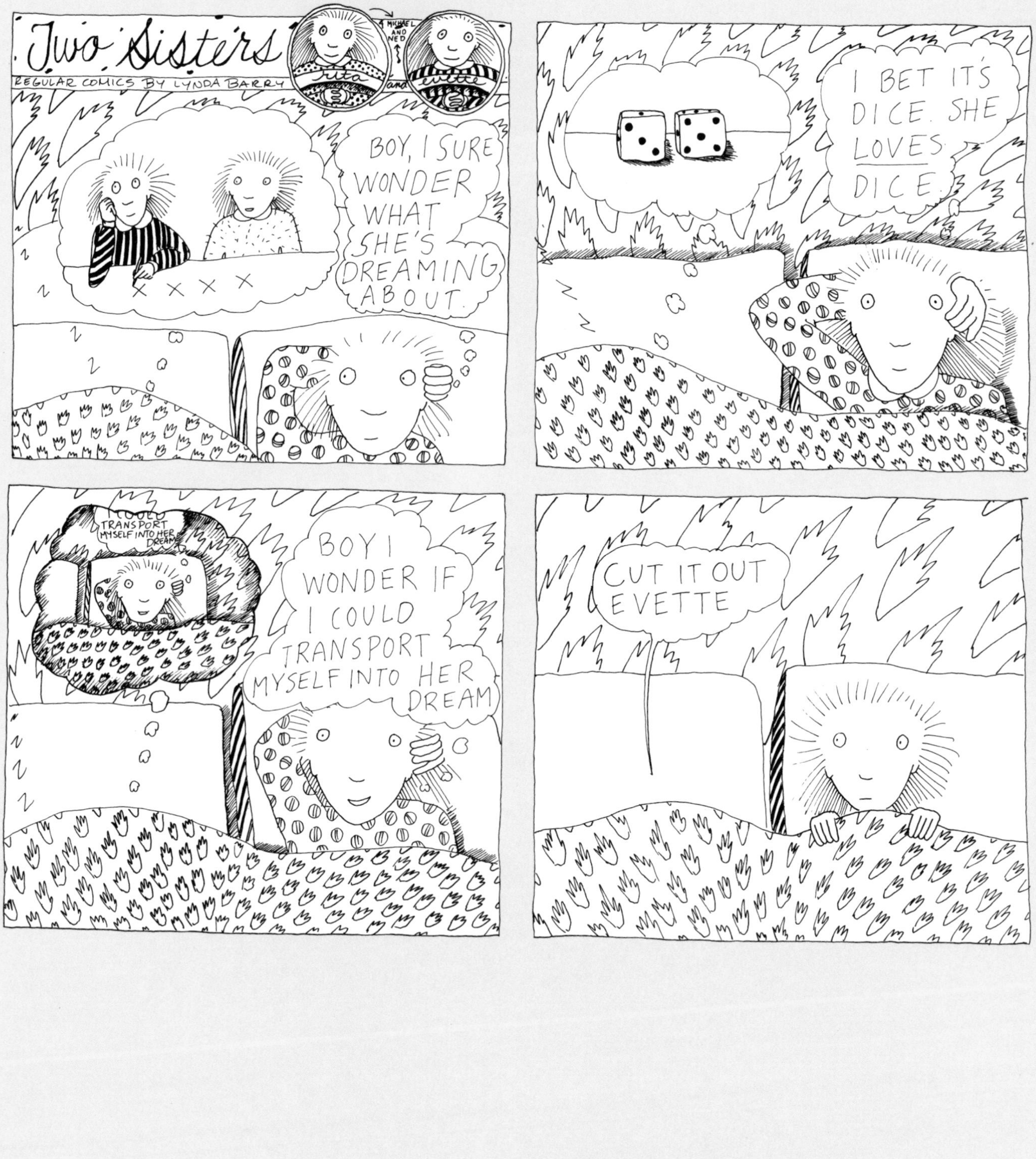
Two Sisters
REGULAR COMICS BY LYNDA BARRY
rita and evette
MICHAEL AND NED
BOY, I SURE WONDER WHAT SHE'S DREAMING ABOUT.
I BET IT'S DICE. SHE LOVES DICE.
TRANSPORT MYSELF INTO HER DREAM
BOY I WONDER IF I COULD TRANSPORT MYSELF INTO HER DREAM
CUT IT OUT EVETTE

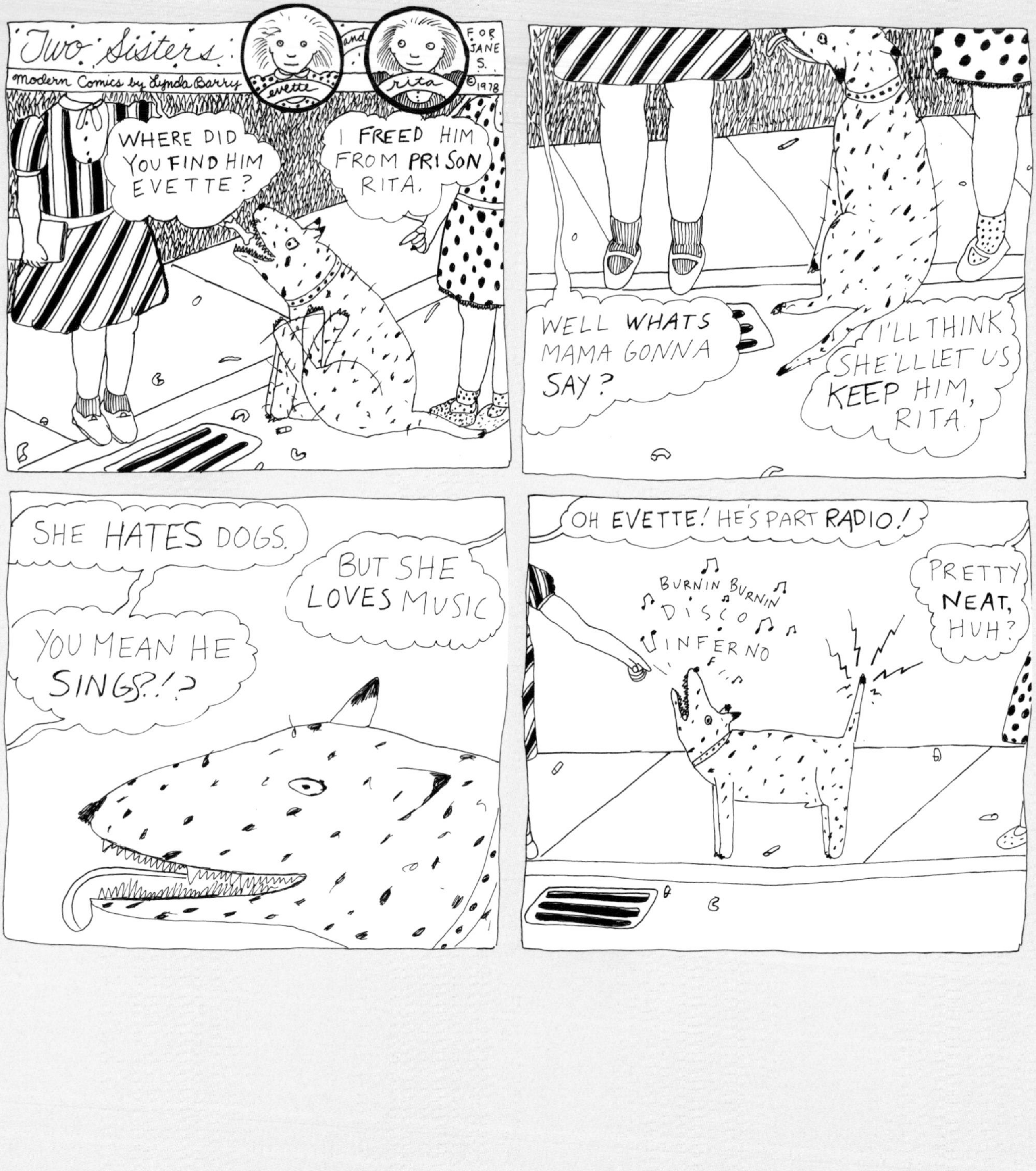

Two Sisters
Modern Comics by Lynda Barry
evette
and
rita
FOR JANE S.
©1978
WHERE DID YOU FIND HIM EVETTE?
I FREED HIM FROM PRISON RITA.
WELL WHATS MAMA GONNA SAY?
I'LL THINK SHE'LL LET US KEEP HIM, RITA.
SHE HATES DOGS.
BUT SHE LOVES MUSIC
YOU MEAN HE SINGS?!?
OH EVETTE! HE'S PART RADIO!
BURNIN BURNIN DISCO INFERNO
PRETTY NEAT, HUH?

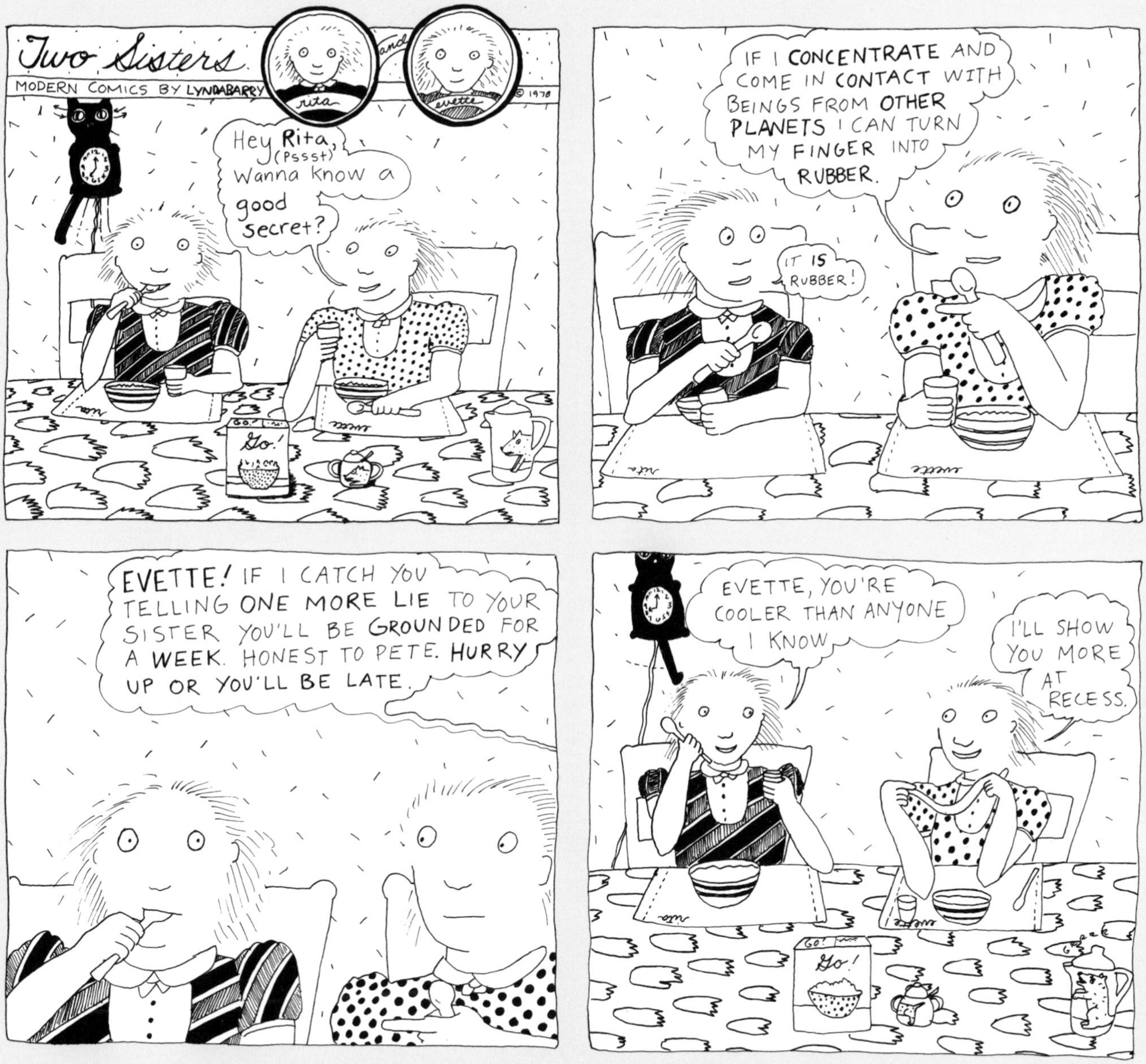
Two Sisters
MODERN COMICS BY LYNDABARRY
rita
and
evette
© 1978
Hey Rita, (Pssst) Wanna know a good secret?
Go!
IF I CONCENTRATE AND COME IN CONTACT WITH BEINGS FROM OTHER PLANETS I CAN TURN MY FINGER INTO RUBBER.
IT IS RUBBER!
EVETTE! IF I CATCH YOU TELLING ONE MORE LIE TO YOUR SISTER YOU'LL BE GROUNDED FOR A WEEK. HONEST TO PETE. HURRY UP OR YOU'LL BE LATE.
EVETTE, YOU'RE COOLER THAN ANYONE I KNOW.
I'LL SHOW YOU MORE AT RECESS.
Go!

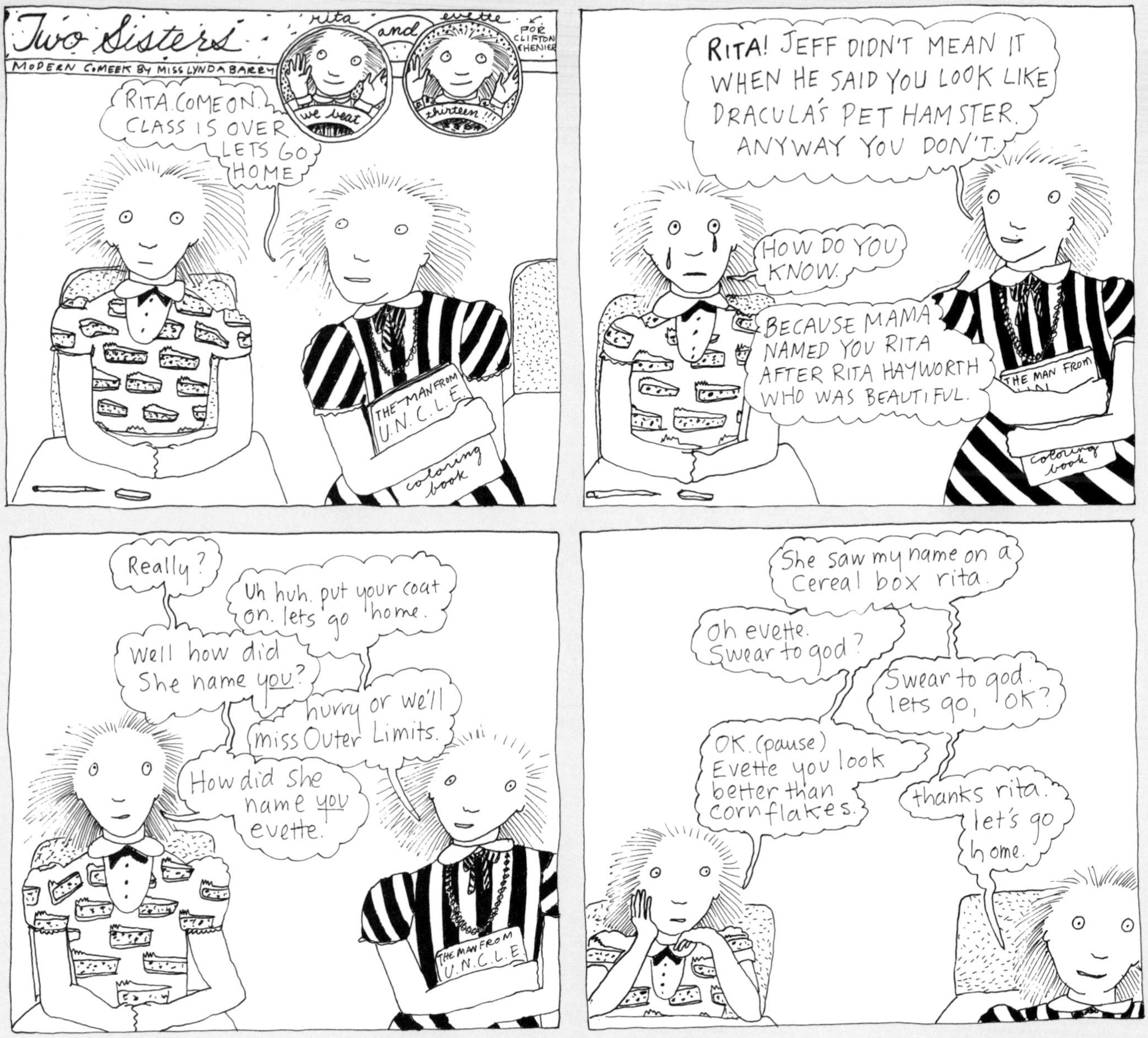
Two Sisters
rita and evette
FOR CLIFTON CHENIER
MODERN COMEEK BY MISS LYNDA BARRY
we beat thirteen!!!
RITA. COME ON. CLASS IS OVER
LETS GO HOME
THE MAN FROM U.N.C.L.E.
coloring book
RITA! JEFF DIDN'T MEAN IT WHEN HE SAID YOU LOOK LIKE DRACULA'S PET HAMSTER. ANYWAY YOU DON'T.
HOW DO YOU KNOW.
BECAUSE MAMA NAMED YOU RITA AFTER RITA HAYWORTH WHO WAS BEAUTIFUL.
THE MAN FROM
coloring book
Really?
Uh huh. put your coat on. lets go home.
Well how did She name you?
hurry or we'll miss Outer Limits.
How did She name you evette.
THE MAN FROM U.N.C.L.E.
She saw my name on a Cereal box rita.
Oh evette. Swear to god?
Swear to god. lets go, OK?
OK. (pause) Evette you look better than cornflakes.
thanks rita. let's go home.

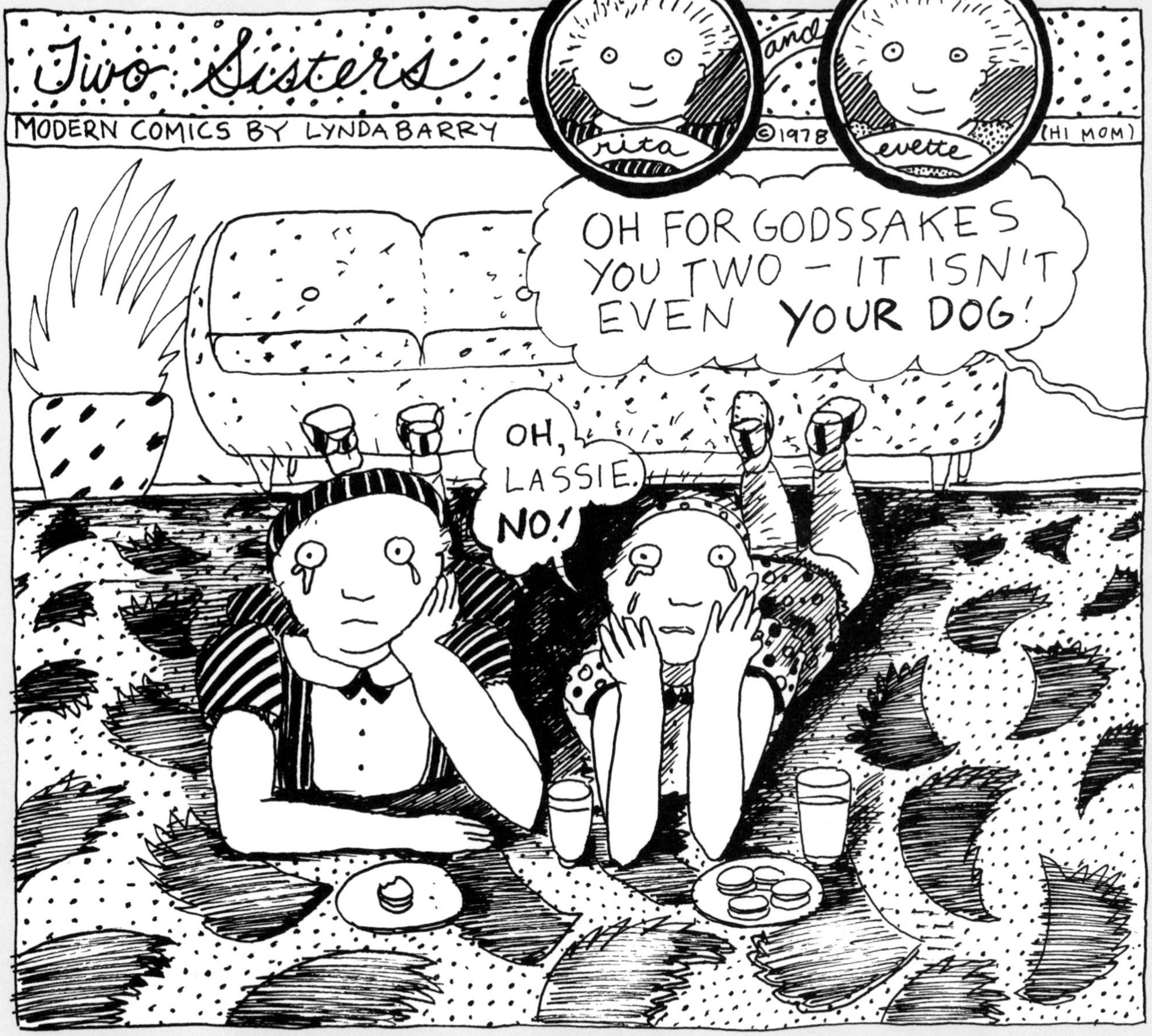
Two Sisters
rita
and
evette
MODERN COMICS BY LYNDA BARRY
©1978
(HI MOM)
OH FOR GODSSAKES YOU TWO - IT ISN'T EVEN YOUR DOG!
OH, LASSIE. NO!

TWO SISTERS
REGULAR COMICKS BY LYNDA BARRY
rita
and
evette
UT'S FEET
HEY RITA. YOU'VE BEEN STARING AT KING TUT'S HEAD FOR AN HOUR. AND YOU'RE LOOKING AT THE BACK- YOU'RE NOT EVEN LOOKING AT HIS FACE! RITA, THE REST OF THE CLASS IS ALREADY IN THE GIFT SHOP.
RITA! CUT IT OUT! IM NOT KIDDING!
"PHAROVER"
RITA FISK! WHERE HAVE YOU BEEN! THE CLASS HAS BEEN WAITING FOR 15 MINUTES!
I WAS HAVING A COSMIC EXPERIENCE MISS LARUE.
RITA WAS ASLEEP IN THE CORNER MISS LARUE.
RITA

Two Sisters
evette
and
rita
REGULAR COMICS BY LYNDA BARRY©1978
FOR ROB PARFET
RITA. THIS IT. WE ARE REALLY GETTING A DOG TODAY. I CAN'T BELIEVE IT.
YEAH.
YOU KNOW HOW YOU WAIT AND WAIT FOR SOMETHING AND THEN ITS ABOUT READY TO HAPPEN - AND IT FEELS SORT OF LIKE IT'S ALL ON T.V., YOU KNOW?
YEAH.
YOU WERE TALKING IN YOUR SLEEP AGAIN RITA. THATS 3 NIGHTS IN A ROW NOW!

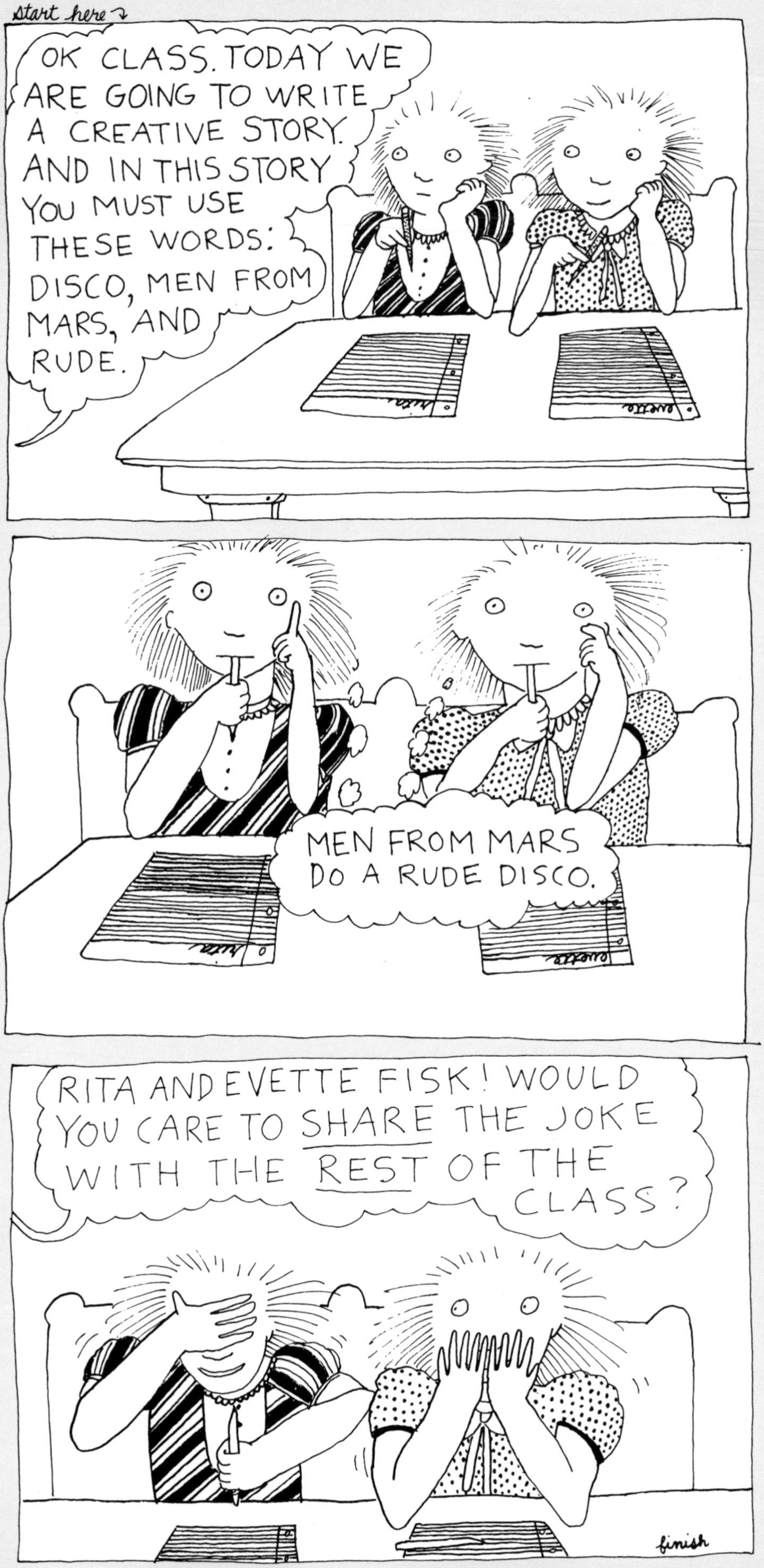
start here
OK CLASS. TODAY WE ARE GOING TO WRITE A CREATIVE STORY. AND IN THIS STORY YOU MUST USE THESE WORDS: DISCO, MEN FROM MARS, AND RUDE.
MEN FROM MARS DO A RUDE DISCO.
RITA AND EVETTE FISK! WOULD YOU CARE TO SHARE THE JOKE WITH THE REST OF THE CLASS?
finish

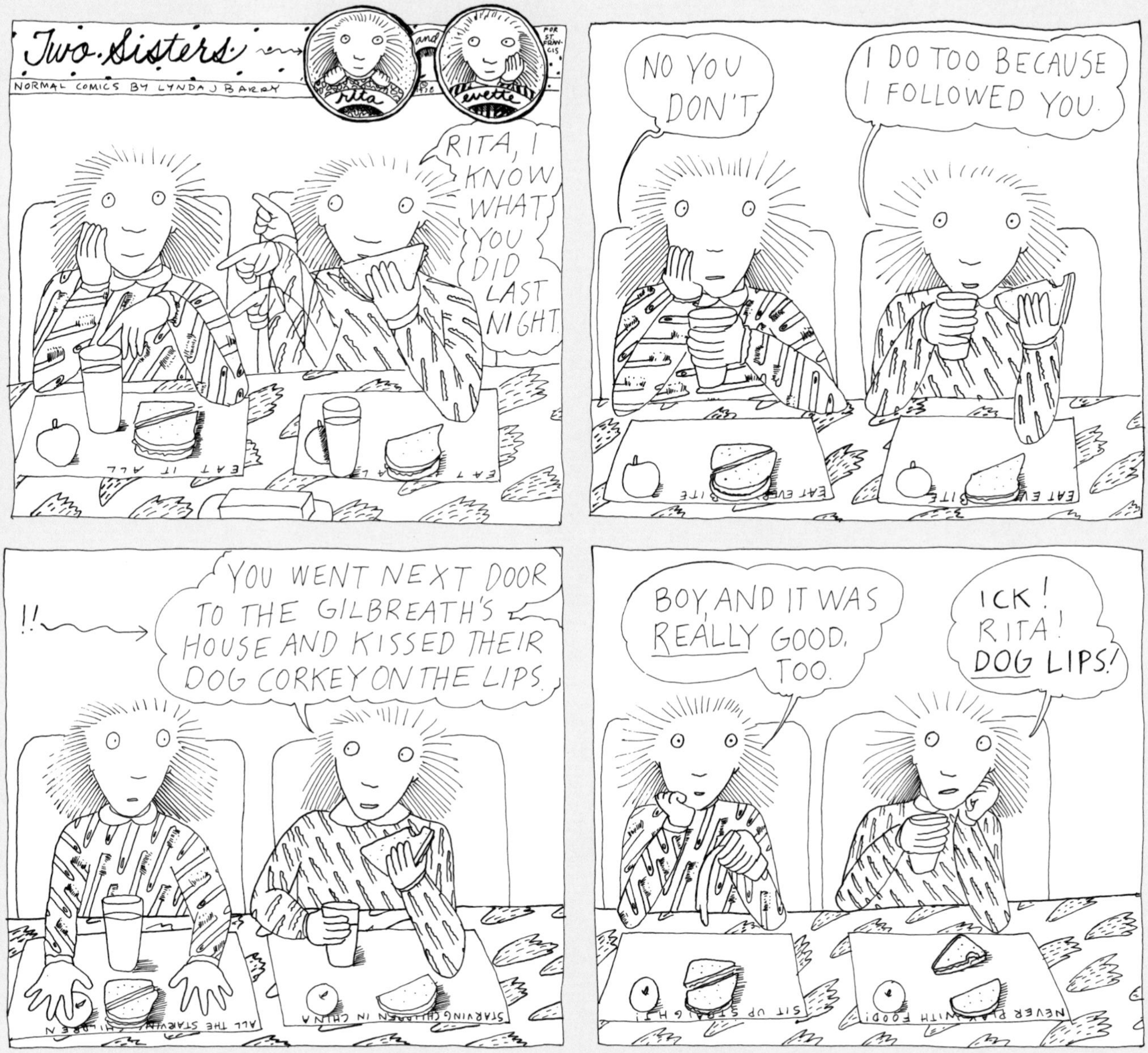
Two Sisters
NORMAL COMICS BY LYNDA J BARRY
rita
and
evette
RITA, I KNOW WHAT YOU DID LAST NIGHT.
NO YOU DON'T
I DO TOO BECAUSE I FOLLOWED YOU.
!!
YOU WENT NEXT DOOR TO THE GILBREATH'S HOUSE AND KISSED THEIR DOG CORKEY ON THE LIPS.
BOY, AND IT WAS REALLY GOOD, TOO.
ICK! RITA! DOG LIPS!

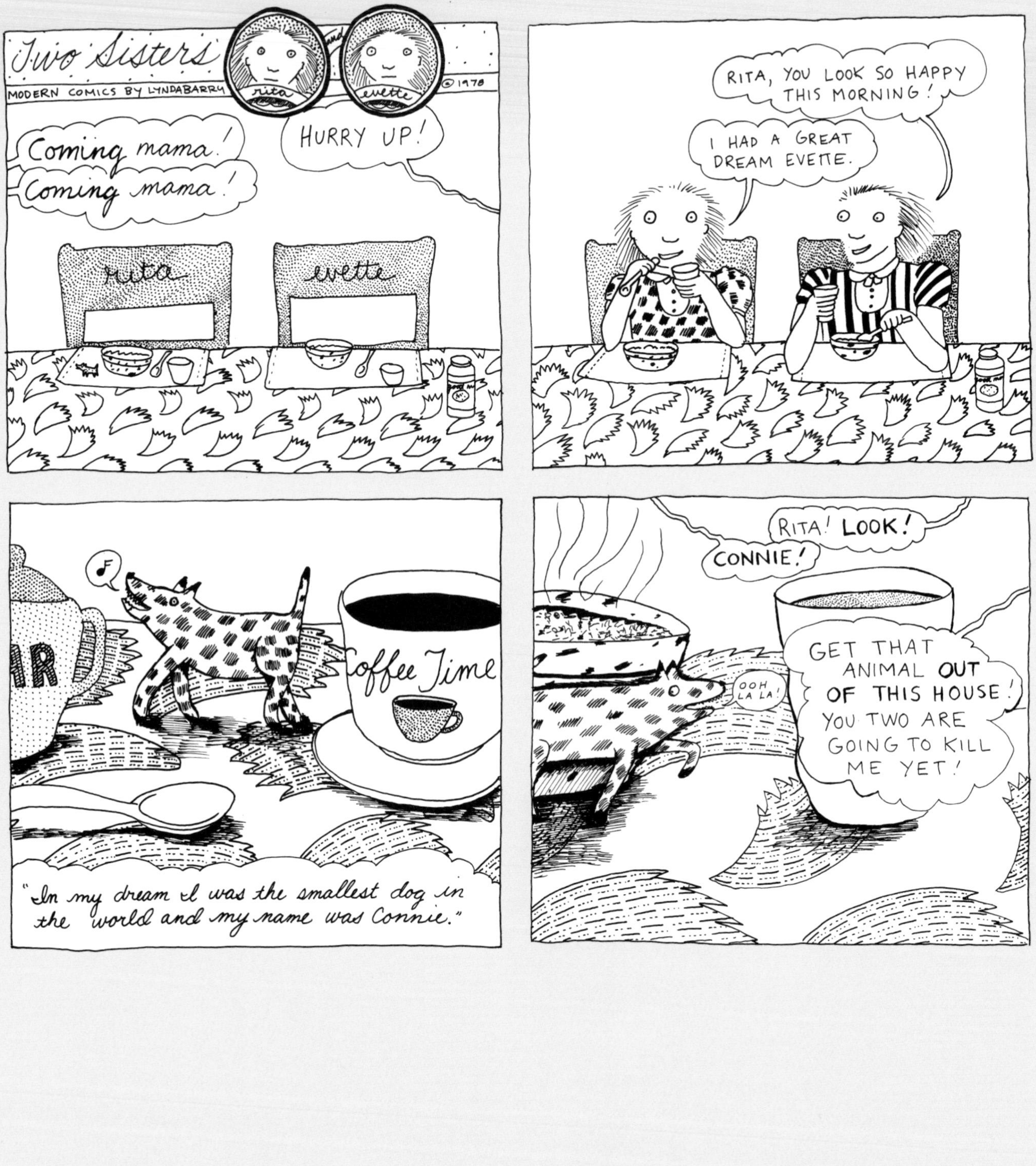
Two Sisters
rita
evette
MODERN COMICS BY LYNDABARRY
© 1978
Coming mama!
Coming mama!
HURRY UP!
rita
evette
RITA, YOU LOOK SO HAPPY THIS MORNING!
I HAD A GREAT DREAM EVETTE.
Coffee Time
"In my dream I was the smallest dog in the world and my name was Connie."
RITA! LOOK!
CONNIE!
OOH LA LA!
GET THAT ANIMAL OUT OF THIS HOUSE! YOU TWO ARE GOING TO KILL ME YET!

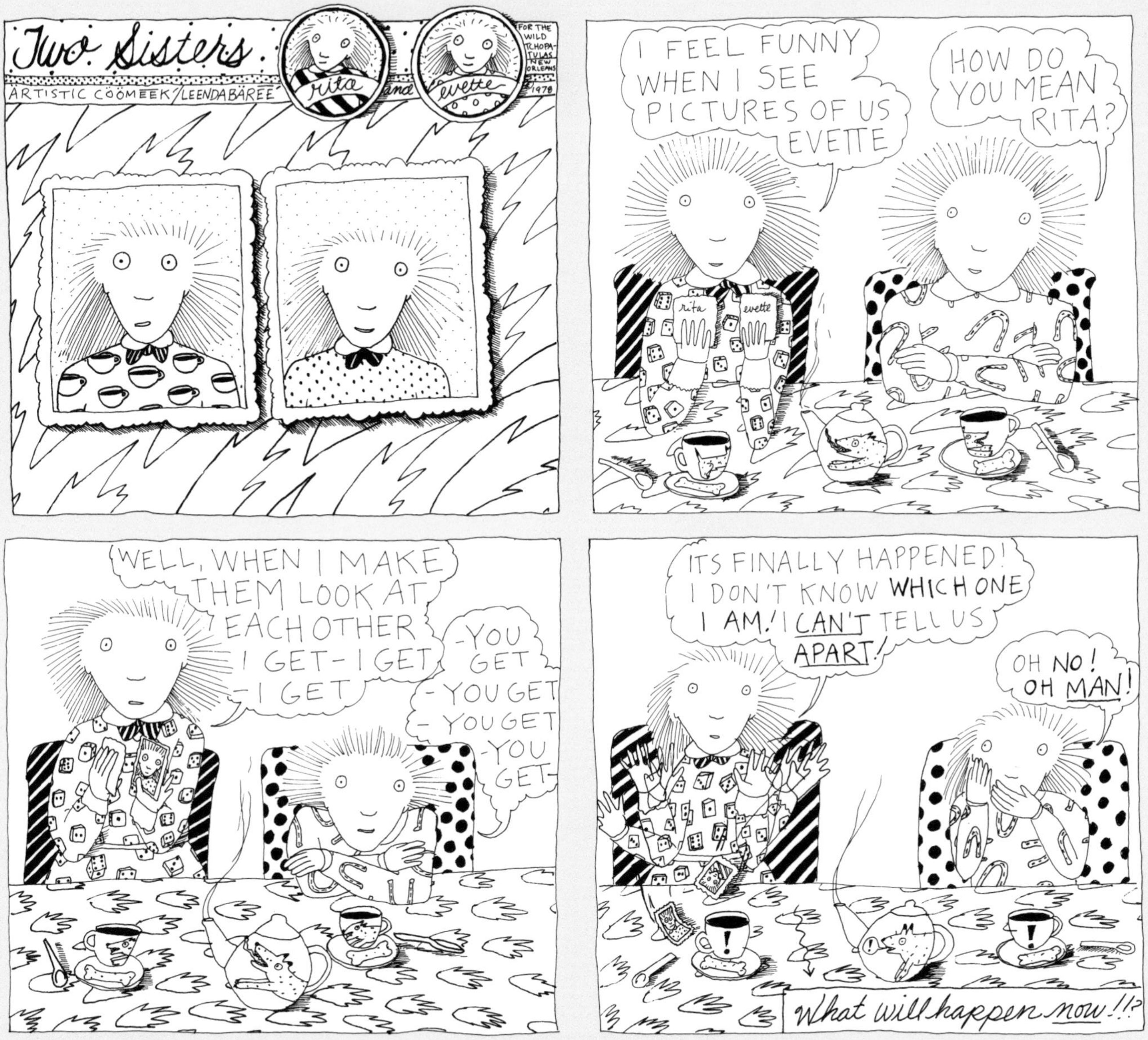

Two Sisters
ARTISTIC CÖÖMEEK / LEENDABÄREE
rita and evette
FOR THE WILD TCHOPATULAS NEW ORLEANS © 1978
I FEEL FUNNY WHEN I SEE PICTURES OF US EVETTE
HOW DO YOU MEAN RITA?
rita
evette
WELL, WHEN I MAKE THEM LOOK AT EACH OTHER I GET—I GET—I GET—I GET
—YOU GET—YOU GET—YOU GET—YOU GET—
ITS FINALLY HAPPENED! I DON'T KNOW WHICH ONE I AM! I CAN'T TELL US APART!
OH NO! OH MAN!
What will happen now!!?

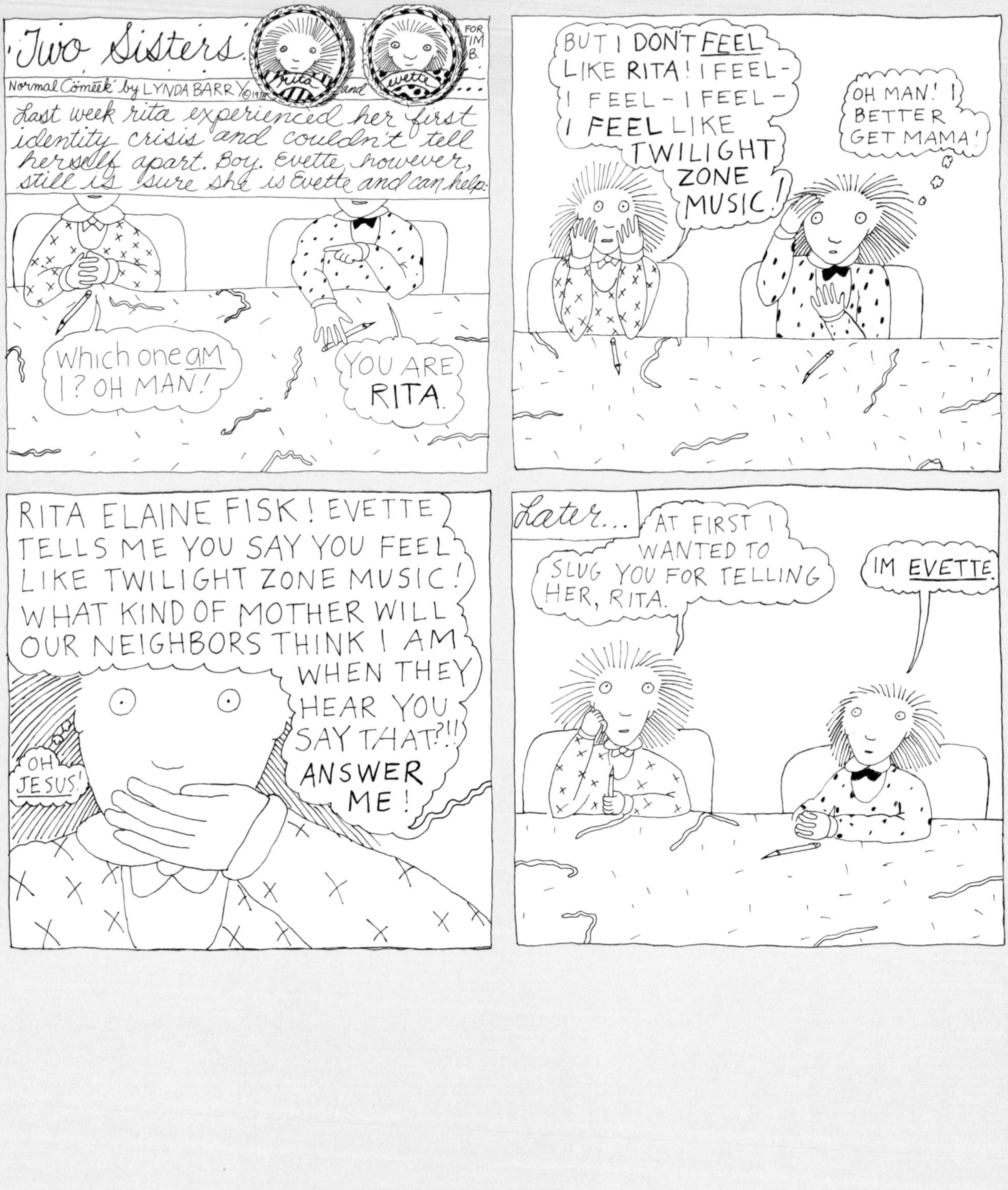
Two Sisters
FOR TIM B.
rita
evette
Normal Cömeek by LYNDA BARRY ©1978
Last week rita experienced her first identity crisis and couldn't tell herself apart. Boy. Evette however, still is sure she is Evette and can help:
Which one AM I? OH MAN!
YOU ARE RITA.
BUT I DON'T FEEL LIKE RITA! I FEEL- I FEEL- I FEEL- I FEEL LIKE TWILIGHT ZONE MUSIC!
OH MAN! I BETTER GET MAMA!
RITA ELAINE FISK! EVETTE TELLS ME YOU SAY YOU FEEL LIKE TWILIGHT ZONE MUSIC! WHAT KIND OF MOTHER WILL OUR NEIGHBORS THINK I AM WHEN THEY HEAR YOU SAY THAT?!! ANSWER ME!
OH JESUS!
Later...
AT FIRST I WANTED TO SLUG YOU FOR TELLING HER, RITA.
IM EVETTE.

Two Sisters
REAL CÖMEK / LYNDA BARRY © 1978
rita
evette
Thanks rita
evette.
Last week rita thought evette was rita and this was a problem.
YOU ARE EVETTE I AM EVETTE MAMA IS EVETTE THIS CHAIR IS EVETTE MY SANDWICH IS EVETTE.
EVERYTHING IS EVETTE! I QUIT!
I QUIT TOO.
IF YOU WON'T BE RITA, I DON'T WANT TO BE EVETTE ANYMORE.
continued next week

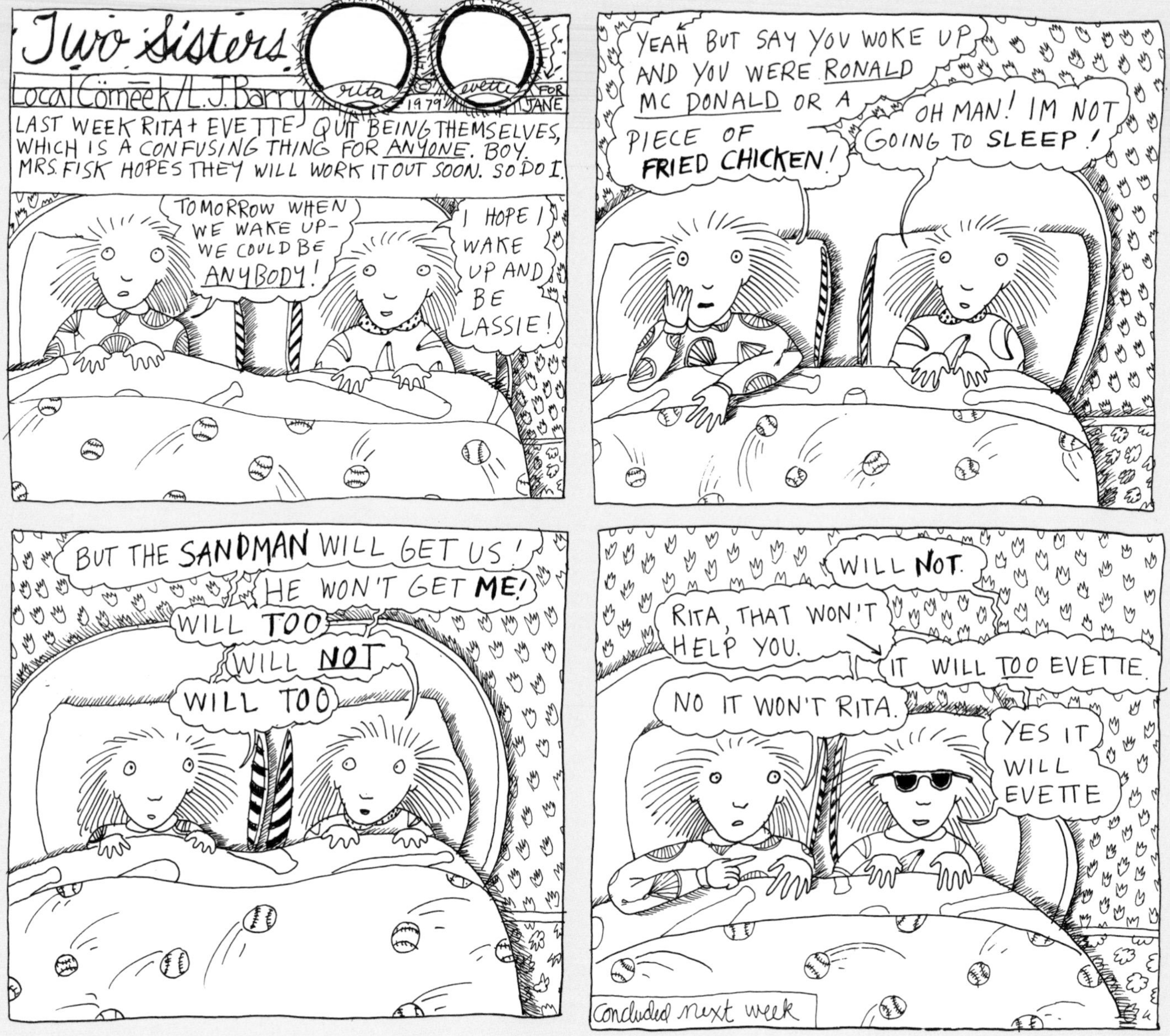
Two Sisters
Local Cömeek / L.J. Barry
rita
evette
© 1979
FOR JANE
LAST WEEK RITA + EVETTE QUIT BEING THEMSELVES, WHICH IS A CONFUSING THING FOR ANYONE. BOY. MRS. FISK HOPES THEY WILL WORK IT OUT SOON. SO DO I.
TOMORROW WHEN WE WAKE UP- WE COULD BE ANYBODY!
I HOPE I WAKE UP AND BE LASSIE!
YEAH BUT SAY YOU WOKE UP AND YOU WERE RONALD MC DONALD OR A PIECE OF FRIED CHICKEN!
OH MAN! IM NOT GOING TO SLEEP!
BUT THE SANDMAN WILL GET US!
HE WON'T GET ME!
WILL TOO
WILL NOT
WILL TOO
WILL NOT.
RITA, THAT WON'T HELP YOU.
IT WILL TOO EVETTE.
NO IT WON'T RITA.
YES IT WILL EVETTE
Concluded next week

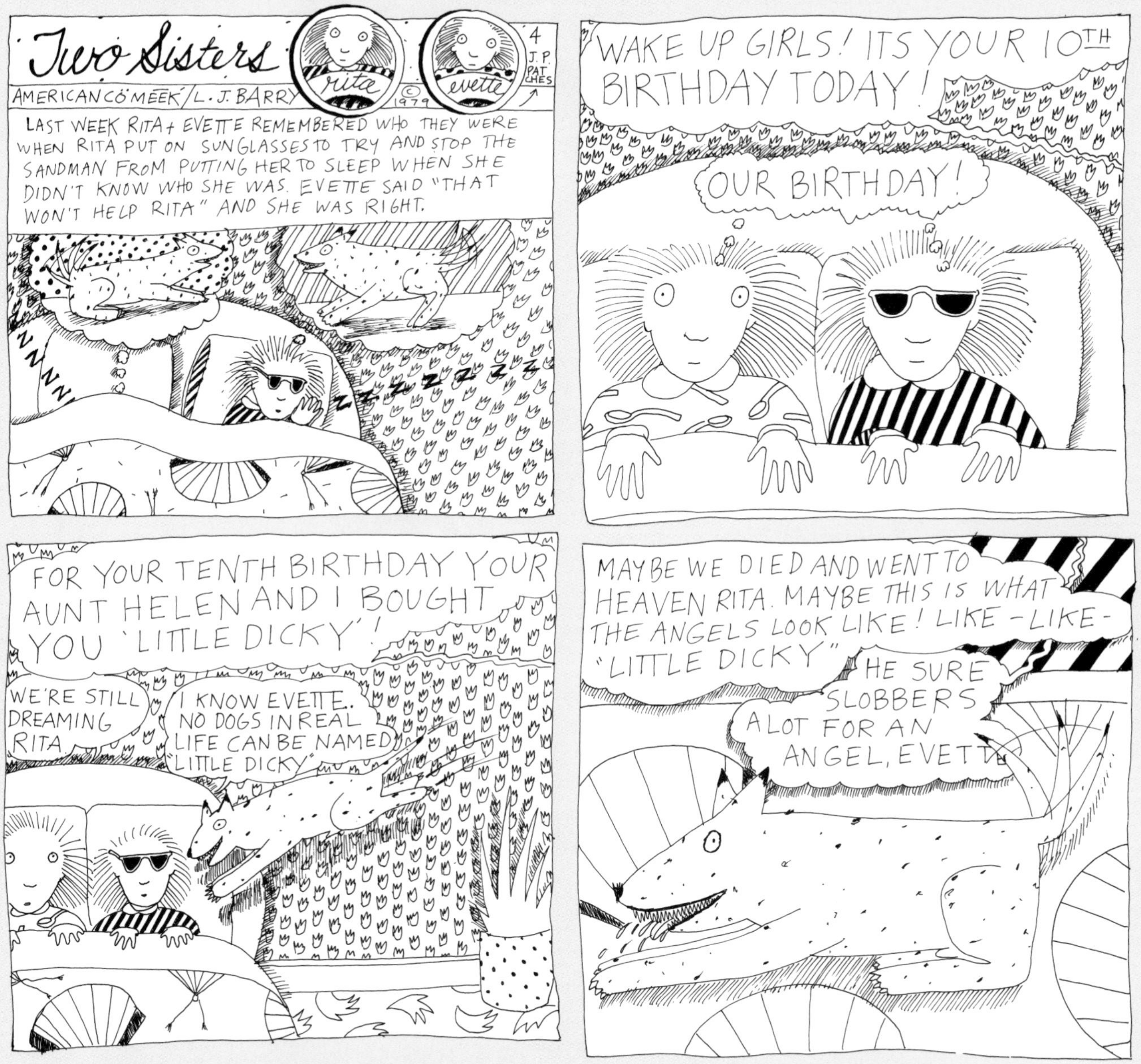
Two Sisters
rita
evette
4
J.P. PATCHES
AMERICAN CÖMEEK / L. J. BARRY
© 1979
LAST WEEK RITA + EVETTE REMEMBERED WHO THEY WERE WHEN RITA PUT ON SUNGLASSES TO TRY AND STOP THE SANDMAN FROM PUTTING HER TO SLEEP WHEN SHE DIDN'T KNOW WHO SHE WAS. EVETTE SAID "THAT WON'T HELP RITA" AND SHE WAS RIGHT.
WAKE UP GIRLS! ITS YOUR 10TH BIRTHDAY TODAY!
OUR BIRTHDAY!
FOR YOUR TENTH BIRTHDAY YOUR AUNT HELEN AND I BOUGHT YOU 'LITTLE DICKY'!
WE'RE STILL DREAMING RITA.
I KNOW EVETTE. NO DOGS IN REAL LIFE CAN BE NAMED "LITTLE DICKY"
MAYBE WE DIED AND WENT TO HEAVEN RITA. MAYBE THIS IS WHAT THE ANGELS LOOK LIKE! LIKE - LIKE - "LITTLE DICKY"
HE SURE SLOBBERS A LOT FOR AN ANGEL, EVETTE

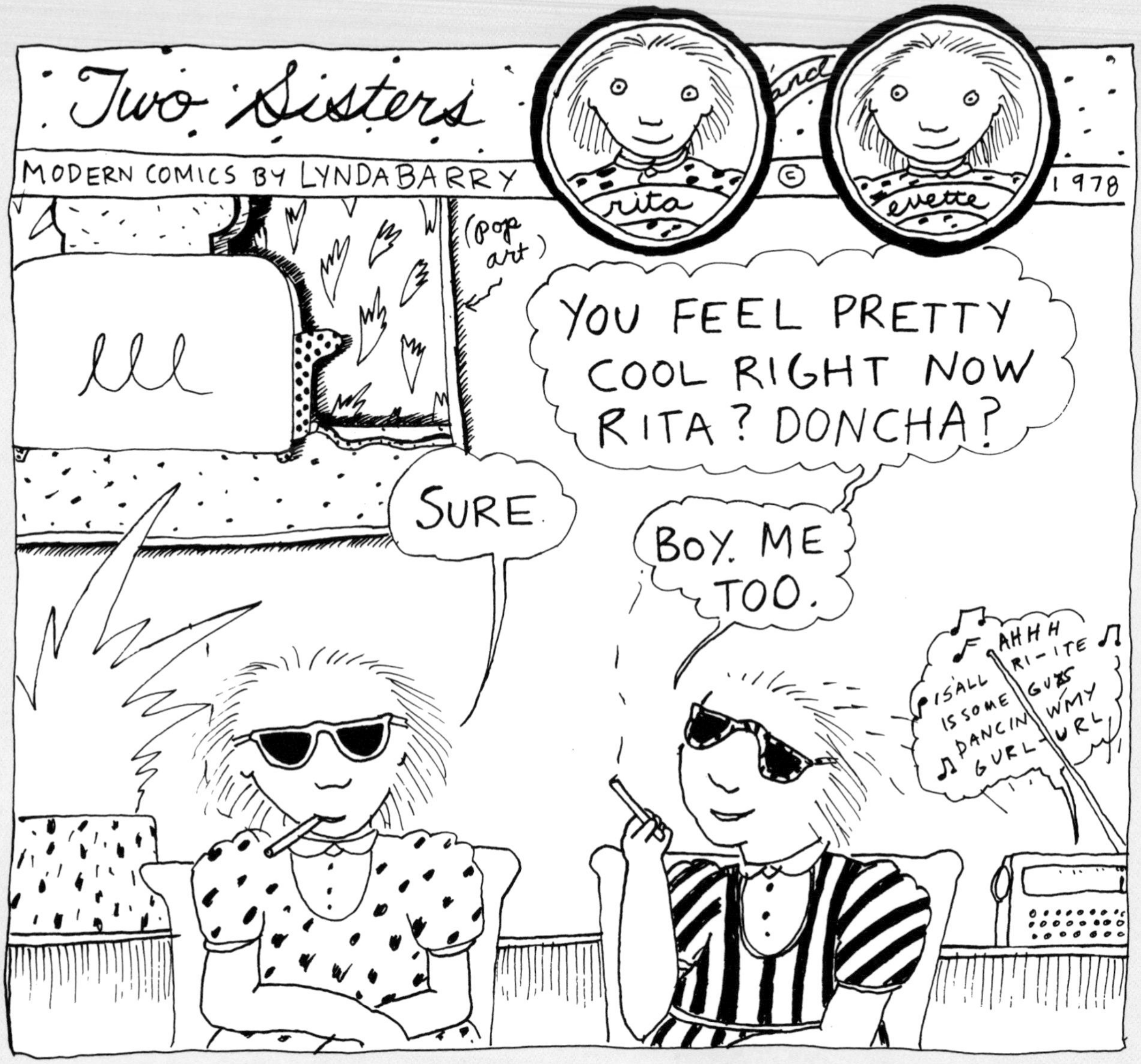
Two Sisters
MODERN COMICS BY LYNDABARRY © 1978
rita
and
evette
(pop art)
YOU FEEL PRETTY COOL RIGHT NOW RITA? DONCHA?
SURE.
BOY. ME TOO.
AHHH
RI-ITE
ISALL
IS SOME GUYS
DANCIN WMY
GURL-URL

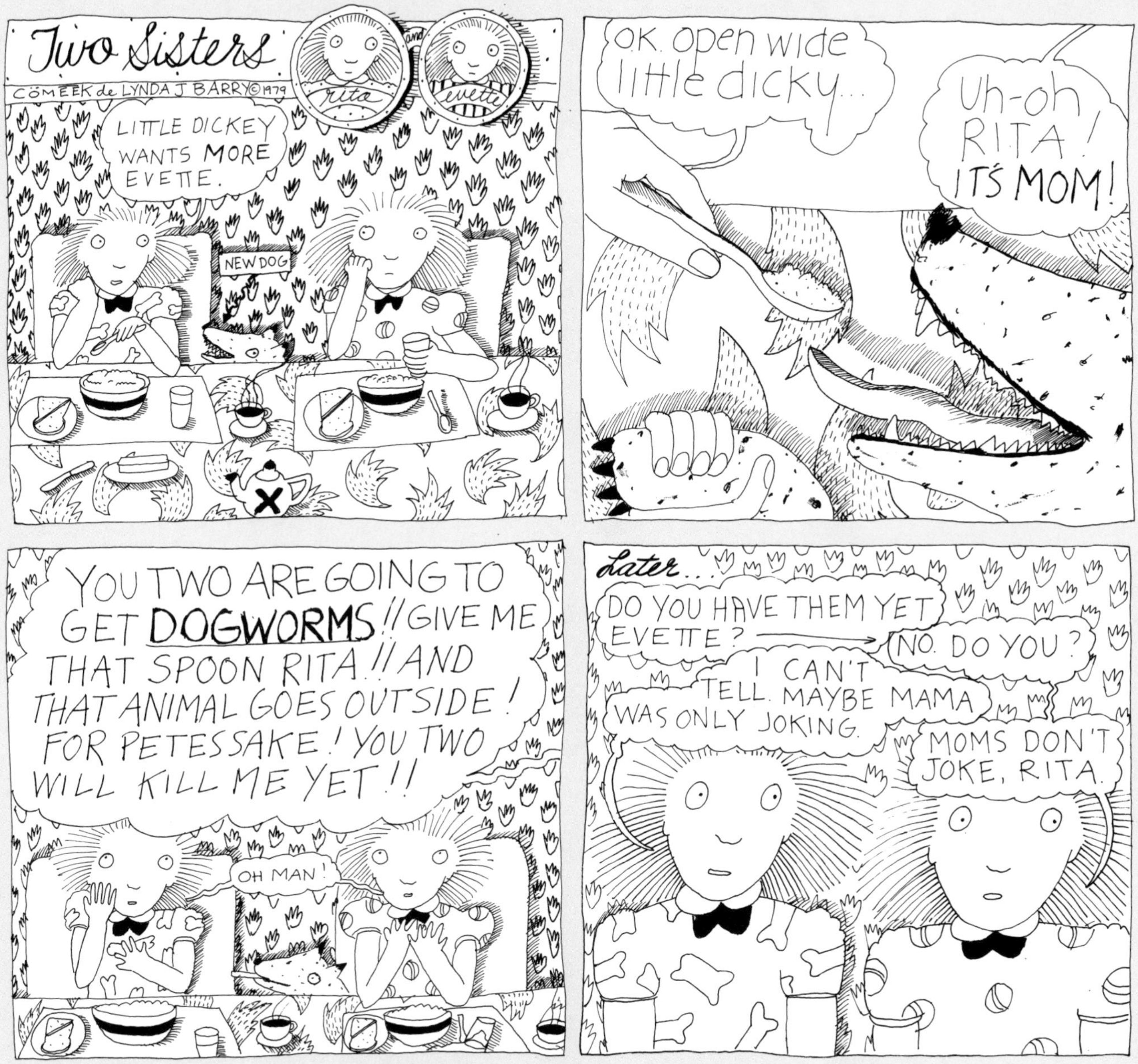
Two Sisters
CÖMEEK de LYNDA J BARRY ©1979
rita
and
evette
LITTLE DICKEY WANTS MORE EVETTE.
NEW DOG
OK. open wide little dicky...
Uh-oh RITA! IT'S MOM!
YOU TWO ARE GOING TO GET DOGWORMS!! GIVE ME THAT SPOON RITA!! AND THAT ANIMAL GOES OUTSIDE! FOR PETESSAKE! YOU TWO WILL KILL ME YET!!
OH MAN!
Later...
DO YOU HAVE THEM YET EVETTE?
NO. DO YOU?
I CAN'T TELL. MAYBE MAMA WAS ONLY JOKING.
MOMS DON'T JOKE, RITA.

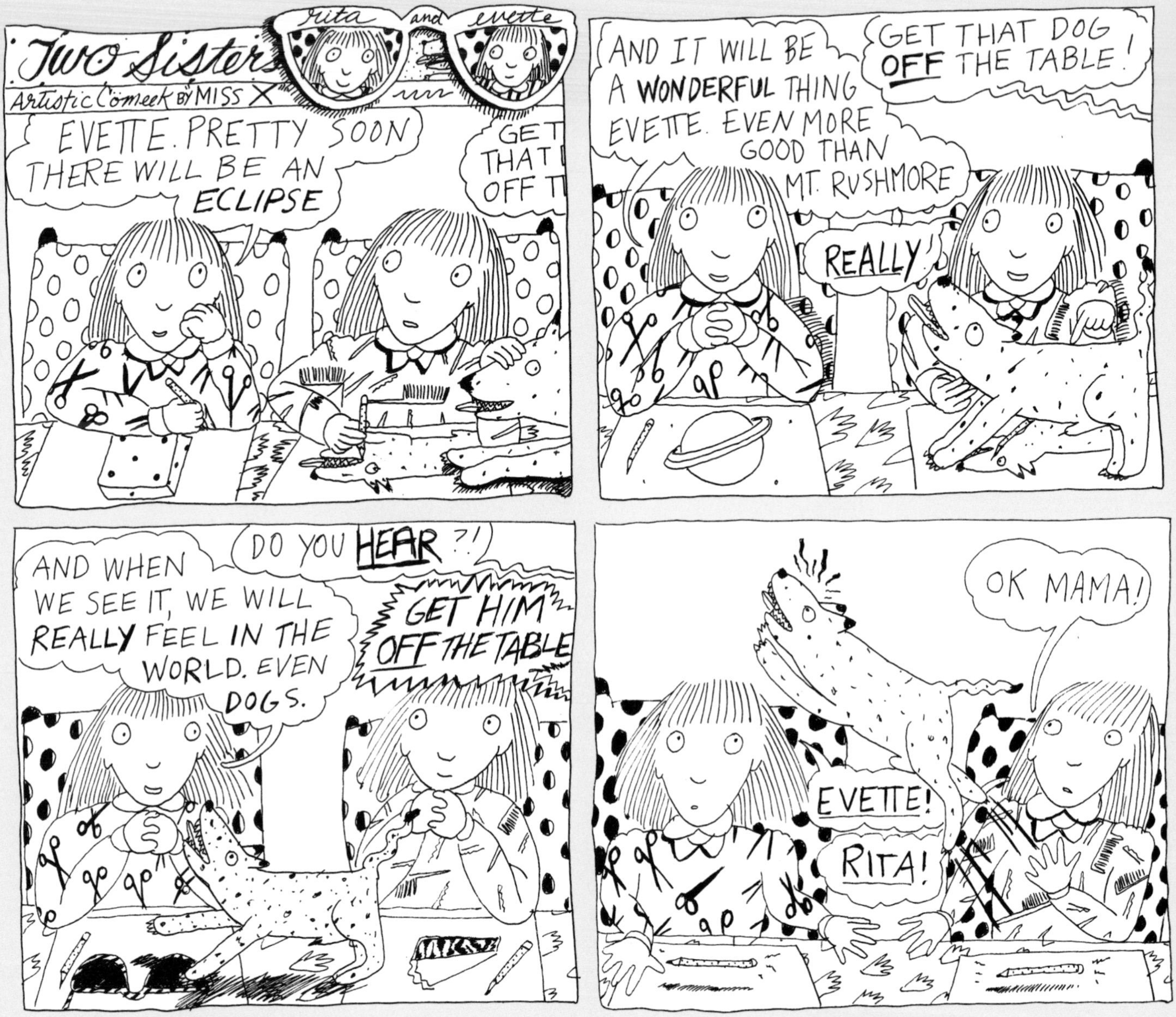
Two Sisters
rita and evette
Artistic Comeek BY MISS X
EVETTE. PRETTY SOON THERE WILL BE AN ECLIPSE
GET THAT OFF T
AND IT WILL BE A WONDERFUL THING EVETTE. EVEN MORE GOOD THAN MT. RUSHMORE
GET THAT DOG OFF THE TABLE!
REALLY
AND WHEN WE SEE IT, WE WILL REALLY FEEL IN THE WORLD. EVEN DOGS.
DO YOU HEAR?!
GET HIM OFF THE TABLE
OK MAMA!
EVETTE!
RITA!

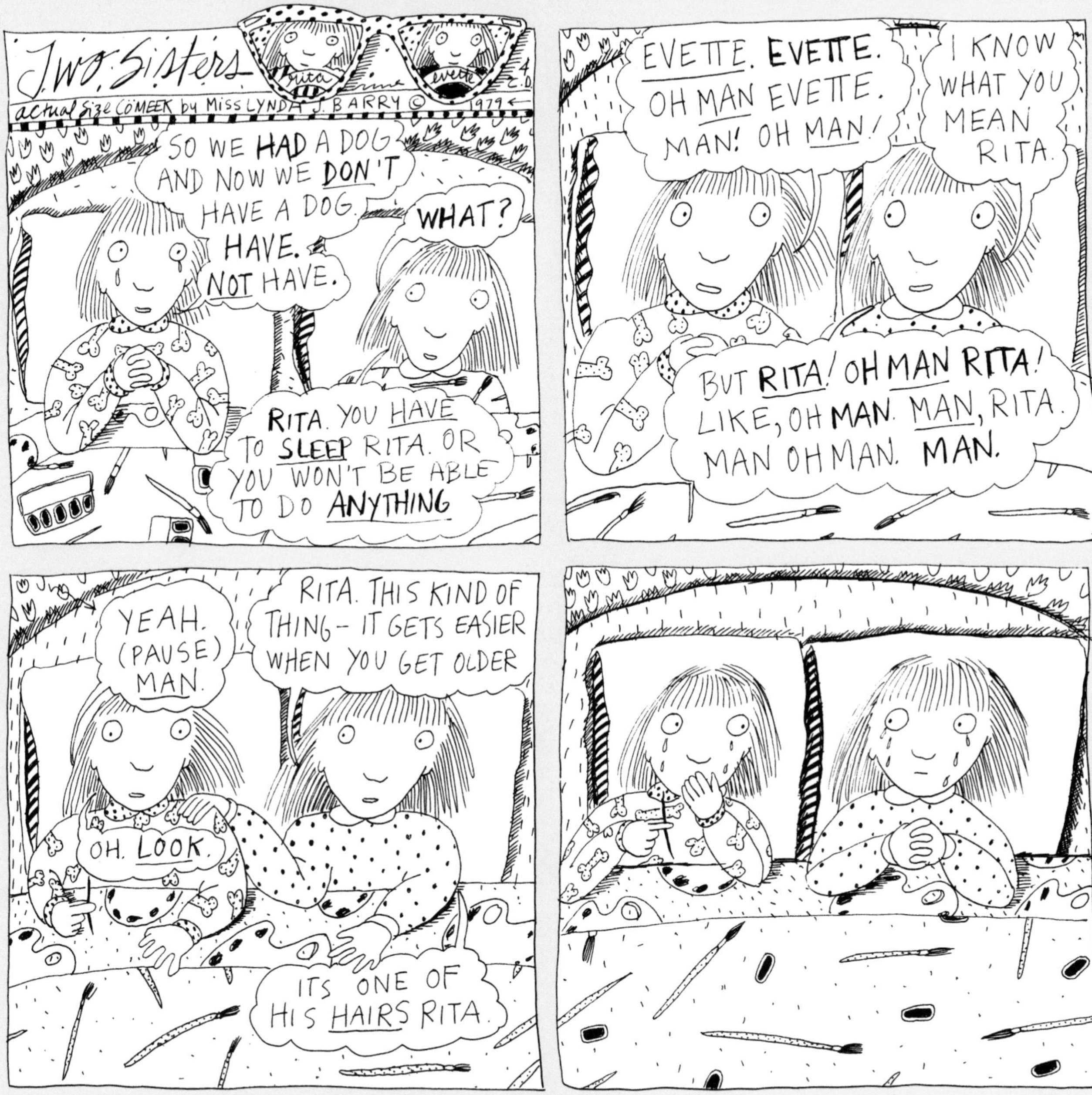

Two Sisters
rita
evette
actual size cömeek by Miss Lynda J. Barry © 1979
SO WE HAD A DOG AND NOW WE DON'T HAVE A DOG. HAVE. NOT HAVE.
WHAT?
RITA. YOU HAVE TO SLEEP RITA. OR YOU WON'T BE ABLE TO DO ANYTHING
EVETTE. EVETTE. OH MAN EVETTE. MAN! OH MAN!
I KNOW WHAT YOU MEAN RITA.
BUT RITA! OH MAN RITA! LIKE, OH MAN. MAN, RITA. MAN OH MAN. MAN.
YEAH. (PAUSE) MAN.
RITA. THIS KIND OF THING-- IT GETS EASIER WHEN YOU GET OLDER
OH. LOOK.
ITS ONE OF HIS HAIRS RITA.

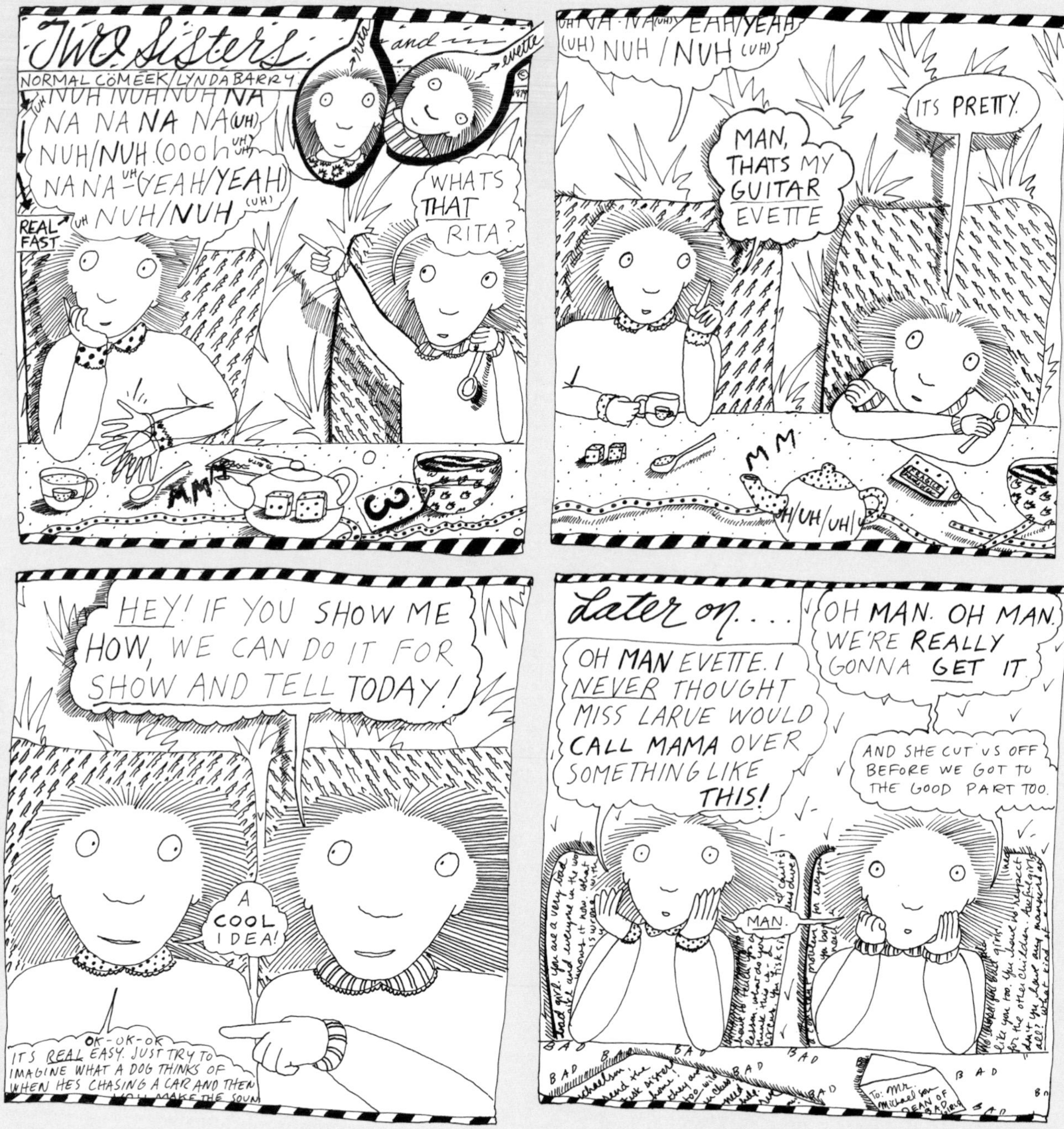
Two Sisters
NORMAL CÖMEEK / LYNDA BARRY
rita
and
evette
UH NUH NUH NUH NA NA NA NA NA (UH) NUH/NUH (oooh UH) NA NA UH (YEAH/YEAH) UH NUH/NUH (UH)
REAL FAST
WHATS THAT RITA?
MM
3
UH NA NA (UH) YEAH/YEAH (UH) NUH / NUH (UH)
MAN, THATS MY GUITAR EVETTE
ITS PRETTY.
MM
UH/UH/UH
HEY! IF YOU SHOW ME HOW, WE CAN DO IT FOR SHOW AND TELL TODAY!
A COOL IDEA!
OK-OK-OK
IT'S REAL EASY. JUST TRY TO IMAGINE WHAT A DOG THINKS OF WHEN HES CHASING A CAR AND THEN
later on....
OH MAN EVETTE. I NEVER THOUGHT MISS LARUE WOULD CALL MAMA OVER SOMETHING LIKE THIS!
OH MAN. OH MAN. WE'RE REALLY GONNA GET IT.
AND SHE CUT US OFF BEFORE WE GOT TO THE GOOD PART TOO.
MAN.
BAD
To: Mr. Michaelson DEAN OF BADNESS

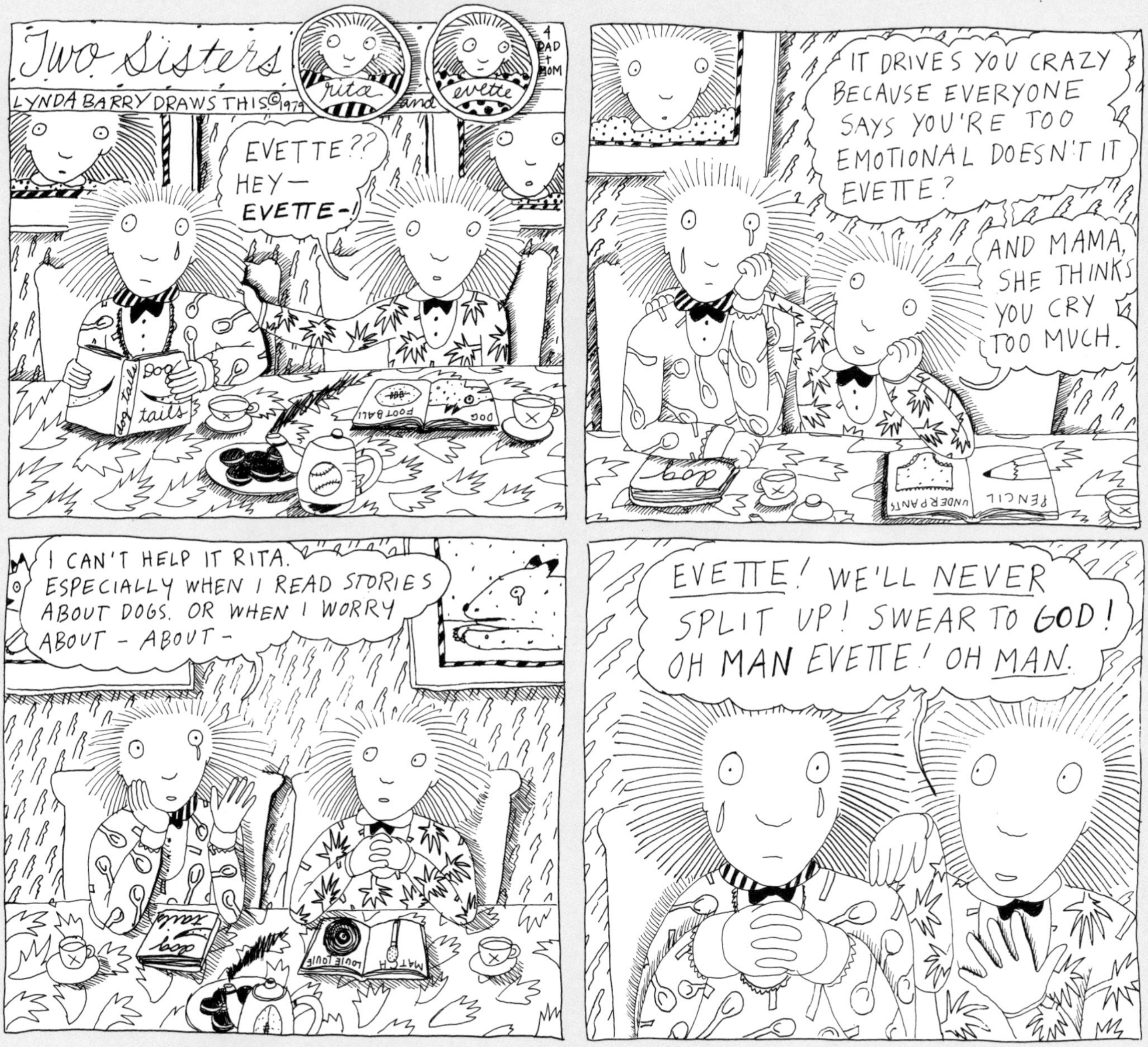
Two Sisters
LYNDA BARRY DRAWS THIS © 1979
rita and evette
4 DAD + MOM
EVETTE?? HEY— EVETTE-!
dog tails
FOOTBALL
DOG
IT DRIVES YOU CRAZY BECAUSE EVERYONE SAYS YOU'RE TOO EMOTIONAL DOESN'T IT EVETTE?
AND MAMA, SHE THINKS YOU CRY TOO MUCH.
dog
UNDERPANTS
PENCIL
I CAN'T HELP IT RITA. ESPECIALLY WHEN I READ STORIES ABOUT DOGS. OR WHEN I WORRY ABOUT - ABOUT -
dog tails
LOUIE LOUIE
MATCH
EVETTE! WE'LL NEVER SPLIT UP! SWEAR TO GOD! OH MAN EVETTE! OH MAN.

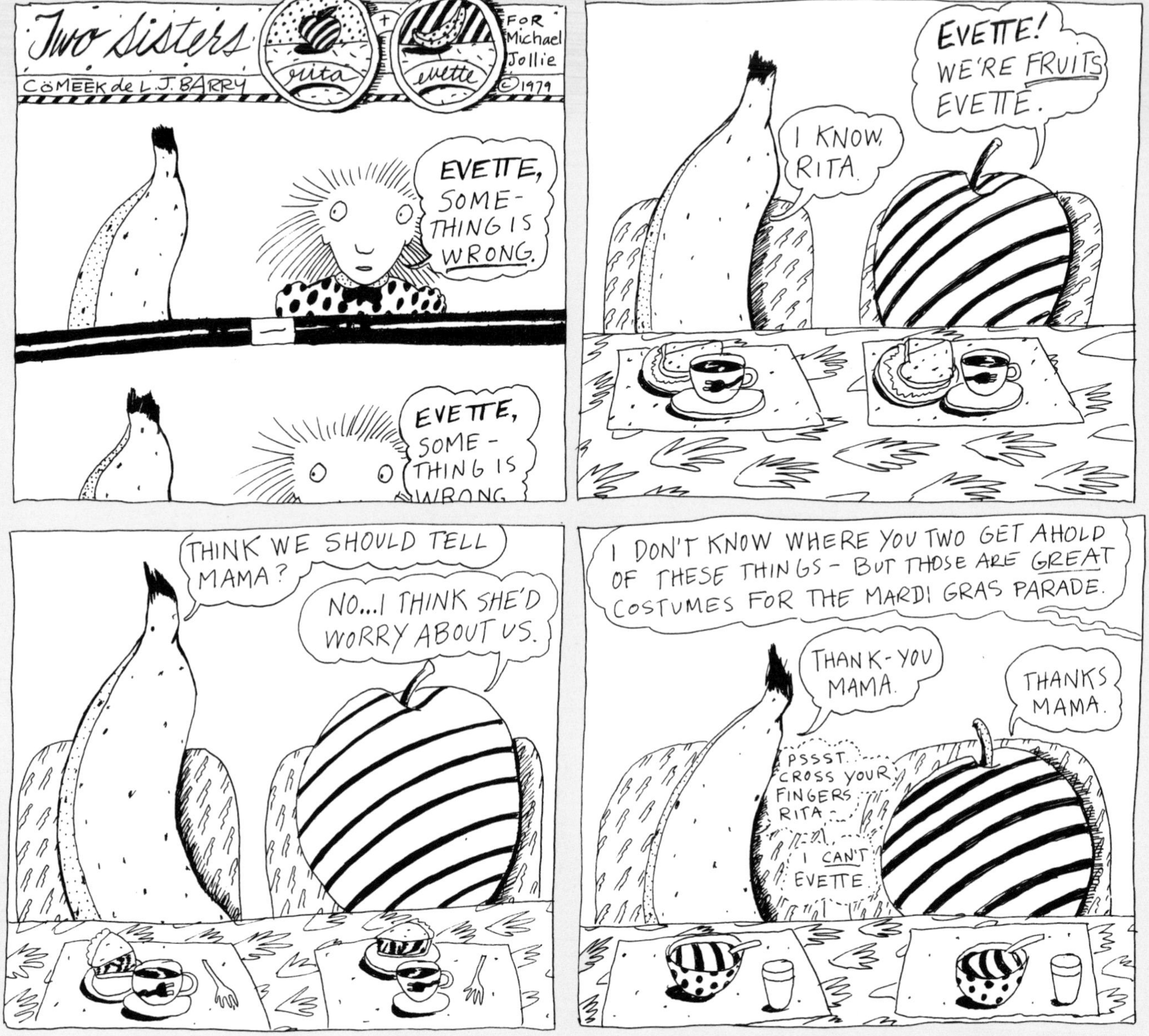
Two Sisters
rita
evette
CöMEEK de L.J. BARRY
FOR Michael Jollie
©1979
EVETTE, SOME-THING IS WRONG.
EVETTE, SOME-THING IS
I KNOW, RITA.
EVETTE! WE'RE FRUITS EVETTE.
THINK WE SHOULD TELL MAMA?
NO...I THINK SHE'D WORRY ABOUT US.
I DON'T KNOW WHERE YOU TWO GET AHOLD OF THESE THINGS - BUT THOSE ARE GREAT COSTUMES FOR THE MARDI GRAS PARADE.
THANK-YOU MAMA.
THANKS MAMA.
PSSST. CROSS YOUR FINGERS RITA.
I CAN'T EVETTE.

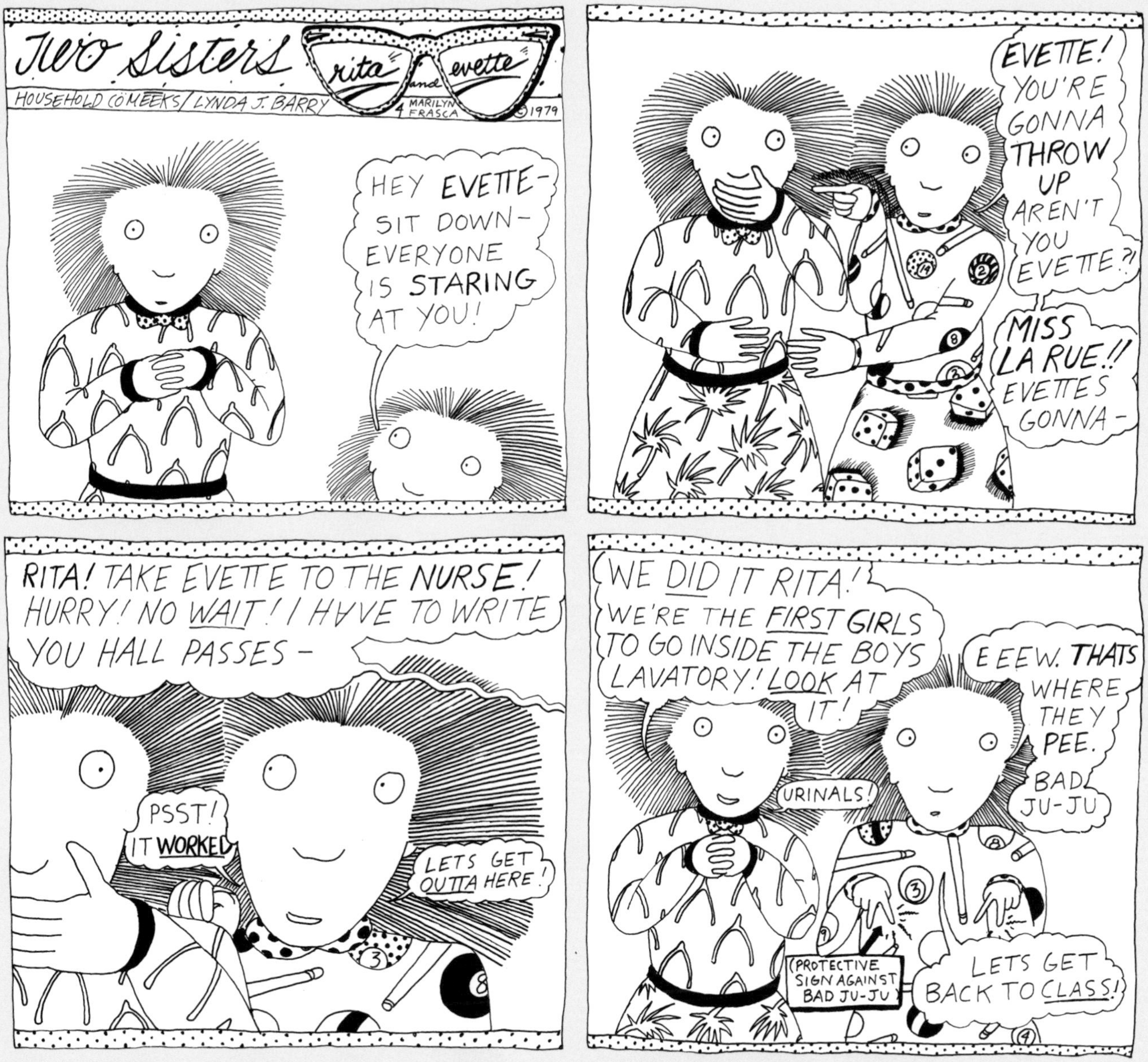
Two Sisters
rita and evette
HOUSEHOLD COMEEKS / LYNDA J. BARRY
4 MARILYN FRASCA
© 1979
HEY EVETTE- SIT DOWN- EVERYONE IS STARING AT YOU!
EVETTE! YOU'RE GONNA THROW UP AREN'T YOU EVETTE?!
MISS LA RUE!! EVETTES GONNA-
RITA! TAKE EVETTE TO THE NURSE! HURRY! NO WAIT! I HAVE TO WRITE YOU HALL PASSES -
PSST! IT WORKED
LETS GET OUTTA HERE!
WE DID IT RITA! WE'RE THE FIRST GIRLS TO GO INSIDE THE BOYS LAVATORY! LOOK AT IT!
EEEW. THATS WHERE THEY PEE.
URINALS!
BAD JU-JU
(PROTECTIVE SIGN AGAINST BAD JU-JU)
LETS GET BACK TO CLASS!

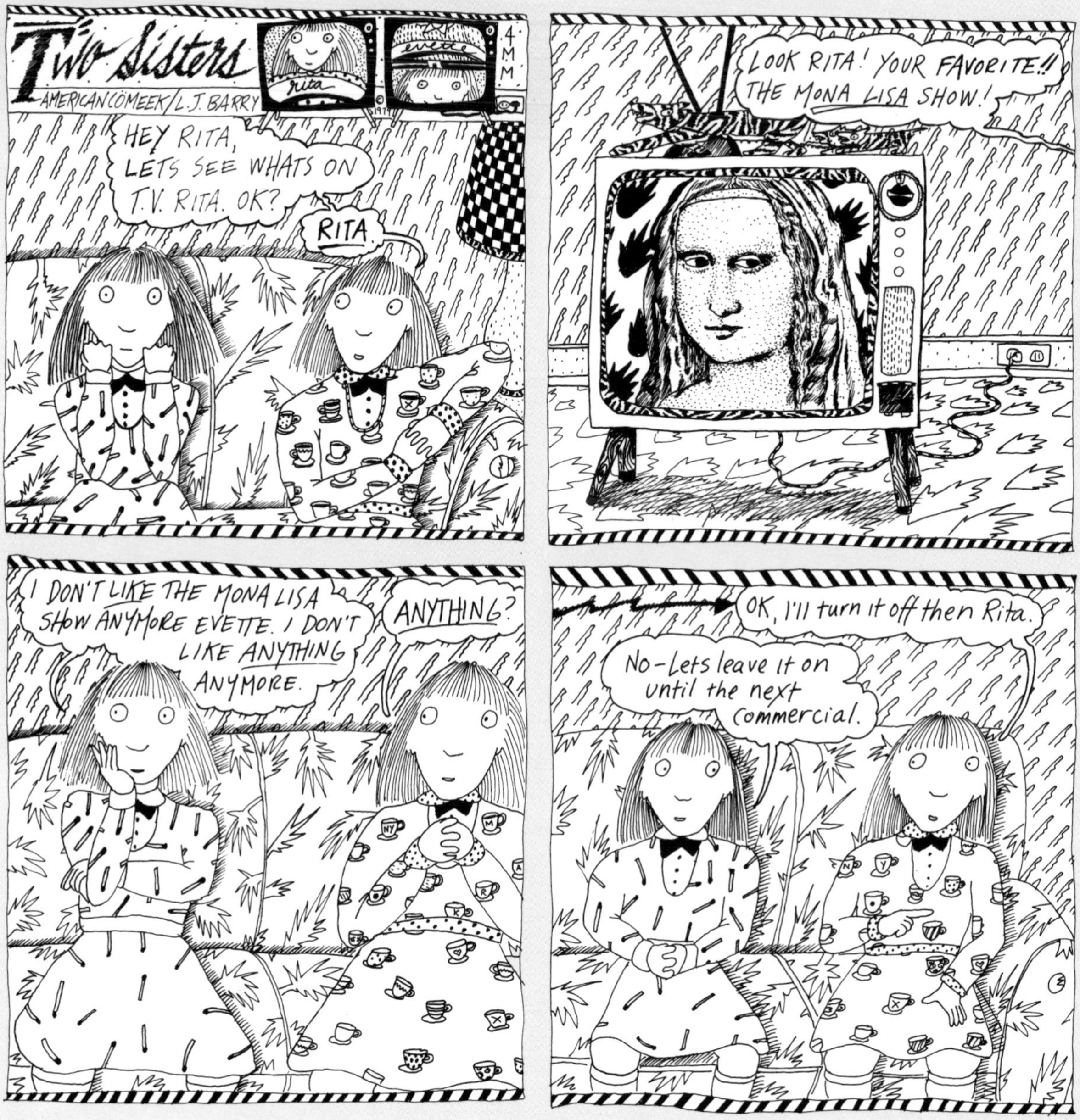
Two Sisters
AMERICAN COMEEK / L.J. BARRY
rita
evette
4MM
HEY RITA, LETS SEE WHATS ON T.V. RITA. OK?
RITA
LOOK RITA! YOUR FAVORITE!! THE MONA LISA SHOW!
I DON'T LIKE THE MONA LISA SHOW ANYMORE EVETTE. I DON'T LIKE ANYTHING ANYMORE.
ANYTHING?
OK, I'll turn it off then Rita.
No-Lets leave it on until the next commercial.

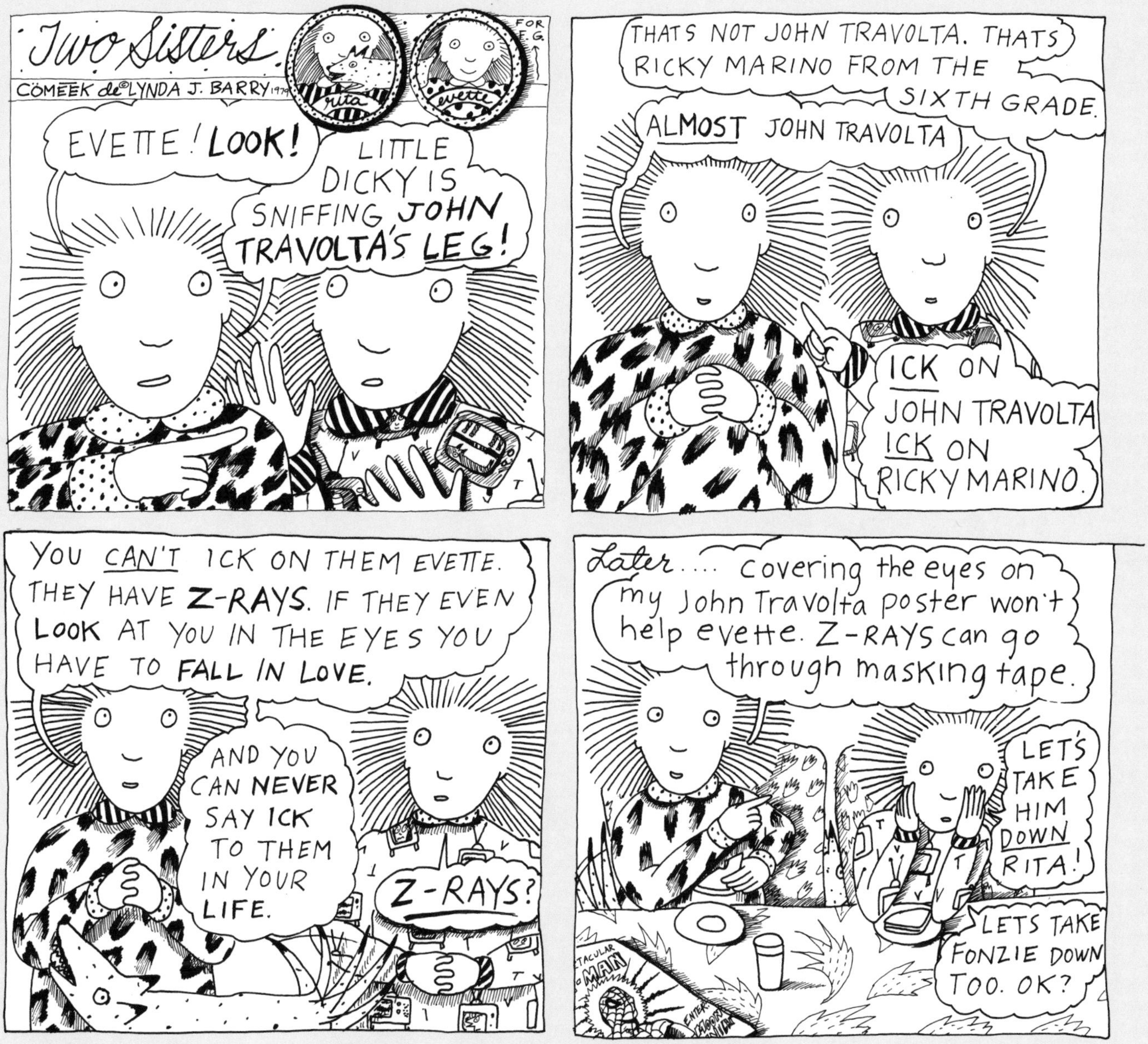
Two Sisters.
CÖMEEK de© LYNDA J. BARRY
FOR E.G.
rita
evette
EVETTE! LOOK!
LITTLE DICKY IS SNIFFING JOHN TRAVOLTA'S LEG!
THATS NOT JOHN TRAVOLTA. THATS RICKY MARINO FROM THE SIXTH GRADE.
ALMOST JOHN TRAVOLTA
ICK ON JOHN TRAVOLTA ICK ON RICKY MARINO.
YOU CAN'T ICK ON THEM EVETTE. THEY HAVE Z-RAYS. IF THEY EVEN LOOK AT YOU IN THE EYES YOU HAVE TO FALL IN LOVE.
AND YOU CAN NEVER SAY ICK TO THEM IN YOUR LIFE.
Z-RAYS?
Later.... Covering the eyes on my John Travolta poster won't help evette. Z-RAYS can go through masking tape.
LET'S TAKE HIM DOWN RITA!
LETS TAKE FONZIE DOWN TOO. OK?

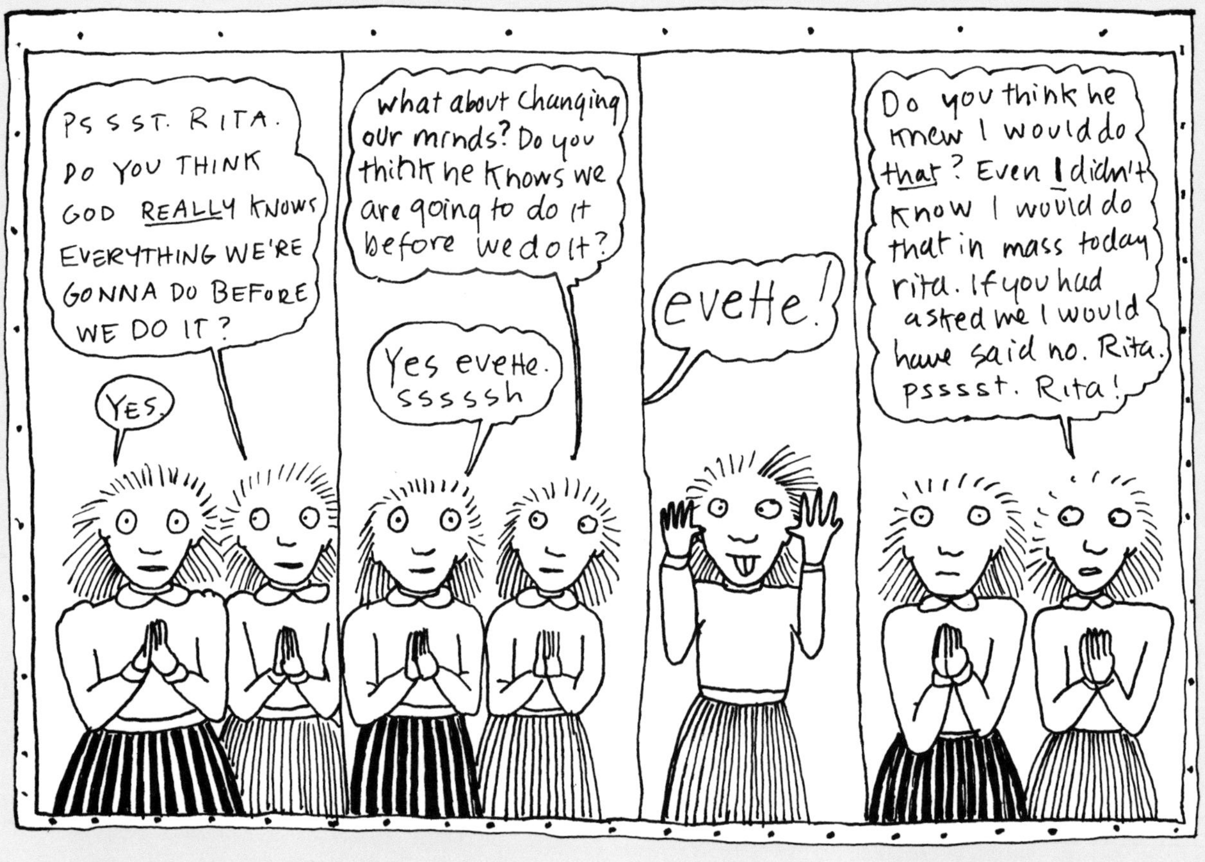
PSSST. RITA. DO YOU THINK GOD REALLY KNOWS EVERYTHING WE'RE GONNA DO BEFORE WE DO IT?
YES.
what about changing our minds? Do you think he knows we are going to do it before we do it?
Yes evette. ssssssh
evette!
Do you think he knew I would do that? Even I didn't know I would do that in mass today rita. If you had asked me I would have said no. Rita. psssst. Rita!

Two Sisters
REGULAR CÖMEEK L.J. BARRY
RITA. WHY ARE YOU UNDER THE TABLE?
IM PRETENDING IM A HORSE
OH.
EVETTE! WHERE IS RITA?
IM IN THE STABLE MAMA.
WHINNY WHINNY NEIGH NEIGH
DON'T YOU THINK YOU'RE A LITTLE OLD FOR THAT RITA? LOOK AT YOUR SISTER EVETTE. YOU DON'T NEED TO SIT UNDER THE TABLE DURING BREAKFAST DO YOU EVETTE?
BUT IM NOT A HORSE THOUGH MAMA
YEAH
YEAH, EVETTE JUST KISSES THE MIRROR AT NIGHT FOR WHEN SHE GETS A BOYFRIEND!
YOU SWORE YOU'D NEVER TELL ANYONE RITA

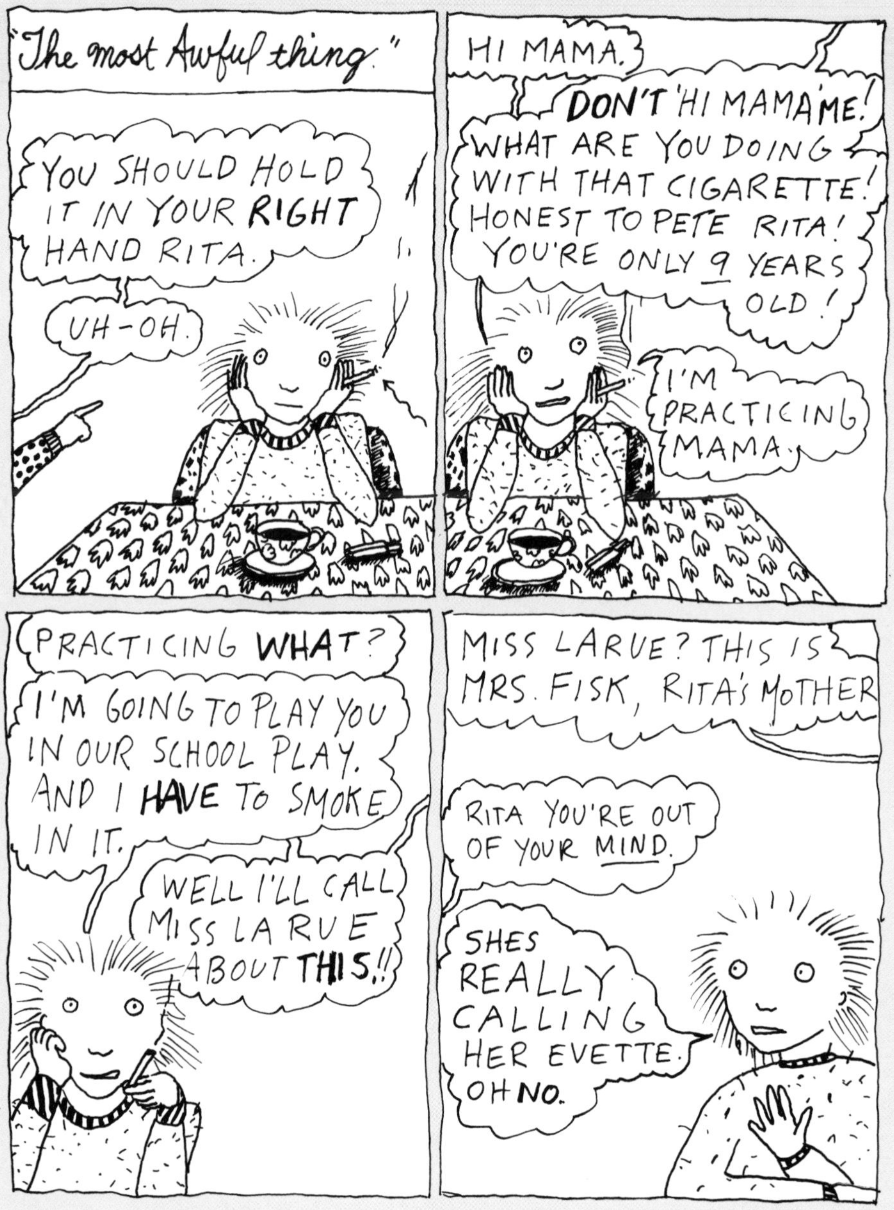
"The most Awful thing."
YOU SHOULD HOLD IT IN YOUR **RIGHT** HAND RITA.
UH-OH.
HI MAMA.
DON'T 'HI MAMA' ME! WHAT ARE YOU DOING WITH THAT CIGARETTE! HONEST TO PETE RITA! YOU'RE ONLY 9 YEARS OLD!
I'M PRACTICING MAMA.
PRACTICING **WHAT**?
I'M GOING TO PLAY YOU IN OUR SCHOOL PLAY. AND I **HAVE** TO SMOKE IN IT.
WELL I'LL CALL MISS LA RUE ABOUT **THIS**!!
MISS LARUE? THIS IS MRS. FISK, RITA'S MOTHER
RITA YOU'RE OUT OF YOUR MIND.
SHES REALLY CALLING HER EVETTE. OH **NO**.

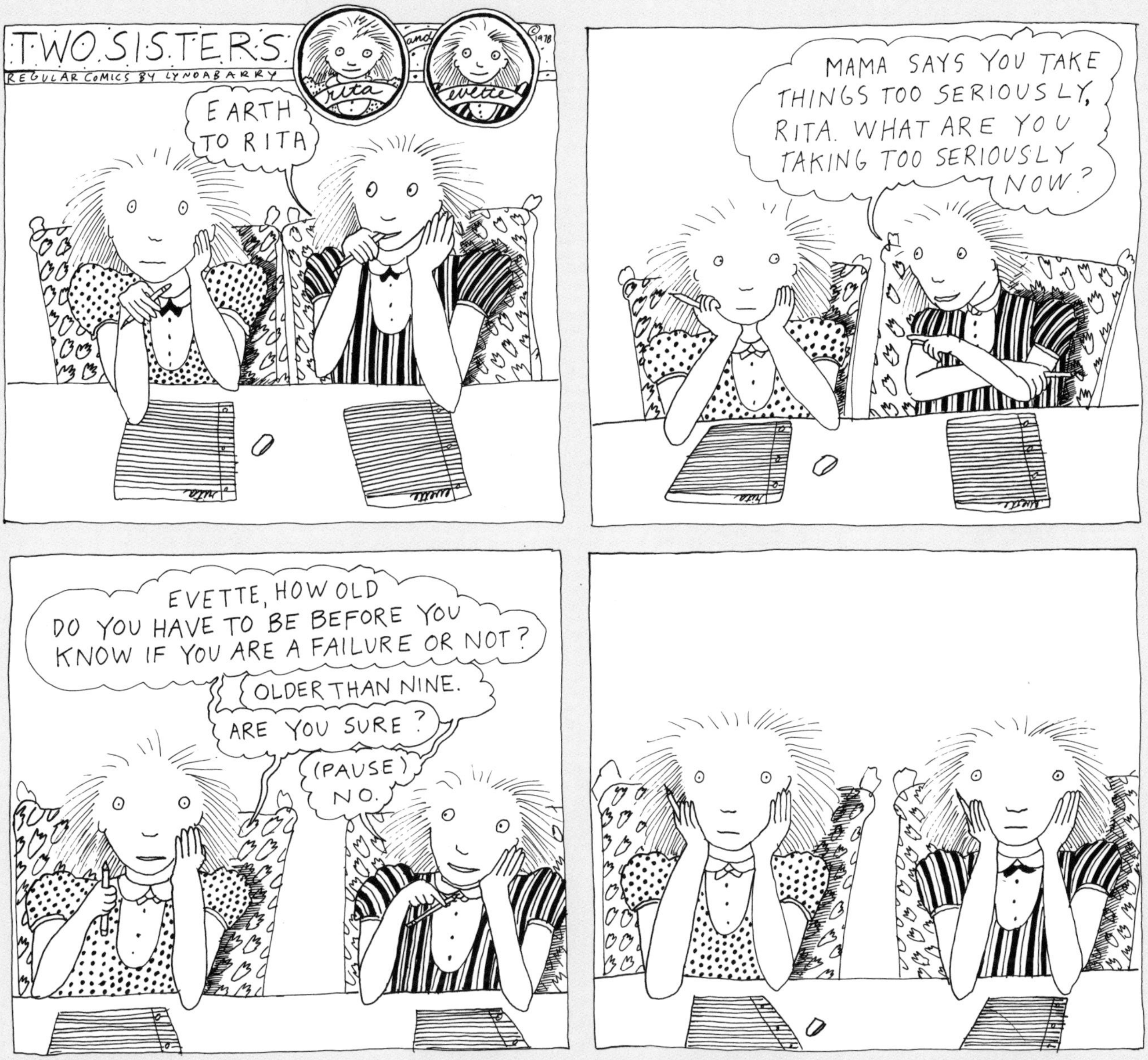
TWO SISTERS
REGULAR COMICS BY LYNDA BARRY
rita
and
evette
© 1978
EARTH TO RITA
MAMA SAYS YOU TAKE THINGS TOO SERIOUSLY, RITA. WHAT ARE YOU TAKING TOO SERIOUSLY NOW?
EVETTE, HOW OLD DO YOU HAVE TO BE BEFORE YOU KNOW IF YOU ARE A FAILURE OR NOT?
OLDER THAN NINE.
ARE YOU SURE?
(PAUSE) NO.

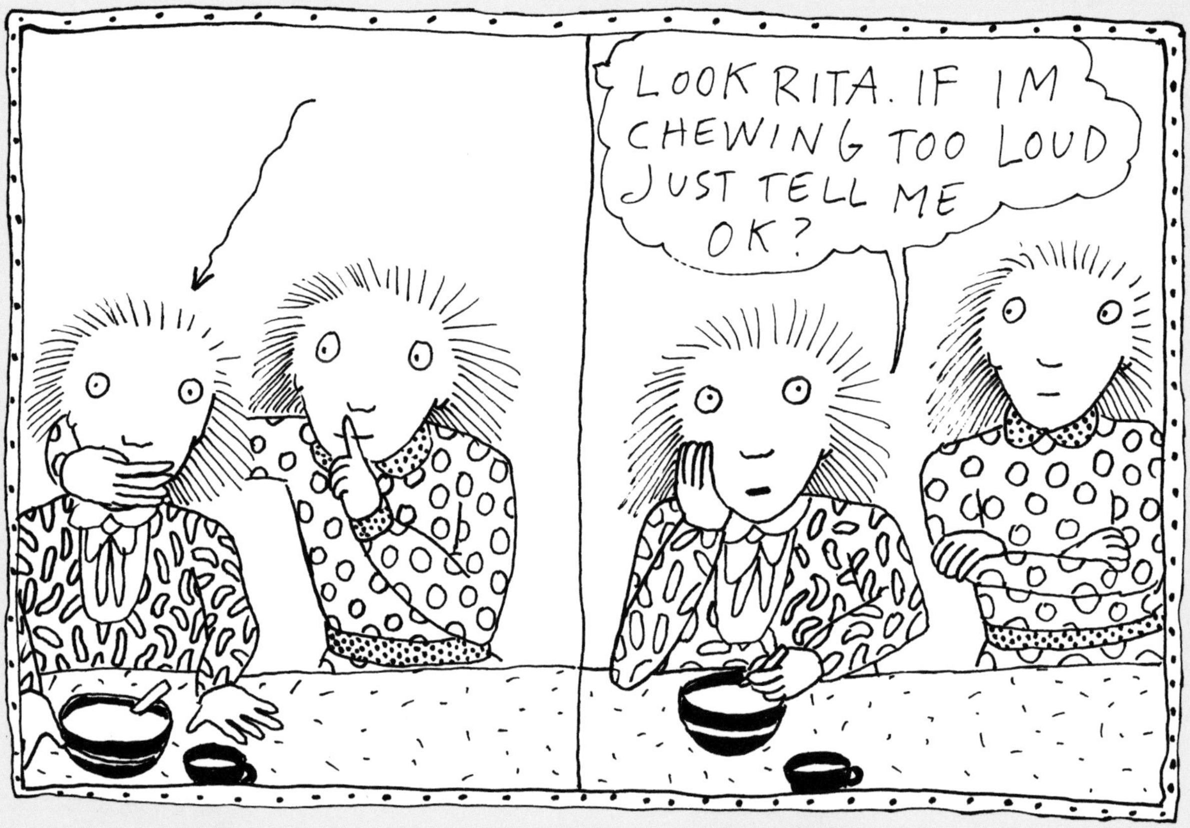
LOOK RITA. IF IM CHEWING TOO LOUD JUST TELL ME OK?

Fiero Sisters
rita and evette
4 D. Feinberg
REGULARCÖMEEK/LYNDABARRY
©
I JUST HAD A SCARY DREAM
ME TWO
I DREAMED I WAS A CARROT
IN MY DREAM YOU WERE A CARROT
EVETTE FISK!!! WHAT WILL YOU TRY NEXT?!!
"and Miss Larve said I was doing it to get attention and avoid doing my math"
GIRLS! WILL YOU PLEASE GO TO SLEEP?!
HELP ME RITA
EVETTE!
RITA! HEY- I WAS JUST GOOFING ON YOU RITA! (OH MAN.)
MAMA! MAMA! EVETTE IS MESSED UP! HELP MAMA!!!
UH-OH
① (MAMA - RITA WAS JUST IMAGINING THINGS - NO -
② MAMA - RITA WAS HAVING A SCARY DREAM - NO - UM
③ MAMA IM REAL SORRY ABOUT TORMENTING RITA - NO -
④ MAYBE I SHOULD JUST PRETEND IM ASLEEP AND I DON'T KNOW WHAT THEY'RE TALKING ABOUT)

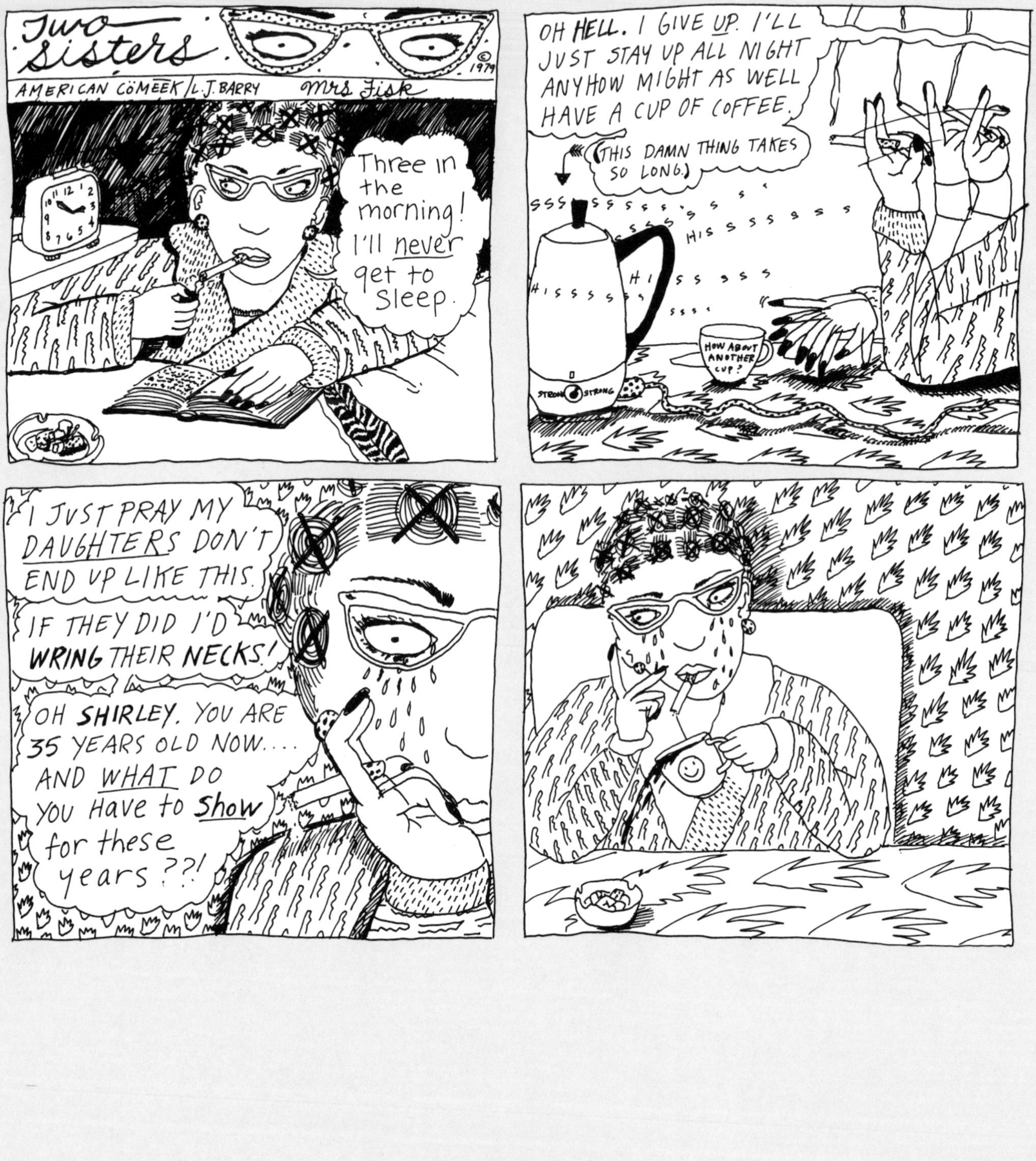
Two Sisters
© 1979
AMERICAN CÖMEEK
L.J. BARRY
Mrs Fisk
Three in the morning! I'll never get to Sleep.
OH HELL. I GIVE UP. I'LL JUST STAY UP ALL NIGHT ANYHOW MIGHT AS WELL HAVE A CUP OF COFFEE.
(THIS DAMN THING TAKES SO LONG.)
SSS SSSSSSSS
HISSSSSSS
HISSSSS
HISSSS SSS
STRONG STRONG
HOW ABOUT ANOTHER CUP?
I JUST PRAY MY DAUGHTERS DON'T END UP LIKE THIS.
IF THEY DID I'D WRING THEIR NECKS!
OH SHIRLEY. YOU ARE 35 YEARS OLD NOW.... AND WHAT DO YOU HAVE to Show for these years??!

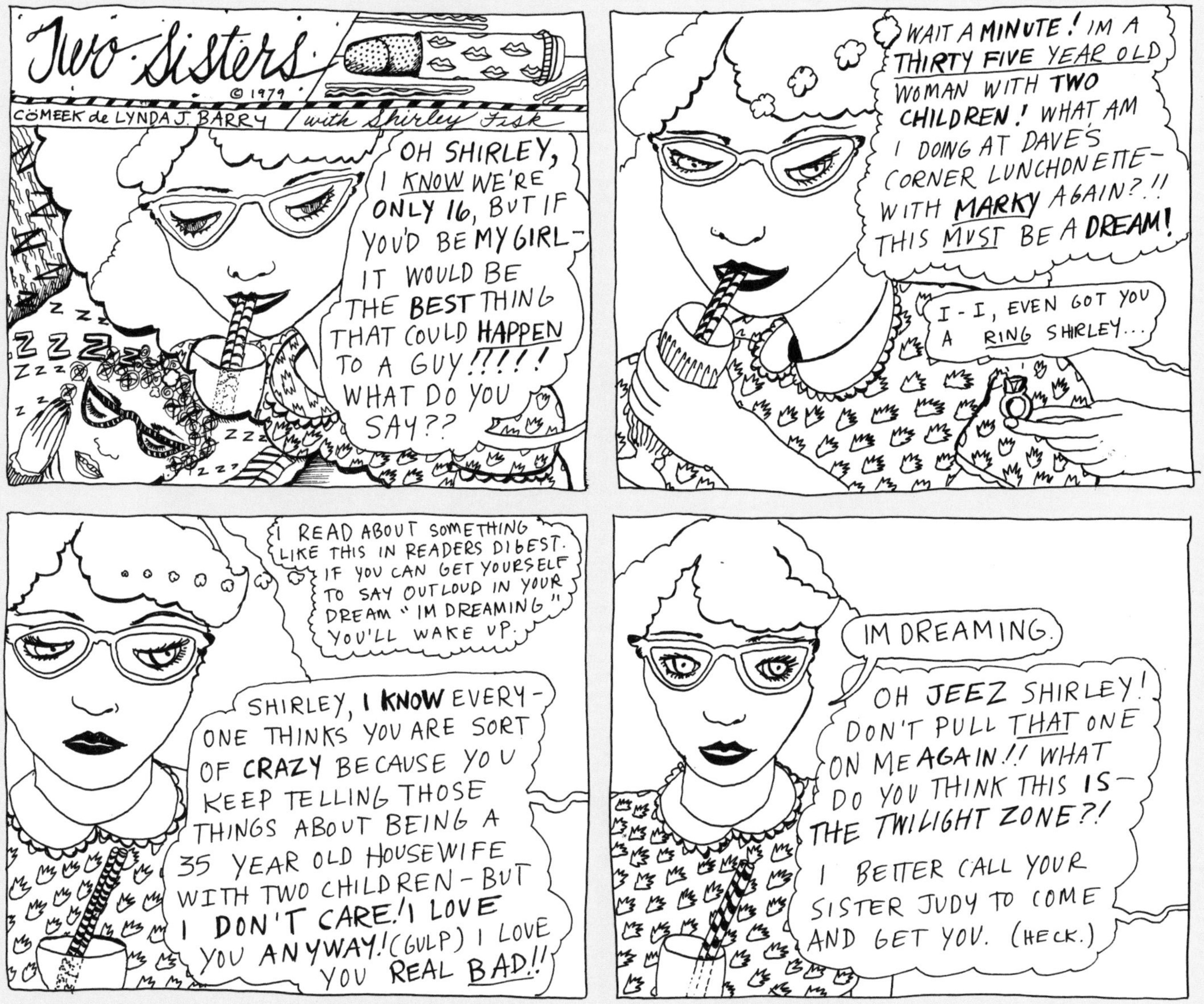
Two Sisters
© 1979
CÖMEEK de LYNDA J. BARRY
with Shirley Fisk
OH SHIRLEY, I KNOW WE'RE ONLY 16, BUT IF YOU'D BE MY GIRL- IT WOULD BE THE BEST THING THAT COULD HAPPEN TO A GUY!!!!! WHAT DO YOU SAY??
WAIT A MINUTE! IM A THIRTY FIVE YEAR OLD WOMAN WITH TWO CHILDREN! WHAT AM I DOING AT DAVE'S CORNER LUNCHONETTE- WITH MARKY AGAIN?!! THIS MUST BE A DREAM!
I-I, EVEN GOT YOU A RING SHIRLEY...
I READ ABOUT SOMETHING LIKE THIS IN READERS DIGEST. IF YOU CAN GET YOURSELF TO SAY OUTLOUD IN YOUR DREAM "IM DREAMING" YOU'LL WAKE UP.
SHIRLEY, I KNOW EVERY-ONE THINKS YOU ARE SORT OF CRAZY BECAUSE YOU KEEP TELLING THOSE THINGS ABOUT BEING A 35 YEAR OLD HOUSEWIFE WITH TWO CHILDREN- BUT I DON'T CARE! I LOVE YOU ANYWAY! (GULP) I LOVE YOU REAL BAD!!
IM DREAMING.
OH JEEZ SHIRLEY! DON'T PULL THAT ONE ON ME AGAIN!! WHAT DO YOU THINK THIS IS- THE TWILIGHT ZONE?! I BETTER CALL YOUR SISTER JUDY TO COME AND GET YOU. (HECK.)

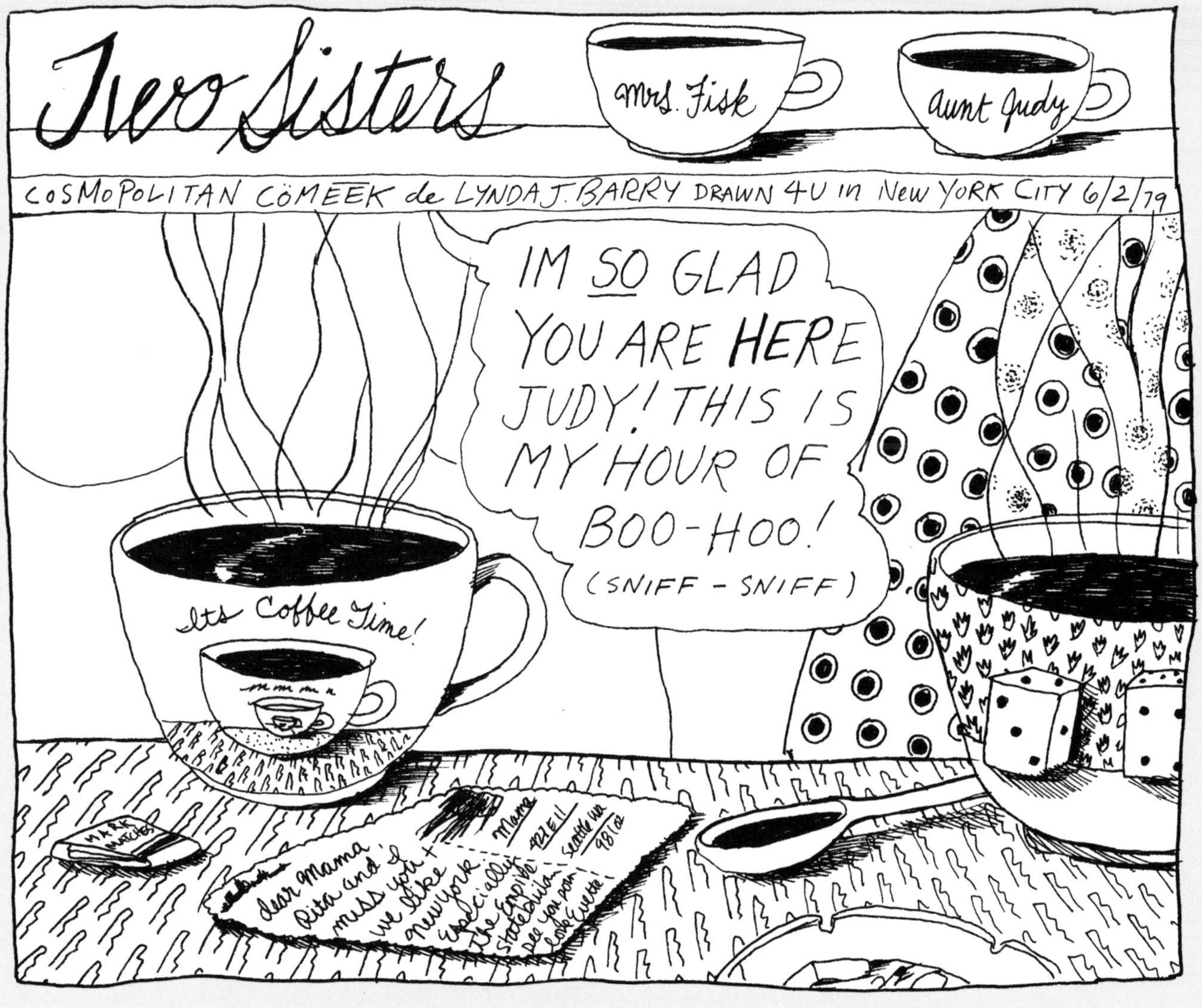
Two Sisters
Mrs. Fisk
Aunt Judy
COSMOPOLITAN CÖMEEK de LYNDA J. BARRY DRAWN 4U in New YORK CITY 6/2/79
IM SO GLAD YOU ARE HERE JUDY! THIS IS MY HOUR OF BOO-HOO! (SNIFF - SNIFF)
Its Coffee Time!
MARK MATCHES

Two Sisters
MODERN MODERN by L. J. BARRY
Shirley and Judy
©1979
SEATTLE. THATS RIGHT. SEATTLE WASHINGTON
SHIRLEY FISK! IF I CATCH YOU MAKING ONE MORE LONG DISTANCE PHONE CALL I BELIEVE I WILL TEAR MY HAIR OUT AND LINE YOUR CASKET WITH IT!!! GET IN HERE AND EAT YOUR BREAKFAST!
YES MAMA
YOU STILL THINK YOU'RE A 35 YEAR OLD WOMAN WITH TWO CHILDREN DON'T YOU SHIRLEY? AND YOU THINK YOU LIVE IN SEATTLE WASHINGTON SO THATS WHY YOU KEEP CALLING THERE TO FIND SOMEONE WHO KNOWS YOU. RIGHT?
POOR SHIRLEY.
OH MAN.
JUDY- I CAN'T TELL WHATS REAL ANYMORE! I FEEL LIKE IM ON T.V. OR IN A BOOK - OR A MOVIE! I JUST DON'T FEEL REAL!
BOY. I KNOW WHAT YOU MEAN SHIRLEY!
NO YOU DON'T.
YES I DO.
YOU DON'T EITHER JUDY
I DO TOO SHIRLEY-
WELL AT LEAST YOU TWO ARE FIGHTING AGAIN AND I CAN GO BACK TO HAVING MY REGULAR HEADACHES INSTEAD OF THESE SPLITTING HEADACHES I'VE HAD SINCE YOU STARTED ACTING CRAZY SHIRLEY.
I FEEL AT LEAST TEN TIMES MORE UNREAL THAN YOU DO
PROVE IT, JU-DITH
MAYBE I DON'T FEEL LIKE IT FOUR EYES

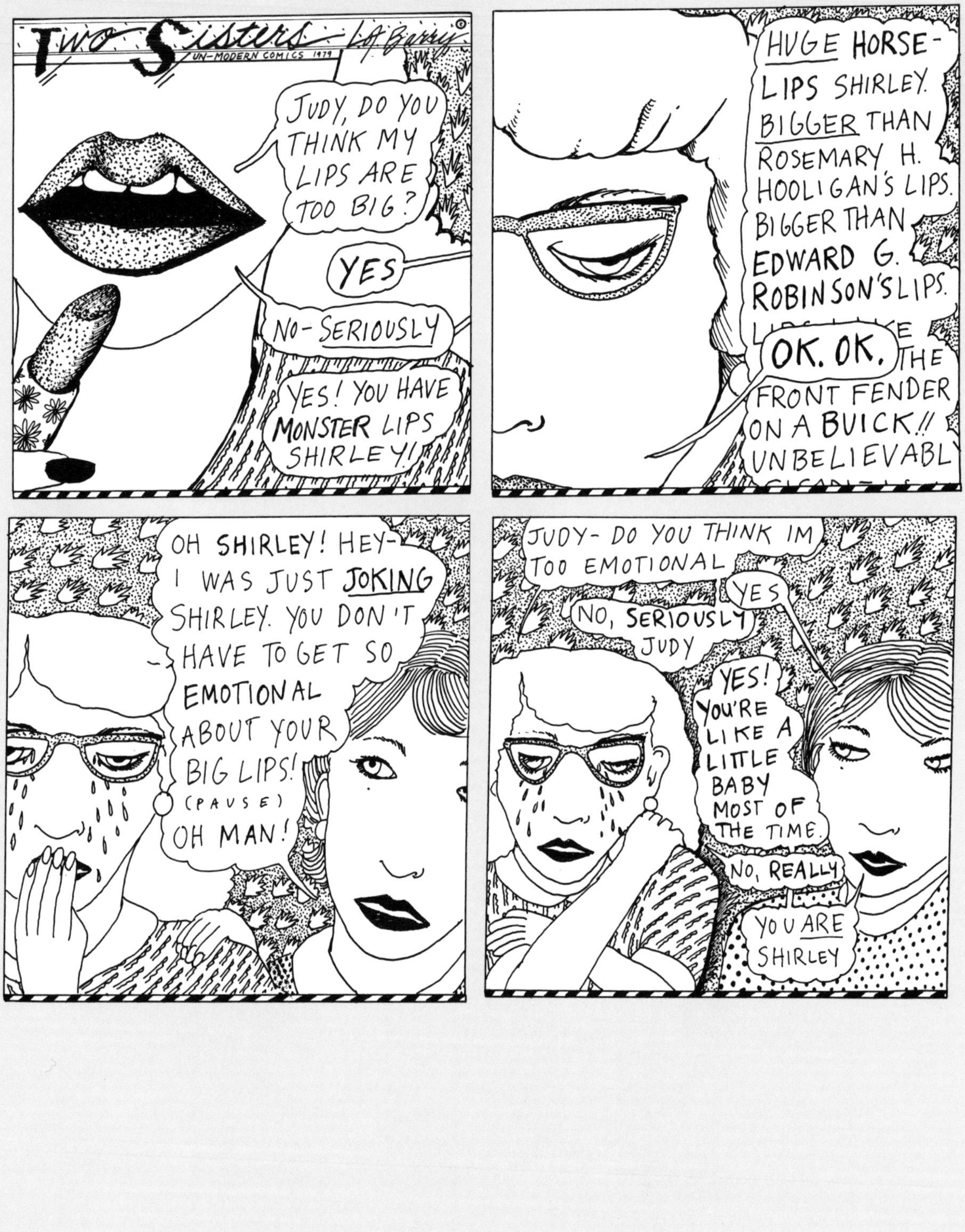
TWO SISTERS
UN-MODERN COMICS 1979
L.A. Barry ©
JUDY, DO YOU THINK MY LIPS ARE TOO BIG?
YES
NO-SERIOUSLY
YES! YOU HAVE MONSTER LIPS SHIRLEY!
HUGE HORSE-LIPS SHIRLEY. BIGGER THAN ROSEMARY H. HOOLIGAN'S LIPS. BIGGER THAN EDWARD G. ROBINSON'S LIPS.
THE FRONT FENDER ON A BUICK!! UNBELIEVABLY
OK. OK.
OH SHIRLEY! HEY- I WAS JUST JOKING SHIRLEY. YOU DON'T HAVE TO GET SO EMOTIONAL ABOUT YOUR BIG LIPS! (PAUSE) OH MAN!
JUDY- DO YOU THINK IM TOO EMOTIONAL
YES
NO, SERIOUSLY JUDY
YES! YOU'RE LIKE A LITTLE BABY MOST OF THE TIME.
NO, REALLY
YOU ARE SHIRLEY

TWO SISTERS
by Lynda Barry
Our Judy and Shirley – Easter
JUDY – YOU KNOW WHEN YOU WERE LITTLE YOU LOOKED SORT OF –
SORT OF WHAT?
– DUMB.
LOOK WHO'S TALKING LITTLE MISS FOUR EYES.
YOU KNOW JUDY THE REASON I HAVE SUCH A POETIC SOUL AND YOU DON'T IS BECAUSE I SUFFERED INTENSELY FROM BEING CALLED FOUR EYES AS A CHILD.
I HAVE A POETIC SOUL TOO SHIRLEY. AND MY CHILDHOOD WAS TEN TIMES MORE PAINFUL THAN YOURS. YOU KNOW HOW MAMA ALWAYS SAID "YOUR FATHER WAS A REAL DOG"? I BELIEVED HER.
THIS PICTURE USED TO GIVE ME AWFUL FEELINGS.
YOU THOUGHT THAT DOG WAS OUR FATHER?
SHIRLEY – YOU'RE THE ONLY ONE I'VE EVER TOLD THIS TO YOU KNOW. YOU'RE NOT GOING TO TELL ANYONE AND, LIKE, MAKE ME LOOK REAL DUMB ARE YOU?
rita and butch

2 Sisters
COMIC STRIP
LYNDA BARRY
JUDY- LIKE YOU KNOW THAT ONE SONG BY MISS JULIE ANDREWS ABOUT HER FAVORITE THINGS?
YEAH
WANT ME TO SING IT TO YOU?
NOT REALLY
RAINDROPS ON ROSES AND WHISKERS ON KITTENS
CUT IT OUT SHIRLEY!
NOT YOUR IDEA OF A GOOD TIME - IS IT JUDY?
TOO CORNEY
YEAH.
OH GOD- NOW I CAN'T GET IT OUT OF MY HEAD.----
BARF! JULIE ANDREWS IN MY BRAIN!
OH MAN! WHAT IF IT STAYS IN MY BRAIN FOREVER!
CALM DOWN JUDY YOU'RE NOT GOING TO GET A TUMOR OR ANYTHING-
A TUMOR! OH SHIRLEY MAYBE THATS HOW IT HAPPENS. YOU CAN'T GET A SONG OUT OF YOUR HEAD - AND - AND-
YOURE THE ONE THAT PUT HER IN MY BRAIN SHIRLEY. I ASKED YOU NOT TO SING THAT SONG AND YOU DID ANYWAY. NOW I MIGHT DIE SHIRLEY
JUDY! CUT IT OUT JUDY!
AND IF I DO ITS YOUR FAULT
IM GETTING FUTURE EMOTIONAL DISORDER FROM YOU JUDY- YOU BETTER QUIT

TWO SISTERS
by L.J. Barry ©1979
BOY, I SURE WONDER WHAT IM GOING TO BE LIKE WHEN IM 21.
I BET YOU'LL BE REAL FAT
OH! OH MAN JUDY! OH MAN DON'T SAY THAT!!
IT WILL PROBABLY HAPPEN REAL SOON TOO. LIKE BY THE TIME FALL QUARTER STARTS AND YOU'RE A SENIOR----
JUDY! CUT IT OUT
EVERYONE WILL SAY "GOD! DID YOU SEE SHIRLEY!
JUDY!
SHIRLEY + JUDY! YOUR AUNT RITA IS COMING OVER FOR DINNER AND THERE ISN'T ENOUGH DESSERT TO GO AROUND. YOU'LL JUST HAVE TO SPLIT YOURS TONIGHT.
YOU PLANNED THIS.
PLANNED WHAT?

Two Sisters Coməək
BY L. BARRY ©
MARKY
LOUIE
MARKY
LOUIE
NOW WHAT DO YOU WANT TO DO, JUDY?
LET'S EAT SOMETHING
AND THEN WHAT?
GUY. JEE. UM. WE COULD-UH-
SHIRLEY AND JUDY! YOU HAVE UNTIL THE COUNT OF THREE TO GET IN HERE AND HELP ME
DISHES!
MARKY
LOUIE
MARKY! MARKY! MARKY! MARKY! MARKY! MARKY! MARKY! MARKY! MARKY! MARKY!
LOUIE! LOUIE! LOUIE! LOUIE! LOUIE! LOUIE! LOUIE! LOUIE! LOUIE! LOUIE! LOUIE! LOUIE!
end

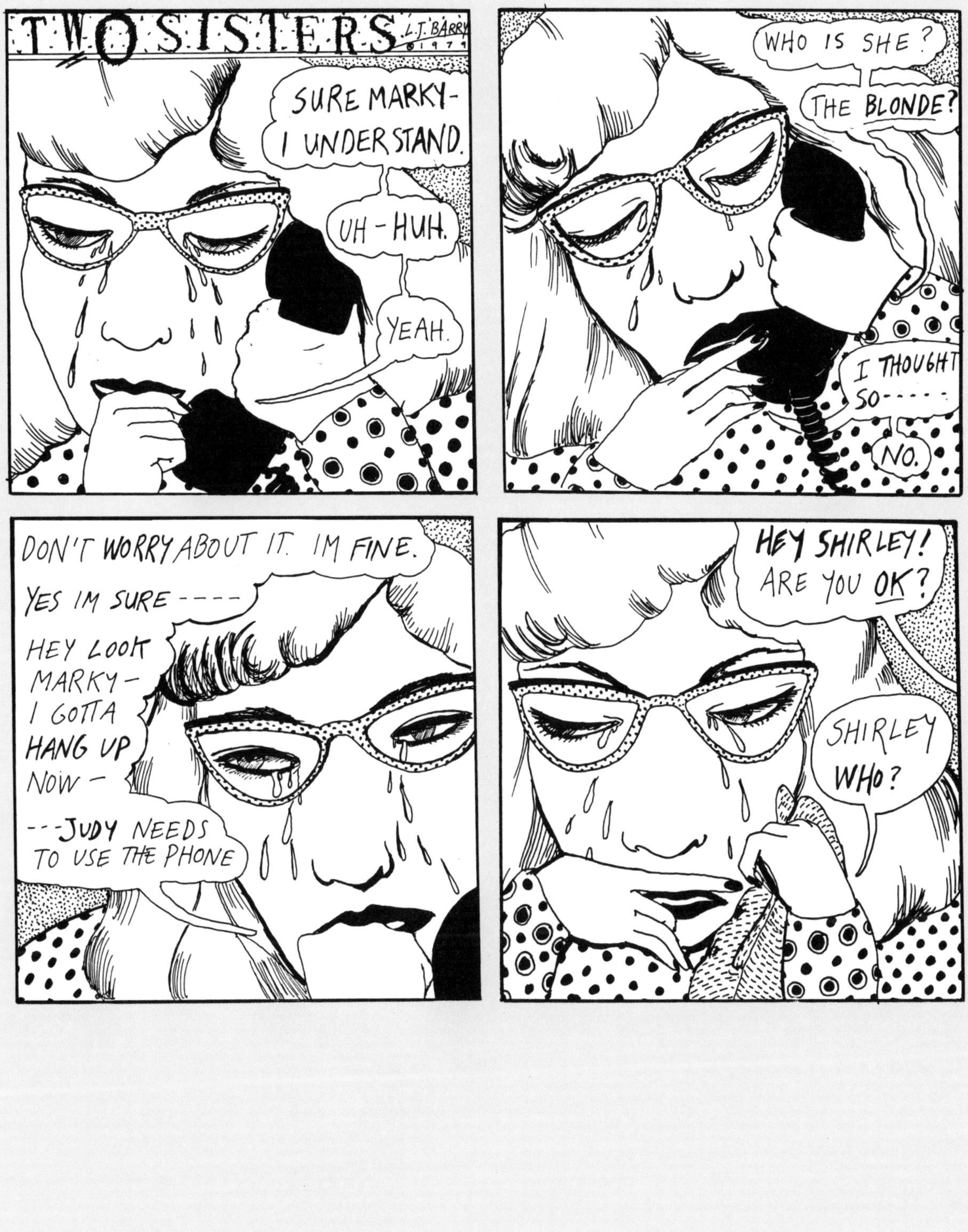
TWO SISTERS
L.J. BARRY ©1979
SURE MARKY- I UNDERSTAND.
UH-HUH.
YEAH.
WHO IS SHE?
THE BLONDE?
I THOUGHT SO----
NO.
DON'T WORRY ABOUT IT. IM FINE.
YES IM SURE----
HEY LOOK MARKY- I GOTTA HANG UP NOW-
---JUDY NEEDS TO USE THE PHONE
HEY SHIRLEY! ARE YOU OK?
SHIRLEY WHO?

TWO SISTERS by L. J. Barry © 1979
HEY LISTEN SHIRLEY- LOU RABINOWITZ AND MARKY WANT TO SNEAK OUT TONIGHT WITH YOU AND ME AFTER MAMAS ASLEEP- WHAT DO YOU THINK?
I THINK IT WOULD BE GREAT! AND JUDY! YOU CAN WEAR THAT NEAT SWEATER WITH THE DIAMONDS ON IT- AND I'LL WEAR- OH MAN- WHAT WILL I WEAR? OH JUDY! IM REAL EXCITED ABOUT THIS!
OH!
SHIRLEY! YOUR AUNT RITA IS VERY SICK! UNCLE MIKE IS ON HIS WAY OVER TO PICK YOU UP SO YOU CAN STAY WITH HER TONIGHT WHILE HE WORKS! GET YOUR PAJAMAS!
SHIRLEY,- JUST DON'T SCREAM SHIRLEY.

TWO SISTERS ©1979 L. BARRY
BRAIN ATTACK! IM HAVING A BRAIN ATTACK!
SHIRLEY! WAKE UP!!! YOU'RE HAVING A NIGHTMARE!
BRAIN ATTACK! BRAIN ATTACK! BRAIN ATTACK!
WHAT?! JUDY? WHAT TIME IS IT?
IT'S NOON SHIRLEY - YOURE A WRECK!!
I JUST CAN'T FACE ANOTHER DAY WITHOUT MARKY - OH! - OH! (CHOKE) (SOB)
GET UP!! CUT IT OUT SHIRLEY!
EVERY NIGHT HAVING THESE DREAMS JUDY! LOVE IS CREEPY!!! LOVE IS FOR JERKS! I HATE HIM! I HATE HIS GUTS! I HATE YOU MARKY!
JUDY! WAKE YOUR SISTER UP AND TELL HER MARKY IS ON THE PHONE AND WANTS TO TALK TO HER!
OH! I LOVE YOU MARKY I LOVE YOU MARKY! I LOVE YOU MARKY!
(YOU'RE A REAL SUCKER SHIRLEY)
(WHAT DO YOU KNOW JUDY?)

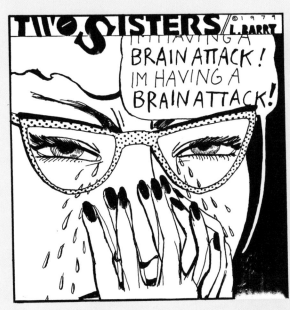

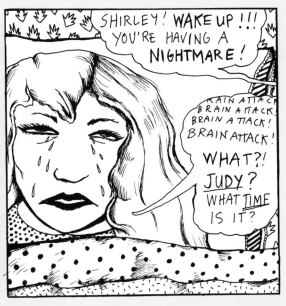

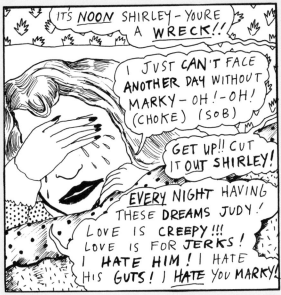

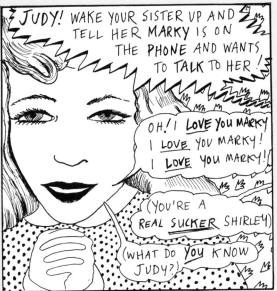

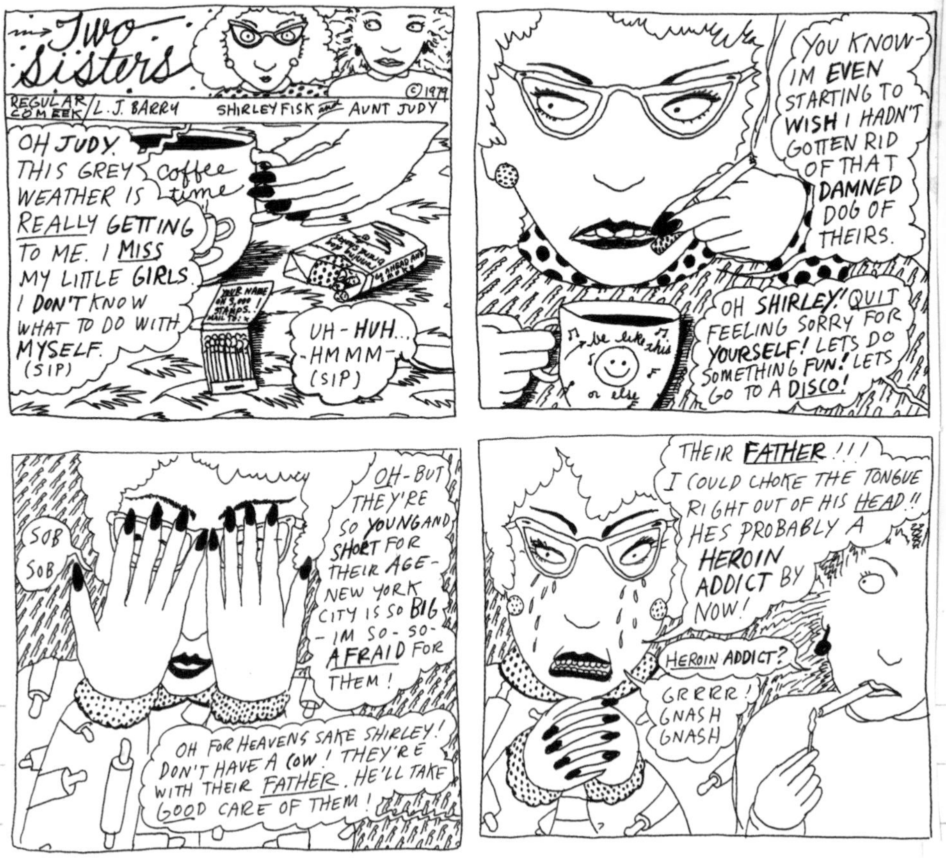
Two Sisters
REGULAR COMEEK
L. J. BARRY
©1979
SHIRLEY FISK and AUNT JUDY
OH JUDY. THIS GREY WEATHER IS REALLY GETTING TO ME. I MISS MY LITTLE GIRLS. I DON'T KNOW WHAT TO DO WITH MYSELF. (SIP)
coffee time
UH-HUH... HMMM (SIP)
YOU KNOW- IM EVEN STARTING TO WISH I HADN'T GOTTEN RID OF THAT DAMNED DOG OF THEIRS.
OH SHIRLEY! QUIT FEELING SORRY FOR YOURSELF! LETS DO SOMETHING FUN! LETS GO TO A DISCO!
SOB SOB
OH- BUT THEY'RE SO YOUNG AND SHORT FOR THEIR AGE- NEW YORK CITY IS SO BIG - IM SO-SO- AFRAID FOR THEM!
OH FOR HEAVENS SAKE SHIRLEY! DON'T HAVE A COW! THEY'RE WITH THEIR FATHER. HE'LL TAKE GOOD CARE OF THEM!
THEIR FATHER!!! I COULD CHOKE THE TONGUE RIGHT OUT OF HIS HEAD!! HES PROBABLY A HEROIN ADDICT BY NOW!
HEROIN ADDICT?
GRRRR! GNASH GNASH

After SEVERAL months OF DRAWING the 'TWO SISTERS' COMICS I FELT trapped BY the CHARACTERS And THE DRAWING STYLE I'd been SO SURE about. IN MY SKETCHBOOKS things WERE CHANGING but I DIDN'T Know how TO change THINGS in 'TWO SISTERS.' SO I ended it SUDDENLY and ABRUPTLY and in a WAY that WAS VERY harsh for 1979. People who LIKED 'TWO SISTERS' were VERY MAD AT ME BUT I was a SMART-ASS PUNK BY THEN. AND IT WAS A SMART-ASS TIME.

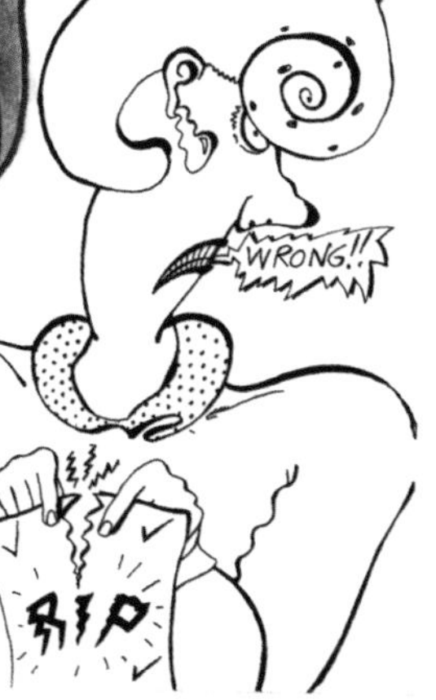
WRONG!!
RIP

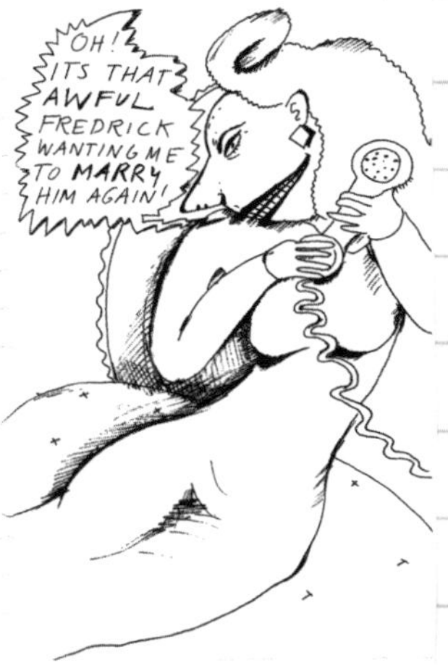
OH! ITS THAT AWFUL FREDRICK WANTING ME TO MARRY HIM AGAIN!

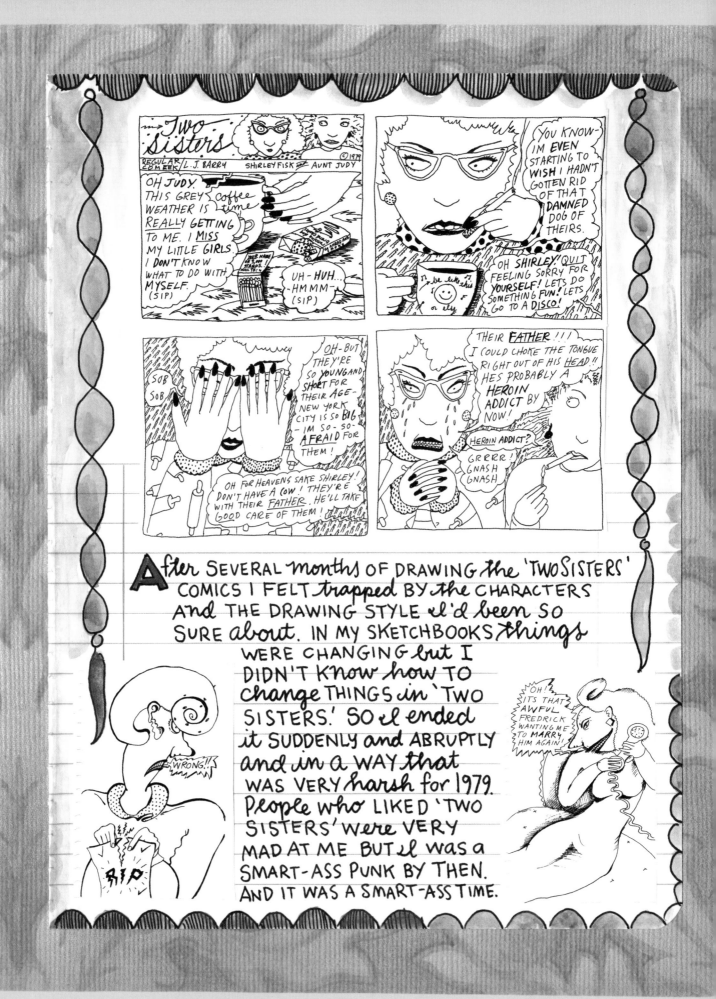

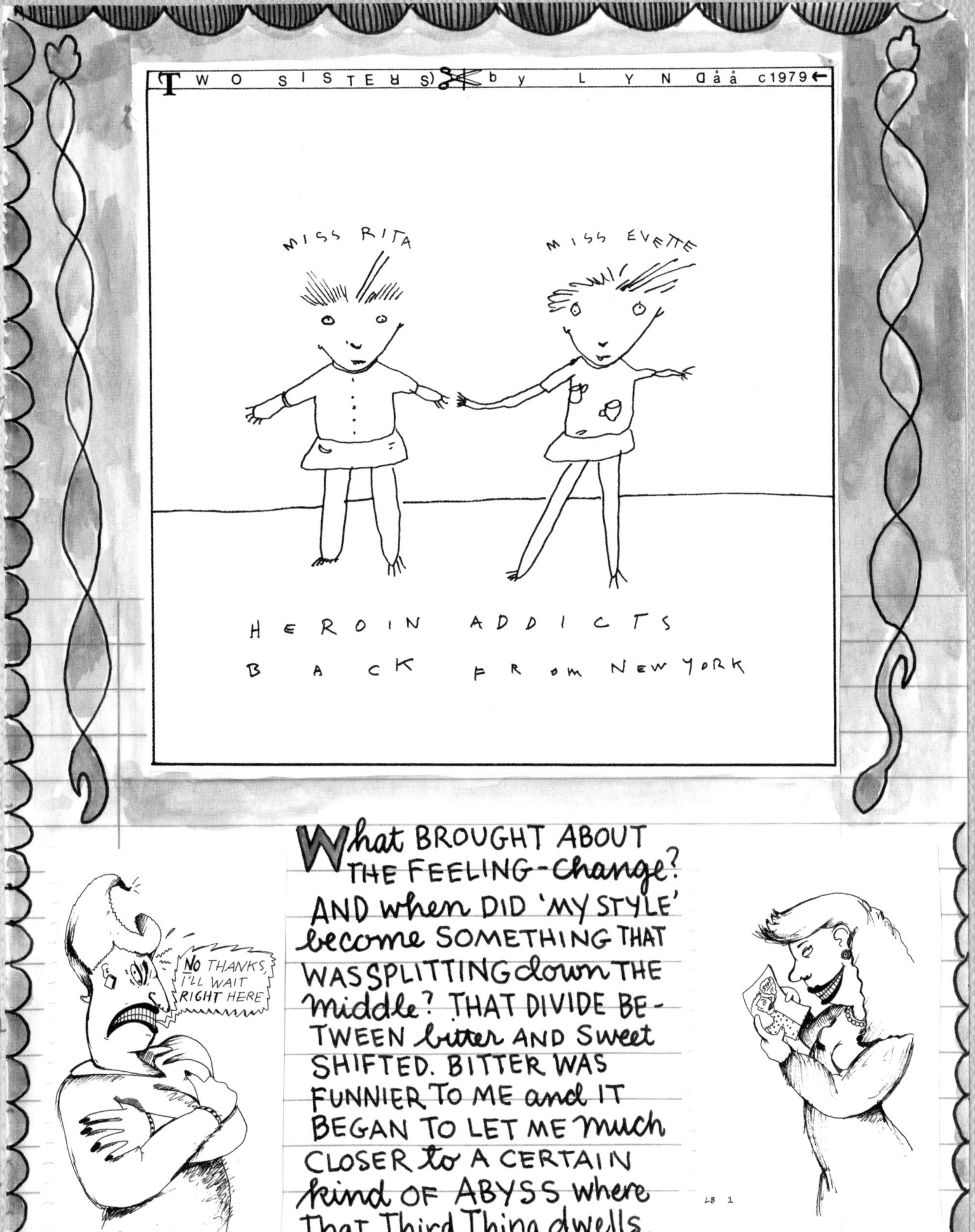
TWO SISTERS by LYN Dåå c1979
MISS RITA
MISS EVETTE
HEROIN ADDICTS
BACK FROM NEW YORK
NO THANKS, I'LL WAIT RIGHT HERE
What BROUGHT ABOUT THE FEELING-Change? AND when DID 'MY STYLE' become SOMETHING THAT WAS SPLITTING down THE middle? THAT DIVIDE BETWEEN bitter AND Sweet SHIFTED. BITTER WAS FUNNIER TO ME and IT BEGAN TO LET ME much CLOSER to A CERTAIN kind OF ABYSS where That Third Thing dwells.

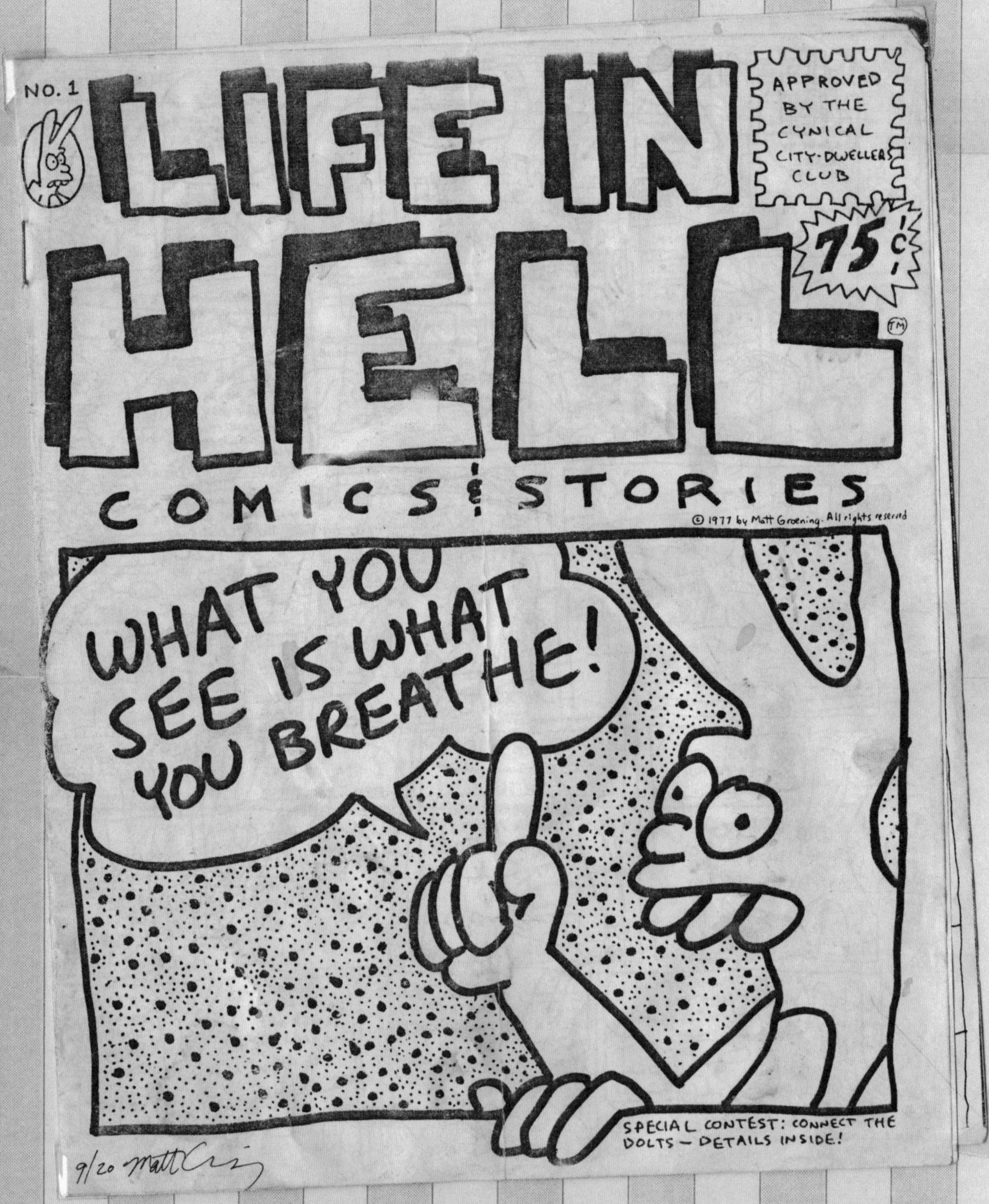
NO. 1
LIFE IN HELL
APPROVED BY THE CYNICAL CITY-DWELLERS CLUB
75¢
TM
COMICS & STORIES
© 1977 by Matt Groening. All rights reserved
WHAT YOU SEE IS WHAT YOU BREATHE!
SPECIAL CONTEST: CONNECT THE DOLTS — DETAILS INSIDE!
9/20 Matt

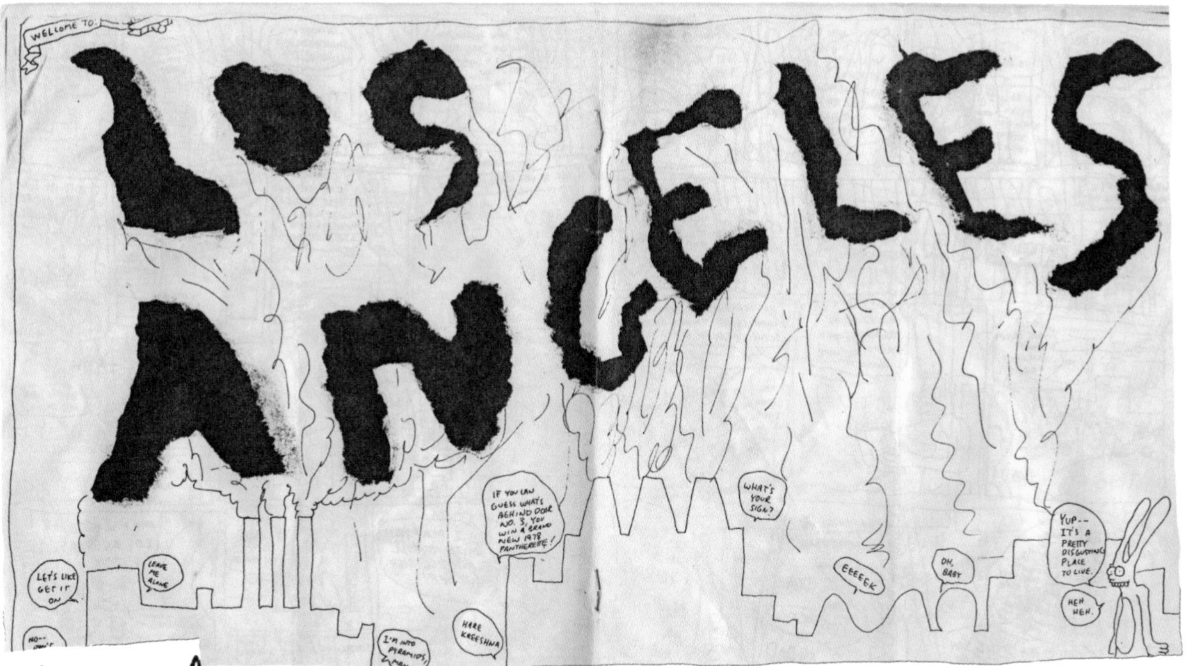
WELCOME TO:
LOS ANGELES
LET'S LIKE GET IT ON
LEAVE ME ALONE
IF YOU CAN GUESS WHAT'S BEHIND DOOR NO. 3, YOU WIN A BRAND NEW 1978 PANTHERETTE!
I'M INTO PYRAMIDS, MAN
HARE KREESHNA
WHAT'S YOUR SIGN?
EEEEEK
OH, BABY
YUP-- IT'S A PRETTY DISGUSTING PLACE TO LIVE.
HEH HEH.

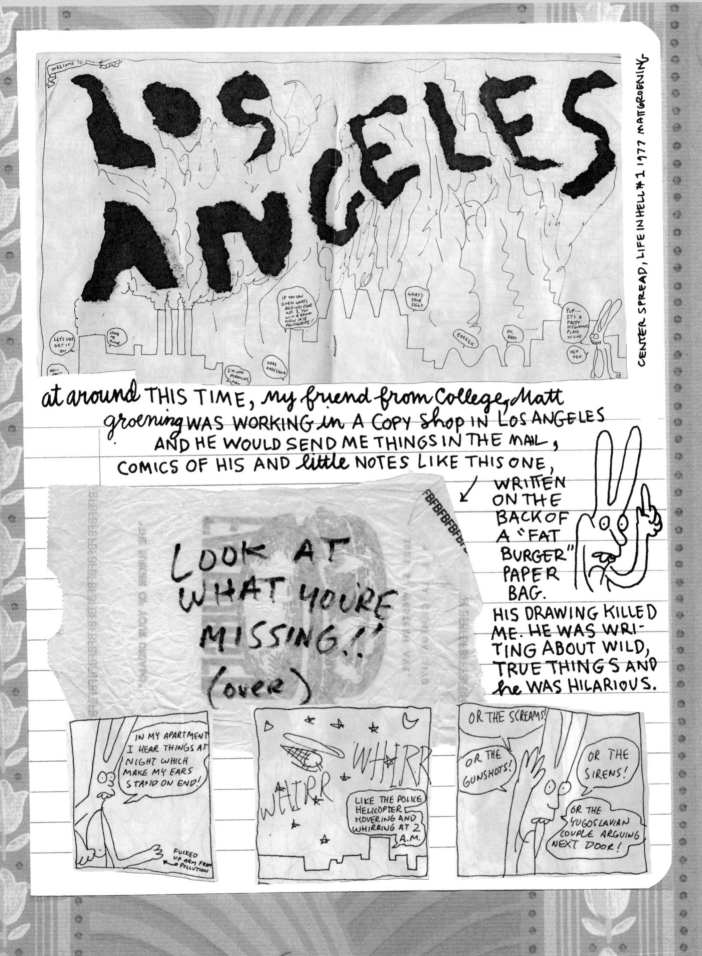

CENTER SPREAD, LIFE IN HELL #1 1977 MATT GROENING

at around THIS TIME, my friend from College, Matt groening WAS WORKING in A COPY Shop IN LOS ANGELES AND HE WOULD SEND ME THINGS IN THE MAIL, COMICS OF HIS AND little NOTES LIKE THIS ONE,

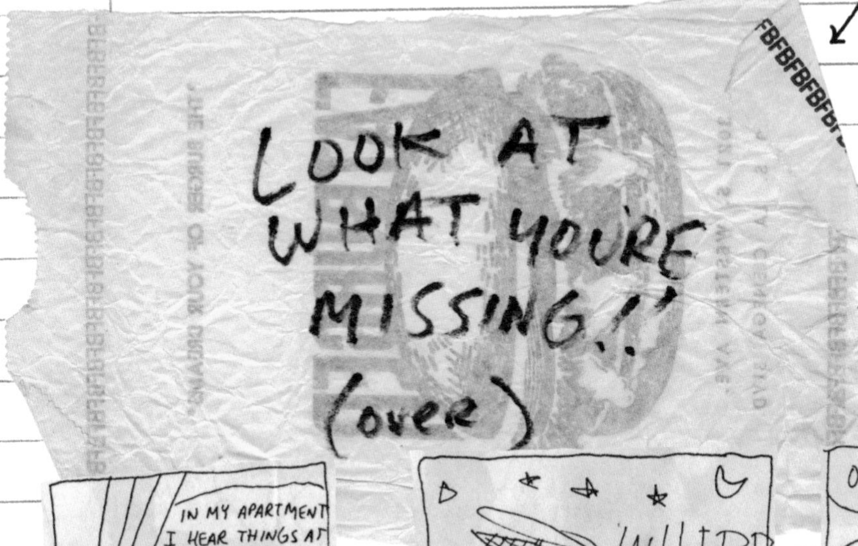
LOOK AT WHAT YOU'RE MISSING!!
(over)

WRITTEN ON THE BACK OF A "FAT BURGER" PAPER BAG.

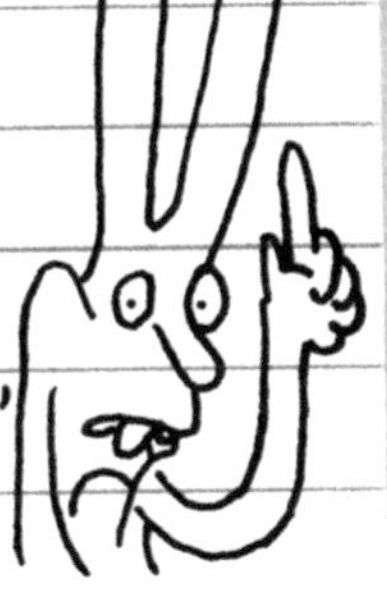

HIS DRAWING KILLED ME. HE WAS WRITING ABOUT WILD, TRUE THINGS AND he WAS HILARIOUS.

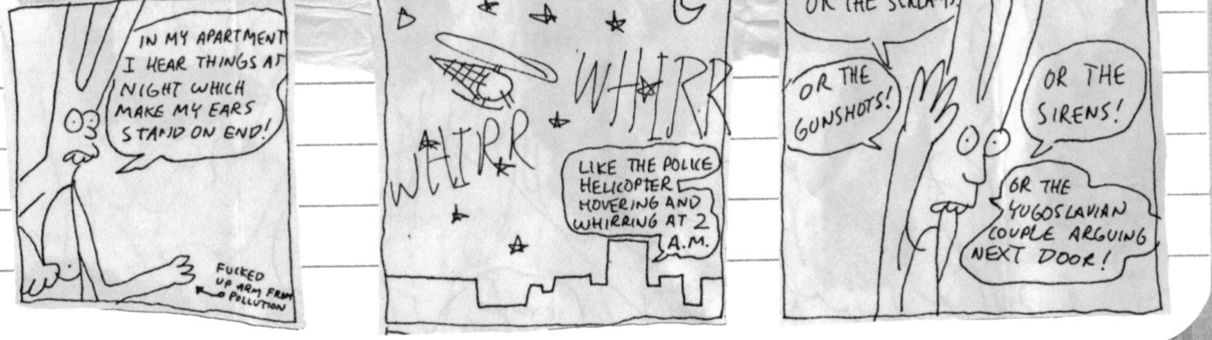
IN MY APARTMENT I HEAR THINGS AT NIGHT WHICH MAKE MY EARS STAND ON END!
FUCKED UP ARM FROM POLLUTION
WHIRR
WHIRR
LIKE THE POLICE HELICOPTER HOVERING AND WHIRRING AT 2 A.M.
OR THE SCREAMS!
OR THE GUNSHOTS!
OR THE SIRENS!
OR THE YUGOSLAVIAN COUPLE ARGUING NEXT DOOR!

HE ALSO SENT ME copies OF COMICS BY GARY PANTER. GARY and MATT used TO GET TOGETHER at NIGHT and DRAW THINGS. WHEN I FIRST SAW the WILLIAM & PERCY → COMICS GARY DID, I felt SO HAPPY. IT was LIKE FINDING THE ESCAPE SLIDE to the BACK YARD and FROM there YOU COULD GET ANYWHERE.

Look at those feet. →

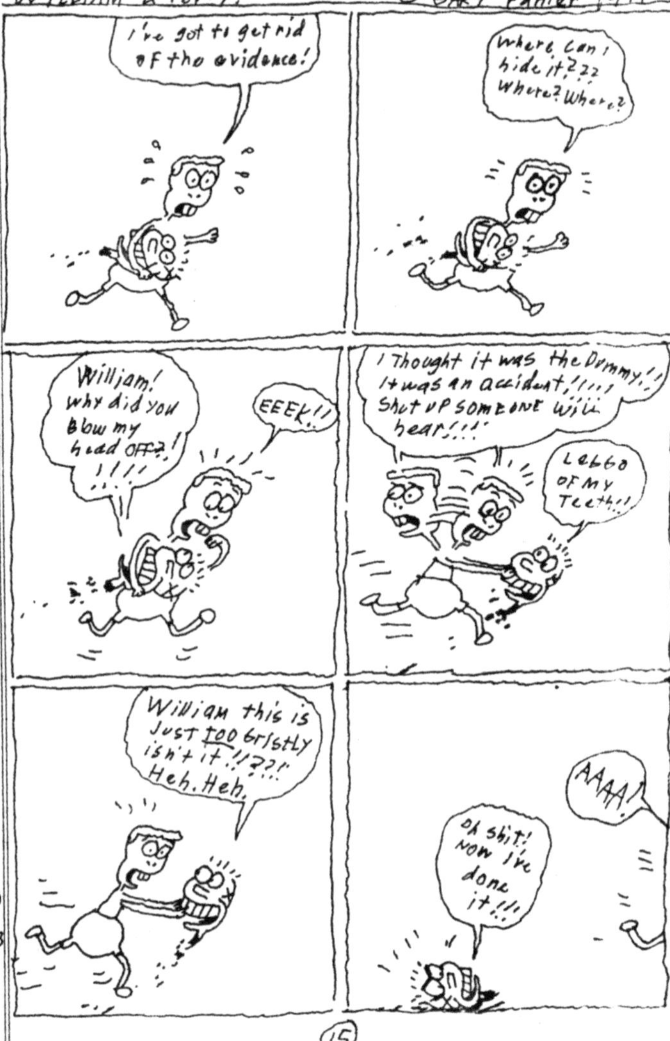

WILLIAM & PERCY.
© GARY PANTER 1979
I've got to get rid of the evidence!
Where can I hide it???? Where? Where?
William! why did you blow my head off?!
EEEK!!
I thought it was the Dummy!! It was an accident!!!! Shut up someone will hear!!!
Lebbo of my Teeth!!
William this is just TOO GRISTLY isn't it!!???! Heh. Heh.
AAAA!
Oh shit! Now I've done it!!!
10
23
15

Both MATT and GARY changed THINGS FOR ME AND ALMOST all OF this HAPPENED VIA THE U.S. MAIL. Long Distance Calls were EXPENSIVE- and WE Were ALL BROKE back Then, as young people OFTEN ARE.

Those feet kill me.

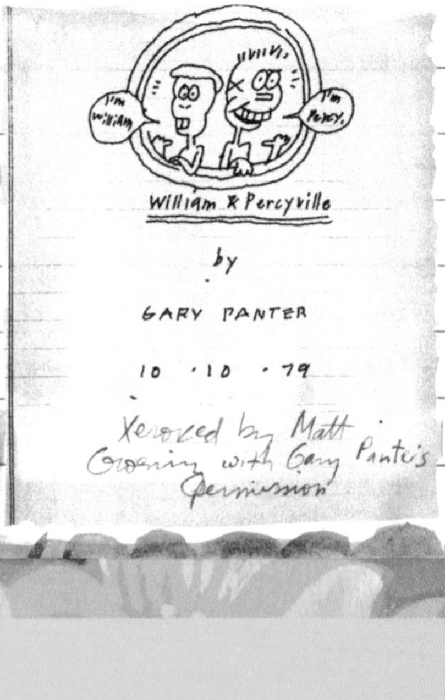

I'm William
I'm Percy.
William & Percyville
by
GARY PANTER
10 · 10 · 79
Xeroxed by Matt Groening with Gary Panter's permission

BUT PHOTO COPIES WERE CHEAP AND stamps were CHEAP and IT WAS MORE FUN TO MAKE SOMETHING when YOU HAD SOMEONE to SEND IT TO.

IT WAS A VERY GOOD WAY TO SEE someone's DRAWINGS FOR the FIRST TIME and A PERFECT WAY TO FIRST SEE A Comic strip.

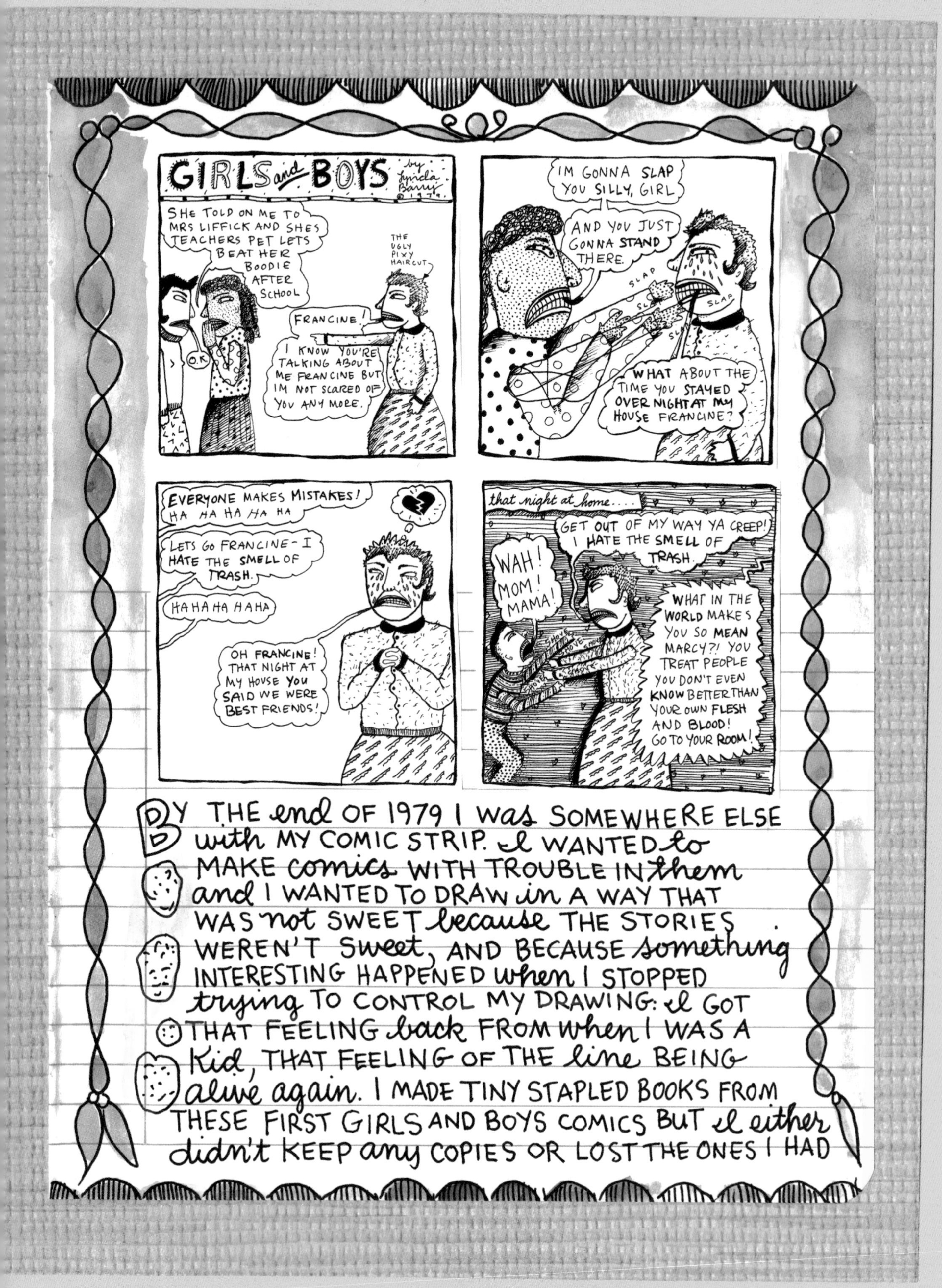
GIRLS and BOYS
by Lynda Barry
SHE TOLD ON ME TO MRS LIFFICK AND SHES TEACHERS PET LETS BEAT HER BOODIE AFTER SCHOOL
O.K.
THE UGLY PIXY HAIRCUT
FRANCINE!
I KNOW YOU'RE TALKING ABOUT ME FRANCINE BUT IM NOT SCARED OF YOU ANY MORE.
IM GONNA SLAP YOU SILLY, GIRL
AND YOU JUST GONNA STAND THERE.
SLAP
SLAP
WHAT ABOUT THE TIME YOU STAYED OVER NIGHT AT MY HOUSE FRANCINE?
EVERYONE MAKES MISTAKES! HA HA HA HA HA
LETS GO FRANCINE - I HATE THE SMELL OF TRASH.
HA HA HA HA HA
OH FRANCINE! THAT NIGHT AT MY HOUSE YOU SAID WE WERE BEST FRIENDS!
that night at home....
GET OUT OF MY WAY YA CREEP! I HATE THE SMELL OF TRASH.
WAH! MOM! MAMA!
SHOVE
WHAT IN THE WORLD MAKES YOU SO MEAN MARCY?! YOU TREAT PEOPLE YOU DON'T EVEN KNOW BETTER THAN YOUR OWN FLESH AND BLOOD! GO TO YOUR ROOM!

BY THE *end* OF 1979 I *was* SOMEWHERE ELSE *with* MY COMIC STRIP. I WANTED *to* MAKE *comics* WITH TROUBLE IN *them* *and* I WANTED TO DRAW *in* A WAY THAT WAS *not* SWEET *because* THE STORIES WEREN'T *sweet*, AND BECAUSE *something* INTERESTING HAPPENED *when* I STOPPED *trying* TO CONTROL MY DRAWING: I GOT THAT FEELING *back* FROM *when* I WAS A *kid*, THAT FEELING OF THE *line* BEING *alive again*. I MADE TINY STAPLED BOOKS FROM THESE FIRST GIRLS AND BOYS COMICS BUT I *either* *didn't* KEEP *any* COPIES OR LOST THE ONES I HAD

Book signing for 'Girls and Boys'   October, 1981

IN 1981 THE GIRLS and BOYS STRIPS were COLLECTED into a BOOK. HERE IS WHAT I KNOW _now_ THAT I DIDN'T KNOW _then_:

- That I WOULD keep drawing comics ALL the WAY PAST THE YEAR 2011.
- THAT I WOULD swing BETWEEN sweet and bitter DRAWING and writing styles AGAIN and AGAIN.
- THAT the FIRST DRAWINGS I copied WOULD LEAVE Traces IN MY work and Drawing style That were UNSHAKABLE and STRONG.
- THAT the QUESTION asked: what BRINGS about a 'feeling-change' when we read CERTAIN KINDS of COMICS? — THIS QUESTION can NEVER be ANSWERED with WORDS ALONE.

| SUN OCT 11 1981 | BOOKSIGNING Party 5-7 Champagne + Cake Groovy party later |
| | 10:30 Tesla → 3:00 Tesla |

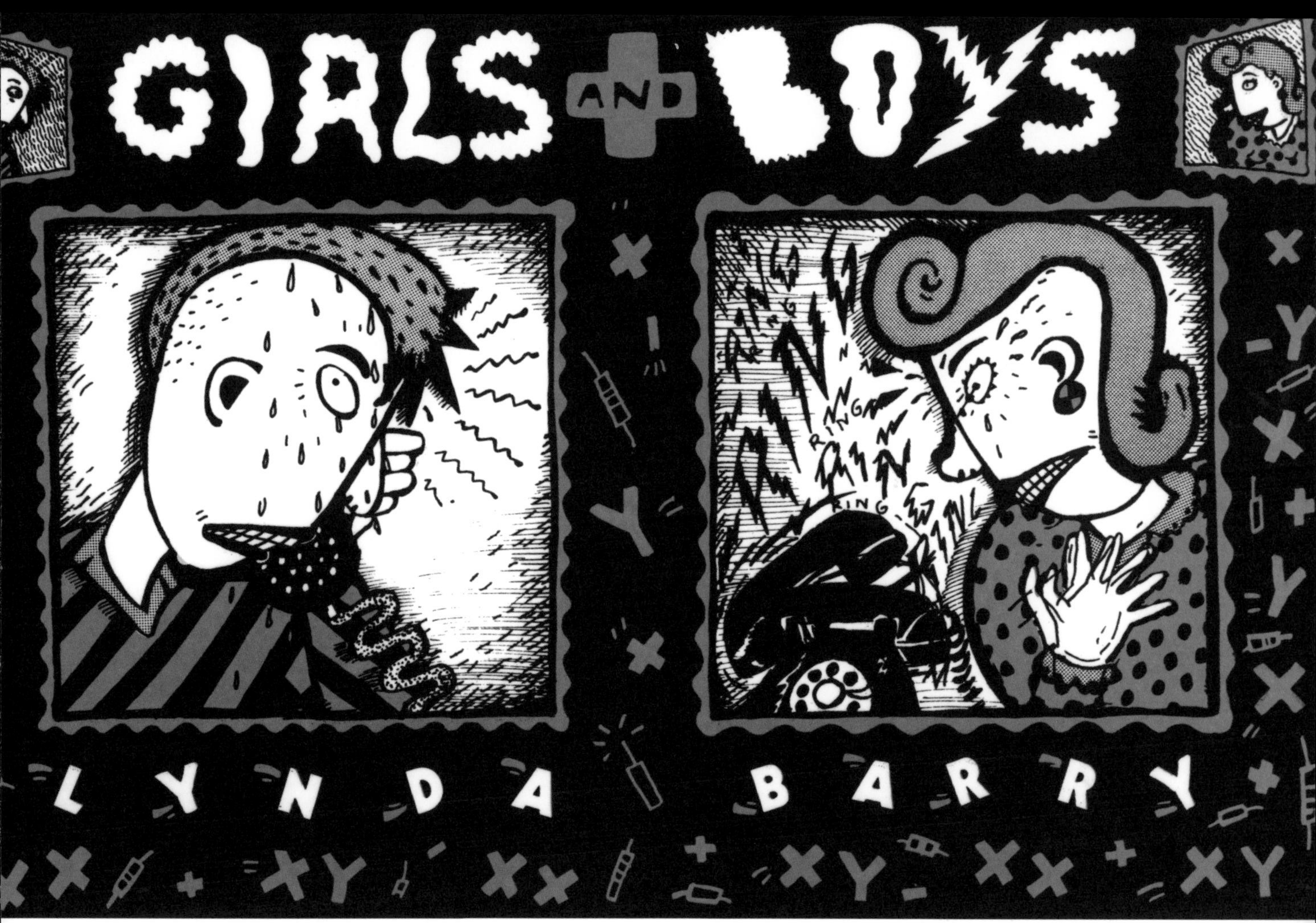
GIRLS AND BOYS
RING
LYNDA BARRY

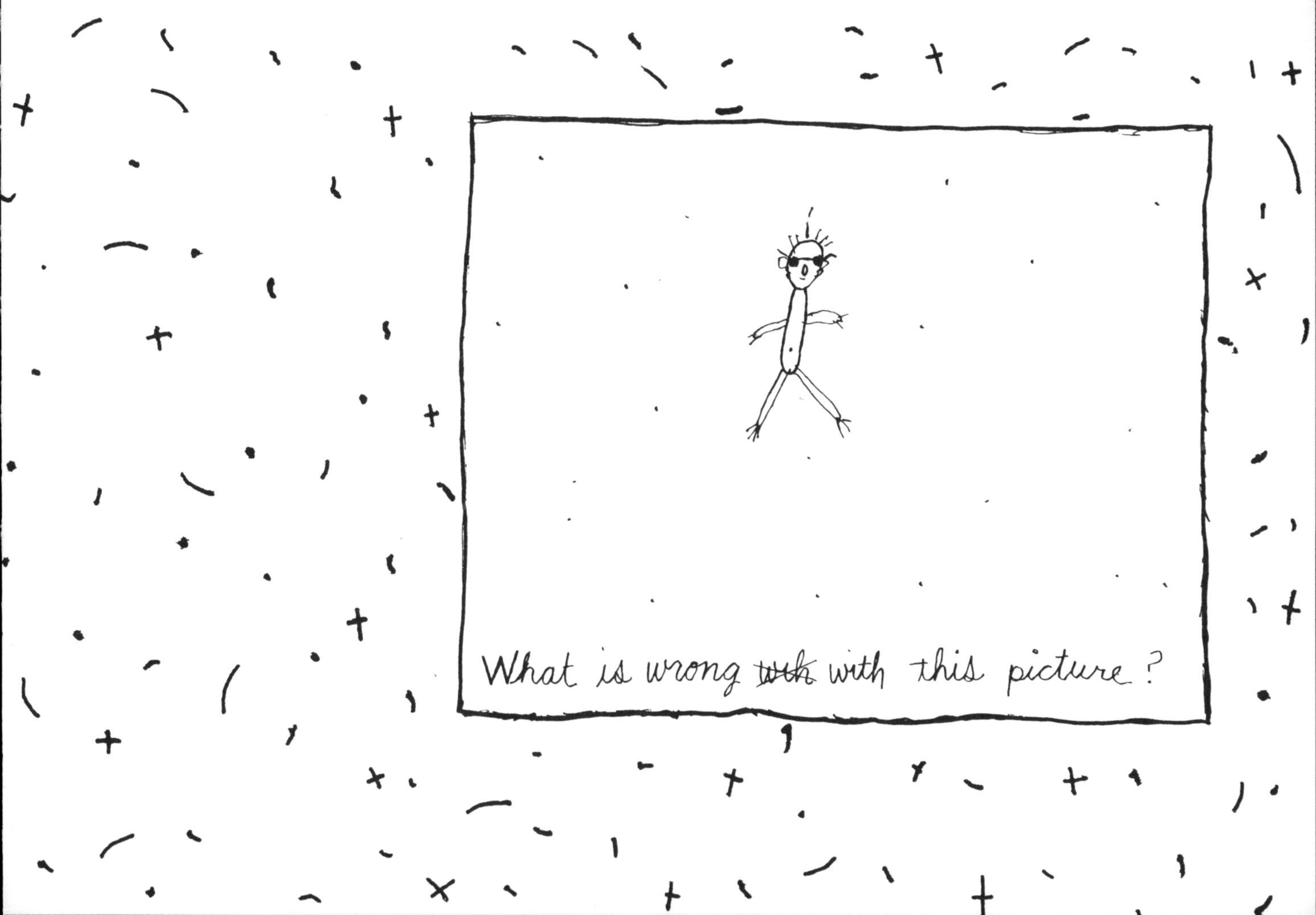
What is wrong with this picture?

GIRLS AND BOYS

LYNDA BARRY

THE REAL COMET PRESS
SEATTLE

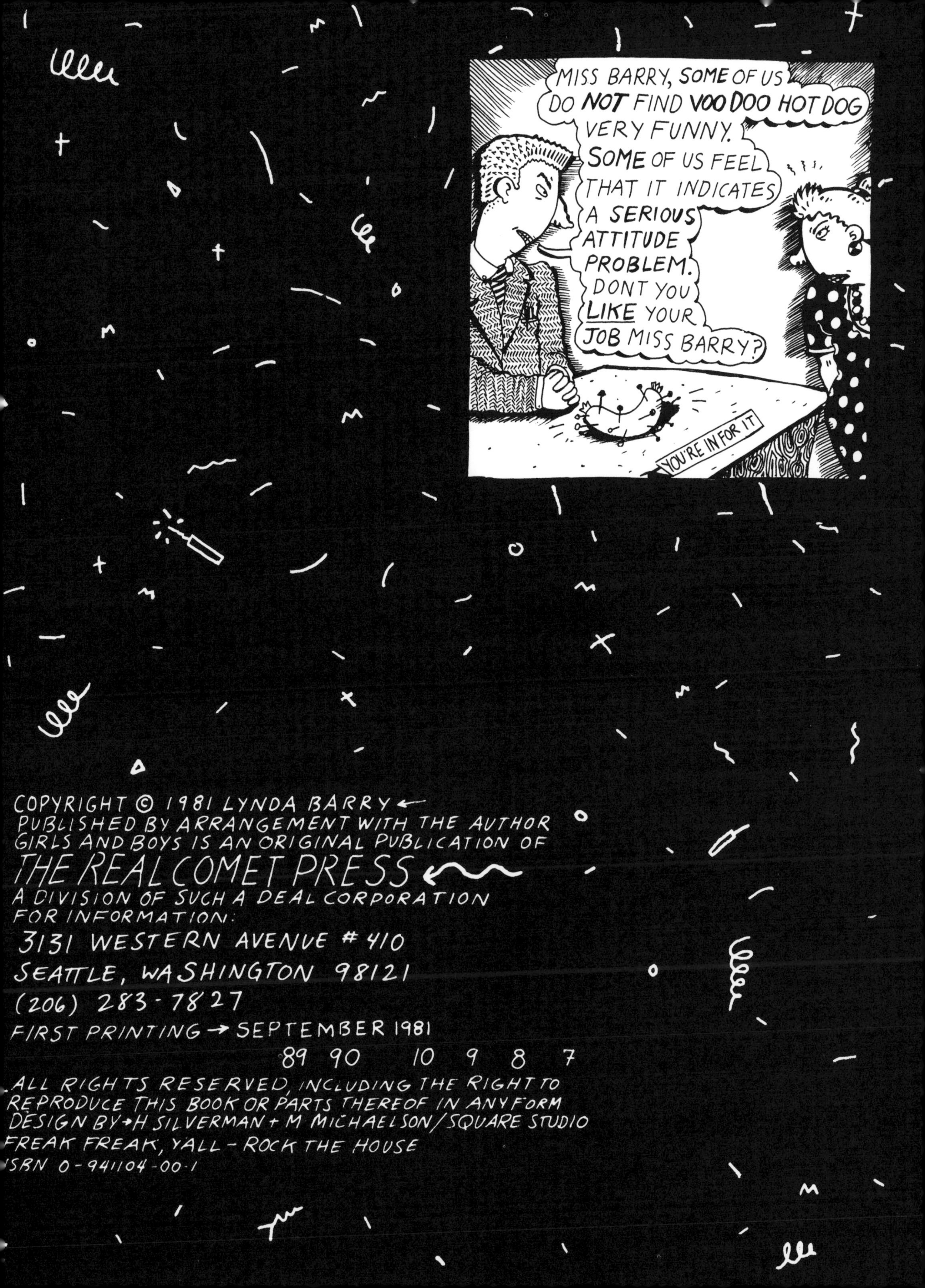
MISS BARRY, SOME OF US DO NOT FIND VOO DOO HOT DOG VERY FUNNY. SOME OF US FEEL THAT IT INDICATES A SERIOUS ATTITUDE PROBLEM. DONT YOU LIKE YOUR JOB MISS BARRY?
YOU'RE IN FOR IT

PUBLISHED BY ARRANGEMENT WITH THE AUTHOR
GIRLS AND BOYS IS AN ORIGINAL PUBLICATION OF
THE REAL COMET PRESS ←
A DIVISION OF SUCH A DEAL CORPORATION
FOR INFORMATION:
3131 WESTERN AVENUE # 410
SEATTLE, WASHINGTON 98121
(206) 283-7827
FIRST PRINTING → SEPTEMBER 1981
89 90 10 9 8 7

DESIGN BY → H SILVERMAN + M MICHAELSON / SQUARE STUDIO
FREAK FREAK, YALL - ROCK THE HOUSE
ISBN 0-941104-00-1

HOW TO DRAW CARTOONS

BY THE FAMOUS ARTIST TEACHER MRS. LYNDA

"I can teach you to draw so that anyone will want to be your partner." —L.B.

ITS FUN! ITS EASY! ALL YOU NEED TO BEGIN IS:
A pencil →
A pen
Paper →
And a HUMAN BRAIN!

WHEN DO WE START!

THIS PARTS EASY!

WADA WE WAITIN FOR! SO: LET'S GO!!!!

The first thing you'll want to think about is what you'll say in the UNDERVIEW with TIME MAGAZINE after they select YOU as CARTOONIST of the YEAR!!! Its sure to happen, so write down some of your PROFOUND THOUGHTS on the subject in the space provided: _ _ _ _ _ _ _ _ _

LEARN FROM OTHERS!
LETS TAKE A LOOK AT HOW OTHERS DO IT!

SHAPE OF THE HEAD

"SPIDER MAN"   "PEANUTS"
"L'il ORPHAN ANNIE"   "NANCY"   "LYNDA BARRY"

NOW YOU TRY

Be SURE to use ALL OF THE SPACE PROVIDED! You have room for 12 DIFFERENT SHAPES SO LET YOUR IMAGINATION "GO-GO" WILD! YOU'RE PROBABLY GOING TO HAVE TO DRAW PRETTY SMALL!! BUT CARTOONISTS MUST DRAW SMALL SO IT WILL ALL FIT IN THAT COMIC STRIP! ON SUNDAYS YOU CAN DRAW "BIGGER!"

FACIAL FEATURES
eyes, nose and mouth

	"SPIDERMAN"	"PEANUTS"	"ANNIE"	"NANCY"	"LYNDA BARRY"
EYES: "DOORWAY to the soul"			00		
NOSE: "GIVES CHARACTER"	NONE	C		—	
MOUTH: "SHOWS FEELING"	NONE			—)	

NOW! MIX 'N' MATCH!
CREATE YOUR OWN CHARACTER! TRY TO FLOW W/ IT!

YOU GIVE IT A TRY! HAVE FUN WITH IT!

use this space for your drawings

NOW: ALL WE NEED IS A STORY

HERES THE KEY: KEEP IT SIMPLE

HMM — THATS SORTA TOUGH

ORIGINALITY! how about one just to help you GET STARTED:

"A young girl has to have extensive dental work. The young dentist finds himself falling in love with the girl. When she falls off the dental chair by accident the young dentist finds himself looking up her skirt. "Dr. Hix!" She exclaims."

OK — GOOD LUCK WITH THIS ONE!

YOUR DIPLOMA

all done?

FRAME 1   FRAME 2   FRAME 3   END   SIGN HERE _ _ _ _

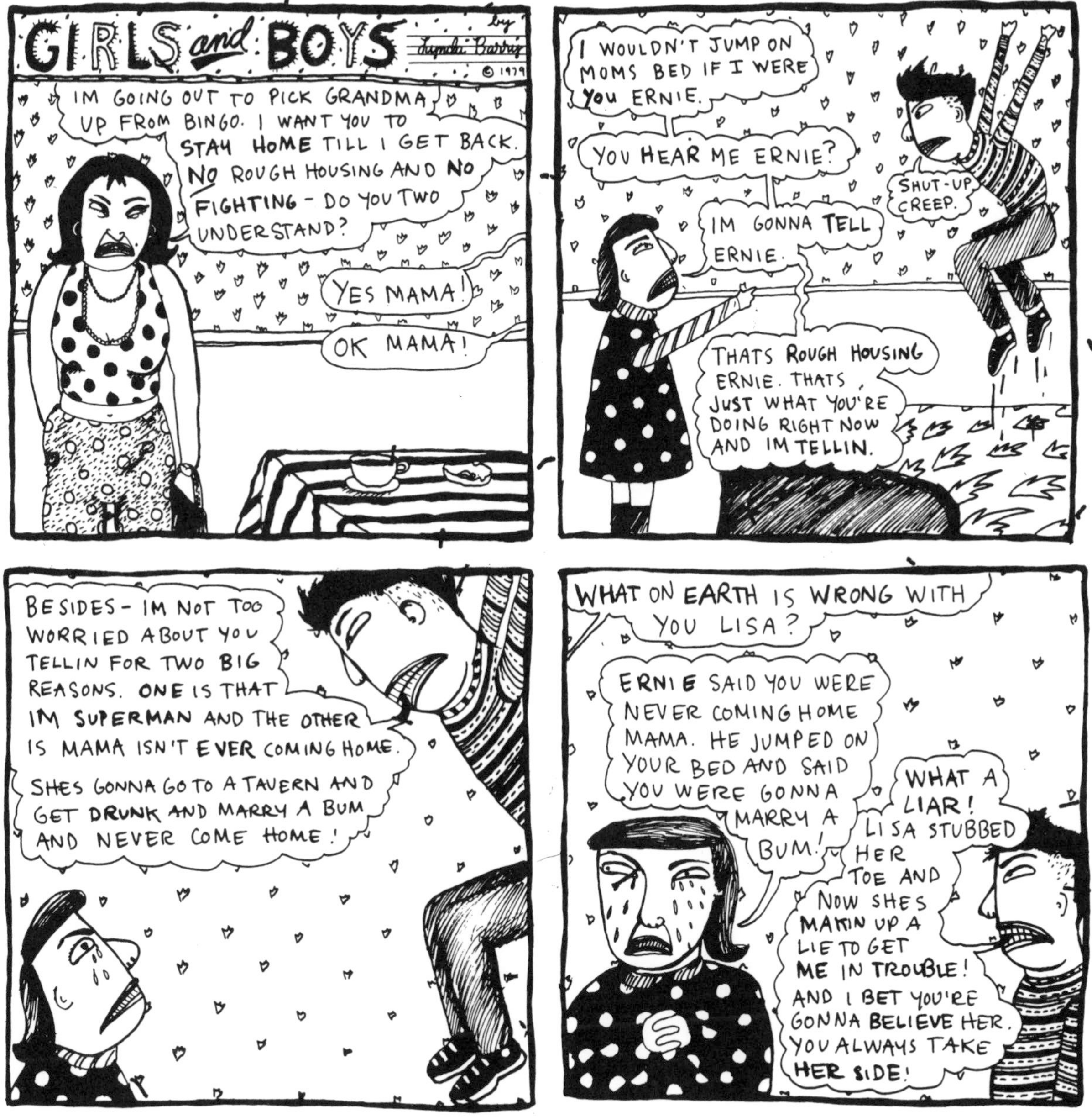
GIRLS and BOYS
by Lynda Barry
© 1979
IM GOING OUT TO PICK GRANDMA UP FROM BINGO. I WANT YOU TO STAY HOME TILL I GET BACK. NO ROUGH HOUSING AND NO FIGHTING - DO YOU TWO UNDERSTAND?
YES MAMA!
OK MAMA!
I WOULDN'T JUMP ON MOMS BED IF I WERE YOU ERNIE.
YOU HEAR ME ERNIE?
SHUT-UP CREEP.
IM GONNA TELL ERNIE.
THATS ROUGH HOUSING ERNIE. THATS JUST WHAT YOU'RE DOING RIGHT NOW AND IM TELLIN.
BESIDES- IM NOT TOO WORRIED ABOUT YOU TELLIN FOR TWO BIG REASONS. ONE IS THAT IM SUPERMAN AND THE OTHER IS MAMA ISN'T EVER COMING HOME.
SHES GONNA GO TO A TAVERN AND GET DRUNK AND MARRY A BUM AND NEVER COME HOME!
WHAT ON EARTH IS WRONG WITH YOU LISA?
ERNIE SAID YOU WERE NEVER COMING HOME MAMA. HE JUMPED ON YOUR BED AND SAID YOU WERE GONNA MARRY A BUM!
WHAT A LIAR! LISA STUBBED HER TOE AND NOW SHES MAKIN UP A LIE TO GET ME IN TROUBLE! AND I BET YOU'RE GONNA BELIEVE HER. YOU ALWAYS TAKE HER SIDE!

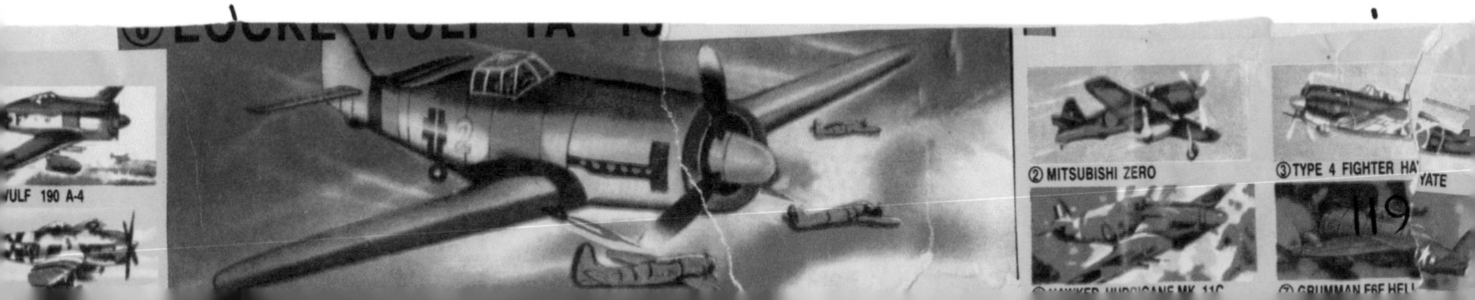
WULF 190 A-4
② MITSUBISHI ZERO
③ TYPE 4 FIGHTER HA
YATE

GIRLS + BOYS!! © 1979
STORY BY: TINA HOGGATT
PICTURES BY: LYNDABARRY
"The New Baby."
WANNA KNOW SOMETHING TINA?
WHAT?
BABIES CANNOT FEEL PAIN.
NUH-UH!
REALLY TINA! A TEACHER TOLD ME THAT IF YOU POKE A BABY WITH A SAFETY PIN BEFORE THE AGE OF 5, THE BABY CAN'T FEEL IT!
YOU'RE TRYING TO GET ME IN TROUBLE LYNN.
IM NOT TRYING TO GET YOU IN TROUBLE! IM TRYING TO TEACH YOU ABOUT SCIENCE! HERE! TRY IT!
REALLY?
SURE!! DO YOU HAVE THE PIN?
UH-HUH
O.K...
MAMA! GET IN HERE!! TINAS GONNA POKE BABY DAWN WITH A SAFETY PIN AND I CAN'T MAKE HER STOP!!
ALL DAY

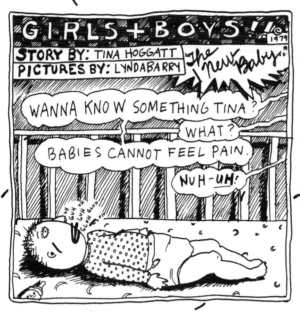

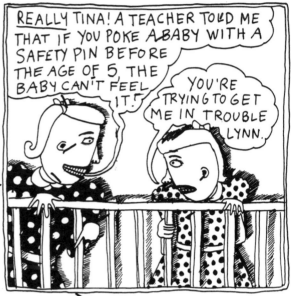

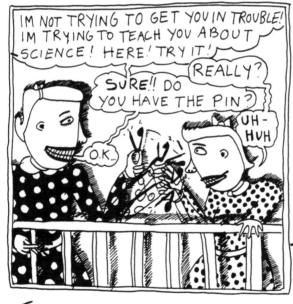

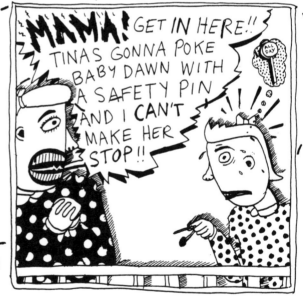

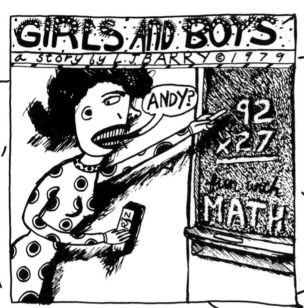

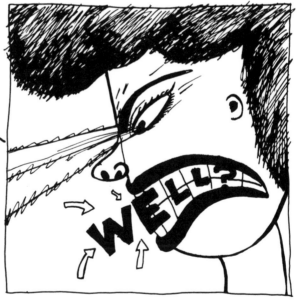

GIRLS AND BOYS
a story by L.J. BARRY ©1979
ANDY?
92
x27
MATH
UH UH UH UH UH UH UH UH
TEACHER'S ICY GAZE
YOU AREN'T PREPARED ARE YOU ANDREW? SUPPOSE YOU TELL US WHAT YOU ARE THINKING ABOUT –
NAKED PICTURES INSIDE THIS BOOK
MATH FOR A-MERI-CANS
HER FREEZING LOOK
CHATTER CHATTER CHATTER
WE ARE ALL WAITING ANDREW. VALUABLE CLASS TIME IS BEING WASTED....
WELL?
WELL?
continued

Mathematics (Expanded notation)

1. Presentation (method and process):
   Used problem 83+2= — Teacher wrote on chalkboard to show (80+3)+2 = □ 80+ (3+2)= □, 80+5 = 85
   Did another -35+3 and had chr. tell what to do.
   Emphasized ...

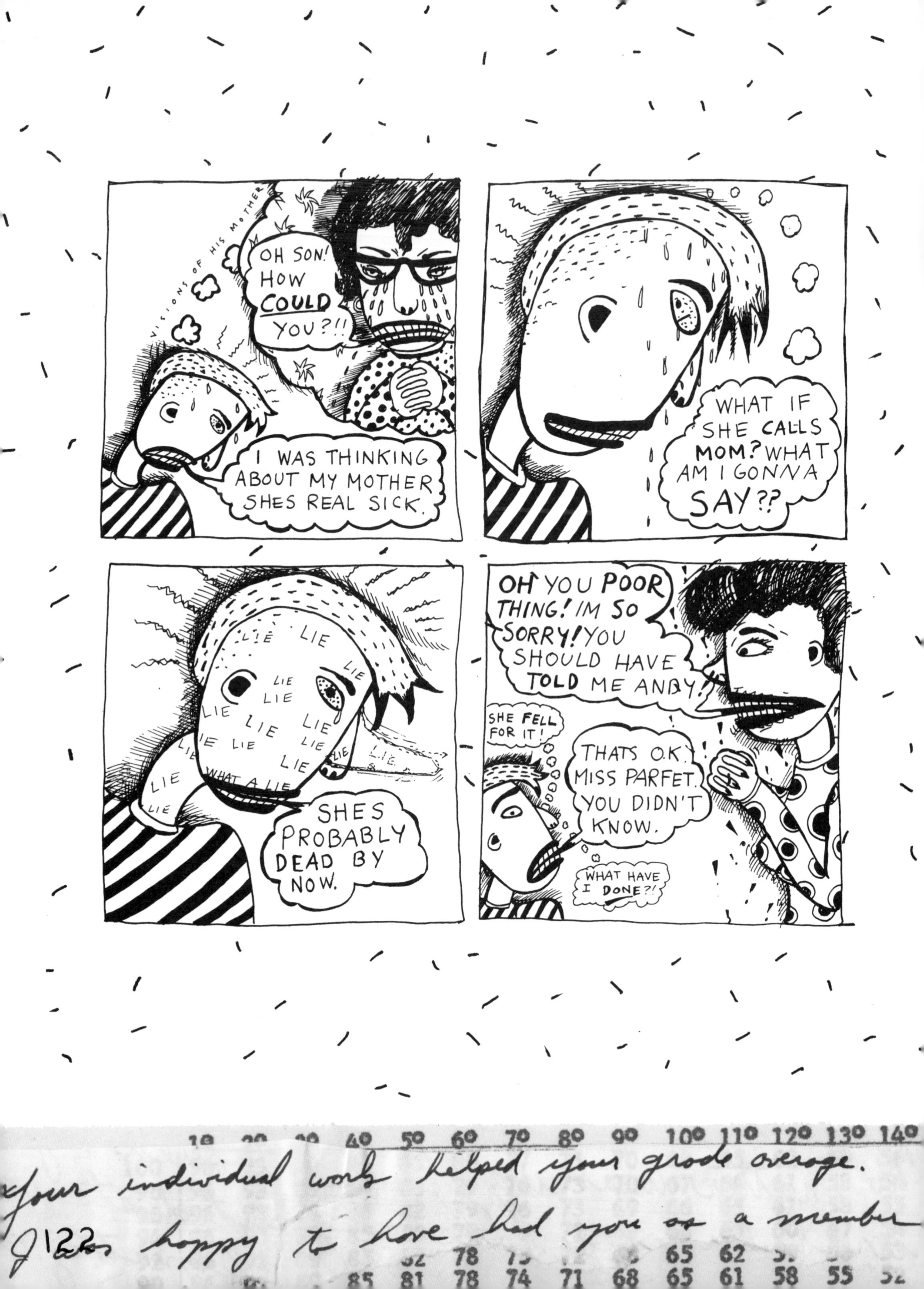
VISIONS OF HIS MOTHER
OH SON! HOW COULD YOU?!!
I WAS THINKING ABOUT MY MOTHER SHES REAL SICK.
WHAT IF SHE CALLS MOM? WHAT AM I GONNA SAY??
LIE LIE LIE LIE LIE LIE LIE LIE LIE LIE LIE LIE LIE LIE
WHAT A LIE
SHES PROBABLY DEAD BY NOW.
OH YOU POOR THING! IM SO SORRY! YOU SHOULD HAVE TOLD ME ANDY!
SHE FELL FOR IT!
THATS O.K. MISS PARFET. YOU DIDN'T KNOW.
WHAT HAVE I DONE?!
your individual work helped your grade average.
happy to have had you as a member

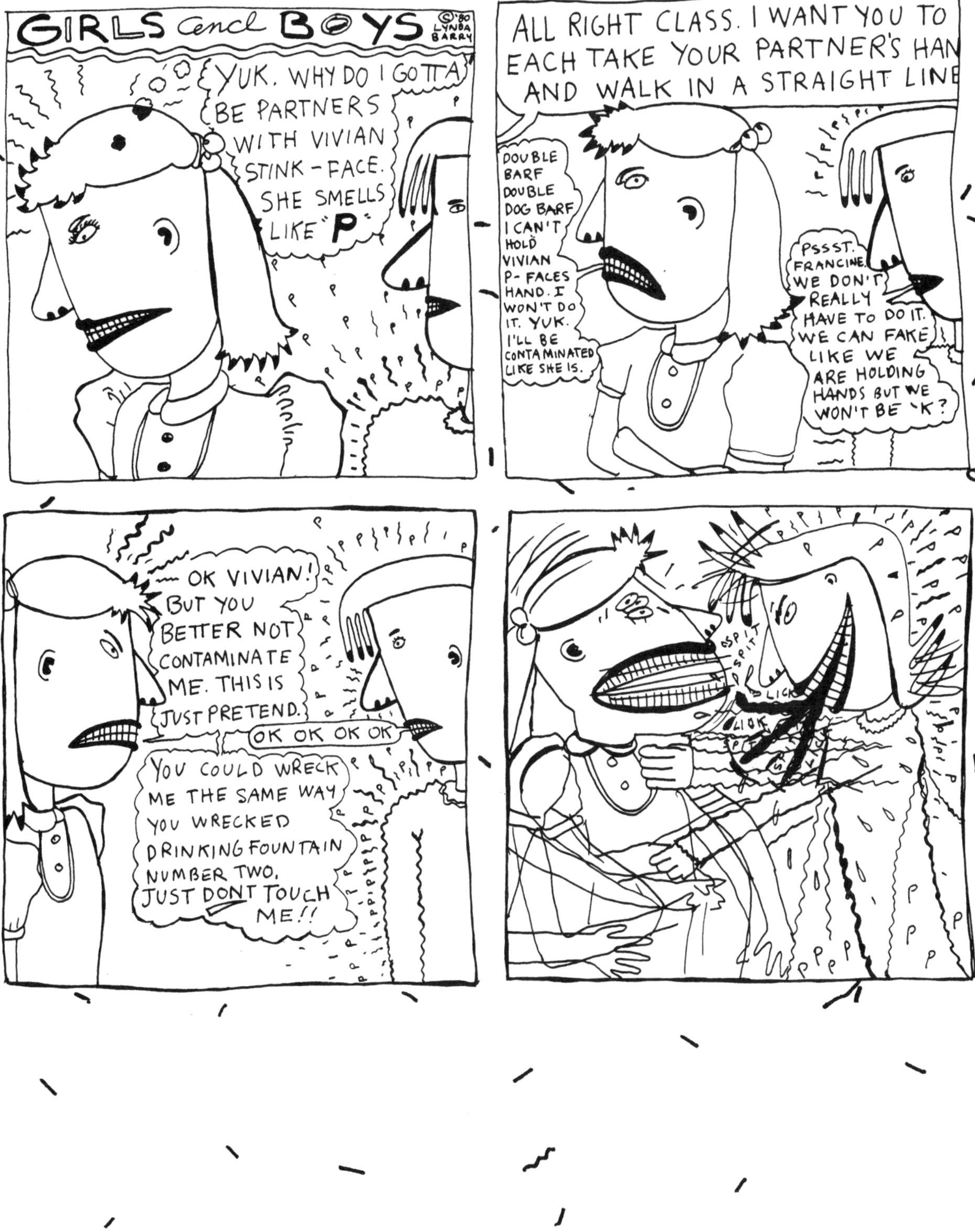

GIRLS and BOYS
©'80 LYNDA BARRY
YUK. WHY DO I GOTTA BE PARTNERS WITH VIVIAN STINK-FACE. SHE SMELLS LIKE "P"
ALL RIGHT CLASS. I WANT YOU TO EACH TAKE YOUR PARTNER'S HAN AND WALK IN A STRAIGHT LINE
DOUBLE BARF DOUBLE DOG BARF I CAN'T HOLD VIVIAN P-FACES HAND. I WON'T DO IT. YUK. I'LL BE CONTAMINATED LIKE SHE IS.
PSSST. FRANCINE. WE DON'T REALLY HAVE TO DO IT. WE CAN FAKE LIKE WE ARE HOLDING HANDS BUT WE WON'T BE 'K?
OK VIVIAN! BUT YOU BETTER NOT CONTAMINATE ME. THIS IS JUST PRETEND.
OK OK OK OK
YOU COULD WRECK ME THE SAME WAY YOU WRECKED DRINKING FOUNTAIN NUMBER TWO. JUST DON'T TOUCH ME!!
SPIT SPIT
LICK
LICK

Vocabulary Test IV

	2.	3.	4.	5.	10.
ch	mustard	salad	hundreds	cockatoo	prince
ch	muddy	sandal	handkerchief	coconut	price

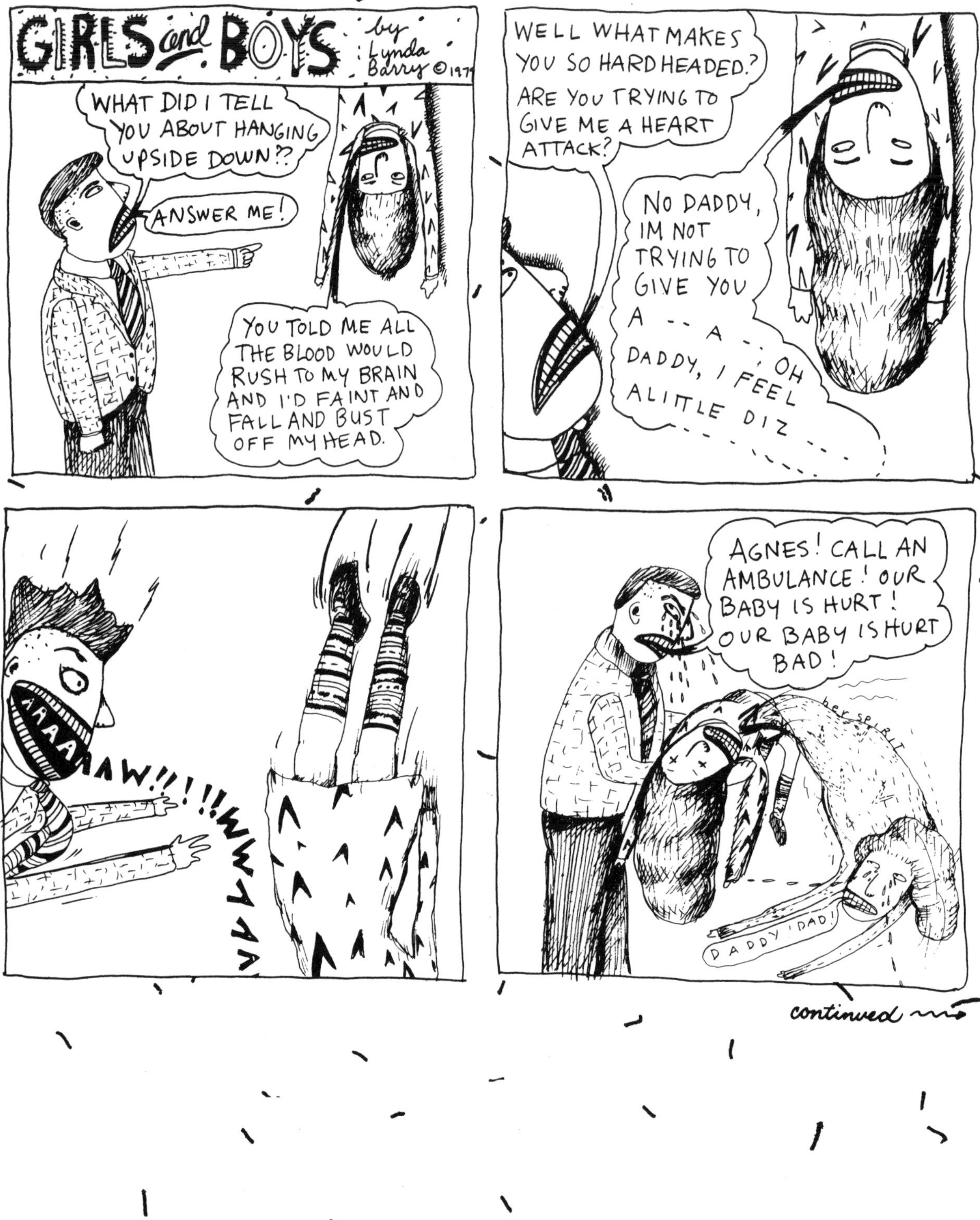
GIRLS and BOYS
by Lynda Barry ©197
WHAT DID I TELL YOU ABOUT HANGING UPSIDE DOWN??
ANSWER ME!
YOU TOLD ME ALL THE BLOOD WOULD RUSH TO MY BRAIN AND I'D FAINT AND FALL AND BUST OFF MY HEAD.
WELL WHAT MAKES YOU SO HARDHEADED? ARE YOU TRYING TO GIVE ME A HEART ATTACK?
NO DADDY, IM NOT TRYING TO GIVE YOU A -- A -- OH DADDY, I FEEL A LITTLE DIZ . . .
AAAAAAW!!!!!!WWAAA
AGNES! CALL AN AMBULANCE! OUR BABY IS HURT! OUR BABY IS HURT BAD!
her SPIRIT
DADDY! DAD!

continued

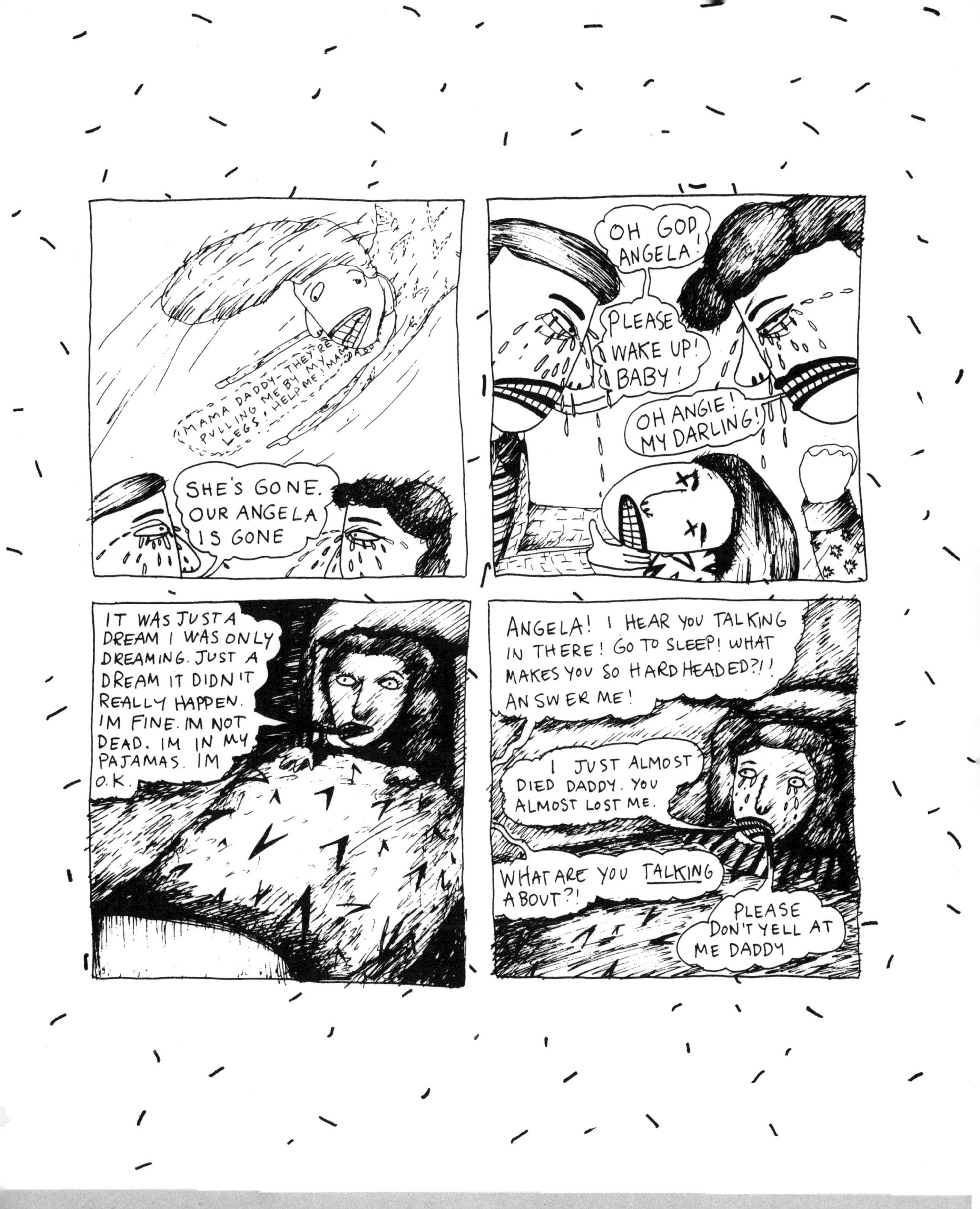
MAMA DADDY- THEY'RE PULLING ME BY MY LEGS! HELP ME! MAMA DADDY
SHE'S GONE. OUR ANGELA IS GONE
OH GOD ANGELA!
PLEASE WAKE UP! BABY!
OH ANGIE! MY DARLING!
IT WAS JUST A DREAM I WAS ONLY DREAMING. JUST A DREAM IT DIDN'T REALLY HAPPEN. IM FINE. IM NOT DEAD. IM IN MY PAJAMAS. IM O.K.
ANGELA! I HEAR YOU TALKING IN THERE! GO TO SLEEP! WHAT MAKES YOU SO HARD HEADED?!! ANSWER ME!
I JUST ALMOST DIED DADDY. YOU ALMOST LOST ME.
WHAT ARE YOU TALKING ABOUT?!
PLEASE DON'T YELL AT ME DADDY

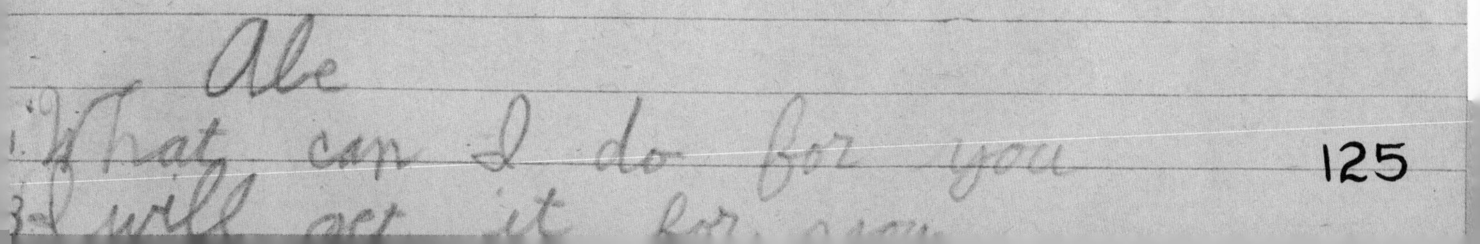
Abe
What can I do for you

GIRLS and BOYS
FUN STORIES OF CHILDHOOD BY LYNDA J. BARRY ©1980
EVELYN EVELYN EVELYN
WELL GEE SARGENT!
DON'T GEE ME GOMER! GET IN THERE!
EVELYN
Relax evelyn... you feel sleepy evelyn... THIS IS THE SPIRIT OF YOUR TV!! YOU SHALL BE MY SLAVE FOR LIFE!!
RRR RRR
GOMER! WHATS WRONG WITH YO GET IN THER
BUT SARGENT! M SCARED!
REMOTE CONTROL
YOU WILL COME TO ME NO MATTER WHATS ON! YOU WILL WATCH ANYTHING!
•BEWITCHED
•F-TROOP
•I DREAM OF JEANN
NO MATTER WHATS ON, I WILL WATCH ANYTHING.
EVELYN HONEY! COME HELP SET THE TABLE. DINNER IS ALMOST READY!
CAN'T. MUST. WATCH. GOMER.
ARE YOU A WHITEMAN WITH A JOB? IF YOU ARE, THIS CAR WILL HELP YOU GET WOMEN TO SLEEP WITH YOU ANYTIME YOU WANT-STARTING NOW. BUY IT FAST.

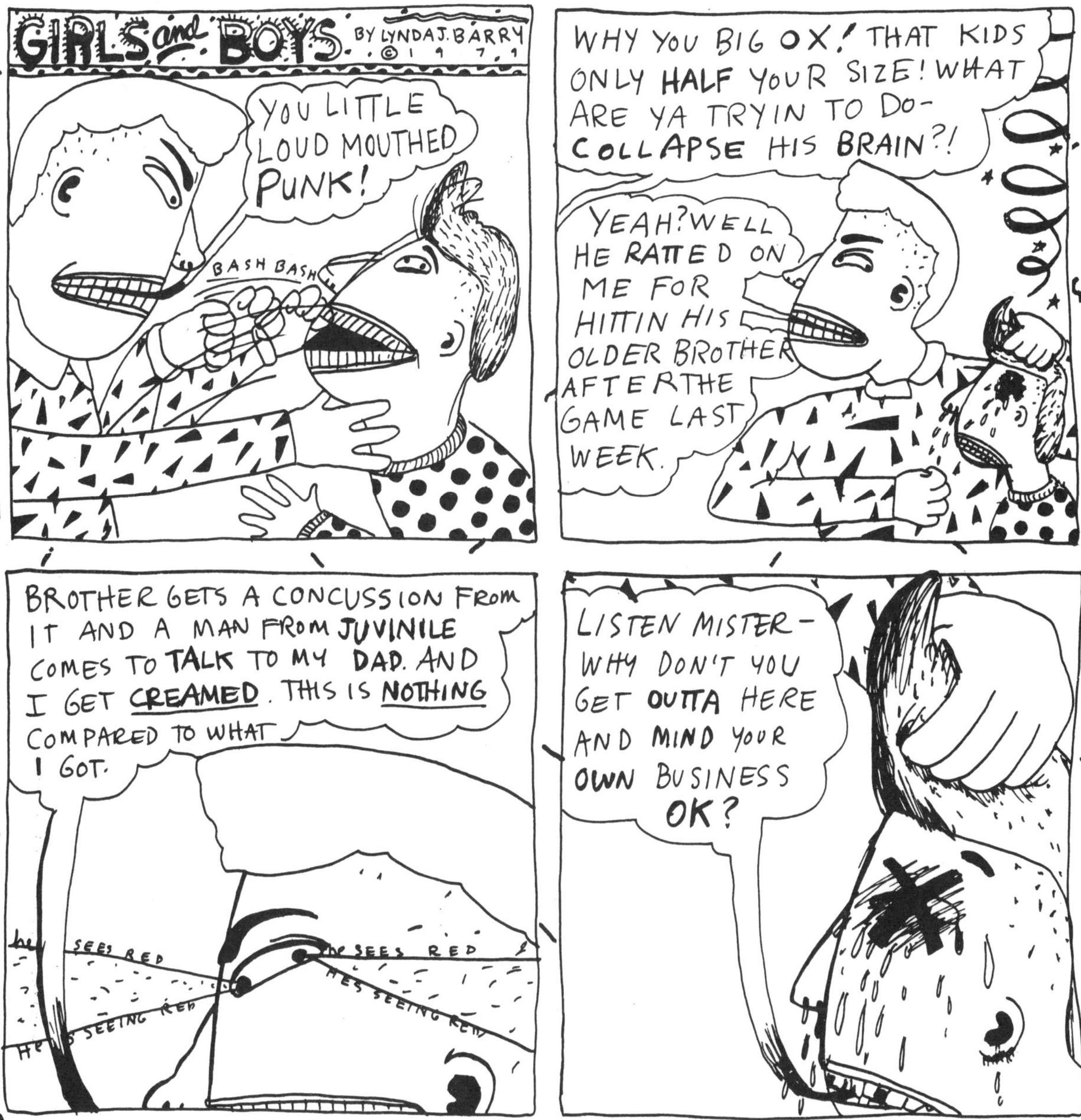
GIRLS and BOYS
BY LYNDA J. BARRY © 1991
YOU LITTLE LOUD MOUTHED PUNK!
BASH BASH
WHY YOU BIG OX! THAT KIDS ONLY HALF YOUR SIZE! WHAT ARE YA TRYIN TO DO- COLLAPSE HIS BRAIN?!
YEAH? WELL HE RATTED ON ME FOR HITTIN HIS OLDER BROTHER AFTER THE GAME LAST WEEK.
BROTHER GETS A CONCUSSION FROM IT AND A MAN FROM JUVINILE COMES TO TALK TO MY DAD. AND I GET CREAMED. THIS IS NOTHING COMPARED TO WHAT I GOT.
HE SEES RED
HE'S SEEING RED
LISTEN MISTER- WHY DON'T YOU GET OUTTA HERE AND MIND YOUR OWN BUSINESS OK?

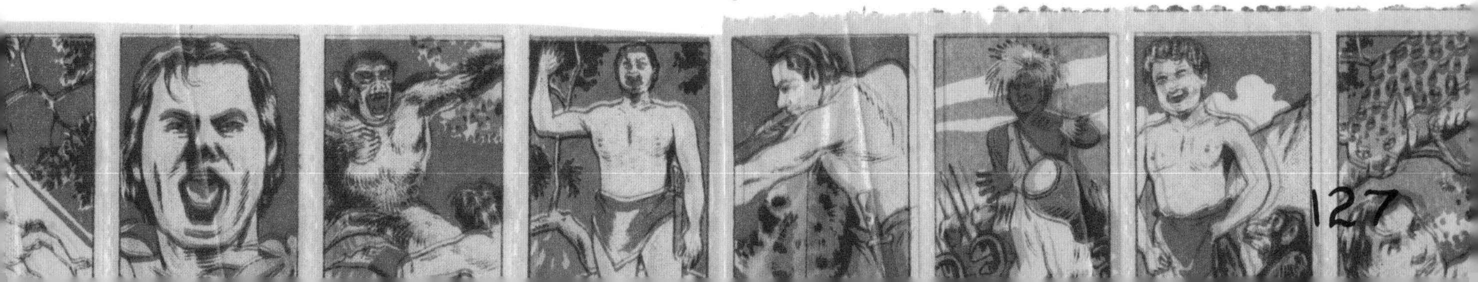

GIRLS and BOYS © 1980
HONEY... DADDY IS ON HIS WAY HOME PUT ON YOUR P.J.s AND-- AND-- UH
MAMA!
MAMA! MAMA! WAKE UP!
SLAM!! STEP STEP STEP
ITS DADDY!
MAMA! WAKE UP! HURRY!
YOU LEAVE HER ALONE DADDY.

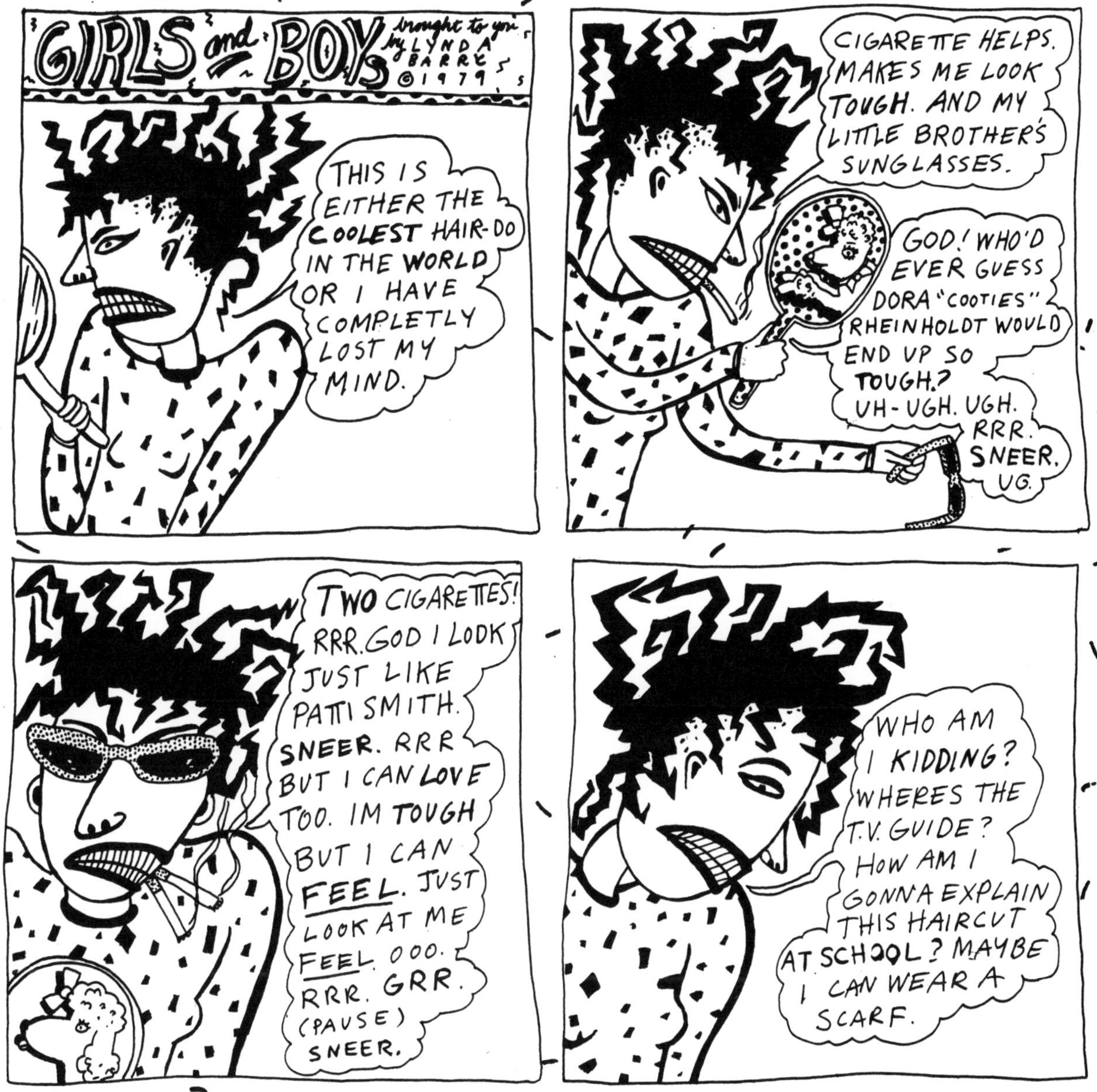
GIRLS and BOYS brought to you by LYNDA BARRY ©1979
THIS IS EITHER THE COOLEST HAIR-DO IN THE WORLD OR I HAVE COMPLETLY LOST MY MIND.
CIGARETTE HELPS. MAKES ME LOOK TOUGH. AND MY LITTLE BROTHER'S SUNGLASSES.
GOD! WHO'D EVER GUESS DORA "COOTIES" RHEINHOLDT WOULD END UP SO TOUGH? UH-UGH. UGH. RRR. SNEER. UG.
TWO CIGARETTES! RRR. GOD I LOOK JUST LIKE PATTI SMITH. SNEER. RRR BUT I CAN LOVE TOO. IM TOUGH BUT I CAN FEEL. JUST LOOK AT ME FEEL OOO. RRR. GRR. (PAUSE) SNEER.
WHO AM I KIDDING? WHERES THE T.V. GUIDE? HOW AM I GONNA EXPLAIN THIS HAIRCUT AT SCHOOL? MAYBE I CAN WEAR A SCARF.

→ When patti smith sings about a space monkey I don'tthink she means Judy. I'm not really sure what she means but whenshe screams ITS JUST MY JACK KNIFE/ITS JUST MY JACK KNIFE I thin she means its just her jack knife.

GIRLS and BOYS © '80 LYNDA BARRY

I remember alot of things about my childhood. Memories of the most ordinary things come to me and I wonder "what made me think of that?" Like my dog's bowl or a T.V. tray that was my favorite.

And then if I think about these things I always become very sad. I think of the people I knew then — and what we did, I think about how I was mean sometimes and I feel sorry. Or I will remember my parents. My mom washing dishes how the water sounded in the sink. Or my dad.

I often feel as if I can go to them again. I will visualize the house, the furniture. But they always seem to be in the next room. It is dim. — I go into each doorway to find them. To say something to them. And then it all fades and I am here. Sitting still.

GIRLS and BOYS
by L. J. Barry
©1977
C'MON KAREN! LETS GO INTO THE DeLEO'S GARAGE AND KISS.
BLONDE + CUTE
I DON'T KNOW BILL. I DON'T KNOW.
AW C'MON. YOU DID IT YESTERDAY
YUK. ICK. BARF. PATOOEY. THIS GARAGE STINKS. THIS WHOLE THING GIVES ME THE CREEPS. WHY AM I EVEN DOING IT?
SHE THINKS
MMM. DO YOU LIKE THIS KAREN?
DO YOU LIKE IT WHEN I DO THIS?
FEEL FEEL
UH, KAREN - IM GONNA BE LATE FOR MY ROUTE - I GUESS I'LL CATCH YOU TOMORROW.
SURE. OK.
I GOT ONE MORE MINUTE
OK! THANKS! SEE YOU TOMORROW! REMEMBER. BE HERE RIGHT AFTER CLASS - OK?
WHY DO I KEEP DOING THIS? IT MAKES ME FEEL SO GROSS. IM NOT GONNA COME HERE TOMORROW. IM GONNA GO STRAIGHT HOME.
BUT WHAT IF HE QUITS LIKING ME.

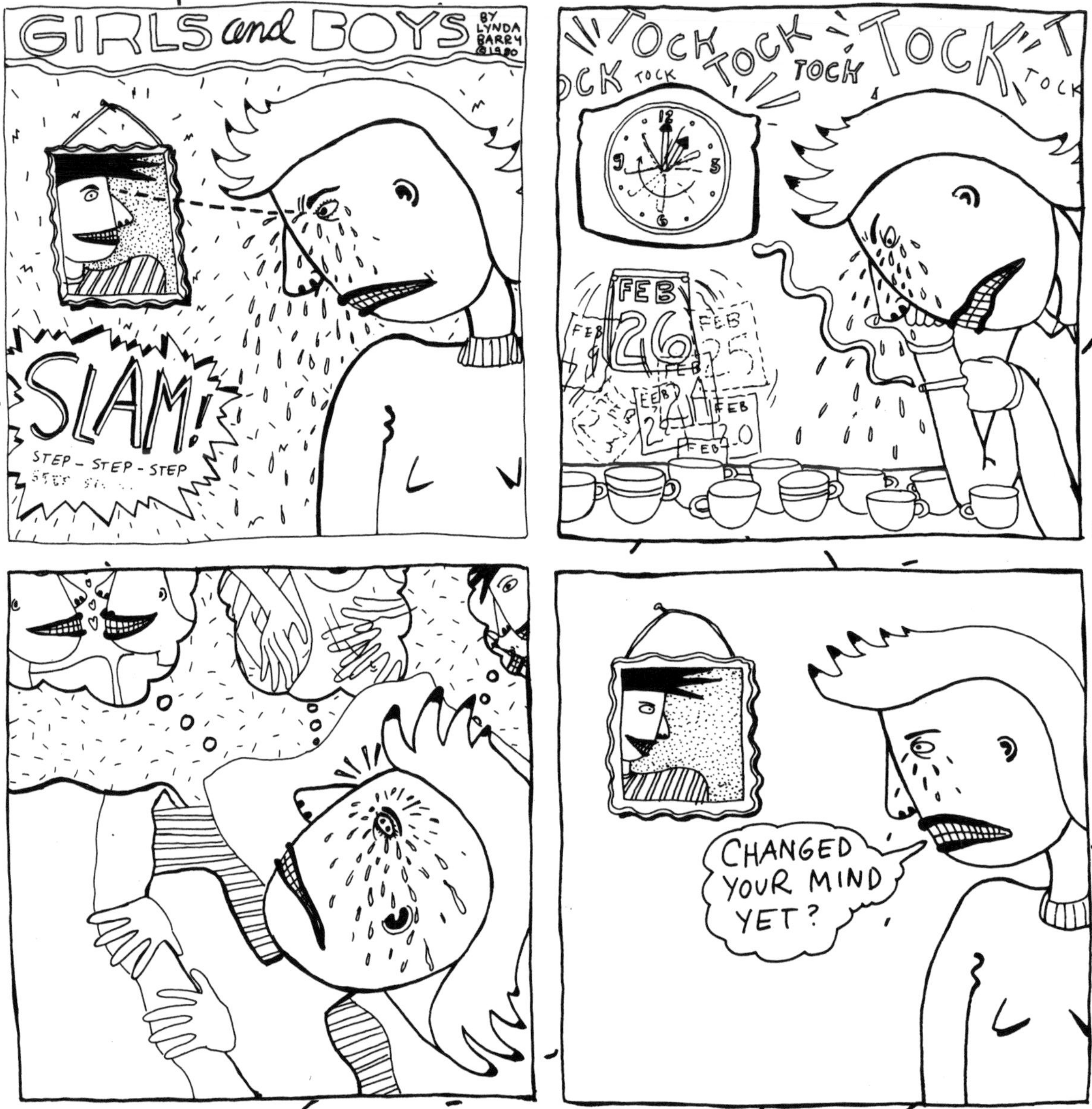
GIRLS and BOYS
BY LYNDA BARRY ©1980
SLAM!
STEP - STEP - STEP
OCK TOCK TOCK TOCK TOCK TOCK T TOCK
FEB 26
FEB 25
FEB 24
FEB 20
CHANGED YOUR MIND YET?

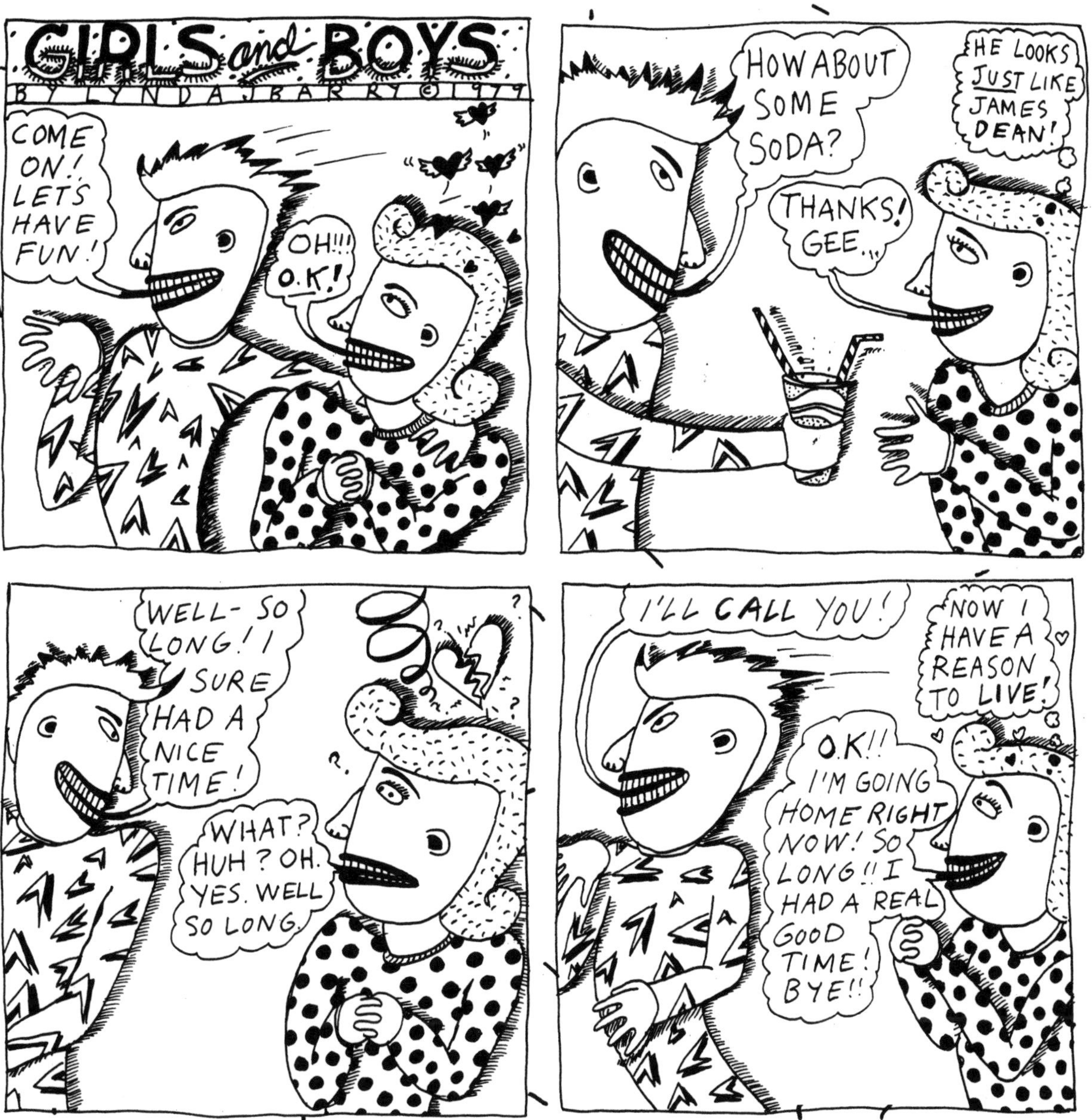
GIRLS and BOYS
BY LYNDA J BARRY ©1979
COME ON! LETS HAVE FUN!
OH!!! O.K!
HOW ABOUT SOME SODA?
HE LOOKS JUST LIKE JAMES DEAN!
THANKS! GEE...
WELL- SO LONG!! I SURE HAD A NICE TIME!
WHAT? HUH? OH. YES. WELL SO LONG.
I'LL CALL YOU!
NOW I HAVE A REASON TO LIVE!
O.K!! I'M GOING HOME RIGHT NOW! SO LONG!! I HAD A REAL GOOD TIME! BYE!!

continued

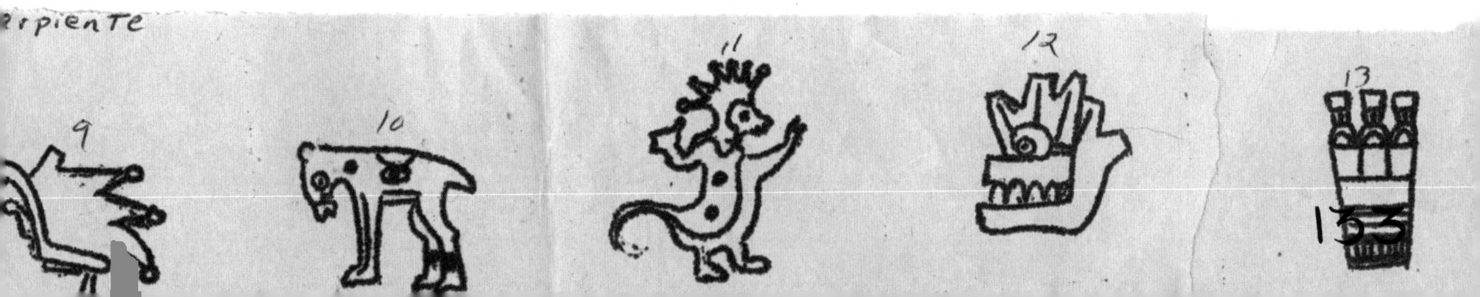
rpiente
9
10
11
12
13

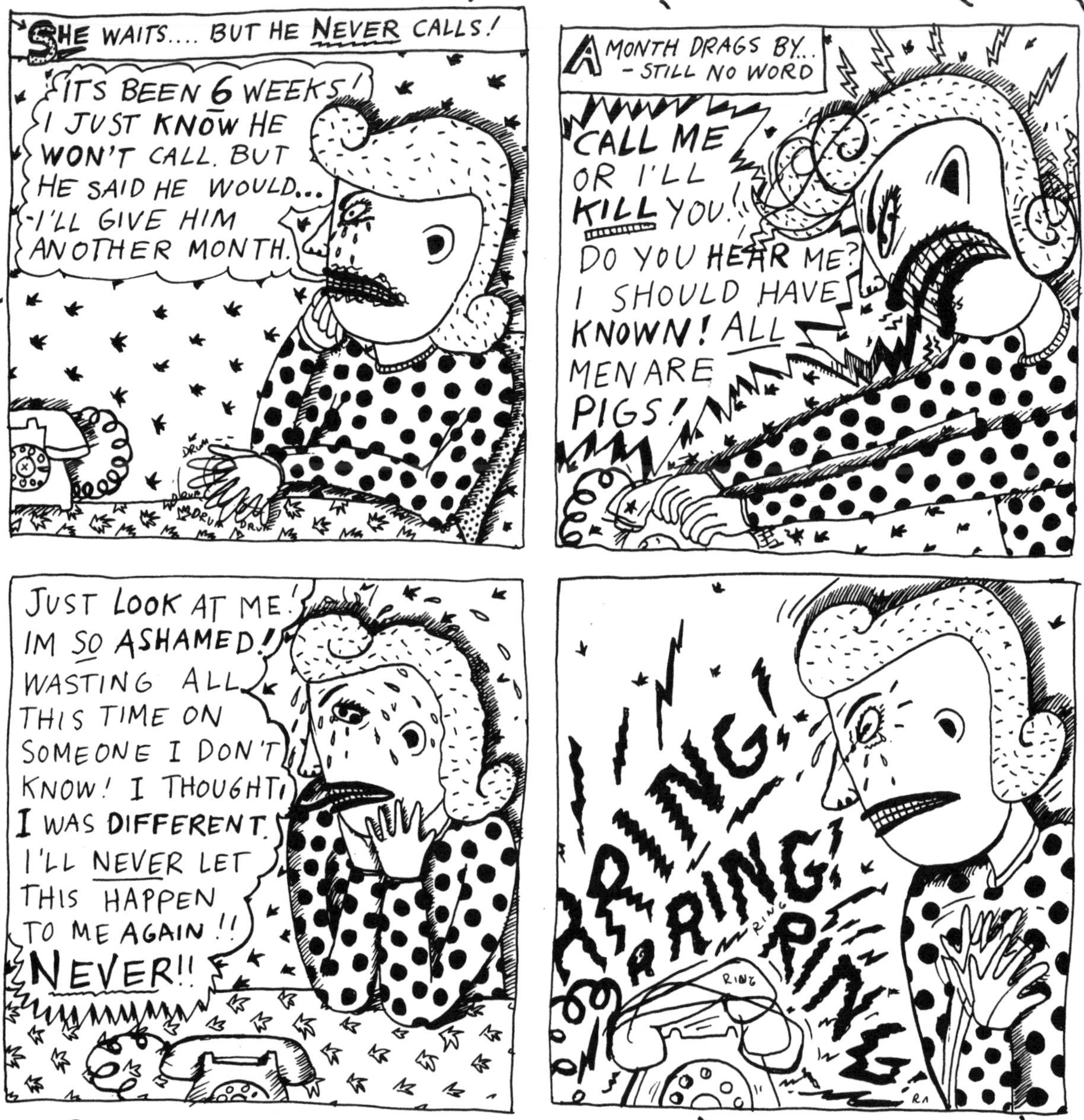
SHE WAITS.... BUT HE NEVER CALLS!
IT'S BEEN 6 WEEKS! I JUST KNOW HE WON'T CALL. BUT HE SAID HE WOULD... -I'LL GIVE HIM ANOTHER MONTH.
DRUM DRUM DRUM DRUM
A MONTH DRAGS BY... - STILL NO WORD
CALL ME OR I'LL KILL YOU! DO YOU HEAR ME? I SHOULD HAVE KNOWN! ALL MEN ARE PIGS!
JUST LOOK AT ME! IM SO ASHAMED! WASTING ALL THIS TIME ON SOMEONE I DON'T KNOW! I THOUGHT I WAS DIFFERENT. I'LL NEVER LET THIS HAPPEN TO ME AGAIN!! NEVER!!
RING! RING! RING! RING!
RING
RING

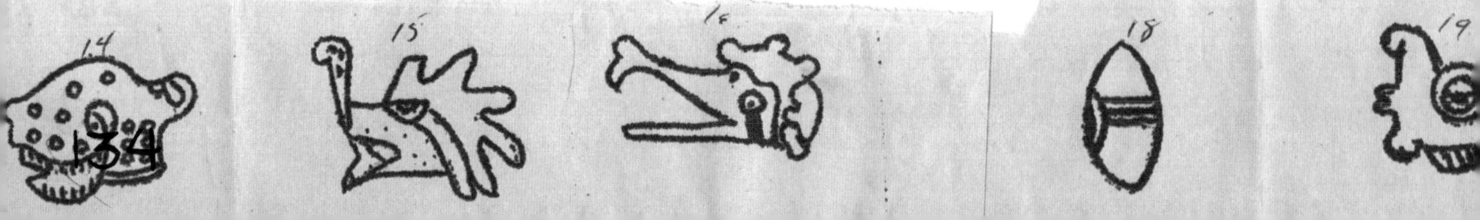
14
15
16
18
19

WONDERFUL NEWS FOR EVERY WOMAN WHO WORRIES ABOUT
FINDING YOUR PERFECT LOVE-MATE
FOR FOR for FOR FOR FOR WOMEN ONLY
Calling all girls! Calling all girls!... Yoo-hoo ladies!!
ITS SPRING AND IF YOU DON'T FIND A LOVE-MATE BY MAY FIRST, YOURE IN FOR IT HONEY, GET ME? IF I WERE YOU I WOULD STEP ON IT. HERE ARE A FEW HINTS TO HELP YOU IN YOUR FABULOUS SEARCH FOR "Mr Right"
SO GRAB A CUP OF COFFEE DEARIE AND PUT ON YOUR THINKING CAP - HERE WE GO!
intelligent
handsome
tall
romantic
Funny
KIND
WRITTEN + DRAWN BY SISTER LYNDA J. BARRY ©'81
Mr "Right"
Ladies ONLY!!
MEN, YOU BETTER STOP READING THIS RIGHT NOW!
SUCCESS BEGINS at HOME!
your keys to happiness.....
Attitude
appearance
FILL out this checklist - ask yourself honestly - where do I need some IMPROVEMENT?
Before You go out looking for that "certain someone, make sure your "house" is in order!!!!
1. Am I cheerful and clean? ☐ yes ☐ no ☐ sort of
2. Do I want a boyfriend for the RIGHT reasons?
☐ I want an intellectual companion.
☐ I have a need to share my life.
☐ I want a man with a big one.
3. How is my personality and my looks?
☐ I am very nice and I am beautiful
☐ I am mean and ugly
4. Am I "too picky" about my future love-mate?
☐ He must be absolutely perfect
☐ I will take any man on earth.
JUST WHO IS Mr Right?
Just what are you looking for in a man? Never mind what others find attractive... what is it that YOU desire. Here is a helpful list to help you define your goals. Check the qualities you feel are important
LOOKS
☐ he MUST BE very handsome
☐ he must be unusually cute
☐ he must not frighten children
BRAINS
☐ he MUST Be a genius
☐ he must be able to read
☐ he must have a big one
Sense of Humor
ha ha ha
☐ he must think my jokes are the funniest ones in the world
☐ he cannot laugh at me
☐ It is OK. if he laughs at others but not to be mean
Penis Size
☐ "I don't really look out for penis size, but I notice it"
☐ Penis size doesn't matter
☐ I want a man with a monster
$ MONEY ?$
☐ He must be solvent
☐ He must be rich
☐ Penis size doesn't matter
JOB
☐ Must have one
☐ Must have one
☐ Must have one
☐ Must have big one
What do I do once I SPOT HIM
Calm down girl. Be cool. Casual. There he is, across the room. At a party, a bar, a cafe, a check out line. THERE HE IS!!!!!
Here are a few TIPS 'N' TRICKS
IDEA "A": always carry a jar with that "too tight" lid in your purse. Take it out and struggle to open it. MAKE SURE YOU FAIL. Walk over to him "nervously" and ask if he would be kind enough to give you "a hand" afterwards, thank him and ask him if he would "take off his pants"
JUST CAN'T OPEN IT
IDEA "B" Shoot a spitwad at him. --- when one "hits," wink and say "Gee. Im sorry. You can "shoot one" at "me" if you'd like to." (This one always gets 'em.)
IDEA "C" Stare at him and smile. Act real "embarassed" when he "catches" you. Offer money. Try to look french.
IDEA "D" Be yourself. Act natural. Let him do the work. If he leaves without speaking to you, follow him to his car and sit on the hood. Let him notice you.
IDEA "E" Go over to him and ask politely "Is this seat taken?" then point to his lap.

What shall we talk ABOUT
Once you've "broken the ice" you want to make "sure" not to "blow it." Alot of women go "wrong" right after they meet a fellow by wanting to talk about doing their hair, their periods, their complexion problems. NIX, gals!! Other girls try to "pal" around with Mr Right by talking about "boy" topics, like salami, trains, cigars, the spaceneedle. No-No, sweets. Lissen up. Remember:
1. Let him pick the conversational topic. Try to figure out just what you think he'll say then timidly say it first - as if you "arent sure"
2. Stare at him while he talks. When you talk look at your hands, embarassed. Interrupt him to feel his muscle. If you have to p, hold it.
3. If he is smart you might try to "impress" him by being smart also. If he is dumb keep feeling his muscles
YES. UH HUH. OH, really?
YA DONT SAY. NO KIDDIN. WELL I'LL BE DAMNED.
BOY ME TOO. IM THE SAME WAY. SAME HERE. I DIG IT.
OK! SURE! LOVE TO!
What Shall we do on OUR 1st DATE
EATING together
is an absolute must!!!! It is said that you can tell what sort of lover a man is by how he eats. Like if he eats real fast then falls asleep right after maybe you better go home. Or if he eats very very slowly and moans each time he puts something in his mouth and talks about what nice food it is and afterwards he pulls the plate gently toward him and strokes its hair and whispers oh baby. Or he might be scared to try different foods. Or he just eats what he wants and leaves the rest unfinished and then picks his teeth and says "gotta go." Maybe he wants to eat only with the lights out or he has to call the food "Mommy"
SO you better go out to eat together. And if you cant, bring a doughnut in your purse and ask him could he please eat it for you.
DOES he like: clams? tacos? twinkies?
IS IT LOVE? HOW CAN I TELL?
LADY, ARE YOU ALL RIGHT?
THUD
1. Which of these things can you no longer do?
☐ anything ☐ everything
2. Do you think about "him" all of the time? ☐ Yes ☐ No
3. Do you think about "him" all of the time? ☐ Yes ☐ No
4. If he wrecks your car through inexcusable carelessness → you say: ☐ Oh. Thats O.K. hon. I didn't like it that much.
☐ Gee ☐ Oh just leave it there, would you like some dinner?
5. Do you find yourself agreeing with everything he says?
☐ Well, he and I have alot in common.
☐ If he says so. ☐ I don't know, ask him.
PLANNING Your FUTURE together
KISS
(ROMEO)
Love nest
matching hula shirts
a cat named "Damien"
FIGHTS
Birth control devices
MAY 1981
NO!

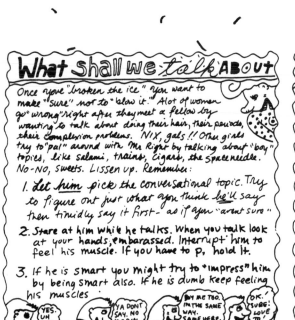

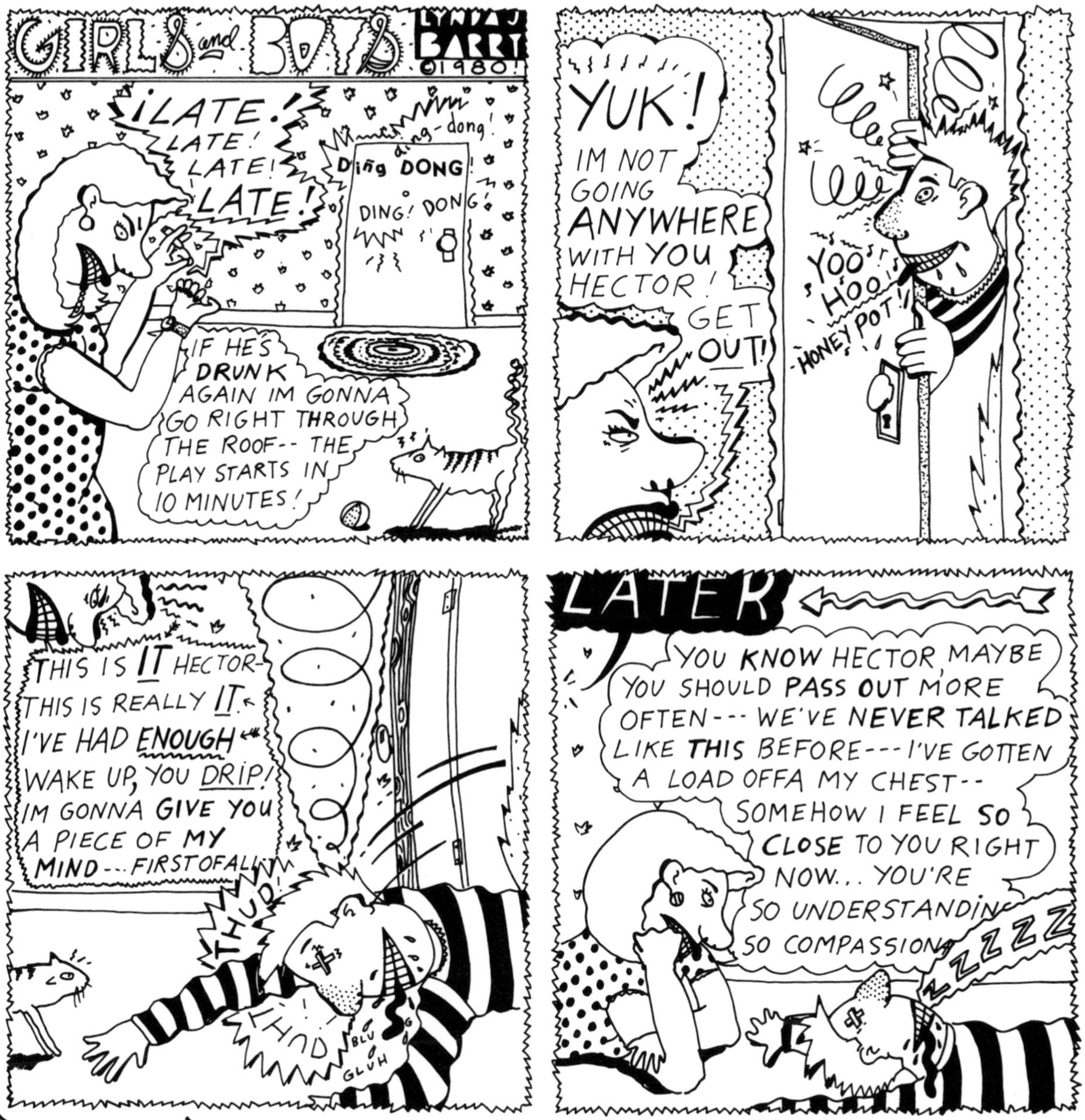
GIRLS and BOYS
LYNDA J. BARRY ©1980!
¡LATE! LATE! LATE! LATE!
ding-dong!
Diñg DONG!
DING! DONG!
IF HE'S DRUNK AGAIN IM GONNA GO RIGHT THROUGH THE ROOF-- THE PLAY STARTS IN 10 MINUTES!
YUK! IM NOT GOING ANYWHERE WITH YOU HECTOR!
GET OUT!
YOO HOO! HONEY POT!
THIS IS IT HECTOR- THIS IS REALLY IT. I'VE HAD ENOUGH WAKE UP, YOU DRIP! IM GONNA GIVE YOU A PIECE OF MY MIND--- FIRSTOFALL
THUD!
THUD
BLU GLUH
LATER
YOU KNOW HECTOR, MAYBE YOU SHOULD PASS OUT MORE OFTEN--- WE'VE NEVER TALKED LIKE THIS BEFORE--- I'VE GOTTEN A LOAD OFFA MY CHEST-- SOMEHOW I FEEL SO CLOSE TO YOU RIGHT NOW... YOU'RE SO UNDERSTANDIN SO COMPASSION
ZZZZZ

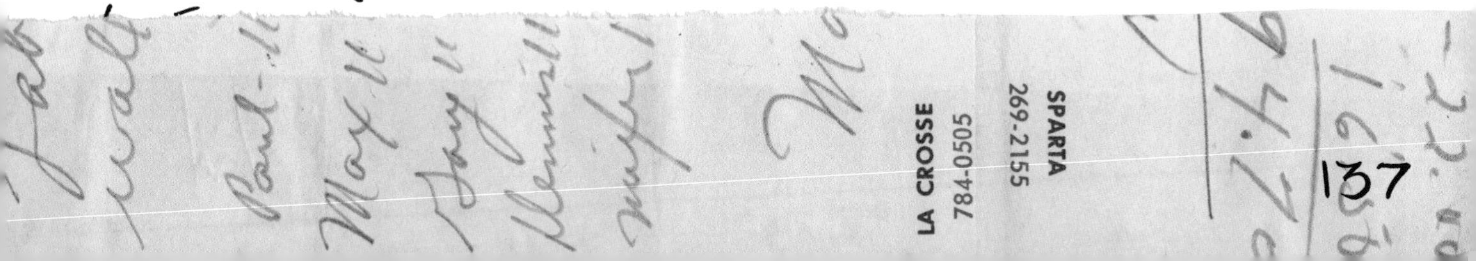
LA CROSSE
784-0505
SPARTA
269-2155

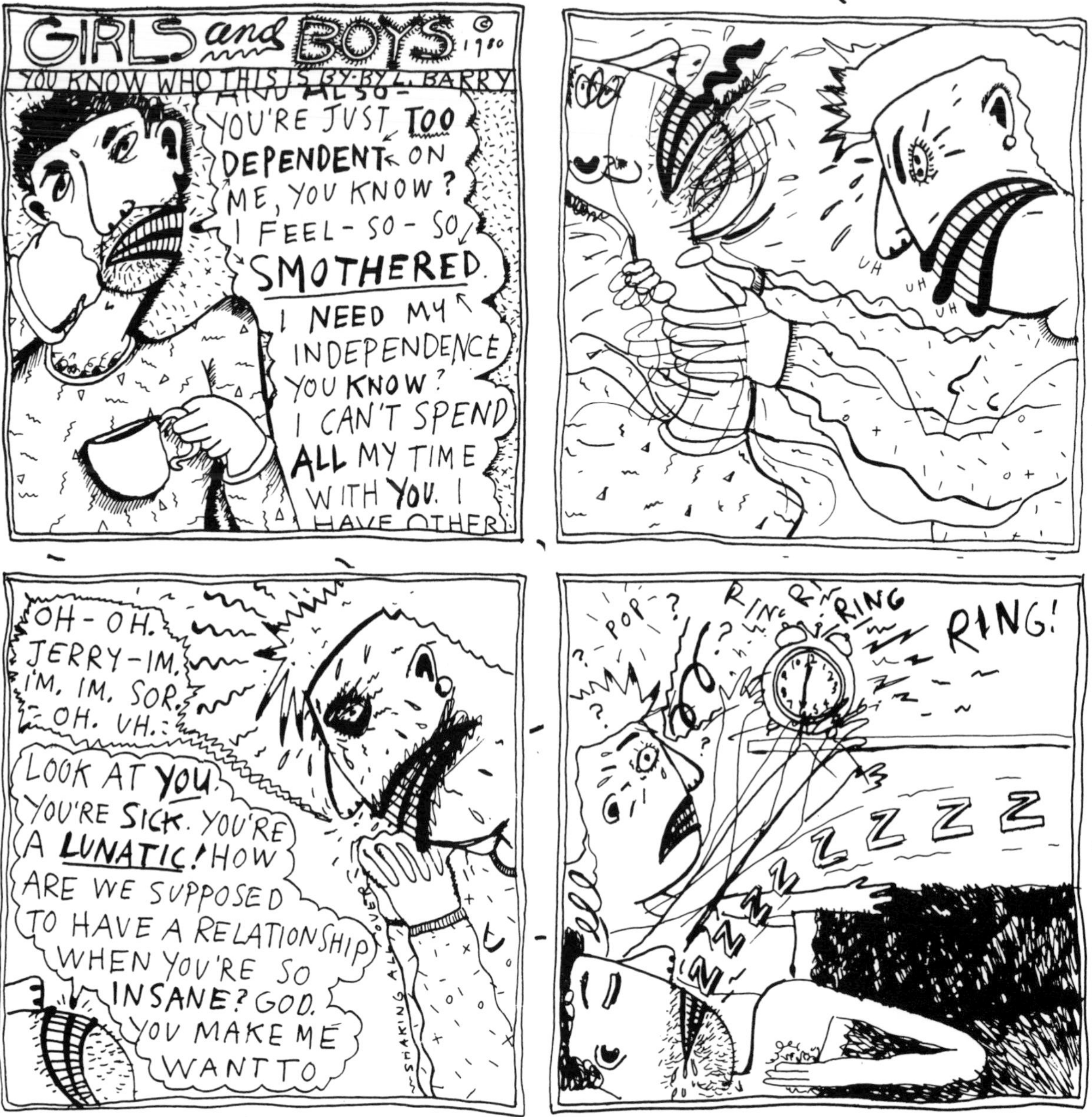
GIRLS and BOYS © 1980
YOU KNOW WHO THIS IS BY·BY L. BARRY
AND ALSO– YOU'RE JUST TOO DEPENDENT ON ME, YOU KNOW? I FEEL–SO–SO SMOTHERED. I NEED MY INDEPENDENCE YOU KNOW? I CAN'T SPEND ALL MY TIME WITH YOU. I HAVE OTHER
UH UH UH
OH-OH. JERRY-IM. IM. IM. SOR. OH. UH.
LOOK AT YOU. YOU'RE SICK. YOU'RE A LUNATIC! HOW ARE WE SUPPOSED TO HAVE A RELATIONSHIP WHEN YOU'RE SO INSANE? GOD. YOU MAKE ME WANT TO
SHAKING ALL OVER
POP
RING RING RING RING!
ZZZZZZ

NOCTURNALITY
(THE NIGHT WORLD)

 Darkness may close the door of one world but it opens the door of another. The night world becomes a world of sounds and smells and of limited sight.

GIRLS + BOYS
DRAWN AT THE LAUNDRO-MAT BY L.J. BARRY © 1980
The Earthwoman has a problem with her wash...
DO YOU THINK YOU CAN CLEAN THIS?
NO ONE CAN CLEAN THAT - IN MY OPINION YOU SHOULD BURN IT, MARY LEE.
THIS SOCK IS ALL HE LEFT ME -- IT SMELLS, BUT ITS ALL I HAVE TO REMEMBER HIM BY.-AT NIGHT I WANT TO EMBRACE IT---
WELL -- MAYBE YOU COULD GET A TETANUS SHOT AND IT WOULD BE ALL RIGHT
SO LONG BABY--- I'LL CALL YA
OH DON,... DONALD... I PRESS THY SOCK TO THESE SAD BREASTS AND LONG ONLY FOR THEE --- DONALDO --- DONNY-- --DON-DON-- WHERE ARE YOU RIGHT NOW? WILL YOU REMEMBER? WILL YOU RETURN?
YOU KNOW, IM EVEN STARTING TO LIKE THE SMELL OF IT--- I GUESS YOU CAN GET USED TO ANYTHING - I GUESS THATS HOW YOU CAN TELL IF ITS REAL LOVE.

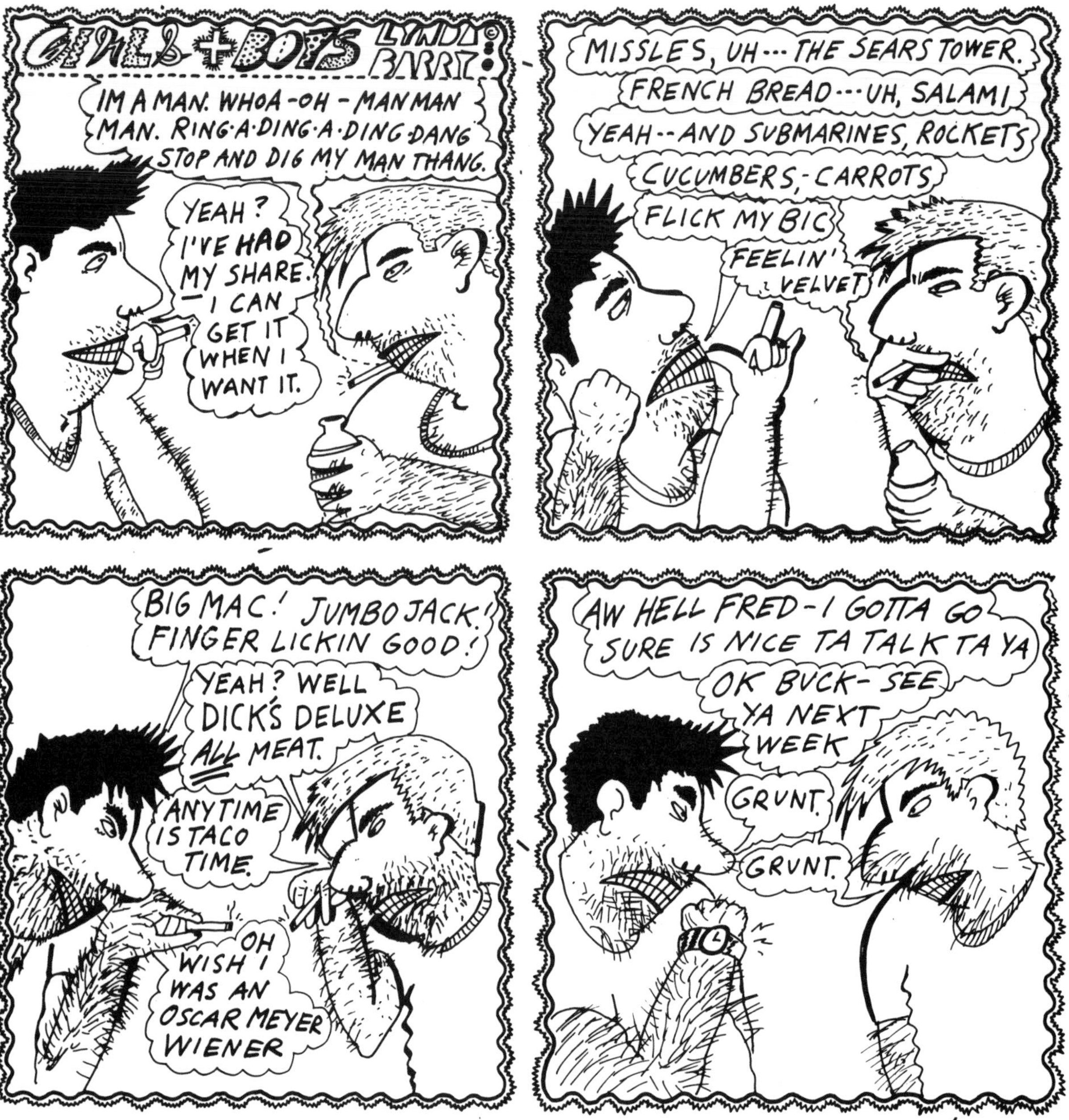
GIRLS + BOYS
LYNDA BARRY ©
IM A MAN. WHOA-OH - MAN MAN MAN. RING·A·DING·A·DING·DANG STOP AND DIG MY MAN THANG.
YEAH? I'VE HAD MY SHARE. — I CAN GET IT WHEN I WANT IT.
MISSLES, UH --- THE SEARS TOWER.
FRENCH BREAD --- UH, SALAMI
YEAH -- AND SUBMARINES, ROCKETS
CUCUMBERS, - CARROTS
FLICK MY BIC
FEELIN' VELVET
BIG MAC! JUMBO JACK! FINGER LICKIN GOOD!
YEAH? WELL DICK'S DELUXE ALL MEAT.
ANYTIME IS TACO TIME.
OH WISH I WAS AN OSCAR MEYER WIENER
AW HELL FRED - I GOTTA GO SURE IS NICE TA TALK TA YA
OK BUCK - SEE YA NEXT WEEK
GRUNT.
GRUNT.

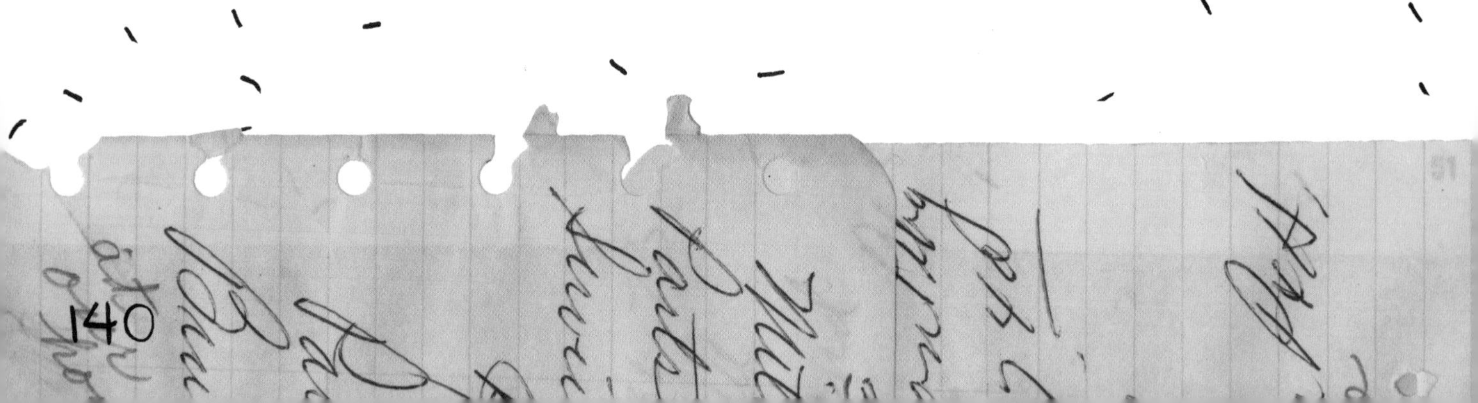

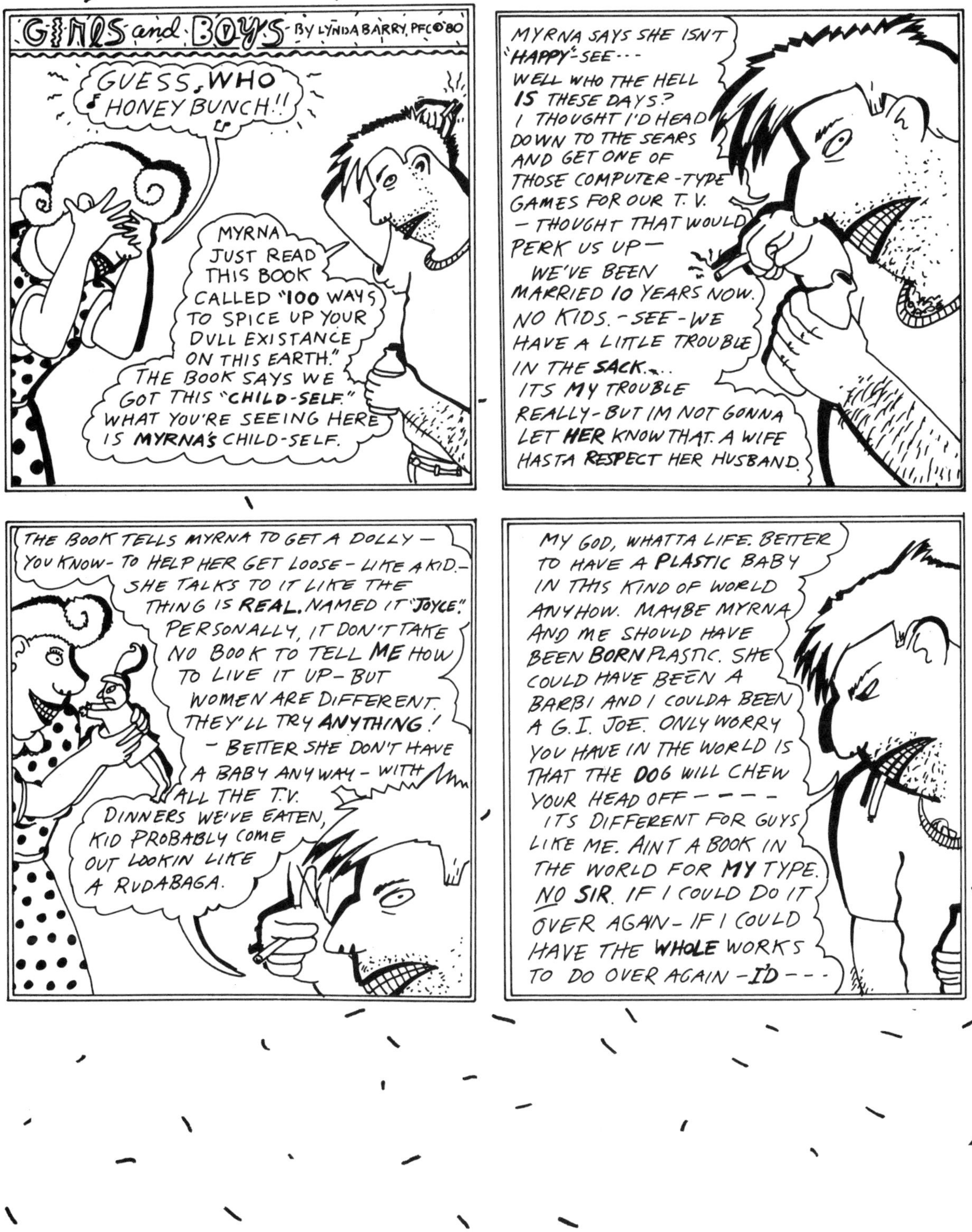
GIRLS and BOYS BY LYNDA BARRY, PFC ©'80
GUESS, WHO HONEY BUNCH!!
MYRNA JUST READ THIS BOOK CALLED "100 WAYS TO SPICE UP YOUR DULL EXISTANCE ON THIS EARTH." THE BOOK SAYS WE GOT THIS "CHILD-SELF." WHAT YOU'RE SEEING HERE IS MYRNA'S CHILD-SELF.
MYRNA SAYS SHE ISN'T "HAPPY"-SEE--- WELL WHO THE HELL IS THESE DAYS? I THOUGHT I'D HEAD DOWN TO THE SEARS AND GET ONE OF THOSE COMPUTER-TYPE GAMES FOR OUR T.V. - THOUGHT THAT WOULD PERK US UP- WE'VE BEEN MARRIED 10 YEARS NOW. NO KIDS.-SEE-WE HAVE A LITTLE TROUBLE IN THE SACK... ITS MY TROUBLE REALLY-BUT IM NOT GONNA LET HER KNOW THAT. A WIFE HASTA RESPECT HER HUSBAND.
THE BOOK TELLS MYRNA TO GET A DOLLY- YOU KNOW- TO HELP HER GET LOOSE-LIKE A KID.- SHE TALKS TO IT LIKE THE THING IS REAL. NAMED IT "JOYCE." PERSONALLY, IT DON'T TAKE NO BOOK TO TELL ME HOW TO LIVE IT UP-BUT WOMEN ARE DIFFERENT. THEY'LL TRY ANYTHING! - BETTER SHE DON'T HAVE A BABY ANYWAY- WITH ALL THE T.V. DINNERS WE'VE EATEN, KID PROBABLY COME OUT LOOKIN LIKE A RUDABAGA.
MY GOD, WHATTA LIFE. BETTER TO HAVE A PLASTIC BABY IN THIS KIND OF WORLD ANYHOW. MAYBE MYRNA AND ME SHOULD HAVE BEEN BORN PLASTIC. SHE COULD HAVE BEEN A BARBI AND I COULDA BEEN A G.I. JOE. ONLY WORRY YOU HAVE IN THE WORLD IS THAT THE DOG WILL CHEW YOUR HEAD OFF---- ITS DIFFERENT FOR GUYS LIKE ME. AINT A BOOK IN THE WORLD FOR MY TYPE. NO SIR. IF I COULD DO IT OVER AGAIN- IF I COULD HAVE THE WHOLE WORKS TO DO OVER AGAIN-I'D---

GIRLS and BOYS ©1980 L. BARRY
OH GOD... JUST LOOK AT HER. SHES SO BEAUTIFUL.
SHUT-UP WILL YA?
SNERT
FREDDY PLEASE.
M-M-M-M-M SMOOTCHIE SMOOTCHIE NUH NUH NUH MMMMMM
YOU KNOW- YOU WOULD'NT KNOW A GOOD TIME IF IT HIT YOU ON THE HEAD. IM GONNA GO OUT AND FIND ME A REAL WOMAN.
THE WORLD ACCORDING TO SNERT
BRING ONE BACK FOR ME TOO, O.K. FREDDY?
SLAM

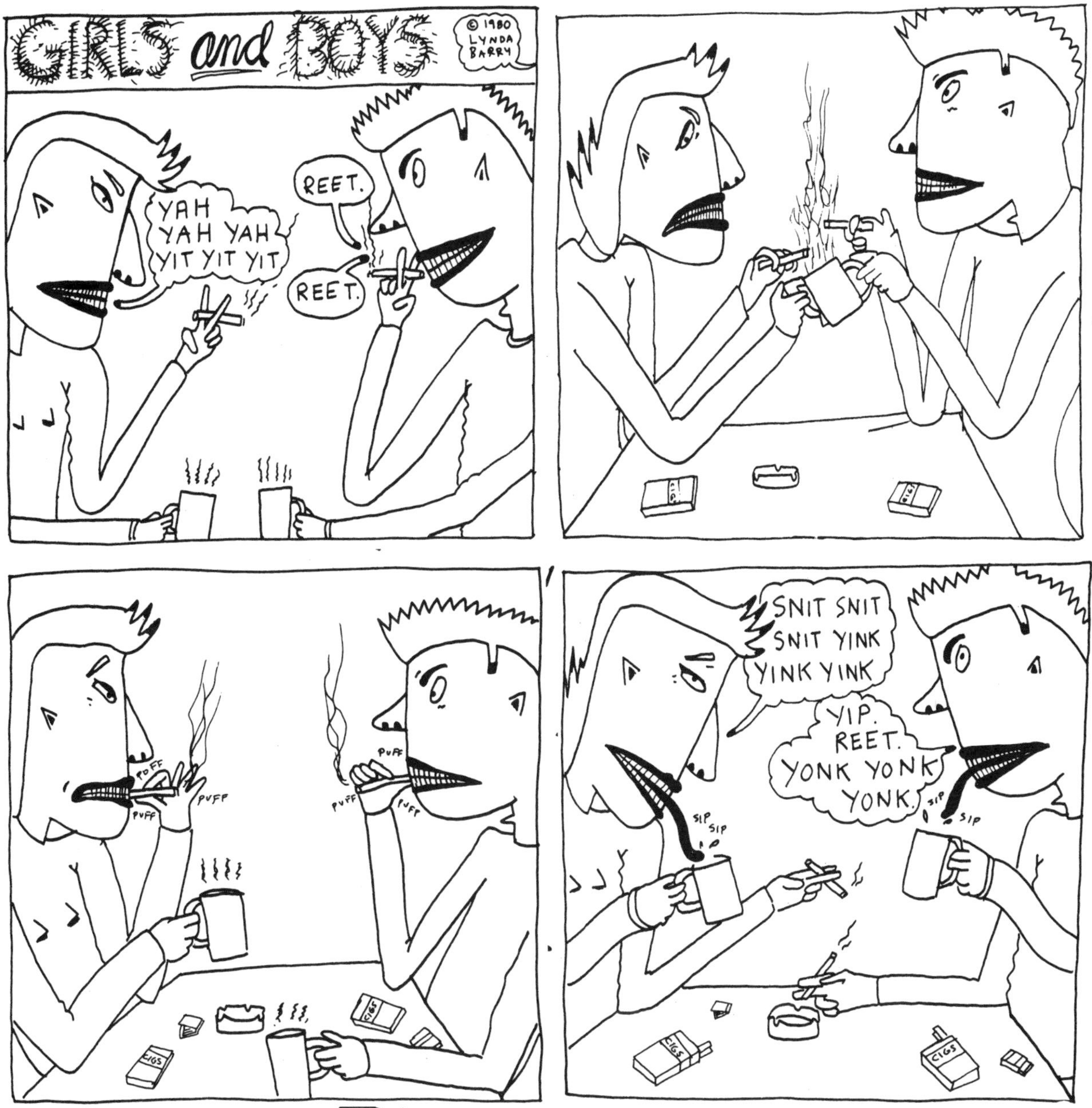
GIRLS and BOYS
© 1980 LYNDA BARRY
YAH YAH YAH YIT YIT YIT
REET.
REET.
CIGS
PUFF
PUFF
PUFF
PUFF
PUFF
PUFF
CIGS
CIGS
SNIT SNIT SNIT YINK YINK YINK
YIP. REET. YONK YONK YONK.
SIP SIP
SIP SIP
CIGS
CIGS

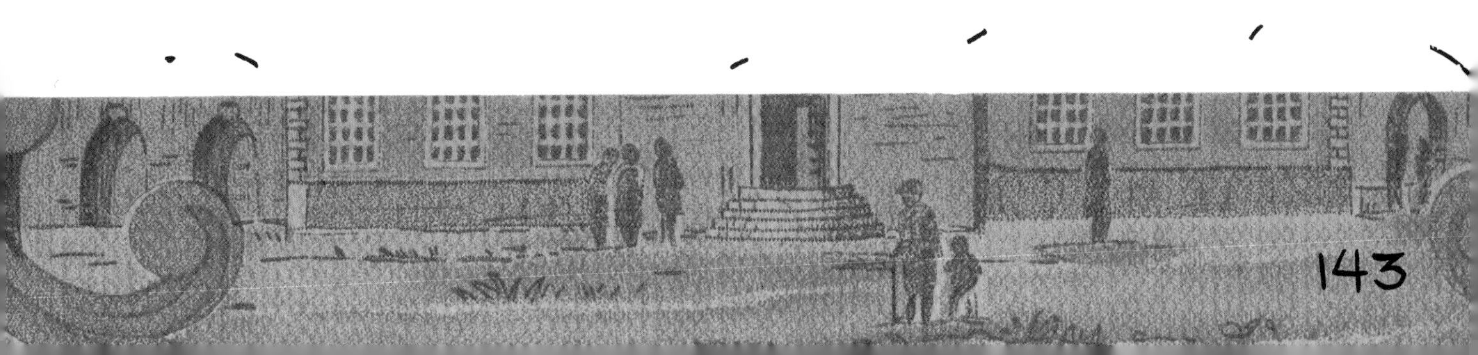

GIRLS and BOYS
© 1980 LYNDA BARRY
NO!!! OH BUT ITS BEEN SUCH A BAD DAY. I'VE FELT SO AWFUL. IM SURE THAT CAKE WOULD MAKE ME FEEL SO MUCH BETTER. ITS SO PRETTY..
MAY I HELP YOU, LADY
NO! HOW MUCH IS THIS CAKE??
30¢
I'LL TAKE IT
IS THIS FOR HERE OR TA GO?
GOD! I MAKE MYSELF SICK. JUST LOOK AT ALL THE PEOPLE IN THE STORE STARING AT ME. I FEEL WORSE THAN I DID.
MAYBE THAT PIE WOULD MAKE ME FEEL BETTER

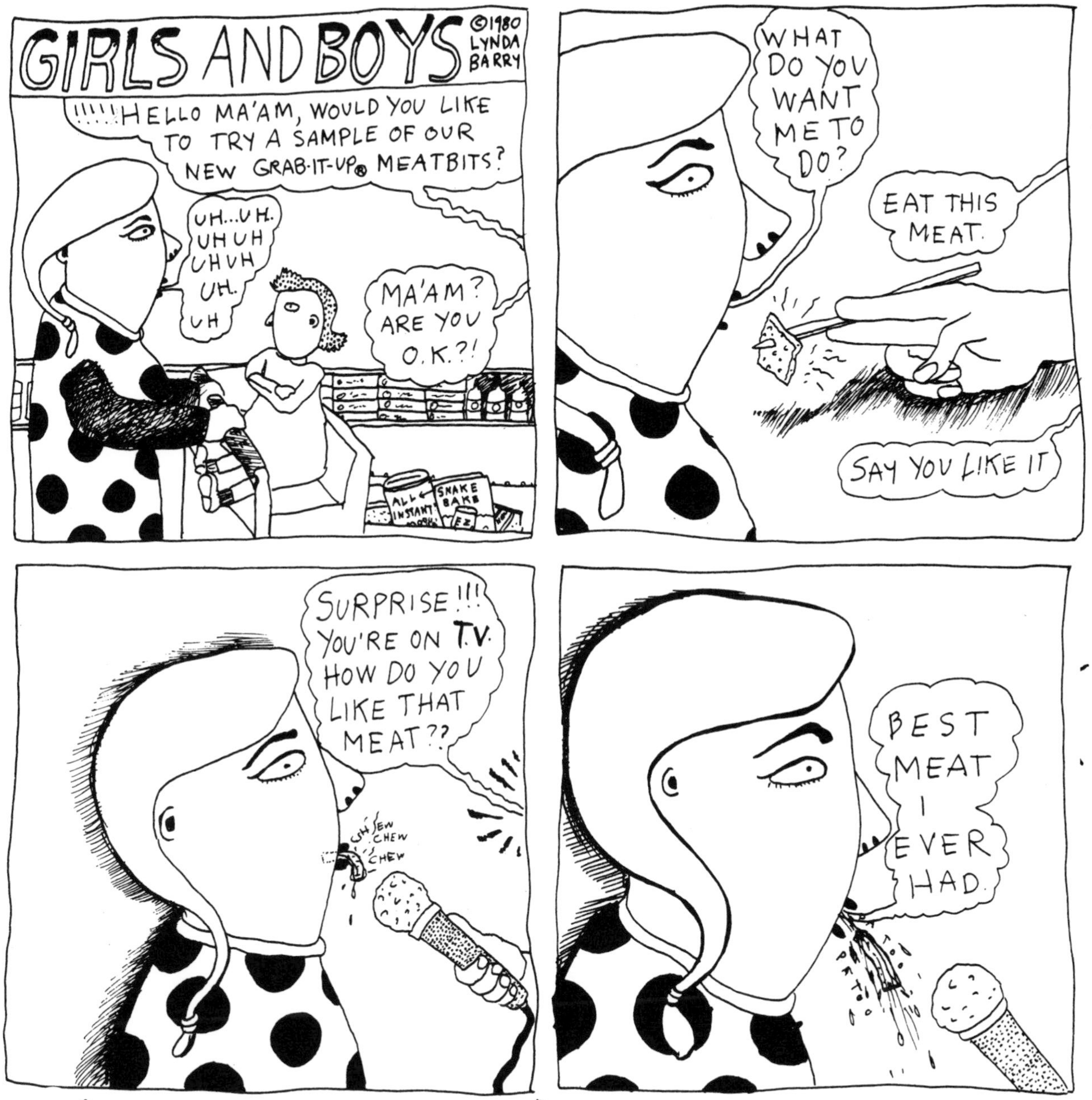

GIRLS AND BOYS
©1980 LYNDA BARRY
!!!!! HELLO MA'AM, WOULD YOU LIKE TO TRY A SAMPLE OF OUR NEW GRAB-IT-UP® MEATBITS?
UH...UH. UHUH UHUH UH. UH
MA'AM? ARE YOU O.K.?!
ALL INSTANT
SNAKE BAKE
WHAT DO YOU WANT ME TO DO?
EAT THIS MEAT.
SAY YOU LIKE IT
SURPRISE!!! YOU'RE ON T.V. HOW DO YOU LIKE THAT MEAT??
BEST MEAT I EVER HAD.

GIRLS and BOYS
©1980 L. BARRY
story by HELEN PARKIN
"This friend of mine bought a pig to fatten up and roast for his company picnic. He bought the pig about six months in advance - it lived in the back -
SHES CRAZY BUT I LOVE HER.
GALLOWS BROS. SAUCE
When the man got drunk he'd go and talk to the pig. He would tell the pig about his wife, Bernice. When they would have a fight he'd go out and sit with the pig --
SURE IS A FRIENDLY FELLA
UNDERSTANDING, TOO.
Friends came by and pretty soon alot of people knew the pig and liked it. Bernice's husband had actually become attatched to it. Pigs are smart animals, you know - -
IS THAT ALL YOU WANT?!
IM JUST HAVING SNIFF SNIFF SNIFF SALAD - IM NOT VERY HUNGRY, BERNICE.
When the time came to kill it, the man just didn't have the heart. So he drove the pig to a place in Renton and they did it there. At the picnic no one would eat it and everyone felt awful.

Girls + Boys
BY LYNDA J. BARRY ©1980
THERE IS NO DOUBT THAT I AM THE SMALLEST WOMAN ON EARTH!
no. 2
(3 TIMES HER ACTUAL SIZE)
MY MOUTH IS SO SMALL I CANNOT EVEN EAT A PEANUT WITH COMFORT. AND FORGET THAT SOMEDAY I SHOULD FIND A HUSBAND! I WILL ALWAYS LIVE ALONE- SMALLER THAN BARBI.
ALTHOUGH IT IS AT TIMES VERY LONELY, I TELL MYSELF "LIZAVITA, YOU ARE THE EARTH'S SMALLEST WOMAN." THERE IS NO ONE SMALLER.
HEY FATSO! GOTTA LIGHT?

THAT HORRIBLE COMIC STRIP! BY L.B. © '80
QUIT YOUR JOB TODAY.
NO! NO! KEEP YOUR JOB! HOW WILL YOU SURVIVE?!? YOU ARE LUCKY TO HAVE A JOB!
YOU SPEND 8 HOURS A DAY COOKING THESE— AND YOU HATE IT! BUT YOU DO IT EVERYDAY. HOW GROSS!
BUT YOU NEED THE MONEY. ALTHOUGH BEING A WEENIE COOKER DOESN'T FULFILL YOU, YOU MUST PAY THE RENT!!!
AT NIGHT YOU LAY IN YOUR BED AND THINK ABOUT ALL OF THE THINGS YOU WANT TO DO IN YOUR LIFE. YOU CURSE THIS STUPID JOB AND WHAT YOU'VE BECOME BECAUSE OF IT. IN THE MORNING YOU GO TO WORK— AND YOU'RE RIGHT ON TIME.
YOU'RE STILL GETTING YOURSELF TOGETHER! IF YOU ARE A BIT NERVOUS, YOU CAN TAKE A CLASS! THIS JOB ISN'T SO BAD. YOU KNOW THAT YOU WON'T BE DOING IT FOREVER... ONE DAY YOU'LL GET YOUR SELF TOGETHER
POP!
WHAT?! WHAT?!
RING

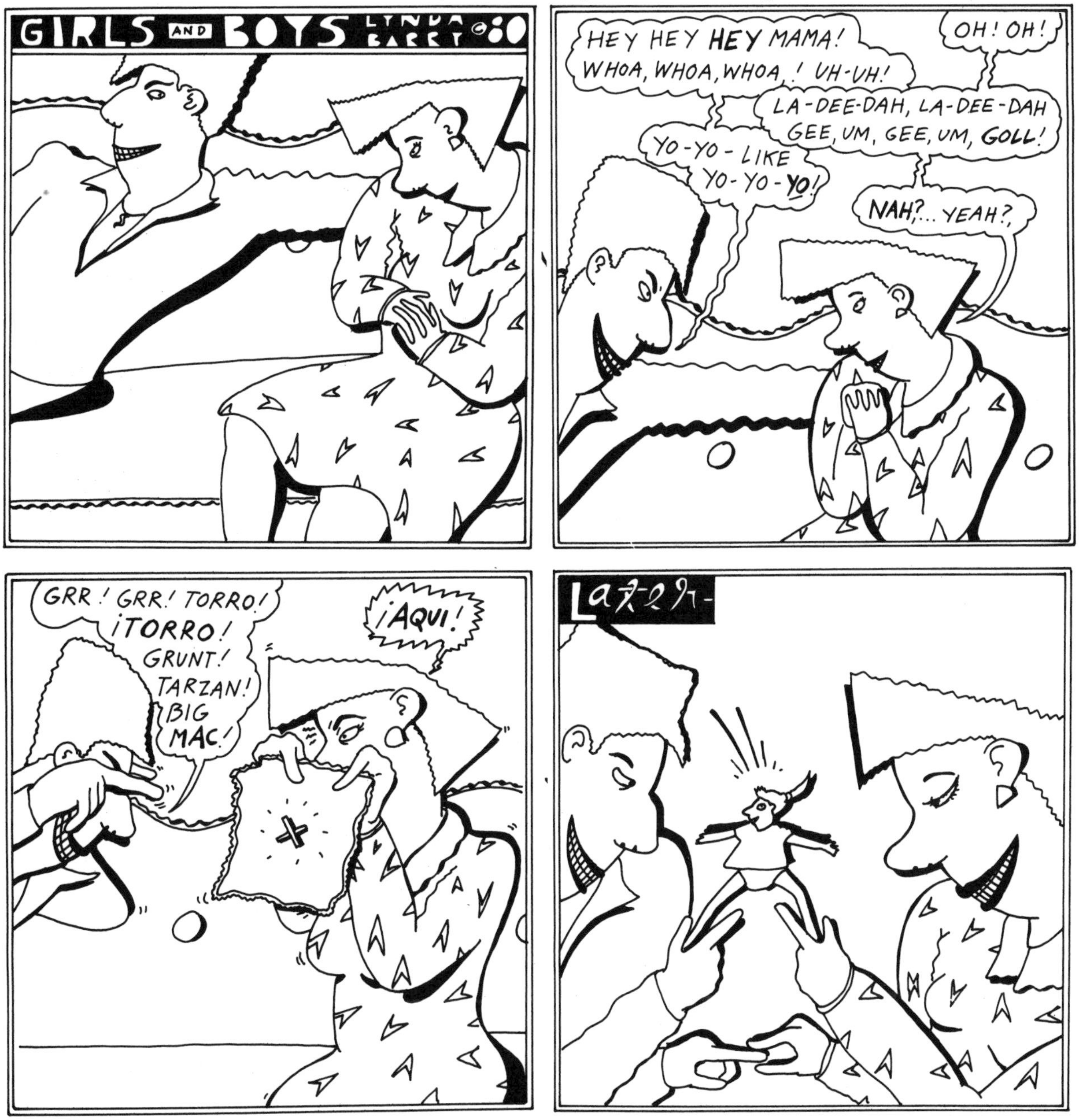
GIRLS AND BOYS
LYNDA BARRY ©80
HEY HEY HEY MAMA! WHOA, WHOA, WHOA! UH-UH!
OH! OH!
LA-DEE-DAH, LA-DEE-DAH GEE, UM, GEE, UM, GOLL!
YO-YO-LIKE YO-YO-YO!
NAH?... YEAH?
GRR! GRR! TORRO! ¡TORRO! GRUNT! TARZAN! BIG MAC!
¡AQUI!

ERNIE POOK COMEEK
BY LYNDA J BARRY
HERES ONE BINKY----"HELP WANTED. WE NEED SOMEONE TO COME AND WORK AT THIS NICE JOB AND MAKE MONEY." BOY THAT SOUNDS OK---"THE HAPPY HOTDOG--9999 WEST 1ST STREET" LETS GO!
GIVE UP.
LATER
OK MAM-THAT SUIT FITS YOU FINE.
LETS SEE HOW YOU HOLD A HOT DOG. VERY GOOD. WE AT THE HAPPY HOT DOG TAKE OUR WEENIES VERY VERY SERIOUSLY. BUT IM SURE YOU'LL DO FINE.
I THINK WE'LL START YOU AT OUR WEINER WINDOW-SEE HOW YA DO THERE
SHE THINKS
BOY-THERE IS SOMETHING KINDA "FUNNY" ABOUT THIS PLACE---EVERYONE LOOKS LIKE A HOT DOG. ITS SORTA CREEPY---
HER THOUGHTS
YOU'RE NEW HERE ARENCHA BABY? NEVER SEEN YOU BEFORE.
HERES YOUR JUMBO DOG SIR-THAT'L BE 99¢
I COULD SHOW YOU A JUMBO DOG MAMA
WEINER WIN
Jumbo dog - 99¢
Deluxe Dog - 99¢
Kitty Dog - 99¢
Show dog - 99¢
Low dog - 99¢
Hard dog - 99¢
Mean dog - 99¢
Dead dog - free
NO MAM-THE HOT DOG SUIT DOESN'T COME OFF--DIDN'T ANY ONE TELL YOU? YOU HAVE TO WEAR IT FOR THE REST OF YOUR LIFE
HA HA HA HA HA HA HA HA
RING RING RING
POP

TRUE COMEEK = CAN YOU HANDLE IT? BY L. J. BARRY © 81
OH FOR PETES SAKE!
NOTHING - I JUST SPILLED THE COFFEE - GO ON, THEN WHAT?
WELL! ID NEVER LET ANY MAN TALK TO ME THAT WAY!!! HOW CAN SHE STAND HIM?! ----- IN PUBLIC TOO! I'D RATHER DIE THAN GO THROUGH THAT KIND OF TORTURE!
(TRIMLINE)
WHAT??
BOY, I'LL SAY. NO KIDDIN. NOT THIS LADY! NO SIR. SINGLE LIFE IS JUST FINE WITH ME. WHO WANTS THAT KIND OF GRIEF FOR CRISSAKES?? SO YOU GOTTA DATE TANITE? WANNA PLAY CARDS? — OH. WITH THAT SCHMOE MARTY? I DON'T KNOW HOW YOU CAN STAND THAT GUY. O.K. ITS YOUR FUNERAL. O.K. I'LL SEE YA GIGI, BYE.
CLICK

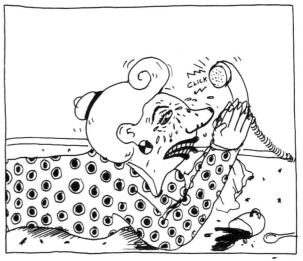

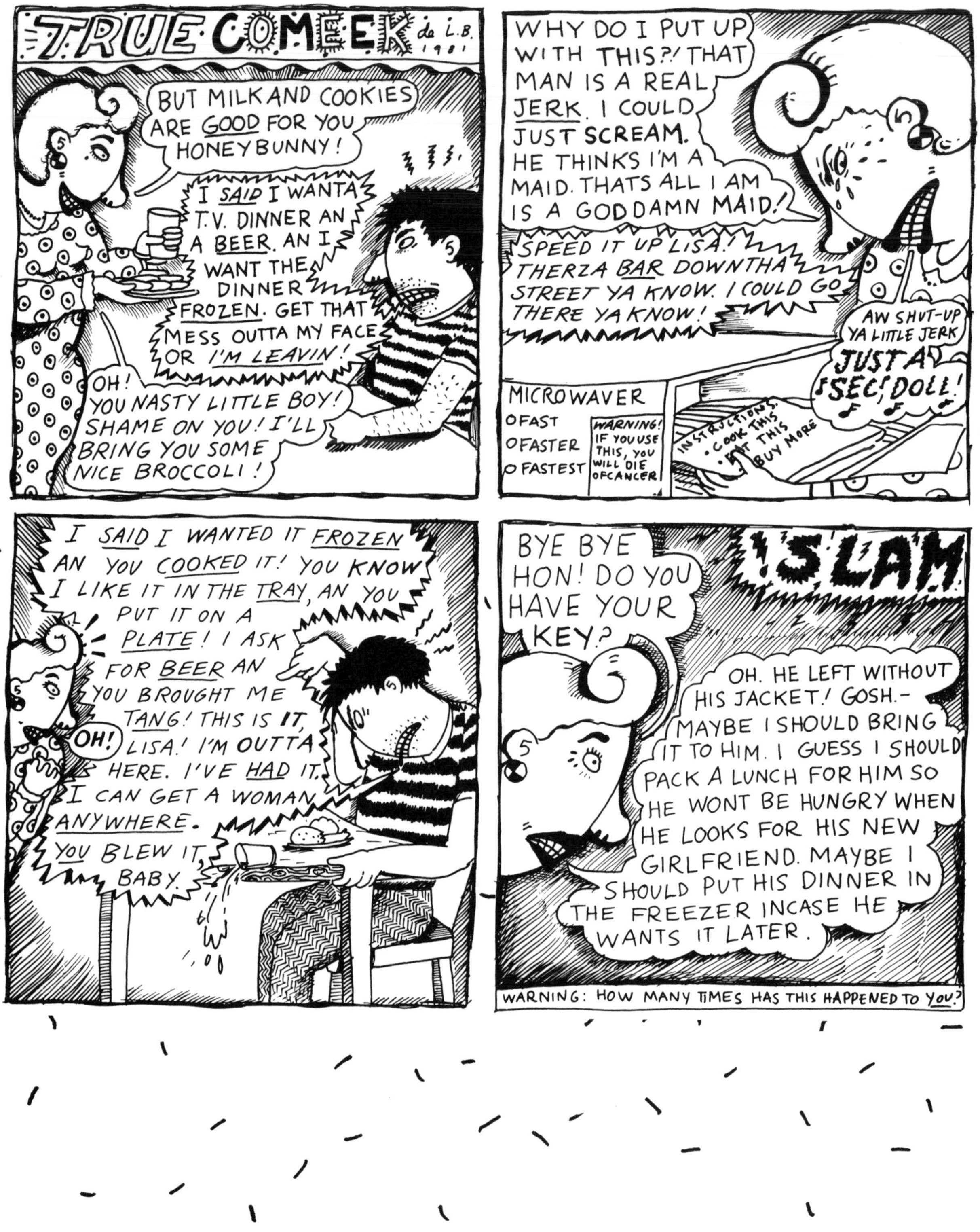
TRUE COMEEK
de L.B. 1981
BUT MILK AND COOKIES ARE GOOD FOR YOU HONEYBUNNY!
I SAID I WANTA T.V. DINNER AN A BEER. AN I WANT THE DINNER FROZEN. GET THAT MESS OUTTA MY FACE OR I'M LEAVIN!
OH! YOU NASTY LITTLE BOY! SHAME ON YOU! I'LL BRING YOU SOME NICE BROCCOLI!
WHY DO I PUT UP WITH THIS?! THAT MAN IS A REAL JERK. I COULD JUST SCREAM. HE THINKS I'M A MAID. THATS ALL I AM IS A GODDAMN MAID!
SPEED IT UP LISA! THERZA BAR DOWNTHA STREET YA KNOW. I COULD GO THERE YA KNOW!
AW SHUT-UP YA LITTLE JERK
JUST A SEC, DOLL!
MICROWAVER
FAST
FASTER
FASTEST
WARNING! IF YOU USE THIS, YOU WILL DIE OF CANCER
INSTRUCTIONS: • COOK THIS • EAT THIS • BUY MORE
I SAID I WANTED IT FROZEN AN YOU COOKED IT! YOU KNOW I LIKE IT IN THE TRAY, AN YOU PUT IT ON A PLATE! I ASK FOR BEER AN YOU BROUGHT ME TANG! THIS IS IT, LISA! I'M OUTTA HERE. I'VE HAD IT. I CAN GET A WOMAN ANYWHERE. YOU BLEW IT, BABY.
OH!
BYE BYE HON! DO YOU HAVE YOUR KEY?
SLAM
OH. HE LEFT WITHOUT HIS JACKET! GOSH.- MAYBE I SHOULD BRING IT TO HIM. I GUESS I SHOULD PACK A LUNCH FOR HIM SO HE WONT BE HUNGRY WHEN HE LOOKS FOR HIS NEW GIRLFRIEND. MAYBE I SHOULD PUT HIS DINNER IN THE FREEZER INCASE HE WANTS IT LATER.
WARNING: HOW MANY TIMES HAS THIS HAPPENED TO YOU?

4 WAYS to HELP CURB your USELESS ANGER
OUTTA MY WAY SQUIRT!
a public service announcement by Mr Lynda J. Barry, PFC
TRUE cömeek de LYNDA J. BARRY © '81
YOU WHAT?
USE Self Control!!
THIS
OH! YOU HAVE BROKEN THE VASE MY DEAD GRANDMOTHER GAVE ME THROUGH INEXCUSABLE CARELESSNESS! OOPSIE-DAISY!!
NOT THIS
USE Cheerfulness!!
THIS
YOU'VE BEEN SLEEPING WITH MY BEST FRIEND? GEE WIZ! WELL I GUESS THATS THE WAY THE BALL BOUNCES!! WELL-HAVE A NICE DAY!
NOT THIS
AUGHH
BE Understanding
THIS
THIS IS SUCH A GOOD MOVIE!! I CAN SEE WHY YOU WANT TO TALK REAL LOUD THROUGH THE WHOLE THING AND CHEW ICE AND TAP YOUR FEET AND SMACK YOUR GUM AND EAT POPCORN WITH YOUR MOUTH OPEN, HONEY.
NOT THIS
SQUIRT
SQUIRT
drink drink!
USE OF SQUIRT GUN IS VERY EFFECTIVE IN DARK THEATERS - Ed.
BE Open Minded!!
YOU'RE LEAVING ME BECAUSE YOU NEED MORE PERSONAL SPACE AND YOU THINK IM OVERBEARING?? THOSE ARE 2 VERY GOOD REASONS DEAR. I CAN DIG IT! TOODALOO!! THANKS! AND WE'LL ALWAYS BE PALS.
HERE THOUGH SWEETIE, HAVE A CUP OF COFFEE BEFORE YOU GO.
PURE POISON
YECH
STOP
DO NOT TURN PAGE

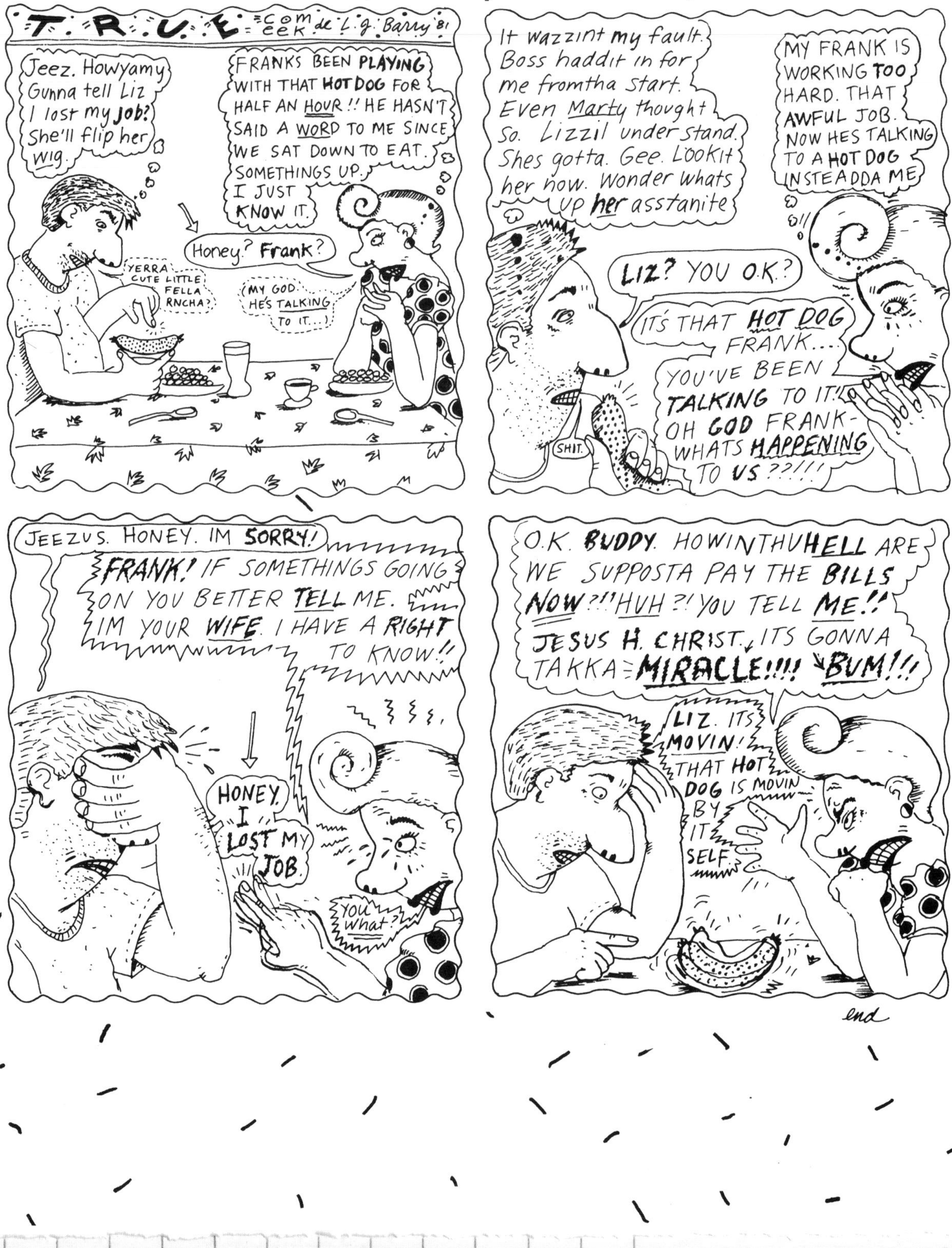
T.R.U.E. comeek de L.g. Barry '81
Jeez. Howyamy Gunna tell Liz I lost my JOB? She'll flip her wig.
FRANKS BEEN PLAYING WITH THAT HOT DOG FOR HALF AN HOUR!! HE HASN'T SAID A WORD TO ME SINCE WE SAT DOWN TO EAT. SOMETHINGS UP. I JUST KNOW IT.
Honey? Frank?
YERRA CUTE LITTLE FELLA RNCHA?
(MY GOD. HE'S TALKING TO IT...)
It wazzint my fault. Boss haddit in for me fromtha start. Even Marty thought so. Lizzil understand. Shes gotta. Gee. Lookit her now. Wonder whats up her asstanite
MY FRANK IS WORKING TOO HARD. THAT AWFUL JOB. NOW HES TALKING TO A HOT DOG INSTEADDA ME
LIZ? YOU O.K?
IT'S THAT HOT DOG FRANK... YOU'VE BEEN TALKING TO IT! OH GOD FRANK- WHATS HAPPENING TO US??!!!
SHIT.
JEEZUS. HONEY. IM SORRY!
FRANK! IF SOMETHINGS GOING ON YOU BETTER TELL ME. IM YOUR WIFE. I HAVE A RIGHT TO KNOW!!
HONEY. I LOST MY JOB.
YOU what?
O.K. BUDDY. HOWINTHUHELL ARE WE SUPPOSTA PAY THE BILLS NOW?!! HUH?! YOU TELL ME!! JESUS H. CHRIST. ITS GONNA TAKKA MIRACLE!!!! BUM!!!
LIZ. ITS MOVIN! THAT HOT DOG IS MOVIN BY IT SELF.
end

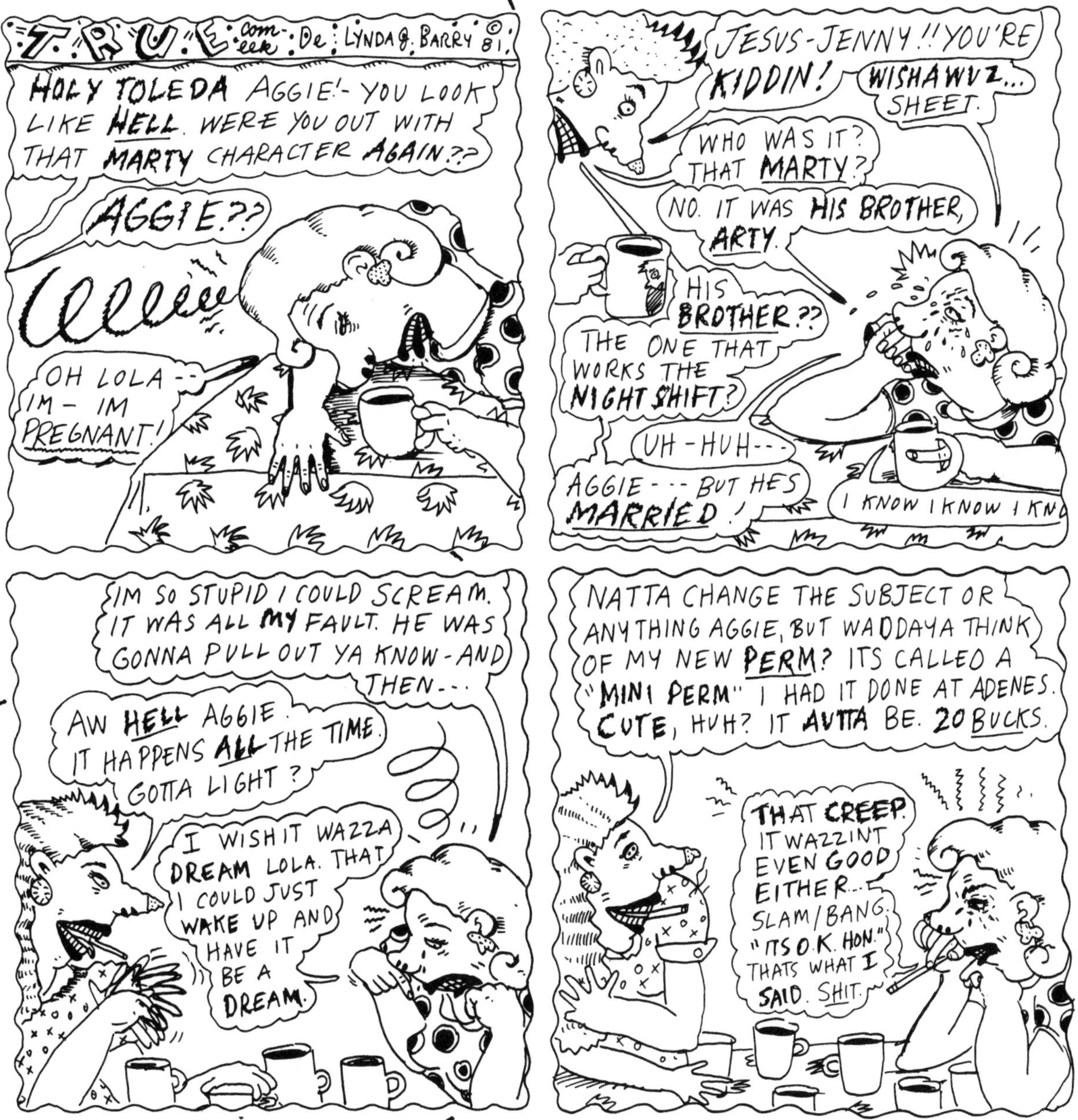
T.R.U.E. com-eek :De: LYNDA J. BARRY © 81.
HOLY TOLEDA AGGIE! - YOU LOOK LIKE HELL. WERE YOU OUT WITH THAT MARTY CHARACTER AGAIN??
AGGIE??
OH LOLA -- IM - IM PREGNANT!
JESUS-JENNY!! YOU'RE KIDDIN!
WISHAWUZ... SHEET.
WHO WAS IT? THAT MARTY?
NO. IT WAS HIS BROTHER, ARTY.
HIS BROTHER?? THE ONE THAT WORKS THE NIGHT SHIFT?
UH-HUH--
AGGIE--- BUT HE'S MARRIED!
I KNOW I KNOW I KN
IM SO STUPID I COULD SCREAM. IT WAS ALL MY FAULT. HE WAS GONNA PULL OUT YA KNOW - AND THEN---
AW HELL AGGIE. IT HAPPENS ALL THE TIME. GOTTA LIGHT?
I WISH IT WAZZA DREAM LOLA. THAT I COULD JUST WAKE UP AND HAVE IT BE A DREAM.
NATTA CHANGE THE SUBJECT OR ANYTHING AGGIE, BUT WADDAYA THINK OF MY NEW PERM? ITS CALLED A "MINI PERM" I HAD IT DONE AT ADENES. CUTE, HUH? IT AUTTA BE. 20 BUCKS.
THAT CREEP. IT WAZZINT EVEN GOOD EITHER... SLAM/BANG. "ITS O.K. HON." THATS WHAT I SAID. SHIT.

TRUE COMIX → L.J. BARRY © 81
GOD! HER CLOTHES!
GOD. I KNOW. SHES THE GROSSEST HOME EC TEACHER OF ALL
I KNOW
O.K. CLASS. — MAY I HAVE YOUR UNDIV ATTENTIC PLEAS
MUFFY VICARS IS A TURD.
SHES GROSS
TOTALLY GROSS
Miss Marfet
HELLO YOUNG WOMEN! AS MANY OF YOU ALL READY KNOW, I AM MISS MARFET AND I WOULD LIKE TO WELCOME YOU TO YOUR "FLOWING AND SEWING" SEMESTER OF HOME ECONOMICS. SO WELCOME TO THE EXCITING WORLD OF WOMANHOOD! SOME OF YOU ARE ALL READY NOTICING YOUR BODYS BEGINNING TO CHANGE. IN THIS CLASS WE WILL LEARN ALL ABOUT THOSE MYSTERIOUS AND WONDERFUL CHANGES AND WE WILL LEARN ALL ABOUT THE SEWING MACHINE. BUT TO BEGIN LETS START WITH AN INFORMATIVE FILM STRIP ENTITLED "THAT SPECIAL DAY" — LUCY, GET THE LIGHTS PLEASE..
"One day, Tina realized She didn't want to climb trees anymore....
KAMON TEEN! LETS GO CLIMB THAT TREE IN HIX'S YARD!
GOSH JOHN- I DON'T FEEL LIKE IT! I WANT TO GO BUY SOME TAMPONS INSTEAD!
1.
Tina purchased some Tampons And quietly awaited "Her Special Day"
GOSH. I KNOW IT WILL BE JUST BEAUTIFUL!
IT WILL TINA! IT WILL BE SO BEAUTIFUL!
2
And then, one morning, Tina found a beautiful red flower in her underpants!
HOW DID THIS GET HERE?
3.
Suddenly, She realized- It was "THAT SPECIAL DAY"!
JANE! GUESS WHAT!! IM A WOMAN! ITS SO BEAUTIFUL! ITS THE HAPPIEST DAY OF MY LIFE!
4.
WASN'T THAT LOVELY?! THATS EXACTLY WHAT ITS LIKE TOO! NOW TO DRAMATICALLY DEMONSTRATE JUST HOW FAST OUR BODIES CHANGE IM GOING TO COME TO EACH TABLE AND MEASURE YOUR BUSTS. WE'LL PUT THE NUMBER ON THAT HUGE CHART OVER THERE THAT FACES THE BOYS PLAYFIELD
OUR FIRST PROJECT WILL BE A REVERSABLE TOTE BAG WITH A SECRET POCKET FOR YOUR "SPECIAL DAY" ACCESSORIES.
HEY- PSST!! PSST - JENNY- YOU GOTTA CIGARETTE ME AN MUFFY CAN SPLIT DURING LUNCH?
IGNOR HER
IGNOR WHO?

TRUE COMEK de LYNDA BARRY © 81
NATURE or NURTURE?
SCIENTISTS BAFFLED!!!
YOU DECIDE!!!
START HERE
I GIVE UP! AND I AM A GENIUS!
I GIVE UP AND I HAVE AN I.Q. OF 283!
I HAVE MANY DEEP CONCEPTS CONCERNING THIS TOPIC.
TOP SCIENTIST
THIS IS REALLY QUITE INTERESTING
THROUGHOUT HISTORY, SCIENTISTS HAVE AGONIZED OVER THE AWFUL QUESTION OF HUMAN NATURE---- DOES IT EXIST?? ARE WE BORN WITH THE DESIRE TO GET A JOB AND EAT TWINKIES, OR IS THIS A LEARNED CONDITION??? AND WHAT ABOUT HOW WE BRED WIENER DOGS TO LOOK THAT WAY???
EVERY NOW + AGAIN THE CIVILIZED WORLD IS GIVEN A RARE OPPORTUNITY TO VEIW MAN IN HIS PRIMAL STATE!! FOR EXAMPLE:
THE DOUGHNUT-BOY of SEATTLE, WASH.
LOST OR ABANDONED IN THE HOSTESS FACTORY IN SEATTLES INDUSTRIAL NEIGHBORHOOD, "LITTLE DUNKIN'" SOMEHOW SURVIVED ---- FOR 9 YEARS!
HIDING FROM THE PLANTS EMPLOYEES BY DAY LIL' DUNKIN KNEW ONLY THE WAYS OF THE CUPCAKES + DOUGHNUTS SURROUNDING HIM! HIS HABITS WERE QUITE UNLIKE OUR OWN! HE WAS VERY ODD
LISSEN HERE YOU ARE MY DISCOVERY SO COME DOWN!!!
PULL
TUG
HERES THE NET BOSS.
HE WAS DISCOVERED BY A TOP SCIENTIST WHILE HIDING IN THE RAFTERS. IT WAS VERY DIFFICULT TO GET HIM DOWN. "THE DOUGHNUT BOY DOES NOT MIND GOOD!" SAID THE SCIENTIST. IT WAS TRUE, INFACT.
HIS NATURAL PARENTS WERE LOCATED BUT THEY REFUSED TO TAKE HIM HOME!
ER, ER. UH HE DOES LOOK A BIT LIKE JAMIE--
OH BILL, ITS NO USE. THINK OF THE NEIGHBORS.
LEFT WITH CONFUSED SOCIAL WORKERS THE DOUGHNUT BOY BECAME LISTLESS AND SULLEN. HE REFUSED TO EAT OR LISTEN TO THE RADIO. THEY GAVE UP HOPE AND THE DOUGHNUT BOY WAS LEFT TO MOLD-
SSSSSS

continued

DAILY DA
WELL YES
YOU BETTER STOP EVERYTHING YOU DO
EVERYONE FIGHTING WITH EVERYONE ELSE
DOG GONE! WELL HELLO THERE SON. YOU'RE COMMIN' WITH ME NOW
A DOCTOR FROM OHIO READ ABOUT THE CASE IN THE NEWSPAPER AND FLEW THERE F=A=S=T
THEY GLADLY GAVE UP LIL' DUNKIN AND THE DOCTOR FLEW HIM TO OHIO FOR TESTS.
IN A SPECIAL NEWS CONFERENCE THE DOCTOR ANNOUNCED---
ACCORDING TO MYSELF, THIS SO CALLED "DOUGHNUT BOY" IS NO DIFFERENT THAN ANY BODY ELSE! AND THIS IS JUST A MEANS OF GETTING ATTENTION AND HAVING AN EXCUSE TO AVOID GETTING A JOB!! BUT IT WON'T WORK. AT LEAST NOT IN AMERICA! I'VE CONTACTED MR. HIX AT THE DOWNTOWN SEARS. HE SAYS HE NEEDS A YOUNG CLERK! NO MORE FREE LUNCH FOR THIS KID, BY GOLLY!
?
MR HIX AT THE SEARS TURNED OUT TO BE A REAL NICE FELLOW...
I USTA BE A DOUGHNUT BOY MYSELF, YOU KNOW. OH YES! AND IT WAS ROUGH BACK THEN, OH YES. BUT I DON'T THINK YOU OUGHT TO WEAR THE CANDLES IN THE STORE, SEE-
THEY GOT DRUNK TOGETHER ONE NIGHT AND POURED THEIR HEARTS OUT
YABBER YABBER BLABBER BLABBER.
STAYS MOIST. SO FRESH. TASTES LIKE HOMEMADE. CRUMBS CLING TO FORK. KIDS LOVE 'EM. MOMS TOO.
XXX
EVENTUALLY THE DOUGHNUT BOY ADJUSTED. HE CHANGED HIS NAME TO DICK RICHARDS AND BOUGHT A HONDA CIVIC. AND HE ALSO GOT A CANARY + STARTED A LITTLE GARDEN. AND THATS ALL.
?
DO YOU THINK THIS STORY IS TRUE??
☐ YES ☐ NO
WHY?

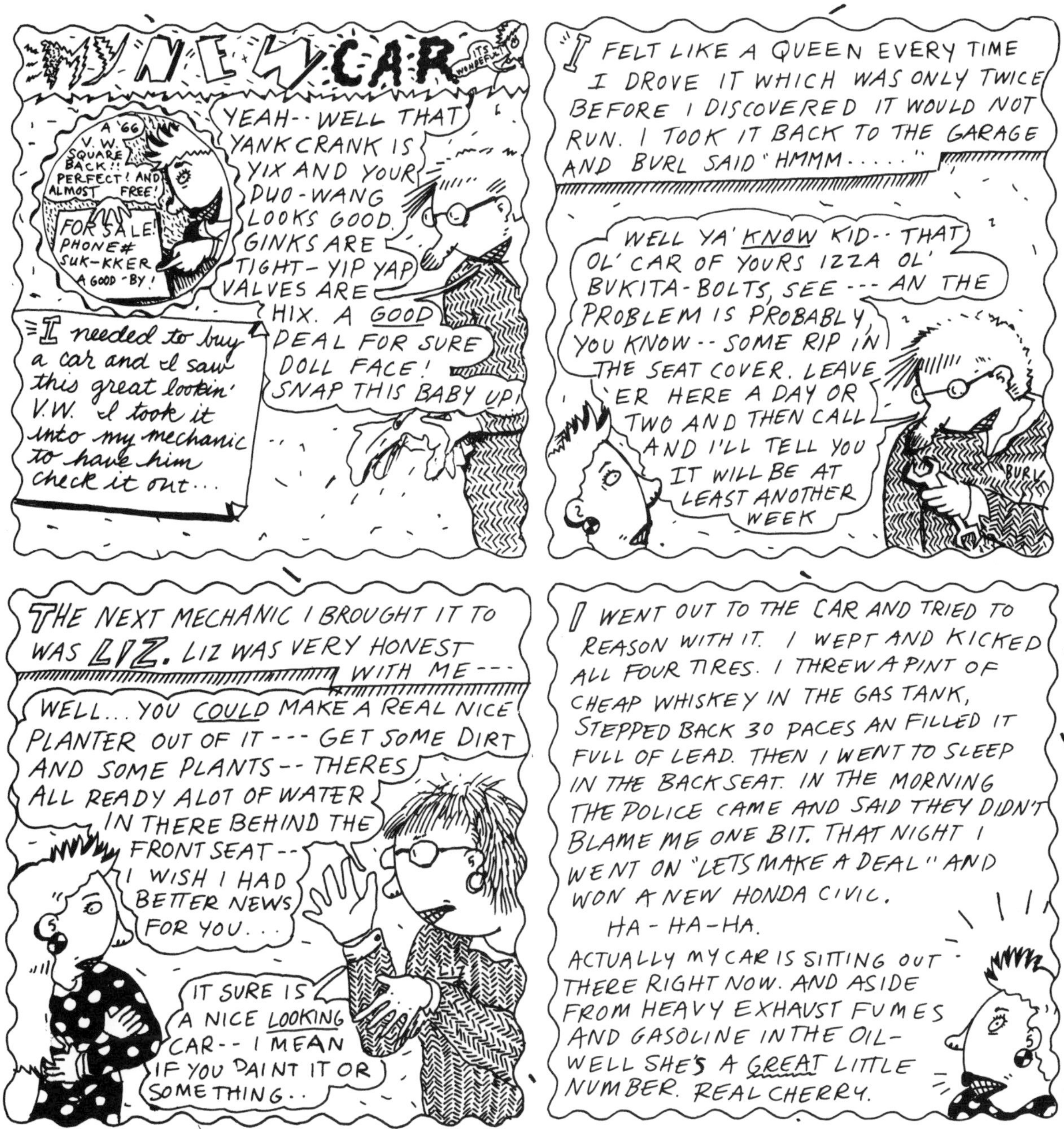
MY NEW CAR
ITS WONDERFUL!
I needed to buy a car and I saw this great lookin' V.W. I took it into my mechanic to have him check it out...
A '66 V.W. SQUARE BACK!! PERFECT! AND ALMOST FREE!
FOR SALE! PHONE# SUK-KKER A GOOD-BY!
YEAH-- WELL THAT YANK CRANK IS YIX AND YOUR DUO-WANG LOOKS GOOD. GINKS ARE TIGHT- YIP YAP VALVES ARE HIX. A GOOD DEAL FOR SURE DOLL FACE! SNAP THIS BABY UP!
I FELT LIKE A QUEEN EVERY TIME I DROVE IT WHICH WAS ONLY TWICE BEFORE I DISCOVERED IT WOULD NOT RUN. I TOOK IT BACK TO THE GARAGE AND BURL SAID "HMMM....."
WELL YA' KNOW KID-- THAT OL' CAR OF YOURS IZZA OL' BUKITA-BOLTS, SEE --- AN THE PROBLEM IS PROBABLY, YOU KNOW -- SOME RIP IN THE SEAT COVER. LEAVE 'ER HERE A DAY OR TWO AND THEN CALL AND I'LL TELL YOU IT WILL BE AT LEAST ANOTHER WEEK
BURL
THE NEXT MECHANIC I BROUGHT IT TO WAS LIZ. LIZ WAS VERY HONEST WITH ME---
WELL... YOU COULD MAKE A REAL NICE PLANTER OUT OF IT --- GET SOME DIRT AND SOME PLANTS -- THERES ALL READY ALOT OF WATER IN THERE BEHIND THE FRONT SEAT -- I WISH I HAD BETTER NEWS FOR YOU...
IT SURE IS A NICE LOOKING CAR-- I MEAN IF YOU PAINT IT OR SOMETHING..
I WENT OUT TO THE CAR AND TRIED TO REASON WITH IT. I WEPT AND KICKED ALL FOUR TIRES. I THREW A PINT OF CHEAP WHISKEY IN THE GAS TANK, STEPPED BACK 30 PACES AN FILLED IT FULL OF LEAD. THEN I WENT TO SLEEP IN THE BACK SEAT. IN THE MORNING THE POLICE CAME AND SAID THEY DIDN'T BLAME ME ONE BIT. THAT NIGHT I WENT ON "LETS MAKE A DEAL" AND WON A NEW HONDA CIVIC.
HA-HA-HA.
ACTUALLY MY CAR IS SITTING OUT THERE RIGHT NOW. AND ASIDE FROM HEAVY EXHAUST FUMES AND GASOLINE IN THE OIL- WELL SHE'S A GREAT LITTLE NUMBER. REAL CHERRY.

FINAL EXAM

MISS BARRY HAS A FAT ASS. FOR REAL

WHO WROTE THIS?!

YOUR INSTRUCTOR: MISS BARRY © 1981 L.J. BARRY

Name - - - - - - - -

Date - - - - - - - -

ESSAY TEST: (PLEASE USE ALL OF SPACE PROVIDED)

I Please name all the things in the world and explain how they got here:

WHAT DID YOU LEARN THIS YEAR? TAKE THIS SIMPLE TEST AND FIND OUT. WOULD YOU SIT DOWN PLEASE? DO YOU UNDERSTAND ENGLISH? NO SHARPENING PENCILS WHILE I'M TALKING- HOW MANY TIMES DO I HAVE TO TELL YOU THIS.?!! O.K CLASS YOU'LL HAVE ALL OF THIS PERIOD TO FINISH THIS- NEATNESS COUNTS.—JIM, THIS MEANS YOU. TINA, WILL YOU PLEASE PUT THAT NOTE AWAY OR READ IT OUT LOUD TO THE CLASS. OK. WORK AT YOUR OWN SPEED, NO COPYING. JAMIE ITS GOING TO BE AWFULLY HARD TO TAKE THIS TEST WITH YOUR SUNGLASSES ON. OK CLASS

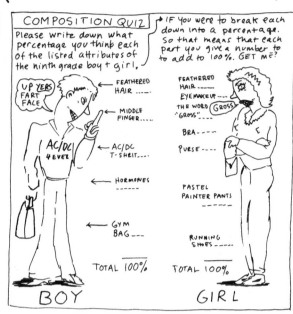

COMPOSITION QUIZ

Please write down what percentage you think each of the listed attributes of the ninth grade boy + girl.

IF YOU were to break each down into a percentage. So that means that each part you give a number to to add to 100%. GET ME?

BOY: UP YERS FART FACE — FEATHERED HAIR — MIDDLE FINGER — AC/DC T-SHIRT (AC/DC 4 EVER) — HORMONES — GYM BAG — TOTAL 100%

GIRL: FEATHERED HAIR — EYE MAKEUP — THE WORD "GROSS" (GROSS) — BRA — PURSE — PASTEL PAINTER PANTS — RUNNING SHOES — TOTAL 100%

BOY   **GIRL**

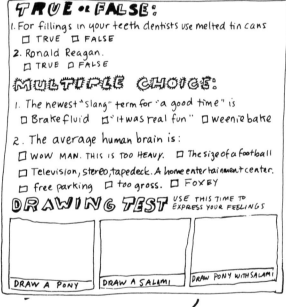

TRUE or FALSE:

1. For fillings in your teeth dentists use melted tin cans
   ☐ TRUE ☐ FALSE
2. Ronald Reagan.
   ☐ TRUE ☐ FALSE

MULTIPLE CHOICE:

1. The newest "slang" term for "a good time" is
   ☐ Brake fluid ☐ "It was real fun" ☐ weenie bake
2. The average human brain is:
   ☐ WOW MAN. THIS IS TOO HEAVY. ☐ The size of a football
   ☐ Television, stereo, tapedeck. A home entertainment center.
   ☐ free parking ☐ too gross. ☐ FOXEY

DRAWING TEST
USE THIS TIME TO EXPRESS YOUR FEELINGS

DRAW A PONY DRAW A SALAMI DRAW PONY WITH SALAMI

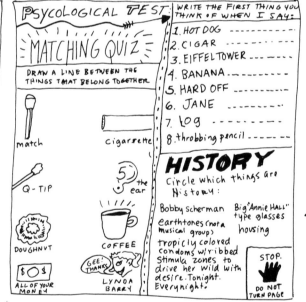

PSYCOLOGICAL TEST

MATCHING QUIZ

DRAW A LINE BETWEEN THE THINGS THAT BELONG TOGETHER

match — cigarrette
Q-TIP — the ear
DOUGHNUT — COFFEE
ALL OF YOUR MONEY — GEE THANKS LYNDA BARRY

WRITE THE FIRST THING YOU THINK OF WHEN I SAY:

1. HOT DOG - - - - -
2. CIGAR - - - - -
3. EIFFEL TOWER - - - - -
4. BANANA - - - - -
5. HARD OFF - - - - -
6. JANE - - - - -
7. LOG - - - - -
8. throbbing pencil - - - - -

HISTORY

Circle which things are History:

Bobby Scherman   Big "Annie Hall" type glasses

earthtones (not a musical group)   housing

tropicly colored condoms w/ribbed stimula zones to drive her wild with desire. Tonight. Every night.

STOP. DO NOT TURN PAGE

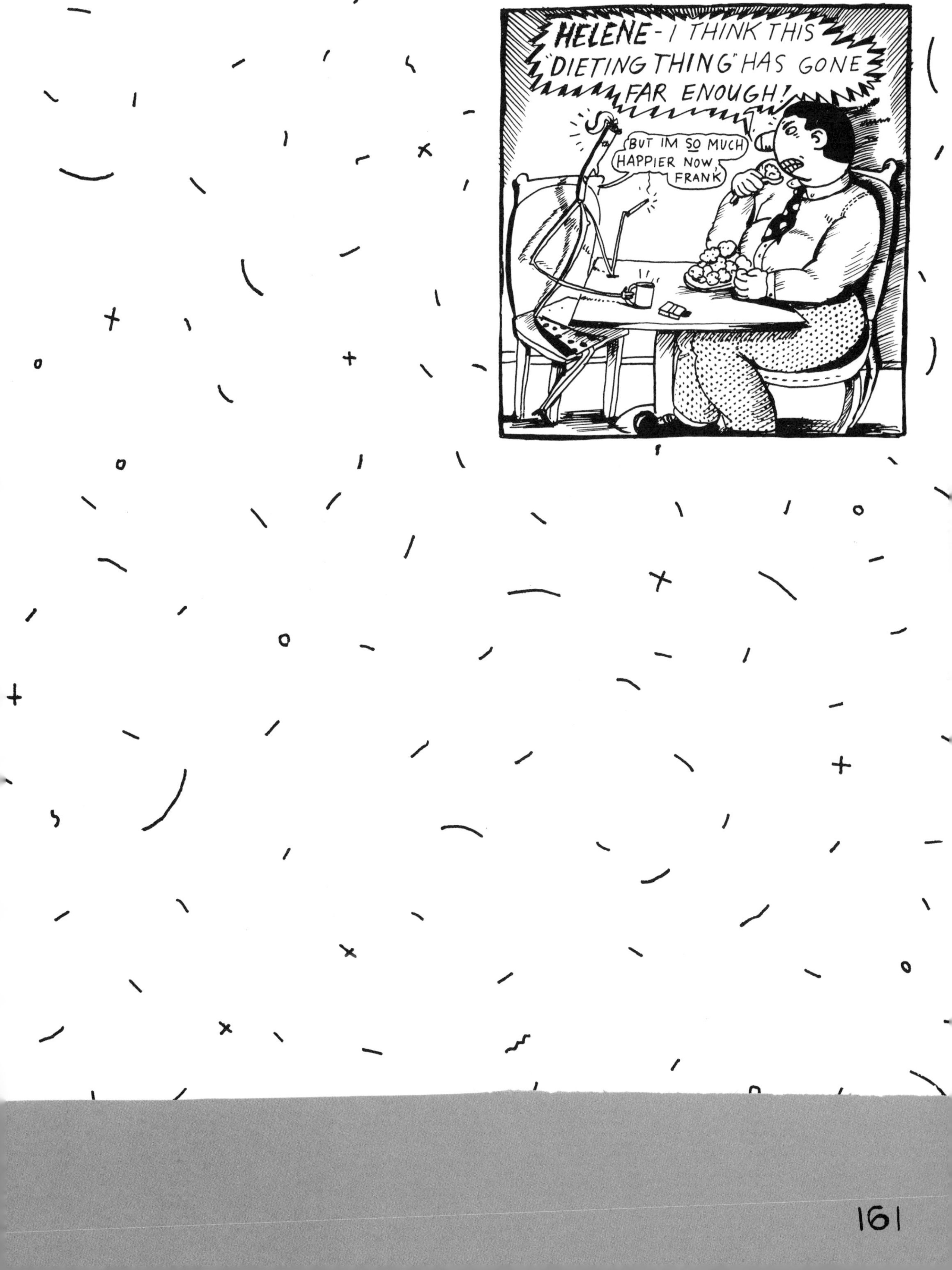
HELENE - I THINK THIS "DIETING THING" HAS GONE FAR ENOUGH!
BUT IM SO MUCH HAPPIER NOW, FRANK

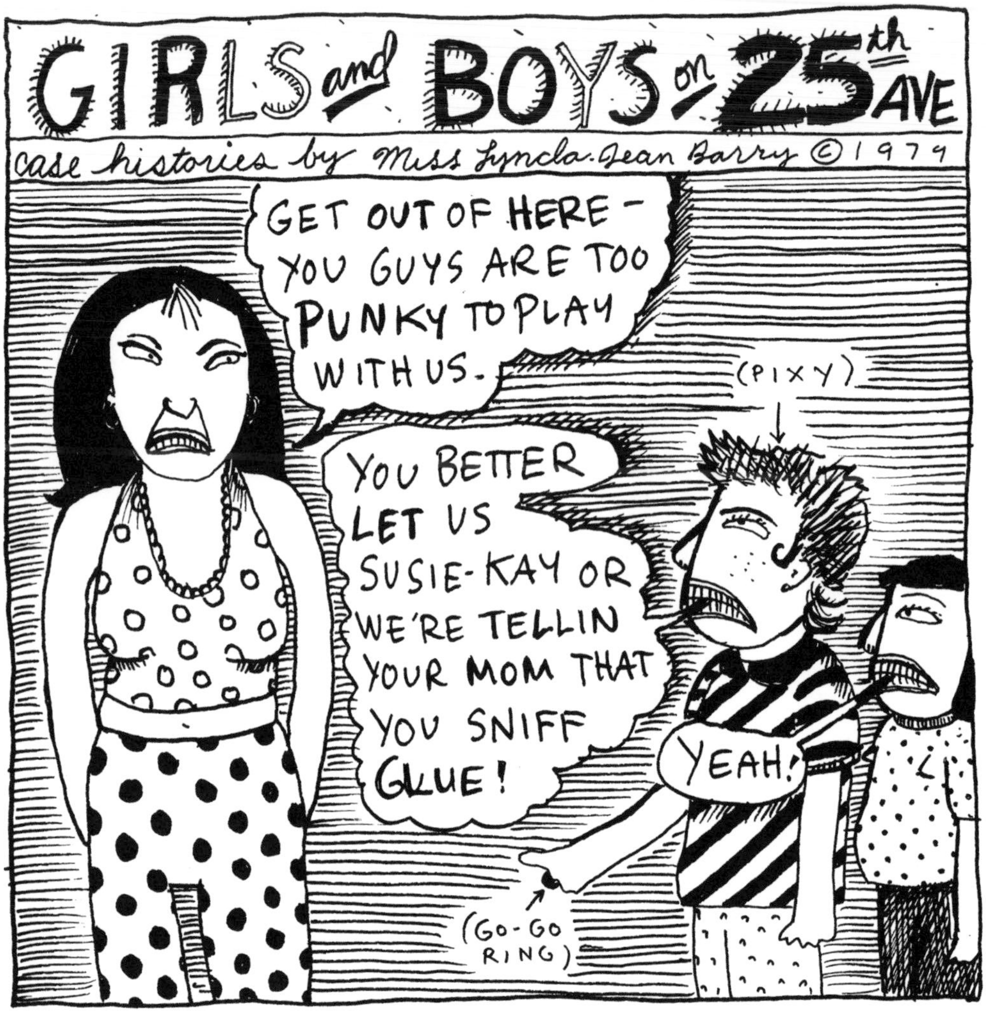
GIRLS and BOYS on 25th AVE
case histories by Miss Lynda Jean Barry ©1979
GET OUT OF HERE - YOU GUYS ARE TOO PUNKY TO PLAY WITH US.
(PIXY)
YOU BETTER LET US SUSIE-KAY OR WE'RE TELLIN YOUR MOM THAT YOU SNIFF GLUE!
YEAH!
(GO-GO RING)

GIRLS and BOYS
as told by LYNDA JEAN BARRY ©1979
WHY JOYCIE H.! THAT IS THE NICEST CUP TO EVER COME OUT OF MY SECOND GRADE CLASS! JUST LOOK AT THAT DELICATE HANDLE!
COIL METHOD
ASH TRAY
FLOWER POT
COIL GO-GO RING
CREATIVE
IM GONNA BREAK THAT SOMEHOW. I CAN JUST TELL.
SHE'LL PASS IT AROUND AND WHEN IT GETS TO MY DESK IT WILL BREAK.
WHY DON'T WE JUST PASS THIS LOVELY CUP AROUND SO EVERYONE CAN SEE! BUT BE CAREFUL! ITS VERY FRAGILE
CONNIE D. WHY DON'T YOU BEGIN.
HERE GOES. I KNEW IT.
MAGNIFYING GLASS
HOW LONG DO I HAVE TO HOLD IT FOR MISS LASANE?
SHAKE
TREMBLE

Girls and Boys
AS TOLD BY LYNDA BARRY ©1979
WILL HE CALL?!!
MAYBE I CAN MAKE HIM CALL WITH MY BRAIN!
RRR GRRR GRR RRR
O.K. IM GONNA COUNT. AND WHEN I GET TO 47 YOU WILL CALL!
1 2 3 4 5 6
8 9 10 11 12
36 37 38 39
40 41 42 43 44
45 46 47 come on 48
49
CREEP!!! PIG!
O.K. IM GIVING YOU ONE MORE CHANCE!! IM COUNTING BACKWARD FROM 100. 99-98-97

GIRLS AND BOYS
©'80 L. J. BARRY
3 O CLOCK IN THE MORNING
¡¿DO YOU KNOW WHAT TIME IT IS?! YOUR FATHER AND I HAVE BEEN WORRIED SICK!!
GLUH GULH GUH
SHE FEELS LIKE GUMBY
¡OH MY GAWD! YOU'RE DRUNK! ADAM! GET IN HERE! OUR DAUGHTER IS DRUNK
ZINK ZINK ZONK ZANK BAY-BEE OH YEAH RINK RANK
¡OH! YOU'RE GETTIN' SICK! NOT ON MOMMY'S CARPET, BABY! ADAM! WILL YOU GET IN HERE! COME ON HONEY. COME WITH ME.
afterwards...
NORMA! DO YOU KNOW WHAT TIME IT IS?? THE KID'S BEEN ASLEEP FOR AN HOUR. COME TO BED. WE'LL DEAL WITH THIS IN THE MORNING.
NORMA! THIS IS NOTHING TO CRY ABOUT. SHE'LL BE ALL RIGHT

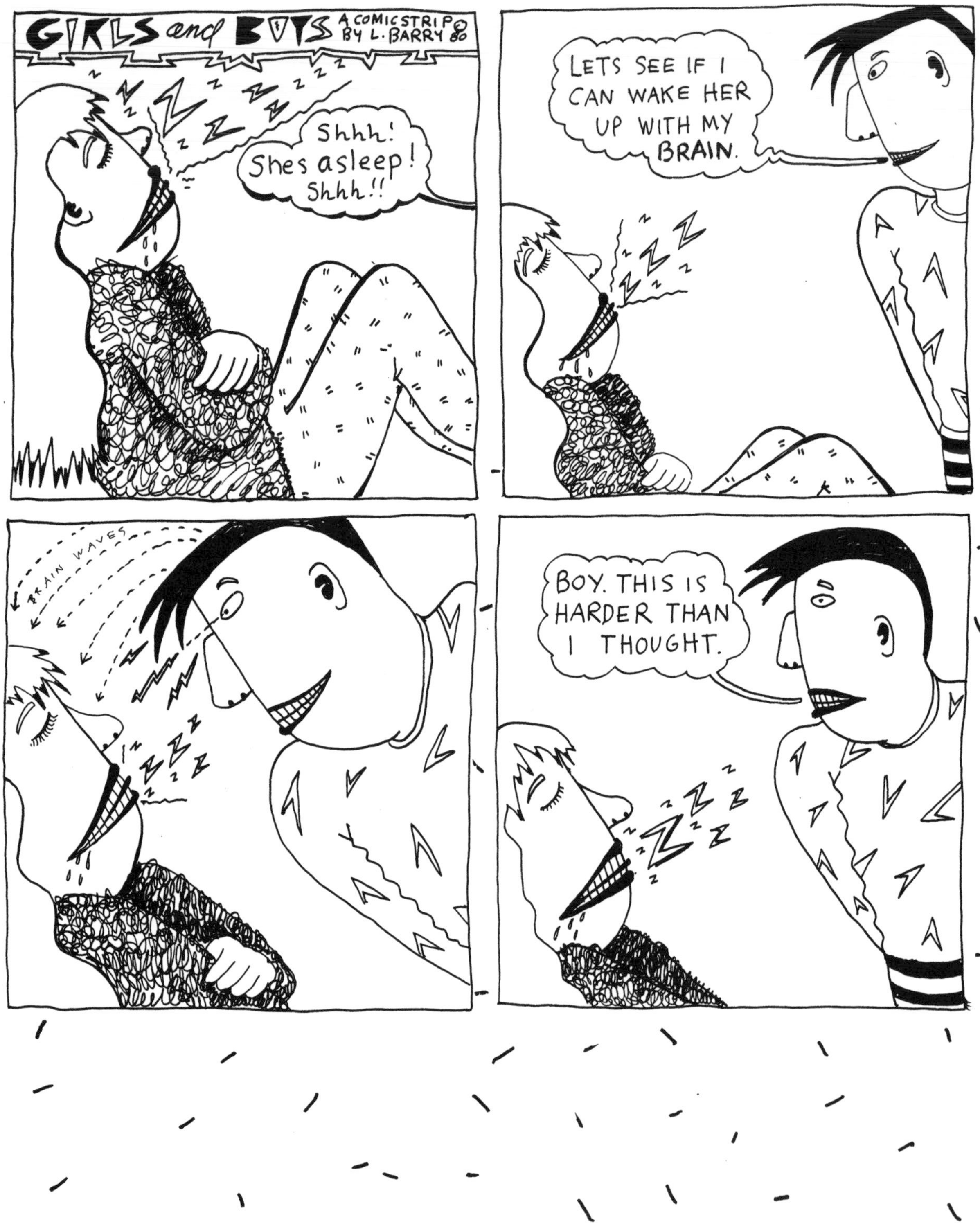
GIRLS and BOYS
A COMICSTRIP BY L. BARRY ©80
Shhh! Shes asleep! Shhh!!
LETS SEE IF I CAN WAKE HER UP WITH MY BRAIN.
BRAIN WAVES
BOY. THIS IS HARDER THAN I THOUGHT.

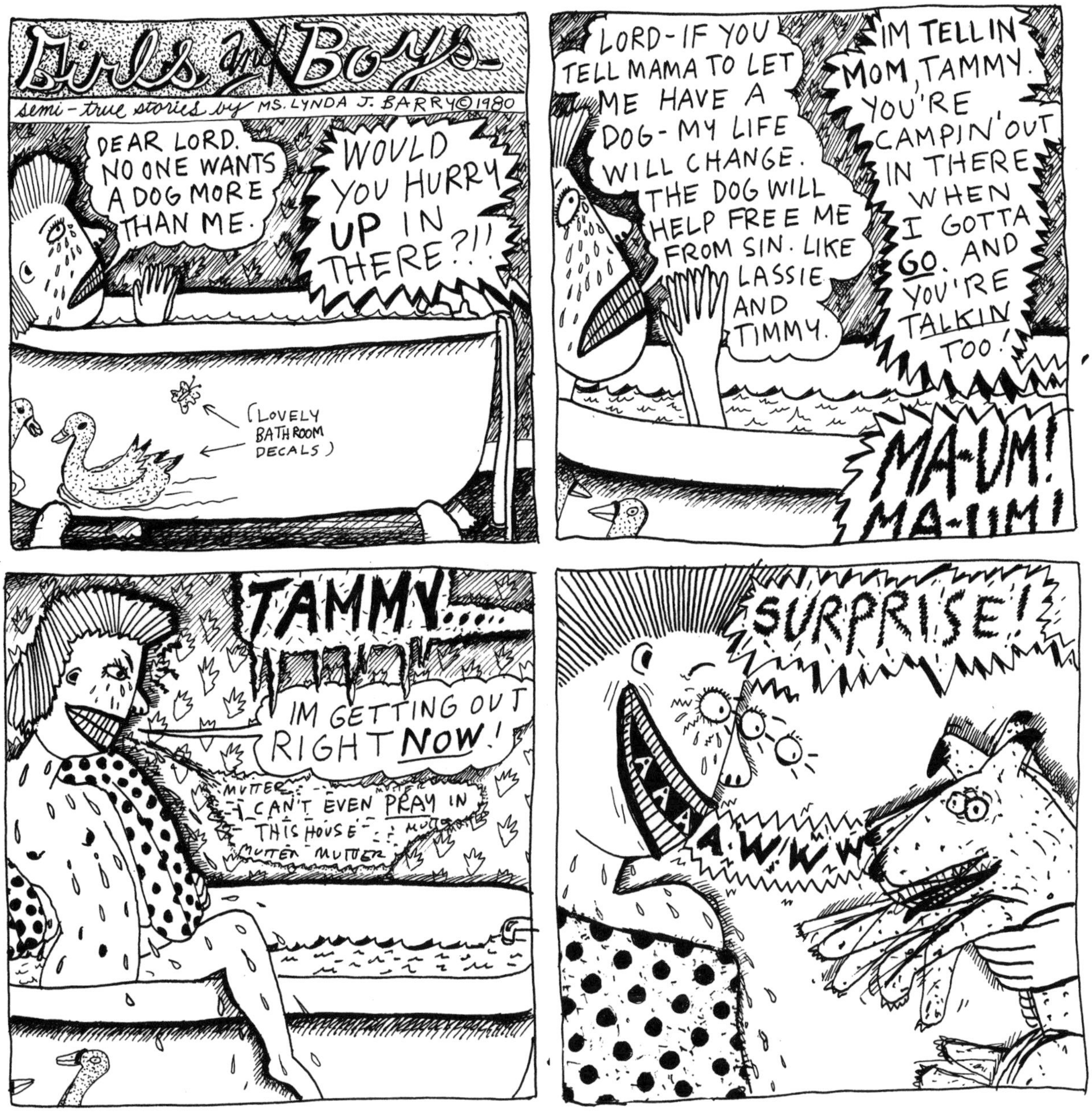
Girls and Boys-
semi-true stories by MS. LYNDA J. BARRY©1980
DEAR LORD. NO ONE WANTS A DOG MORE THAN ME.
WOULD YOU HURRY UP IN THERE?!!
(LOVELY BATHROOM DECALS)
LORD-IF YOU TELL MAMA TO LET ME HAVE A DOG-MY LIFE WILL CHANGE. THE DOG WILL HELP FREE ME FROM SIN. LIKE LASSIE AND TIMMY.
IM TELLIN MOM, TAMMY. YOU'RE CAMPIN' OUT IN THERE WHEN I GOTTA GO. AND YOU'RE TALKIN TOO!
MA-UM! MA-UM!
TAMMY.....
IM GETTING OUT RIGHT NOW!
MUTTER I CAN'T EVEN PRAY IN THIS HOUSE MUTTER MUTTER MUTTER
SURPRISE!
AAAAAWWWW

NOCTURNALITY
(THE NIGHT WORLD)

Darkness may close the door of one world but it opens the door of another. The night world becomes a world of sounds and smells and of limited sight.

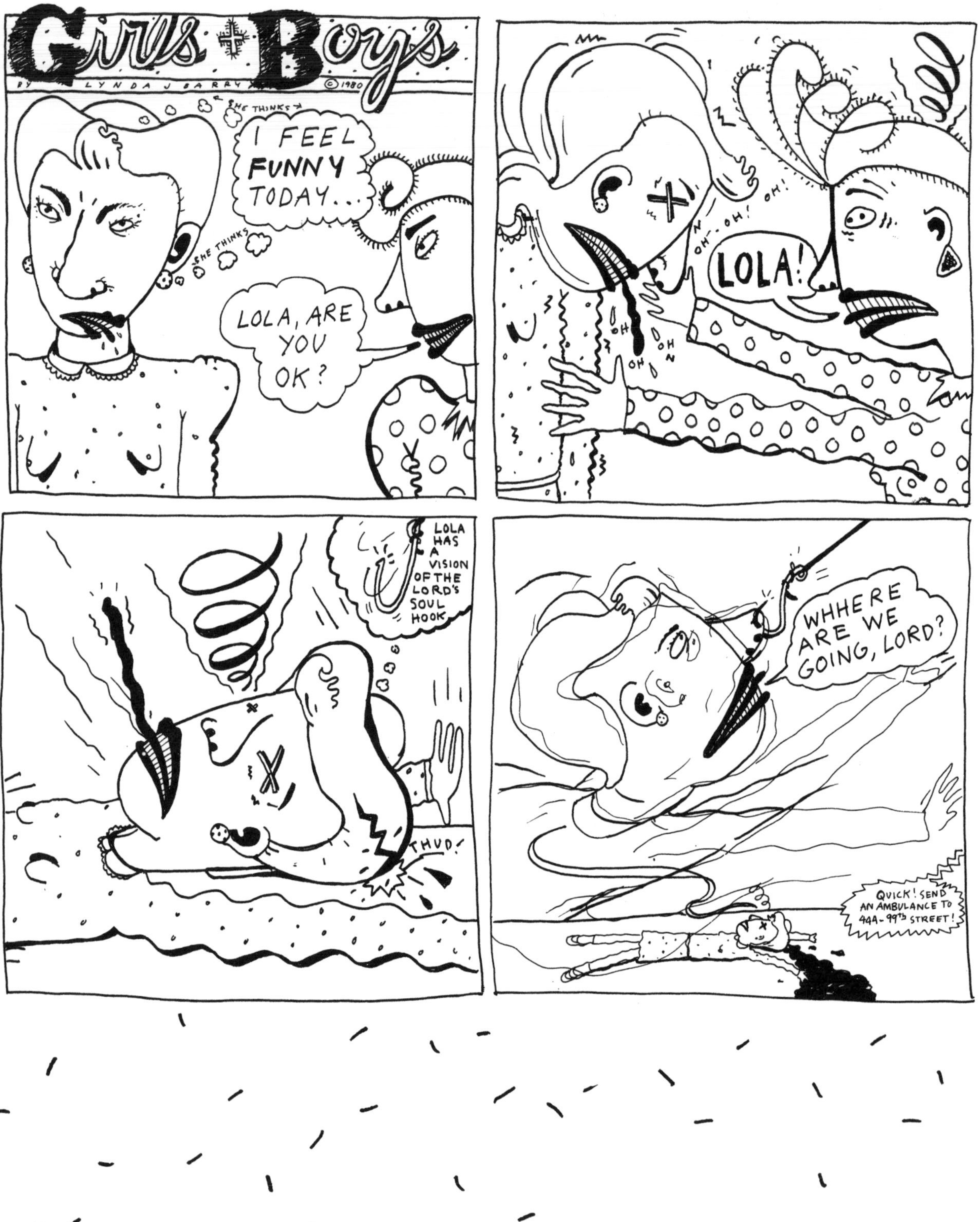
Girls + Boys
BY LYNDA J BARRY ©1980
SHE THINKS
I FEEL FUNNY TODAY...
SHE THINKS
LOLA, ARE YOU OK?
OH-OH! OH!
LOLA!
OH OH OH
LOLA HAS A VISION OF THE LORD'S SOUL HOOK
THUD!
WHHERE ARE WE GOING, LORD?
QUICK! SEND AN AMBULANCE TO 444-99TH STREET!

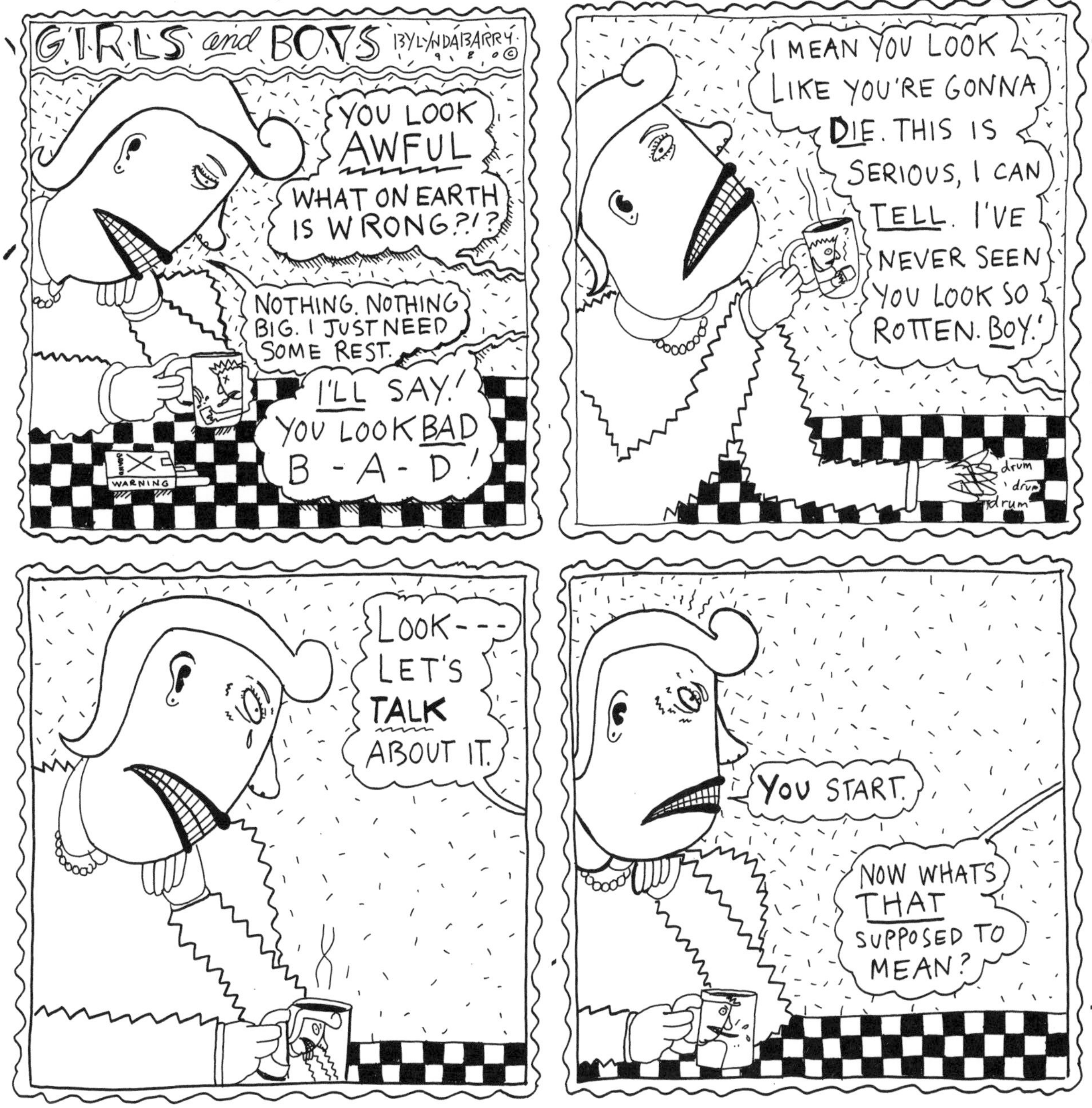
GIRLS and BOYS
BY LYNDA BARRY
YOU LOOK AWFUL
WHAT ON EARTH IS WRONG?!?
NOTHING. NOTHING BIG. I JUST NEED SOME REST.
I'LL SAY! YOU LOOK BAD B-A-D!
WARNING
I MEAN YOU LOOK LIKE YOU'RE GONNA DIE. THIS IS SERIOUS, I CAN TELL. I'VE NEVER SEEN YOU LOOK SO ROTTEN. BOY!
drum drum drum
LOOK--- LET'S TALK ABOUT IT.
YOU START.
NOW WHATS THAT SUPPOSED TO MEAN?

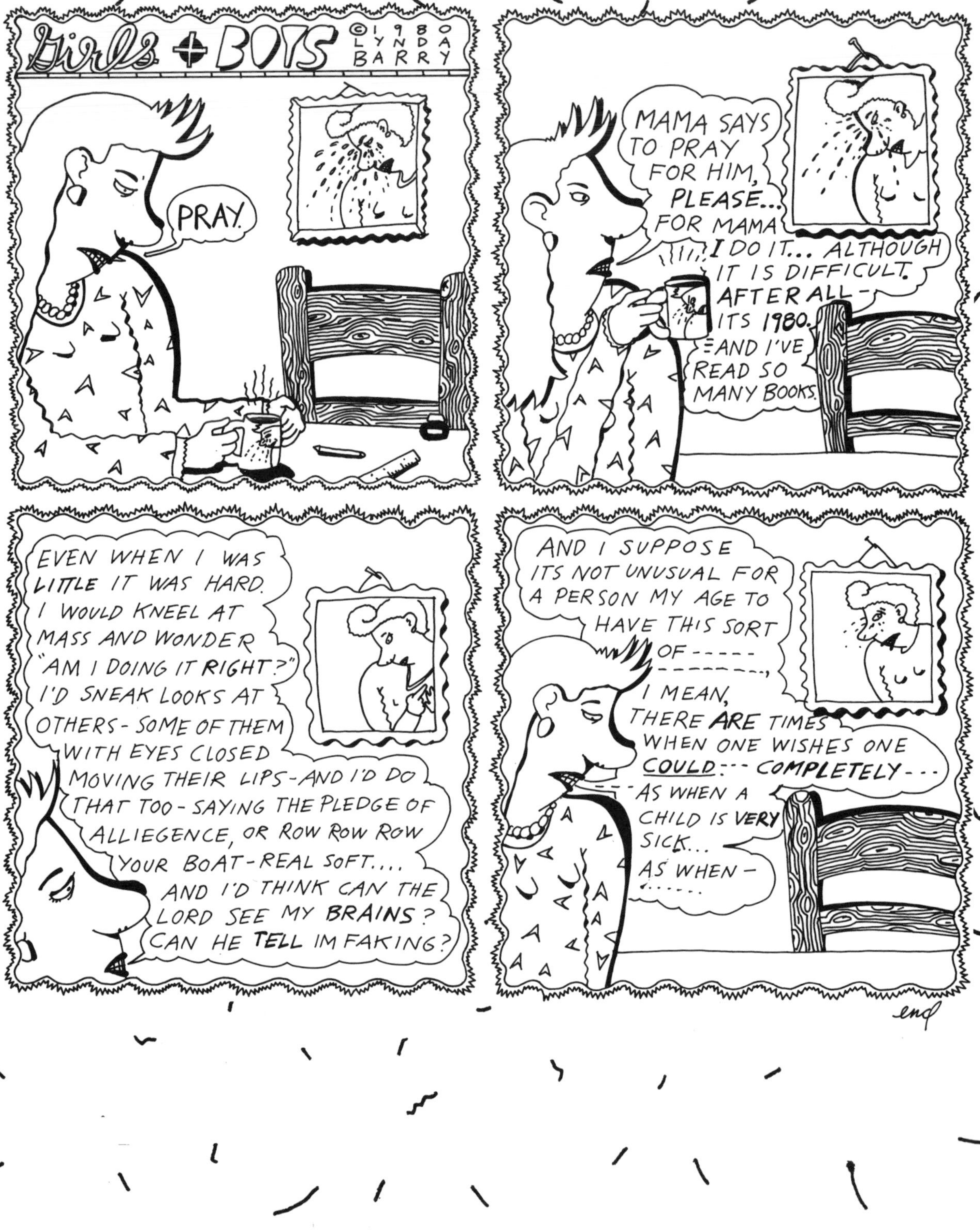
GIRLS + BOYS
©1980 LYNDA BARRY
PRAY.
MAMA SAYS TO PRAY FOR HIM, PLEASE... FOR MAMA I DO IT... ALTHOUGH IT IS DIFFICULT. AFTER ALL– ITS 1980. AND I'VE READ SO MANY BOOKS.
EVEN WHEN I WAS LITTLE IT WAS HARD. I WOULD KNEEL AT MASS AND WONDER "AM I DOING IT RIGHT?" I'D SNEAK LOOKS AT OTHERS - SOME OF THEM WITH EYES CLOSED MOVING THEIR LIPS - AND I'D DO THAT TOO - SAYING THE PLEDGE OF ALLIEGENCE, OR ROW ROW ROW YOUR BOAT - REAL SOFT....
AND I'D THINK CAN THE LORD SEE MY BRAINS? CAN HE TELL IM FAKING?
AND I SUPPOSE ITS NOT UNUSUAL FOR A PERSON MY AGE TO HAVE THIS SORT OF -----
I MEAN, THERE ARE TIMES WHEN ONE WISHES ONE COULD --- COMPLETELY ---
AS WHEN A CHILD IS VERY SICK...
AS WHEN –
end

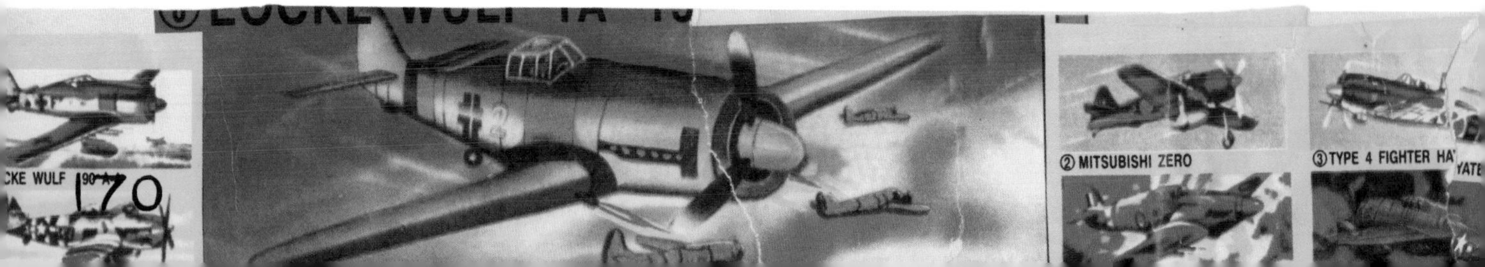
② MITSUBISHI ZERO

GIRLS and BOYS
LYNDA BARRY 80 ©
BILL JUST ISN'T RESPONDING TONIGHT--- MAYBE A BIT OF PERFUME WILL BRING HIM AROUND, SOMETHING SHY, YET SEXY, LETS SEE HERE, "ULTRA SNIFF" THAT SOUNDS ALLURING....
your Favorite Fragrance ONLY 10¢
CHANEL #5
ULTRA SNIFF
WHITE SUGAR
INSERT COIN →
PULL LEVER AND PERFUME WILL SPRAY ALL OVER YOU AND HELP TO GET A BOYFRIEN
SIXTY-FIVE BUCKS FOR THIS PERM AND HE DOESN'T EVEN NOTICE - WHY DO I BOTHER?? NOTHING CAUGHT IN MY TEETH I HOPE. AND THE WAY HE LOOKS AT MY FRIEND LIZ! IF I DIDN'T KNOW BETTER, ID SAY THEY'VE ALREADY.... DAMN CHAPPED LIPS. - NEVER REALLY TRUSTED HER ANYHOW ---
AW HELL - WHO CARES ANYMORE? THIS LIPSTICK DRIVES ME NUTS, TOO DRY. BUNCH OF NAIVE, OLD FASHIONED IDEAS ANYWAY. ANYTHING GOES NOW. ALLS FAIR. OH GOD. A WHITEHEAD. BEEN THERE ALL THROUGH DINNER IM SURE. IF I TRY TO GET RID OF IT NOW, BILL WILL THINK I DID IT JUST FOR HIM. SHOULD I LEAVE IT ALONE OR POP IT? IF I POP IT HE MIGHT THINK IM INSECURE. HES PROBABLY WONDERING WHY I'VE BEEN IN HERE SO LONG. I BETTER GET OUT THERE ON THE DOUBLE!
HI DARLING! IM BA-ACK! SORRY I TOOK SO LONG!
WHADDAYA MEAN? YOU GO SOMEWHERE? TA THE CAN?
select-a-tune! Yes!
Menu
LIEING + CHEATING UP 90%
GIANT ANT FOUND IN RENTON
MORE RAIN

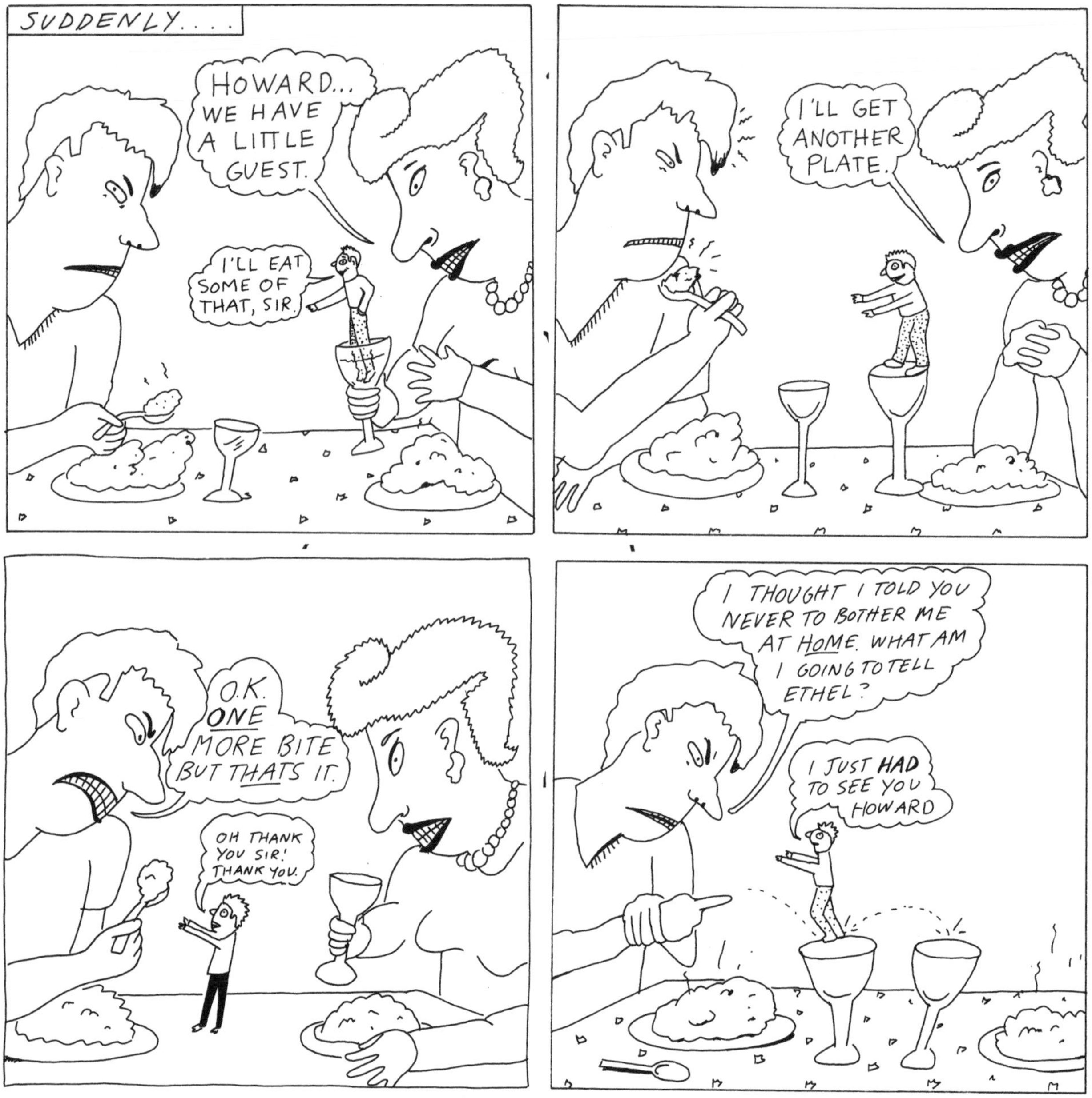
SUDDENLY....
HOWARD... WE HAVE A LITTLE GUEST.
I'LL EAT SOME OF THAT, SIR.
I'LL GET ANOTHER PLATE.
O.K. ONE MORE BITE BUT THATS IT.
OH THANK YOU SIR! THANK YOU.
I THOUGHT I TOLD YOU NEVER TO BOTHER ME AT HOME. WHAT AM I GOING TO TELL ETHEL?
I JUST HAD TO SEE YOU HOWARD

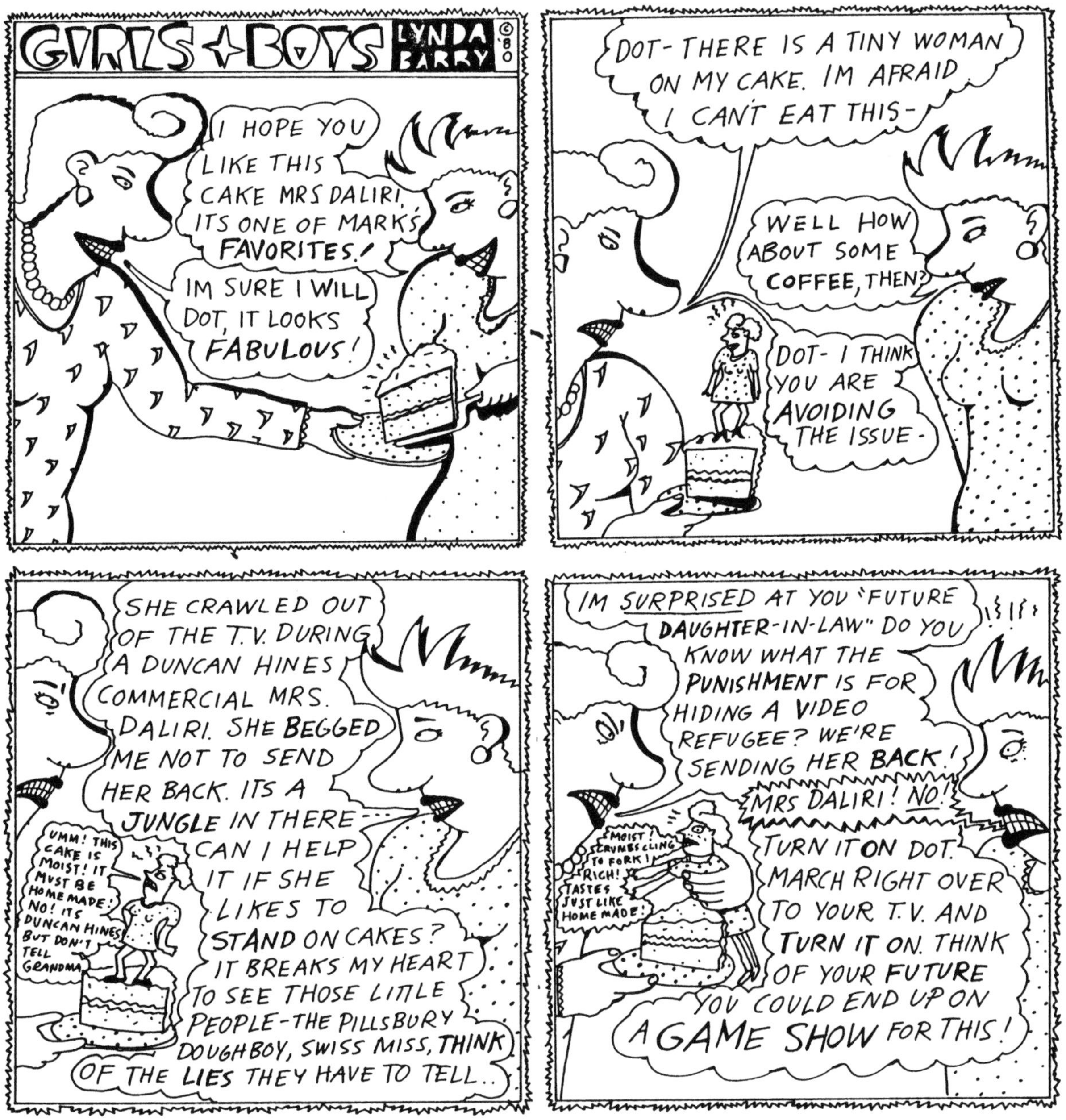
GIRLS + BOYS
LYNDA BARRY ©'80
I HOPE YOU LIKE THIS CAKE MRS DALIRI, ITS ONE OF MARK'S FAVORITES!
IM SURE I WILL DOT, IT LOOKS FABULOUS!
DOT - THERE IS A TINY WOMAN ON MY CAKE. IM AFRAID I CAN'T EAT THIS -
WELL HOW ABOUT SOME COFFEE, THEN?
DOT - I THINK YOU ARE AVOIDING THE ISSUE -
SHE CRAWLED OUT OF THE T.V. DURING A DUNCAN HINES COMMERCIAL MRS. DALIRI. SHE BEGGED ME NOT TO SEND HER BACK. ITS A JUNGLE IN THERE CAN I HELP IT IF SHE LIKES TO STAND ON CAKES? IT BREAKS MY HEART TO SEE THOSE LITTLE PEOPLE - THE PILLSBURY DOUGHBOY, SWISS MISS, THINK OF THE LIES THEY HAVE TO TELL..
UMM! THIS CAKE IS MOIST! IT MUST BE HOMEMADE! NO! ITS DUNCAN HINES BUT DON'T TELL GRANDMA
IM SURPRISED AT YOU "FUTURE DAUGHTER-IN-LAW" DO YOU KNOW WHAT THE PUNISHMENT IS FOR HIDING A VIDEO REFUGEE? WE'RE SENDING HER BACK!
MRS DALIRI! NO!
MOIST! CRUMBS CLING TO FORK! RICH! TASTES JUST LIKE HOMEMADE!
TURN IT ON DOT. MARCH RIGHT OVER TO YOUR T.V. AND TURN IT ON. THINK OF YOUR FUTURE YOU COULD END UP ON A GAME SHOW FOR THIS!

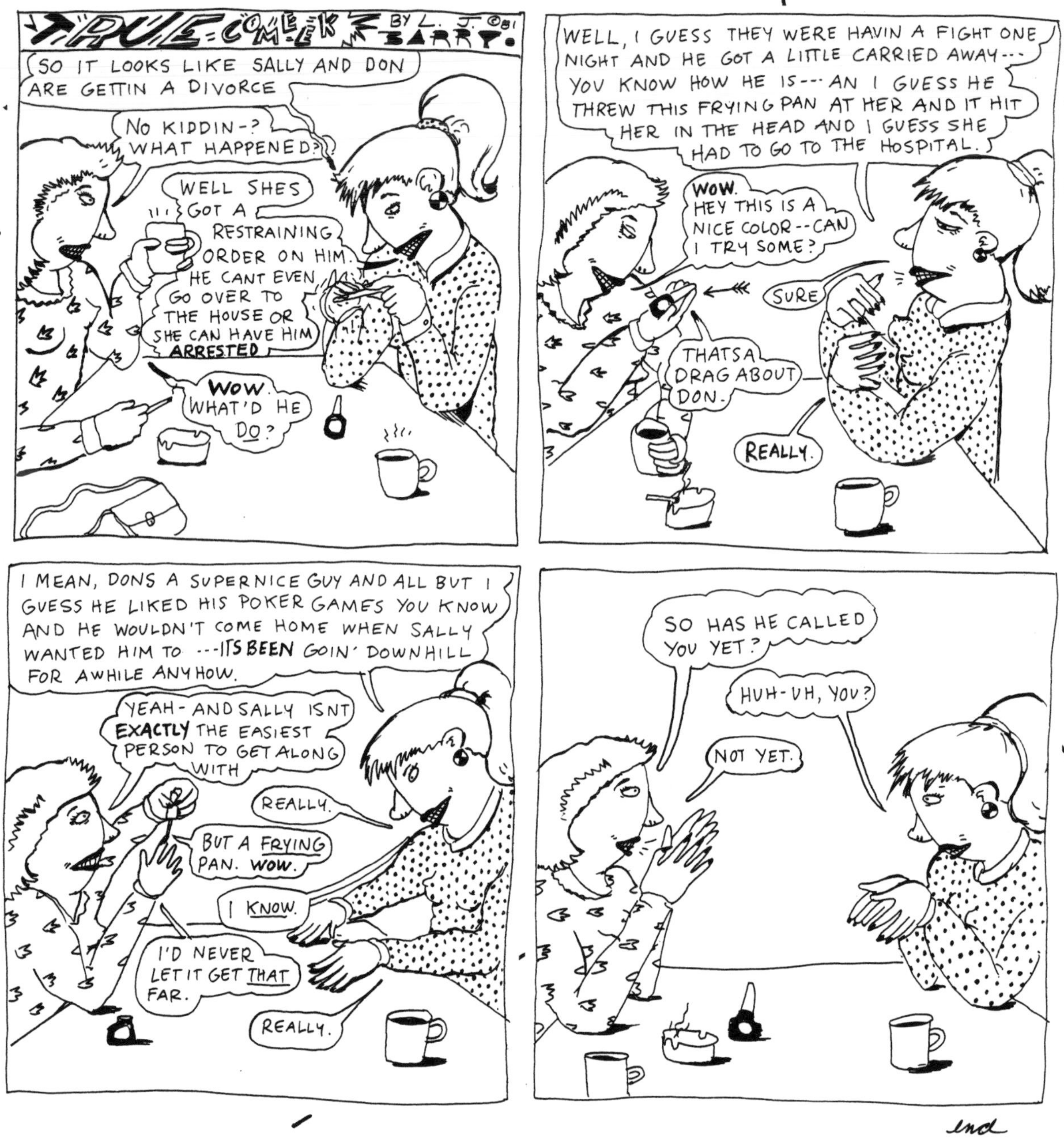
TRUE COMEEK BY L. J. BARRY ©81
SO IT LOOKS LIKE SALLY AND DON ARE GETTIN A DIVORCE
No KIDDIN-? WHAT HAPPENED?
WELL SHES GOT A RESTRAINING ORDER ON HIM. HE CANT EVEN GO OVER TO THE HOUSE OR SHE CAN HAVE HIM ARRESTED
WOW. WHAT'D HE DO?
WELL, I GUESS THEY WERE HAVIN A FIGHT ONE NIGHT AND HE GOT A LITTLE CARRIED AWAY--- YOU KNOW HOW HE IS--- AN I GUESS HE THREW THIS FRYING PAN AT HER AND IT HIT HER IN THE HEAD AND I GUESS SHE HAD TO GO TO THE HOSPITAL.
WOW. HEY THIS IS A NICE COLOR--CAN I TRY SOME?
SURE
THATS A DRAG ABOUT DON.
REALLY.
I MEAN, DONS A SUPERNICE GUY AND ALL BUT I GUESS HE LIKED HIS POKER GAMES YOU KNOW AND HE WOULDN'T COME HOME WHEN SALLY WANTED HIM TO ---ITS BEEN GOIN' DOWNHILL FOR AWHILE ANYHOW.
YEAH- AND SALLY ISNT EXACTLY THE EASIEST PERSON TO GET ALONG WITH
REALLY.
BUT A FRYING PAN. WOW.
I KNOW.
I'D NEVER LET IT GET THAT FAR.
REALLY.
SO HAS HE CALLED YOU YET?
HUH-UH, YOU?
NOT YET.
end

Girls and Boys
by LYNDA BARRY
HAVE YOU EVER WONDERED IF YOU SHOULD SEE A THERAPIST? I HAVE
HERE WE GO AGAIN!
MY PROBLEM IS THAT I DON'T HAVE A PROBLEM. SOMETIMES I THINK I MIGHT HAVE A SECRET ONE, AN AWFUL ONE, AND MAYBE I JUST DON'T KNOW ABOUT IT. THIS POSSIBILITY EVEN THRILLS ME A LITTLE...
LIKE, WOW MAN.
MAKES ME FEEL COMPLEX. YOU KNOW, "DEEP." SORTA LIKE THAT "ANNIE HALL" TYPE. AND THEN I THINK "HEY! IM A LITTLE "ECCENTRIC."! IT MAKES ME FEEL MORE FASHIONABLE- AND MORE INTELLIGENT! AW, YEAH!
A REGULAR EINSTEIN.
WHAT ABOUT ME? A SIX INCH WOMAN WHO APPEARS OUTTA NOWHERE, AND TALKS TO YOU, NOW THATS WHAT I CALL A PROBLEM, SISTER!!!
LOOK- WE'VE BEEN THROUGH THIS. YOU'RE TOO PASSE. IF I TOLD A THERAPIST ABOUT YOU, THEY'D THINK I WAS SOME KIND OF NUT. I WANT A PROBLEM THATS HIP!

FOR MY MOTHER, PEARL LANDON
AND MY FATHER, BOB BARRY
AND MY BROTHERS, MICHAEL+MARK

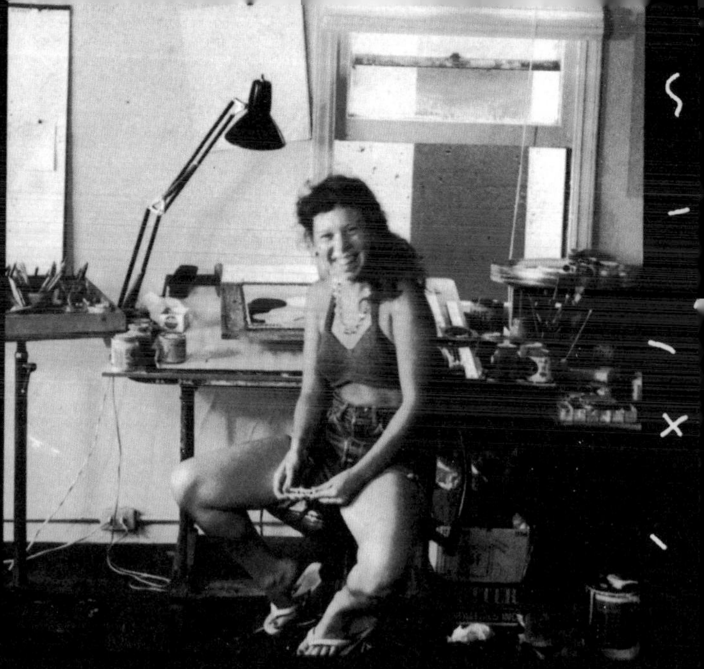

SUMMER 1981

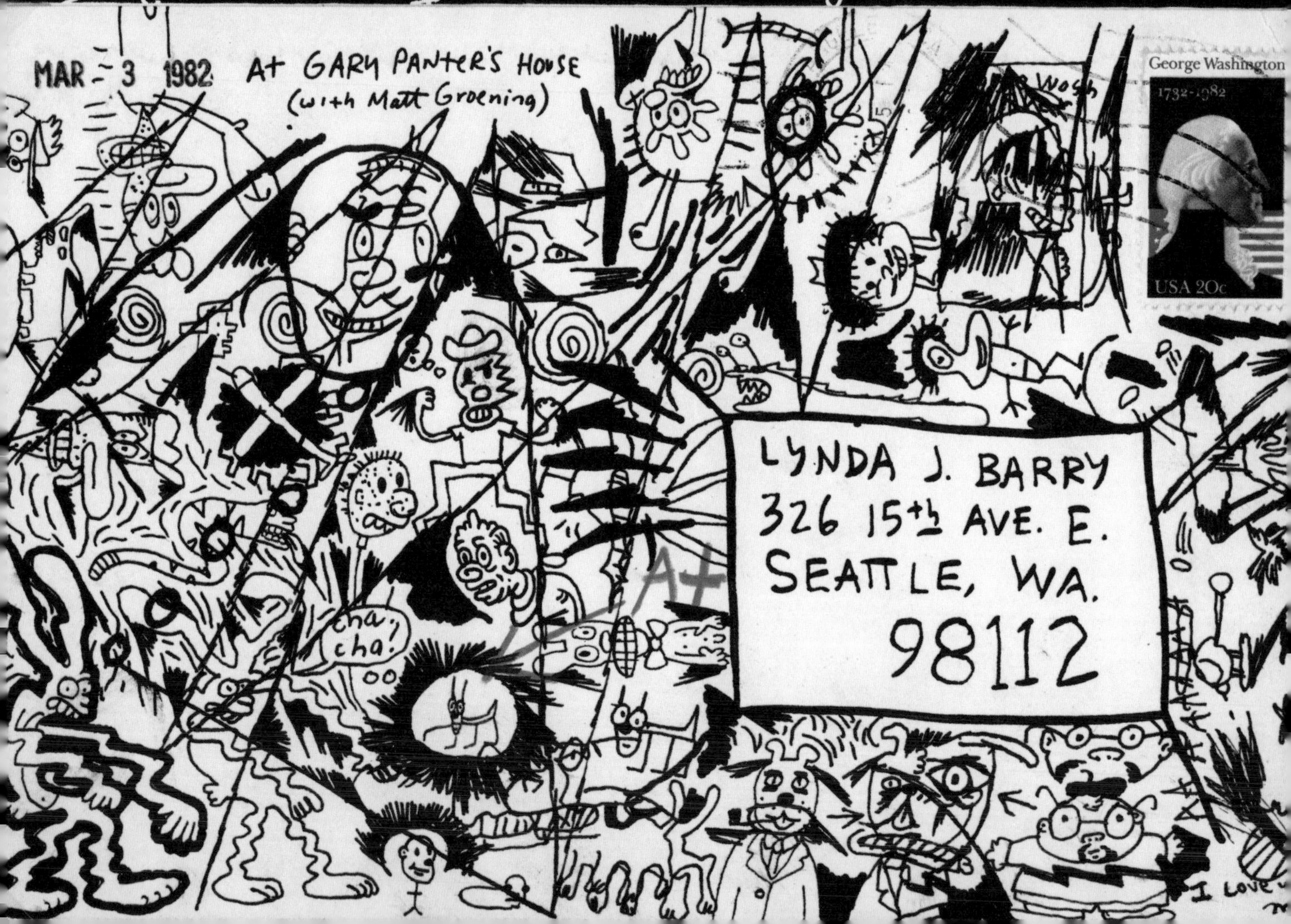
MAR 3 1982
At GARY PANTER'S HOUSE
(with Matt Groening)
George Washington
1732-1982
USA 20c
LYNDA J. BARRY
326 15th AVE. E.
SEATTLE, WA.
98112
cha cha!
I LOVE